KUROGANE 5

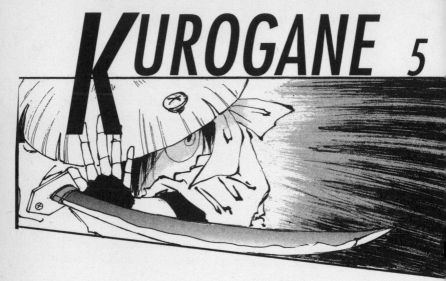

Kei Toume

Translated and adapted by Ikoi Hiroe
Lettered by Takka Takka

DEL
REY

Ballantine Books ★ New York

Kurogane volume 5 is a work of fiction. Names, characters, places, and incidents are the products of the author's imagination or are used fictitiously. Any resemblance to actual events, locales, or persons, living or dead, is entirely coincidental.

A Del Rey Trade Paperback Original

Kurogane volume 5 copyright ©2001 by Kei Toume
English translation copyright © 2007 by Kei Toume

All rights reserved.

Published in the United States by Del Rey Books, an imprint of The Random House Publishing Group, a division of Random House, Inc., New York.

DEL REY is a registered trademark and the Del Rey colophon is a trademark of Random House, Inc.

Publication rights arranged through Kodansha Ltd.

First published in Japan in 2001 by Kodansha Ltd., Tokyo.

ISBN 978 0 345 49207 4

Printed in the United States of America

www.delreymanga.com

2 4 6 8 9 7 5 3 1

Translator and adapter—Ikoi Hiroe
Lettering—Takka Takka

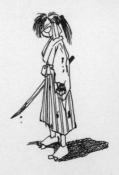

CONTENTS

A Note from the Author...iv
Honorifics Explained...v

Chapter 12: Swords Man
(Fighting over a target on Nakasen Road)
Episode 1...5
Episode 2...27
Chapter 13: A Dense Fog
(Kurogane of Kasumi Pass)
Episode 1...51
Episode 2...75
Chapter 14: Chaser
(Blue Dusk Wanderings)
Episode 1...103
Episode 2...129
Episode 3...149
Episode 4...169
Episode 5...187

Translation Notes...215

A NOTE FROM THE AUTHOR

To be continued...

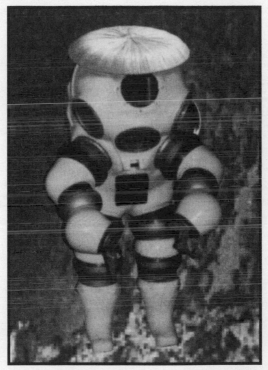

Recent photograph of the author

HONORIFICS EXPLAINED

Throughout the Del Rey Manga books, you will find Japanese honorifics left intact in the translations. For those not familiar with how the Japanese use honorifics and, more important, how they differ from American honorifics, we present this brief overview.

Politeness has always been a critical facet of Japanese culture. Ever since the feudal era, when Japan was a highly stratified society, use of honorifics—which can be defined as polite speech that indicates relationship or status—has played an essential role in the Japanese language. When addressing someone in Japanese, an honorific usually takes the form of a suffix attached to one's name (example: "Asuna-san"), or as a title at the end of one's name, or in place of the name itself (example: "Negi-sensei" or simply "Sensei!").

Honorifics can be expressions of respect or endearment. In the context of manga and anime, honorifics give insight into the nature of the relationship between characters. Many English translations leave out these important honorifics, and therefore distort the feel of the original Japanese. Because Japanese honorifics contain nuances that English honorifics lack, it is our policy at Del Rey not to translate them. Here, instead, is a guide to some of the honorifics you may encounter in Del Rey Manga.

-san: This is the most common honorific and is equivalent to Mr., Miss, Ms., or Mrs. It is the all-purpose honorific and can be used in any situation where politeness is required.

-sama: This is one level higher than "-san" and is used to confer great respect.

-dono: This comes from the word "tono," which means "lord." It is an even higher level than "-sama" and confers utmost respect.

-kun: This suffix is used at the end of boys' names to express familiarity or endearment. It is also sometimes used by men among friends, or when addressing someone younger or of a lower station.

-chan: This is used to express endearment, mostly toward girls. It is also used for little boys, pets, and even among lovers. It gives a sense of childish cuteness.

Bozu: This is an informal way to refer to a boy, similar to the English terms "kid" or "squirt."

**Sempai/
Senpai:** This title suggests that the addressee is one's senior in a group or organization. It is most often used in a school setting, where underclassmen refer to their upperclassmen as "sempai." It can also be used in the workplace, such as when a newer employee addresses an employee who has seniority in the company.

Kohai: This is the opposite of "-sempai," and is used toward underclassmen in school or newcomers in the workplace. It connotes that the addressee is of a lower station.

Sensei: Literally meaning "one who has come before," this title is used for teachers, doctors, or masters of any profession or art.

-[blank]: This is usually forgotten in these lists, but it is perhaps the most significant difference between Japanese and English. The lack of honorific means that the speaker has permission to address the person in a very intimate way. Usually, only family, spouses, or very close friends have this kind of permission. Known as *yobisute*, it can be gratifying when someone who has earned the intimacy starts to call one by one's name without an honorific. But when that intimacy hasn't been earned, it can be very insulting.

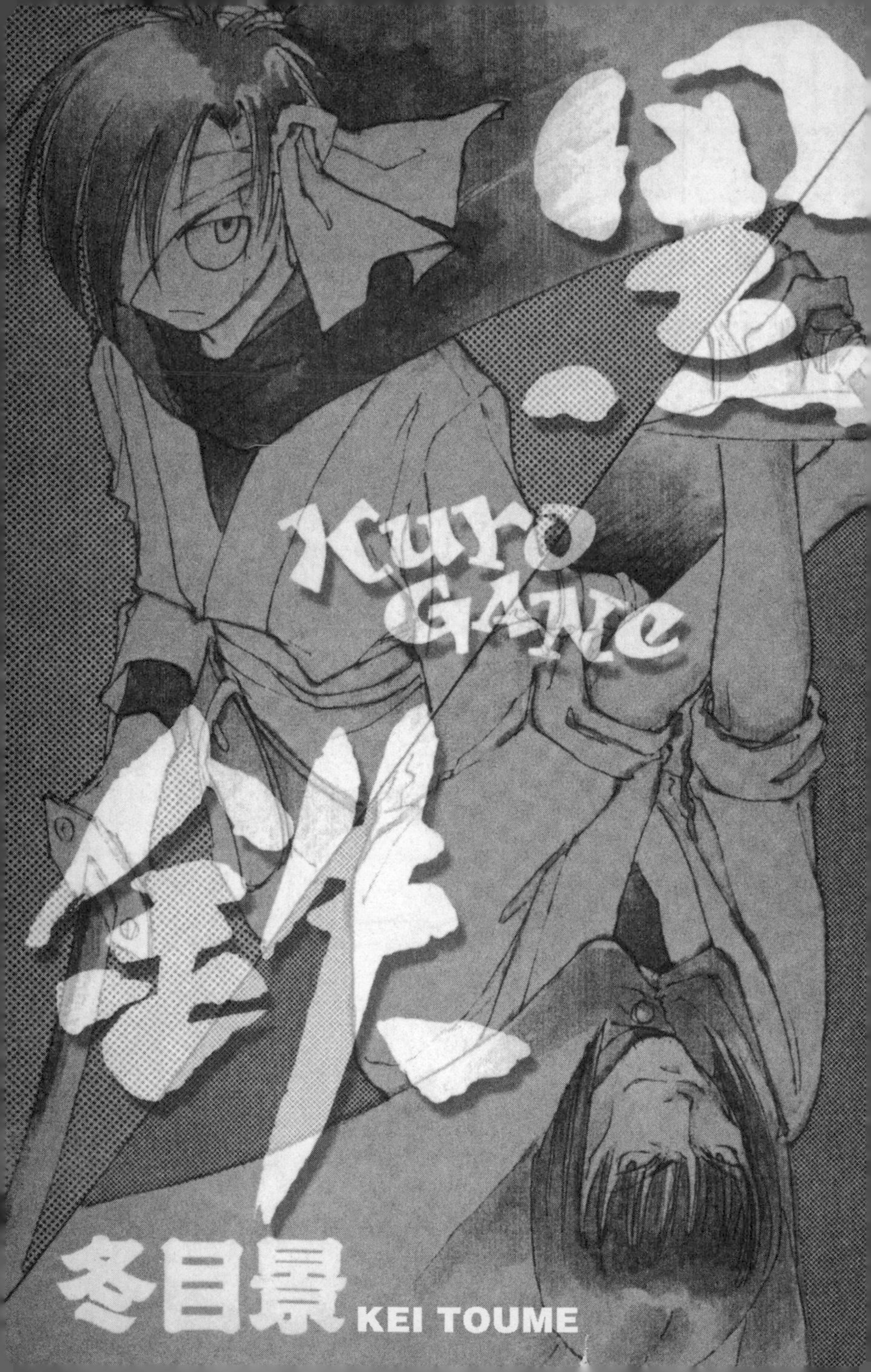
Kuro GANe
冬目景
KEI TOUME

Introduction

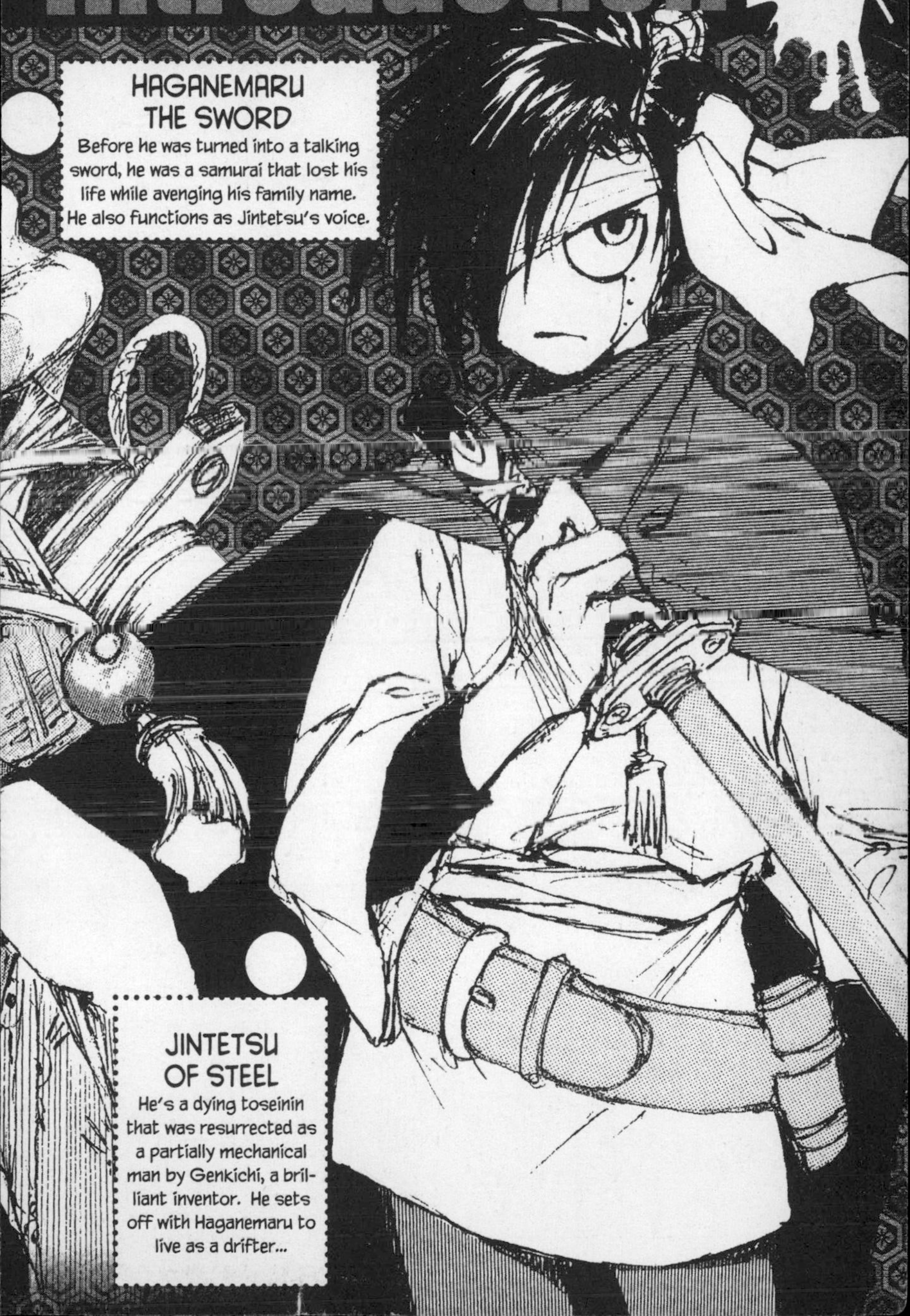
HAGANEMARU THE SWORD
Before he was turned into a talking sword, he was a samurai that lost his life while avenging his family name. He also functions as Jintetsu's voice.
JINTETSU OF STEEL
He's a dying toseinin that was resurrected as a partially mechanical man by Genkichi, a brilliant inventor. He sets off with Haganemaru to live as a drifter...

黒鉄Characters

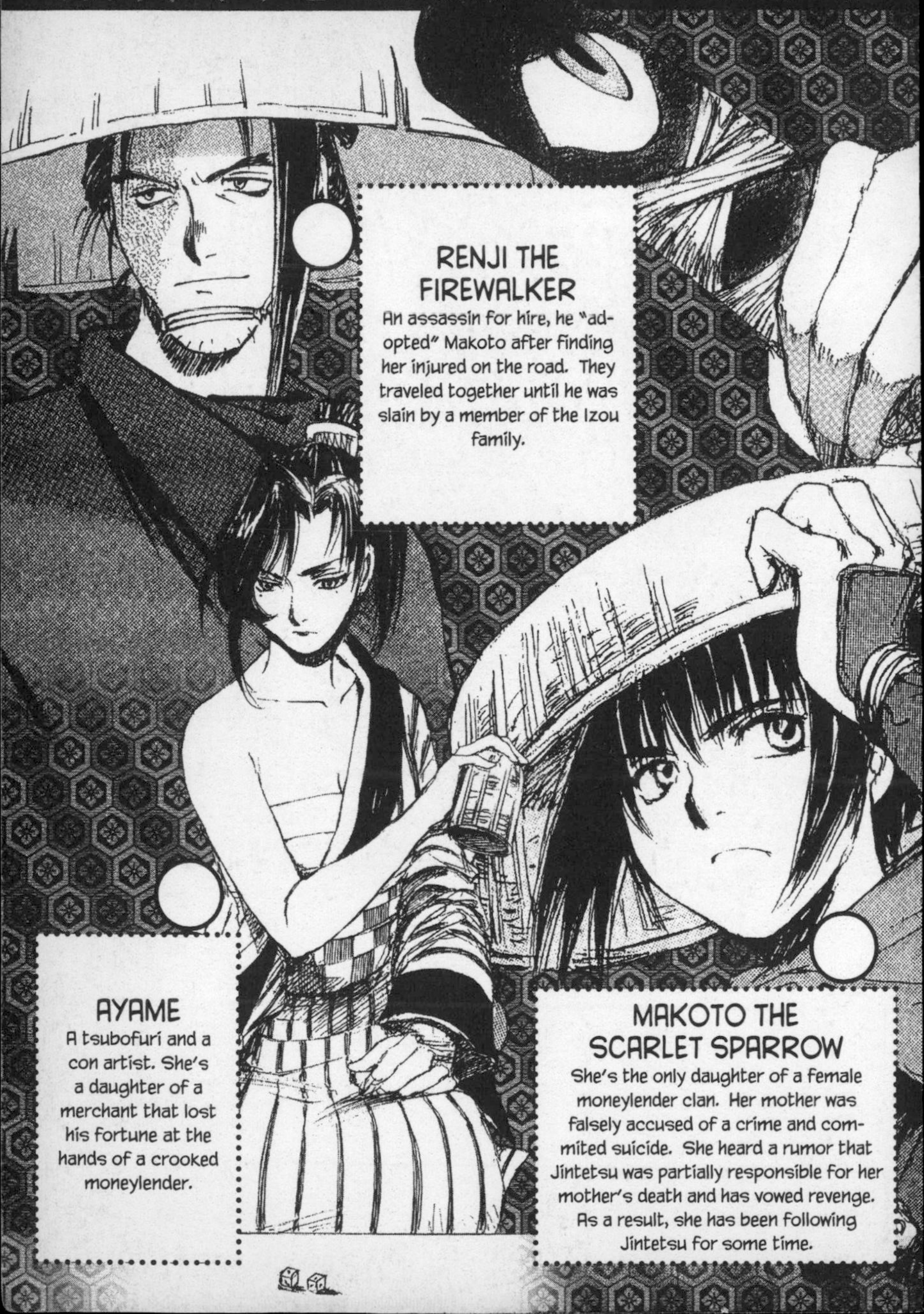

RENJI THE FIREWALKER

An assassin for hire, he "adopted" Makoto after finding her injured on the road. They traveled together until he was slain by a member of the Izou family.

AYAME

A tsubofuri and a con artist. She's a daughter of a merchant that lost his fortune at the hands of a crooked moneylender.

MAKOTO THE SCARLET SPARROW

She's the only daughter of a female moneylender clan. Her mother was falsely accused of a crime and commited suicide. She heard a rumor that Jintetsu was partially responsible for her mother's death and has vowed revenge. As a result, she has been following Jintetsu for some time.

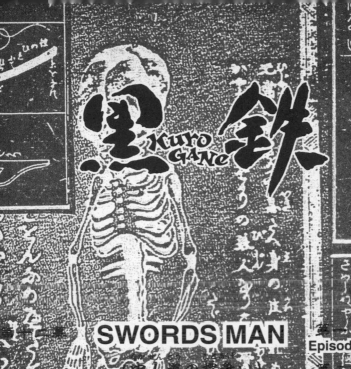

黒鉄
Kuro GANe

SWORDS MAN
(Fighting over a target on Nakasen Road)

第十二景　Episode 1 5
　　　　　Episode 2 27

A DENSE FOG
(Kurogane of Kasumi Pass)

第十三景　Episode 1 51
　　　　　Episode 2 75

CHASER
(Blue Dusk Wanderings)

第十四景　Episode 1 103
　　　　　Episode 2 129
　　　　　Episode 3 149
　　　　　Episode 4 169
　　　　　Episode 5 187

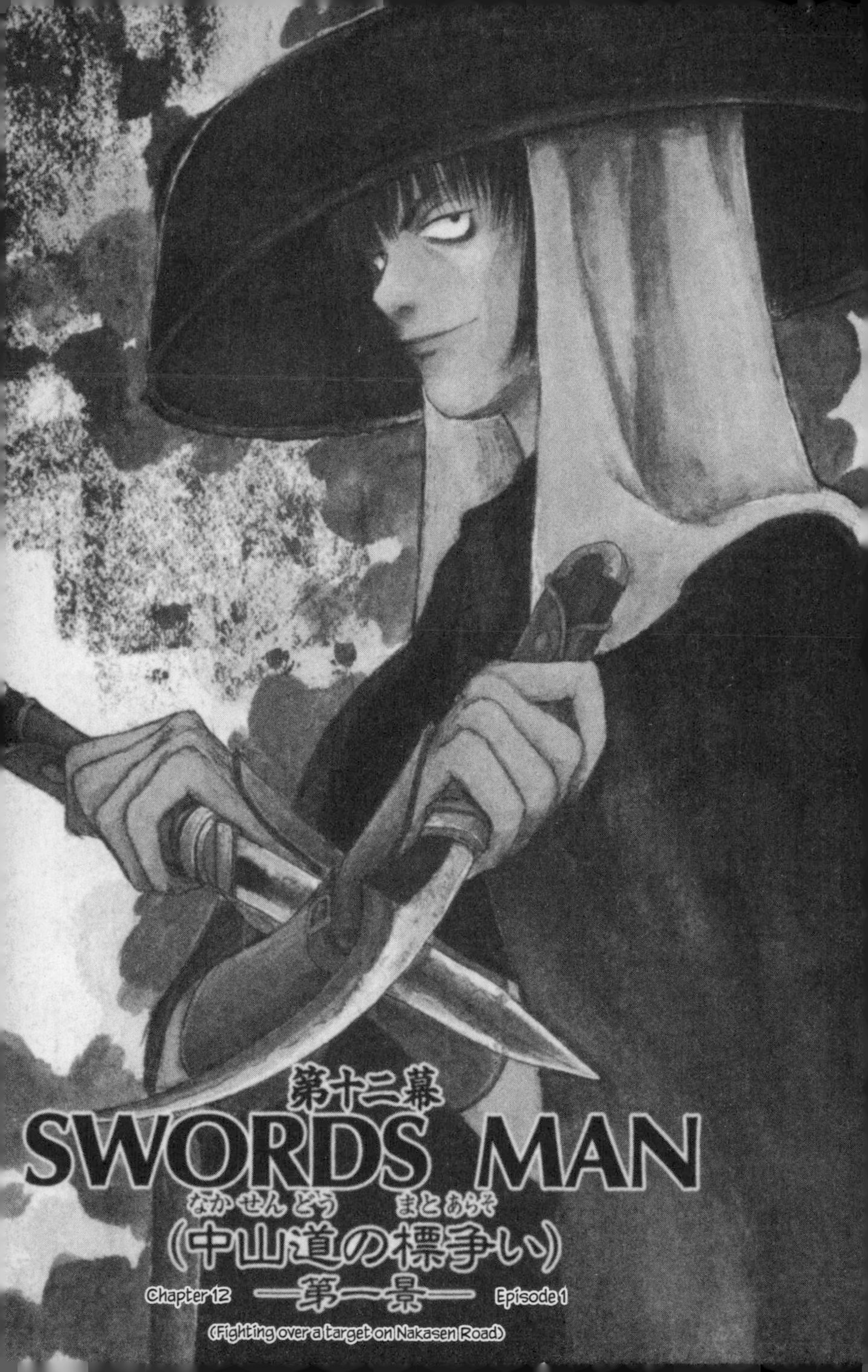
第十二幕
SWORDS MAN
なかせんどう まとあらそ
(中山道の標争い)
Chapter 12 —第一景— Episode 1
(Fighting over a target on Nakasen Road)

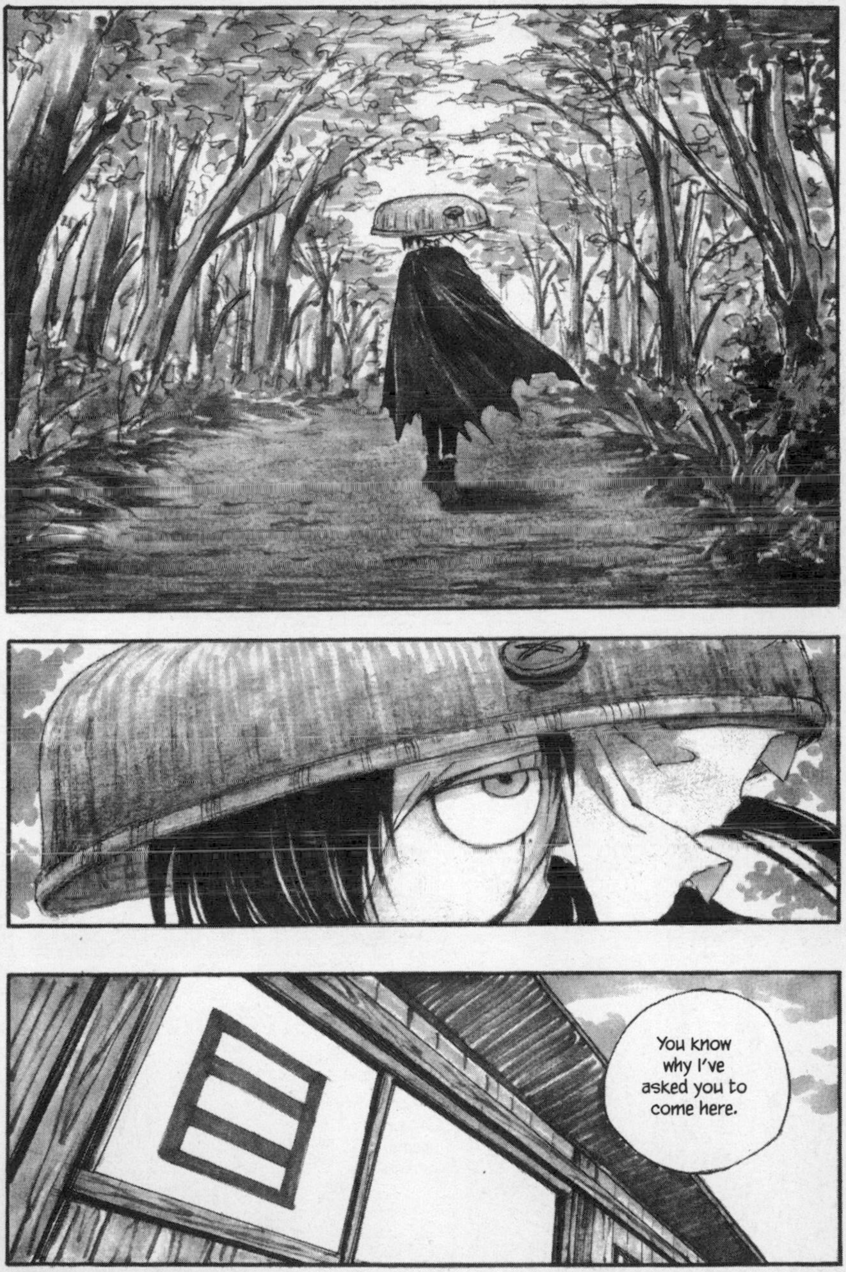
You know why I've asked you to come here.

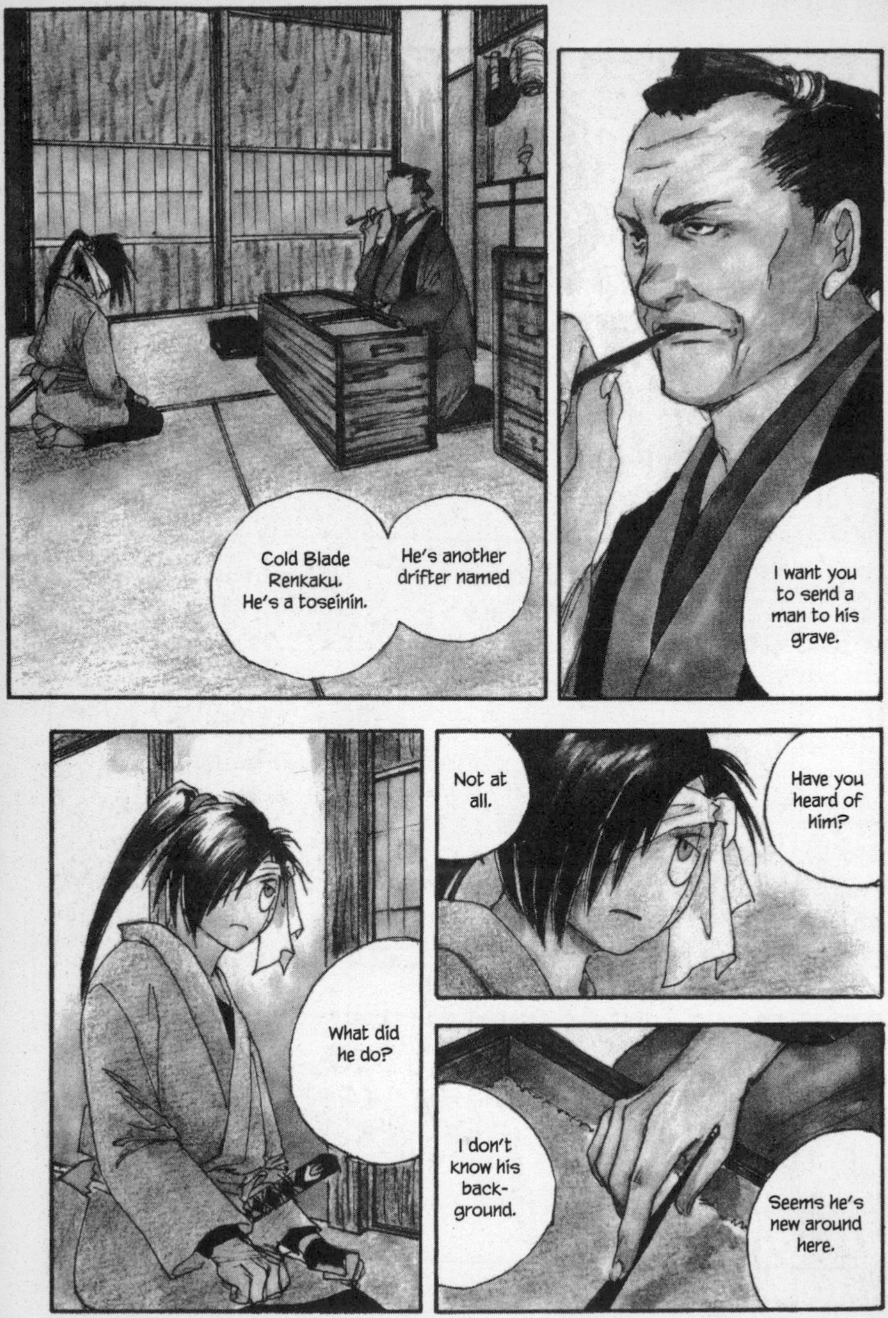
I want you to send a man to his grave.
He's another drifter named
Cold Blade Renkaku. He's a toseinin.
Have you heard of him?
Not at all.
Seems he's new around here.
I don't know his background.
What did he do?

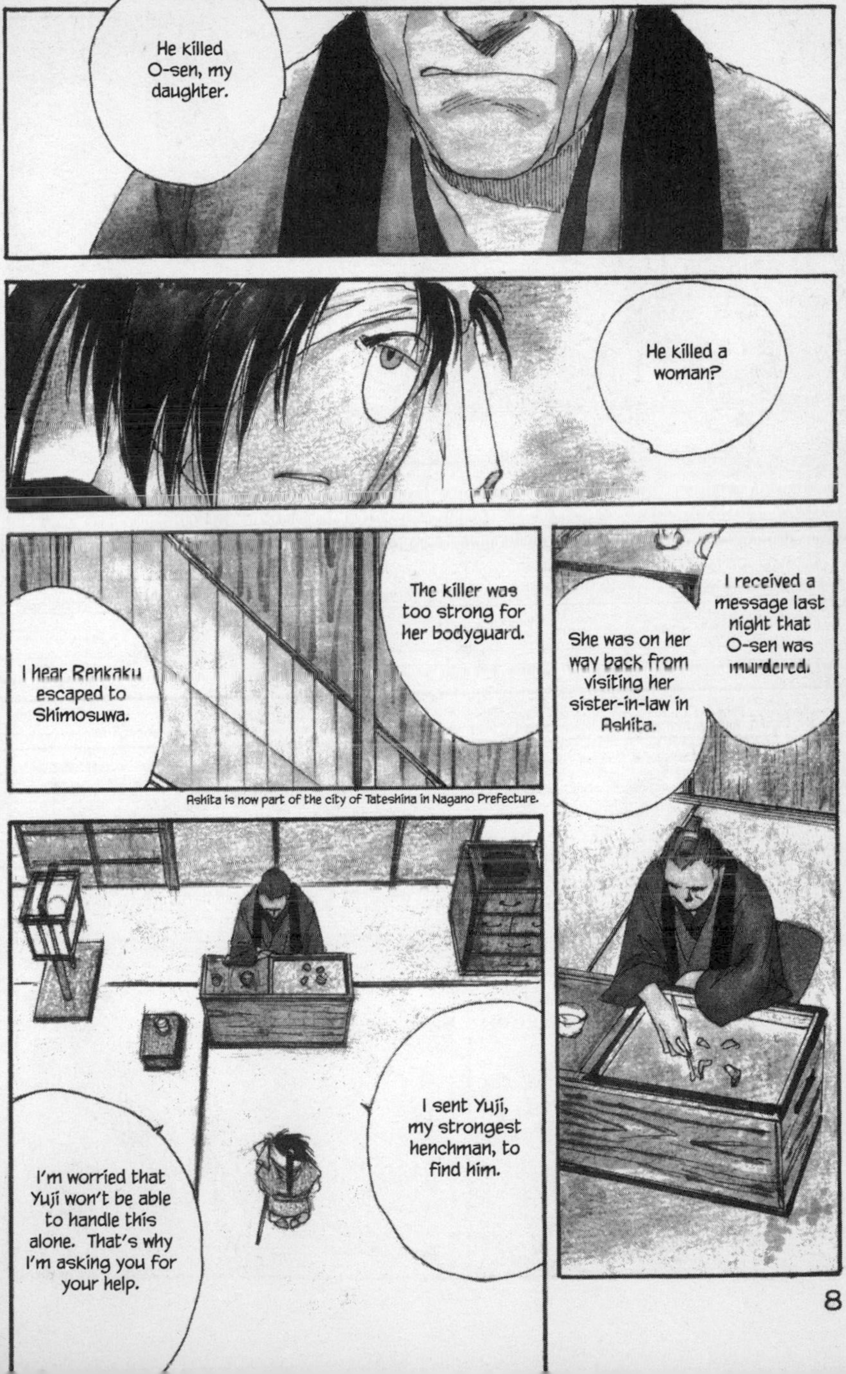
He killed O-sen, my daughter.
He killed a woman?
I received a message last night that O-sen was murdered.
She was on her way back from visiting her sister-in-law in Ashita.
The killer was too strong for her bodyguard.
I hear Renkaku escaped to Shimosuwa.
I sent Yuji, my strongest henchman, to find him.
I'm worried that Yuji won't be able to handle this alone. That's why I'm asking you for your help.

Ashita is now part of the city of Tateshina in Nagano Prefecture.

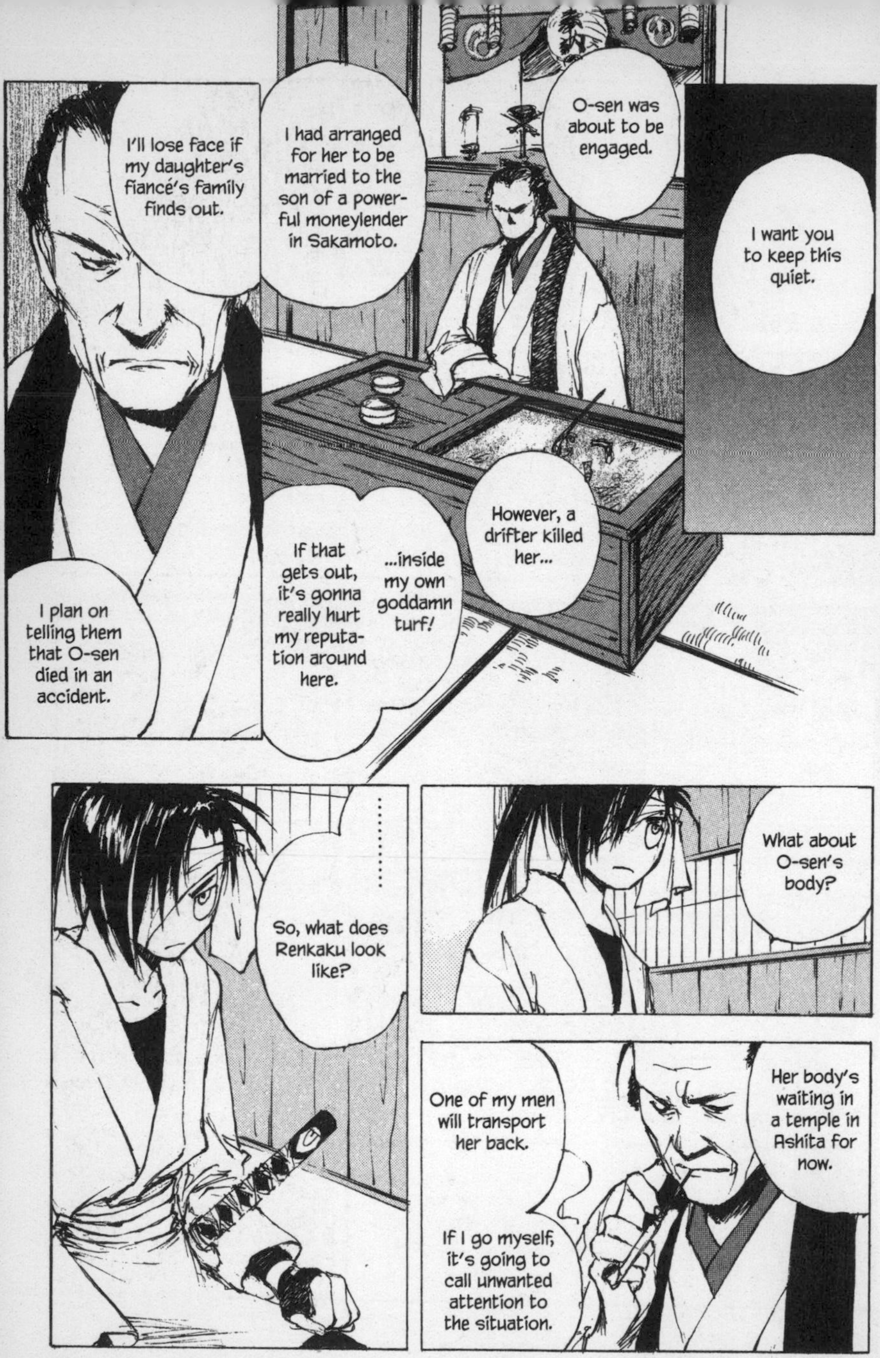
I want you to keep this quiet.
O-sen was about to be engaged.
I had arranged for her to be married to the son of a powerful moneylender in Sakamoto.
I'll lose face if my daughter's fiancé's family finds out.
However, a drifter killed her...
...inside my own goddamn turf!
If that gets out, it's gonna really hurt my reputation around here.
I plan on telling them that O-sen died in an accident.
What about O-sen's body?
Her body's waiting in a temple in Ashita for now.
One of my men will transport her back.
If I go myself, it's going to call unwanted attention to the situation.
......
So, what does Renkaku look like?

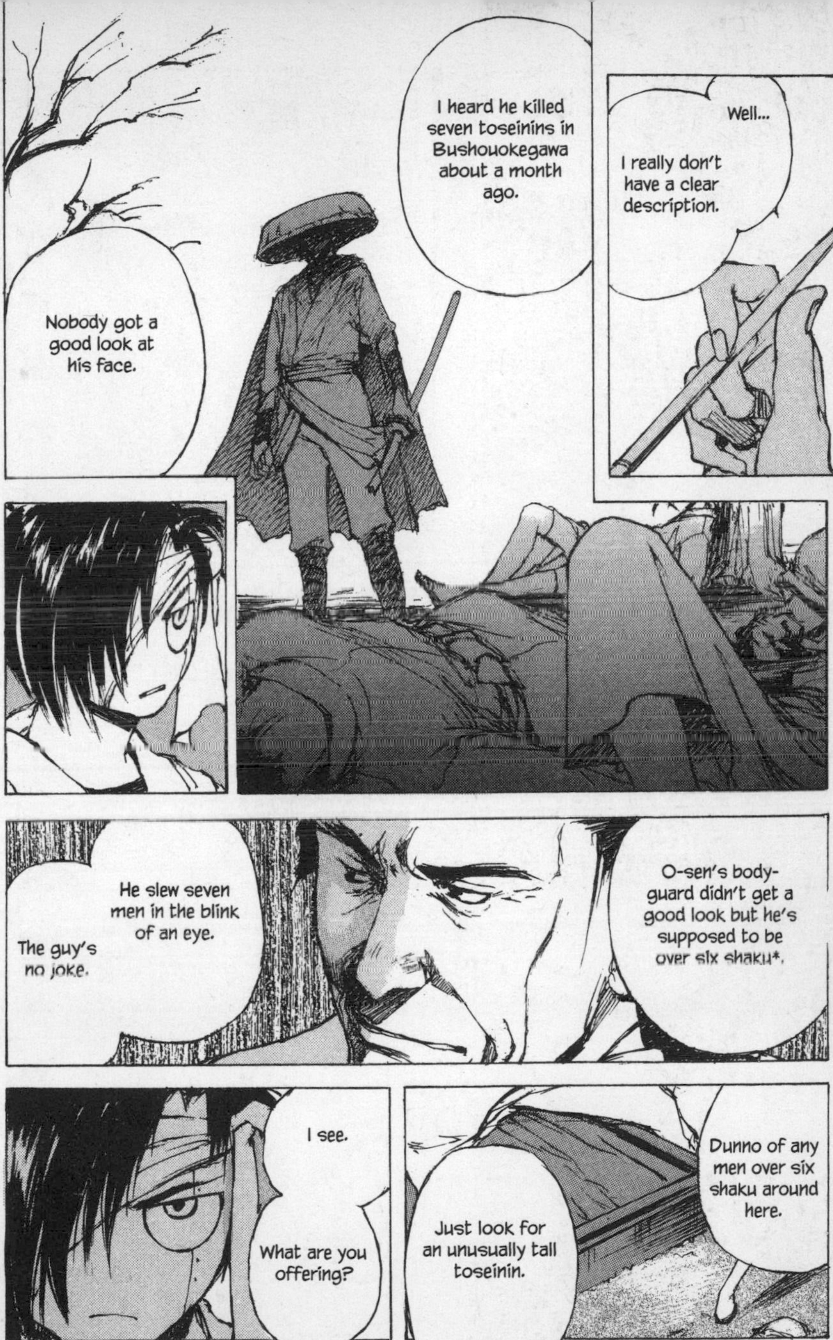
Well...
I really don't have a clear description.
I heard he killed seven toseinins in Bushouokegawa about a month ago.
Nobody got a good look at his face.
O-sen's body-guard didn't get a good look but he's supposed to be over six shaku*.
He slew seven men in the blink of an eye.
The guy's no joke.
Dunno of any men over six shaku around here.
Just look for an unusually tall toseinin.
I see.
What are you offering?

*1 shaku = 30 cm (12 inches)

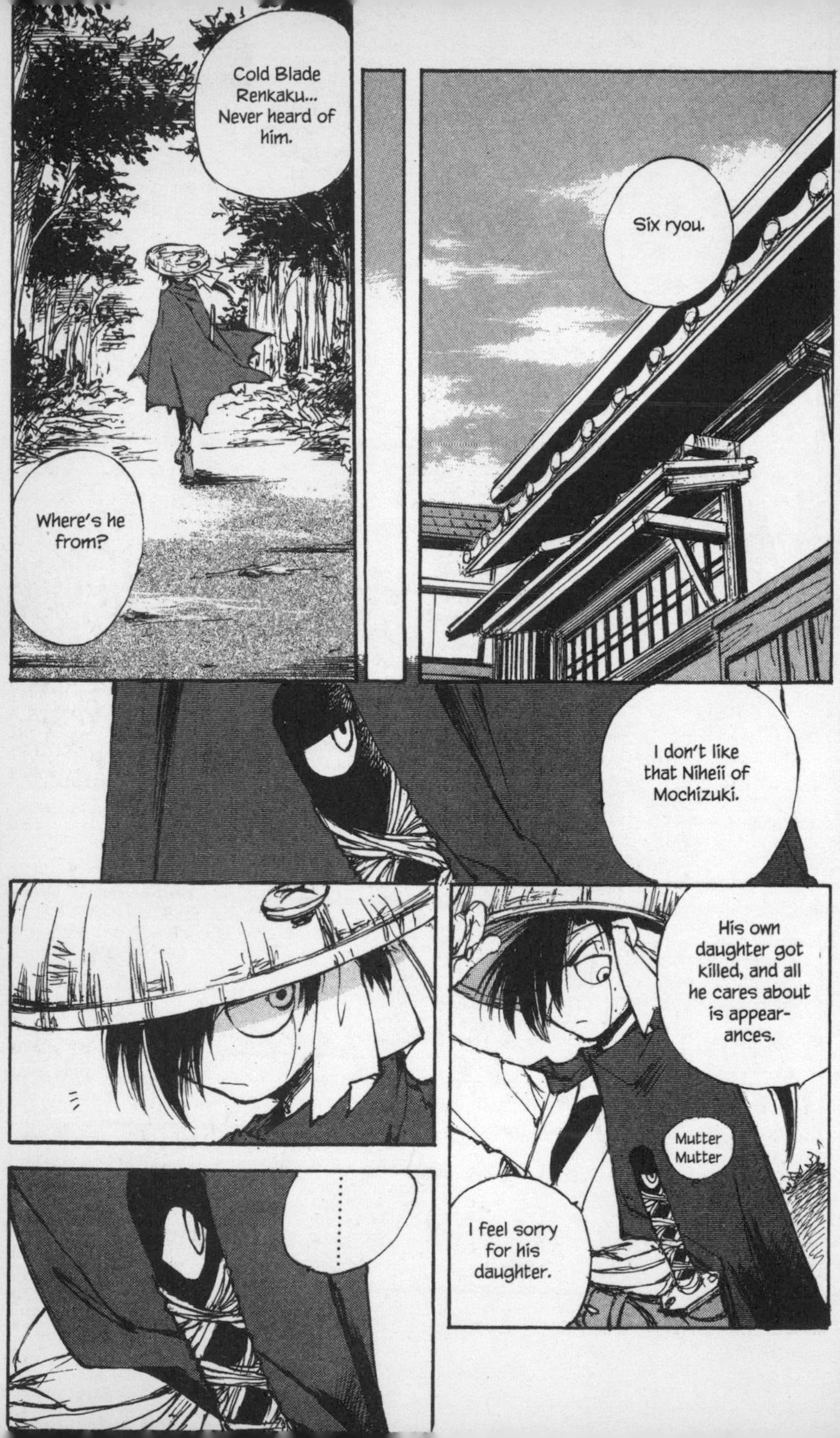
Six ryou.
Cold Blade Renkaku... Never heard of him.
Where's he from?
I don't like that Niheii of Mochizuki.
His own daughter got killed, and all he cares about is appearances.
Mutter Mutter
I feel sorry for his daughter.
......

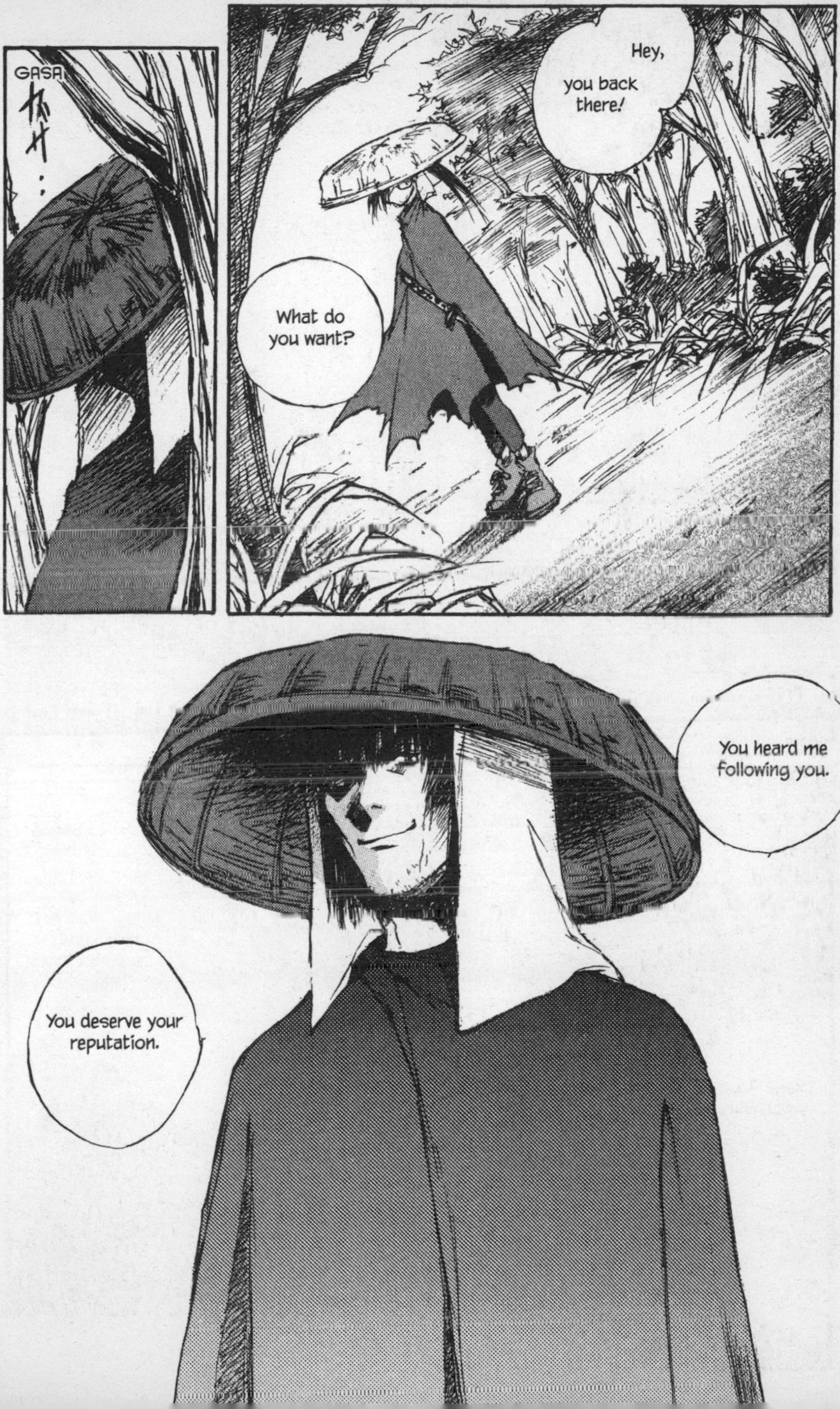
Hey, you back there!
What do you want?
GASA
You heard me following you.
You deserve your reputation.

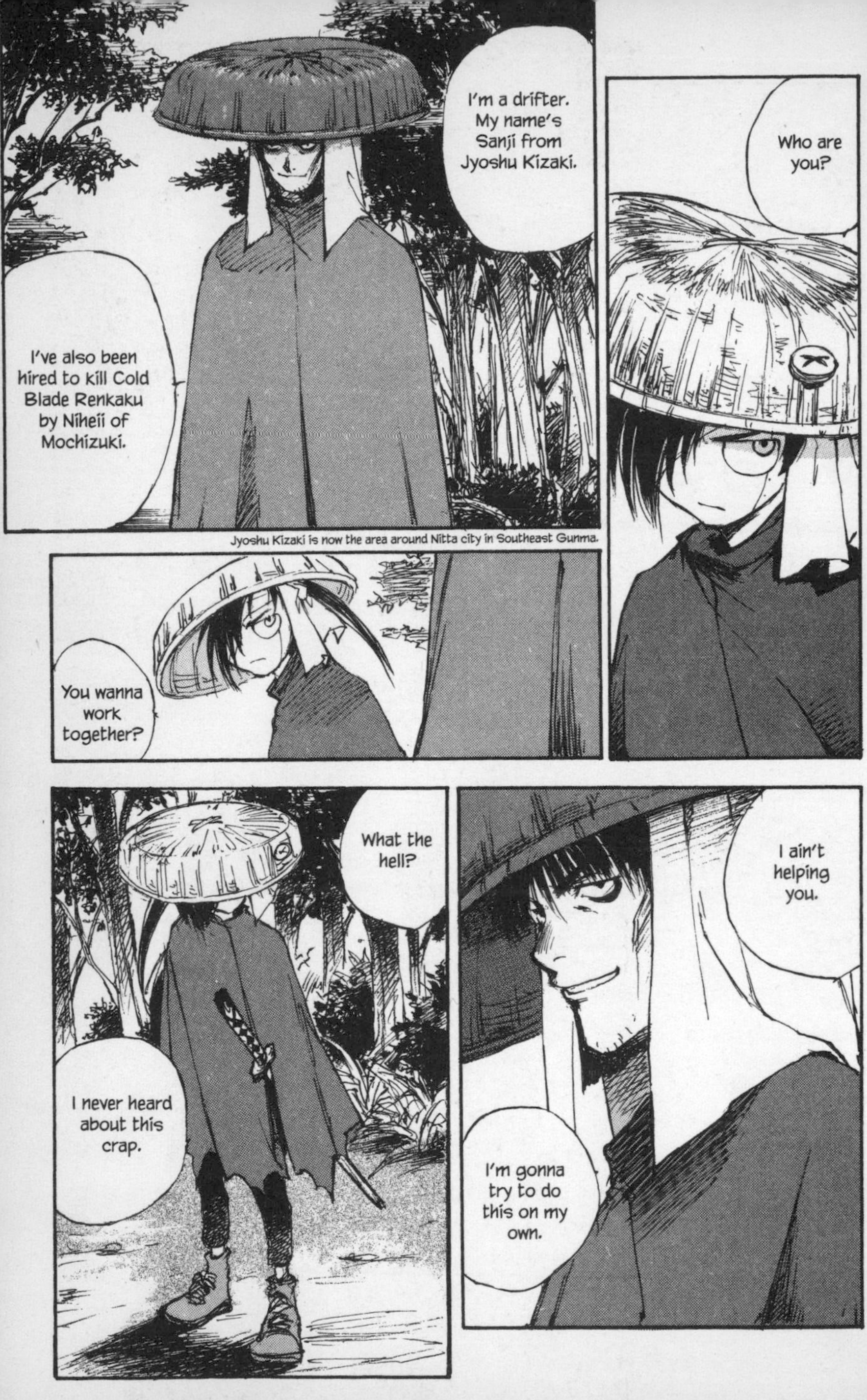
Who are you?
I'm a drifter. My name's Sanji from Jyoshu Kizaki.
I've also been hired to kill Cold Blade Renkaku by Niheii of Mochizuki.
Jyoshu Kizaki is now the area around Nitta city in Southeast Gunma.
You wanna work together?
I ain't helping you.
I'm gonna try to do this on my own.
What the hell?
I never heard about this crap.

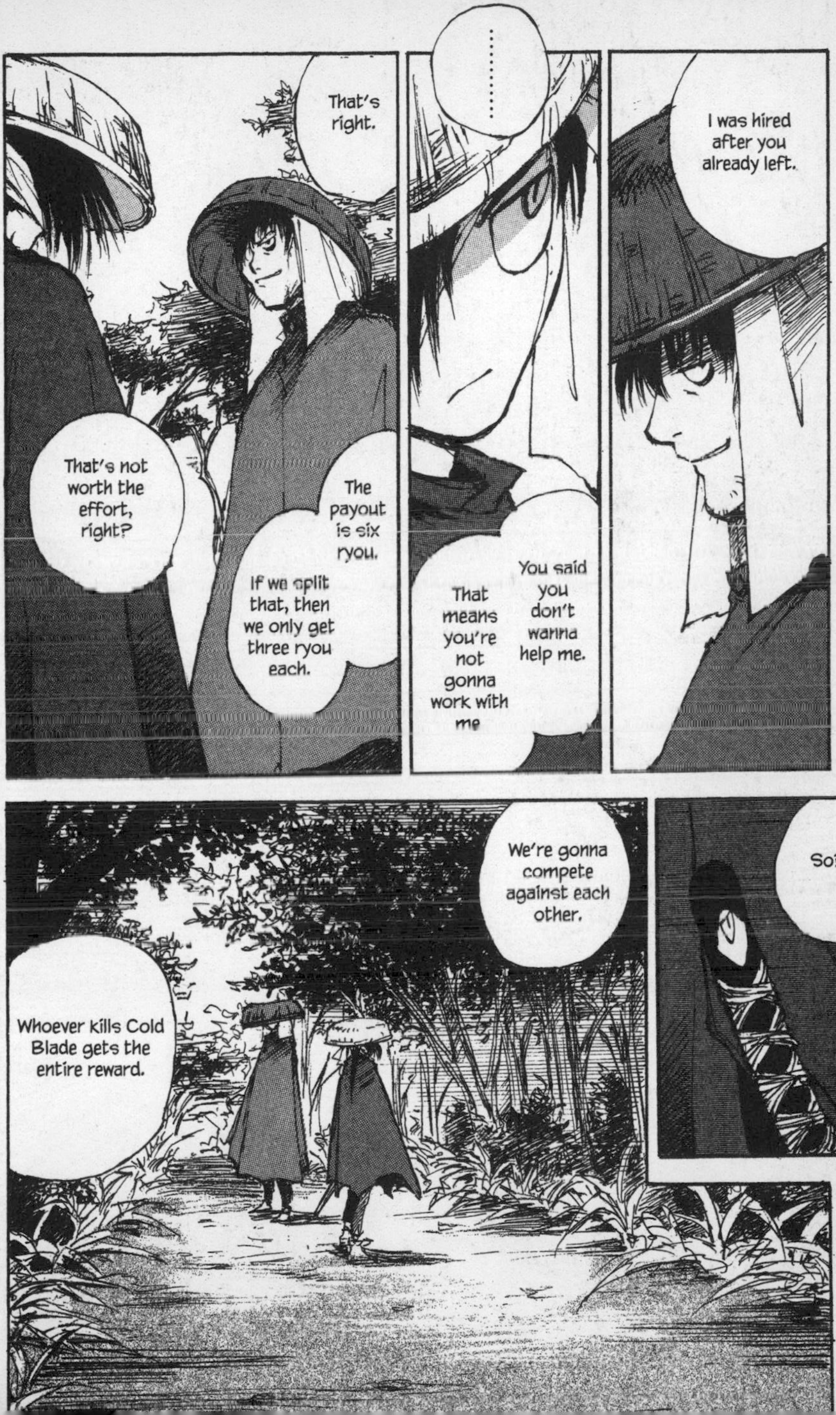
I was hired after you already left.
......
You said you don't wanna help me.
That means you're not gonna work with me
That's right.
The payout is six ryou.
If we split that, then we only get three ryou each.
That's not worth the effort, right?
So?
We're gonna compete against each other.
Whoever kills Cold Blade gets the entire reward.

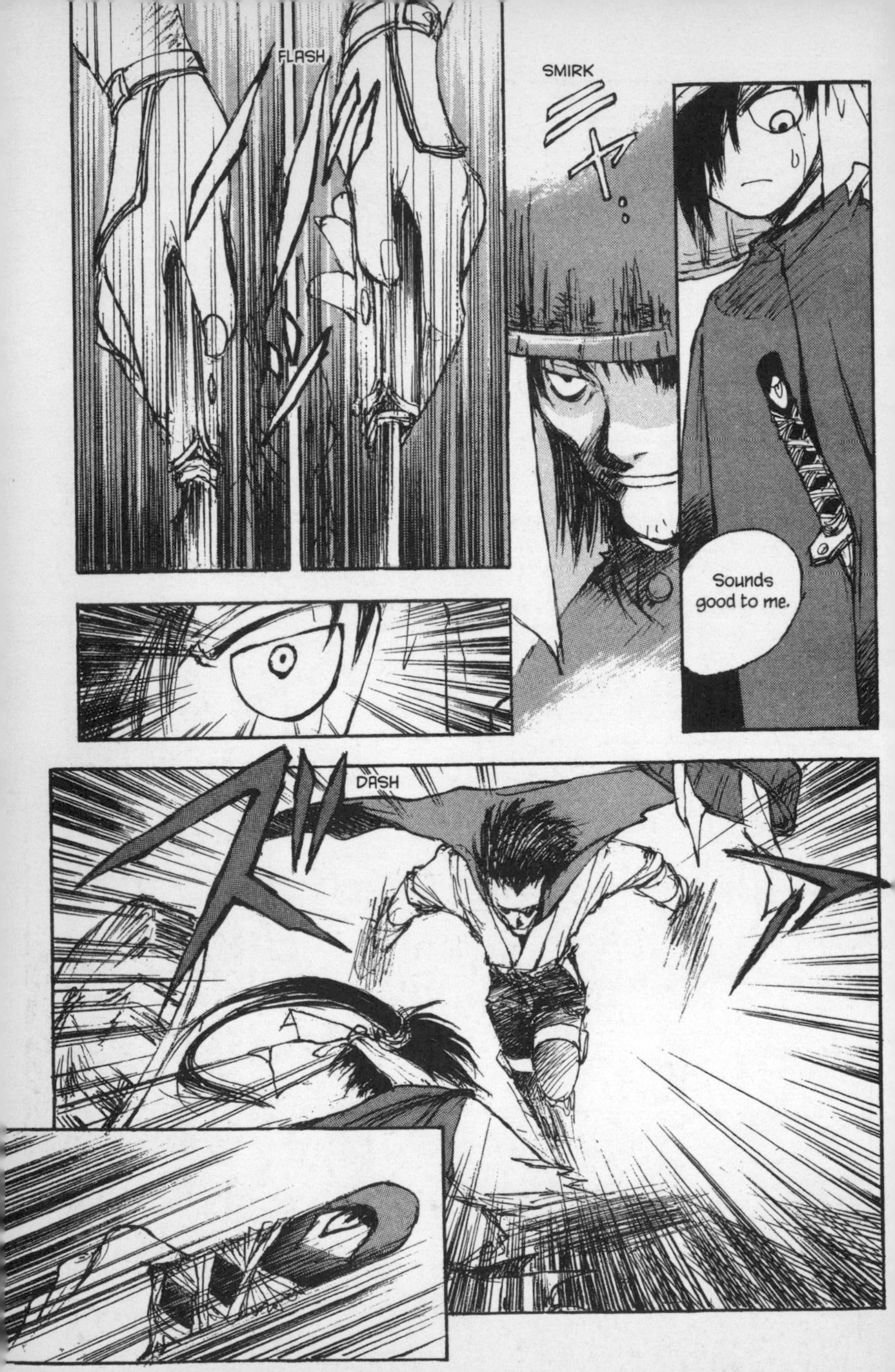
SMIRK
Sounds good to me.
FLASH
DASH

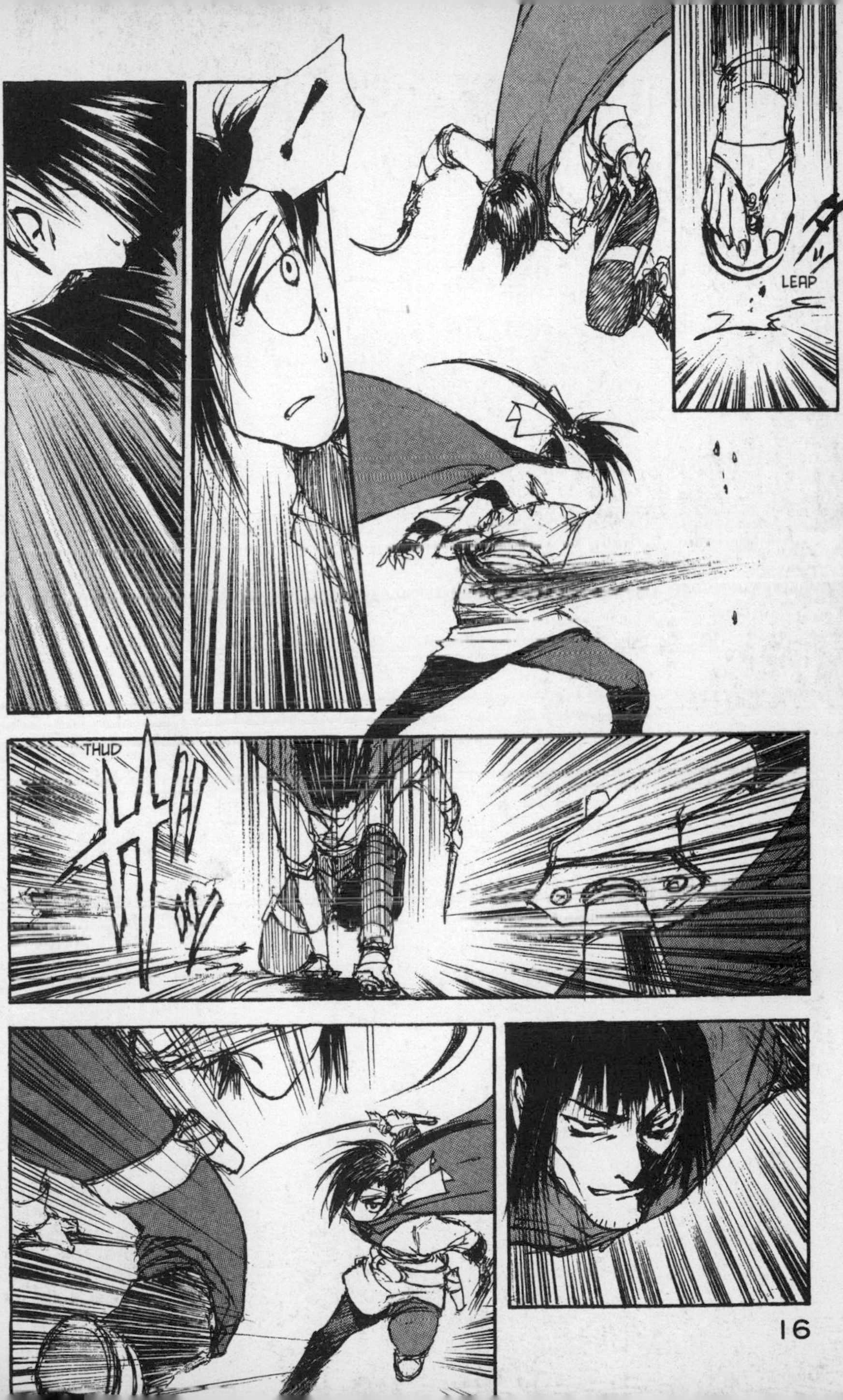
LEAP
!
THUD

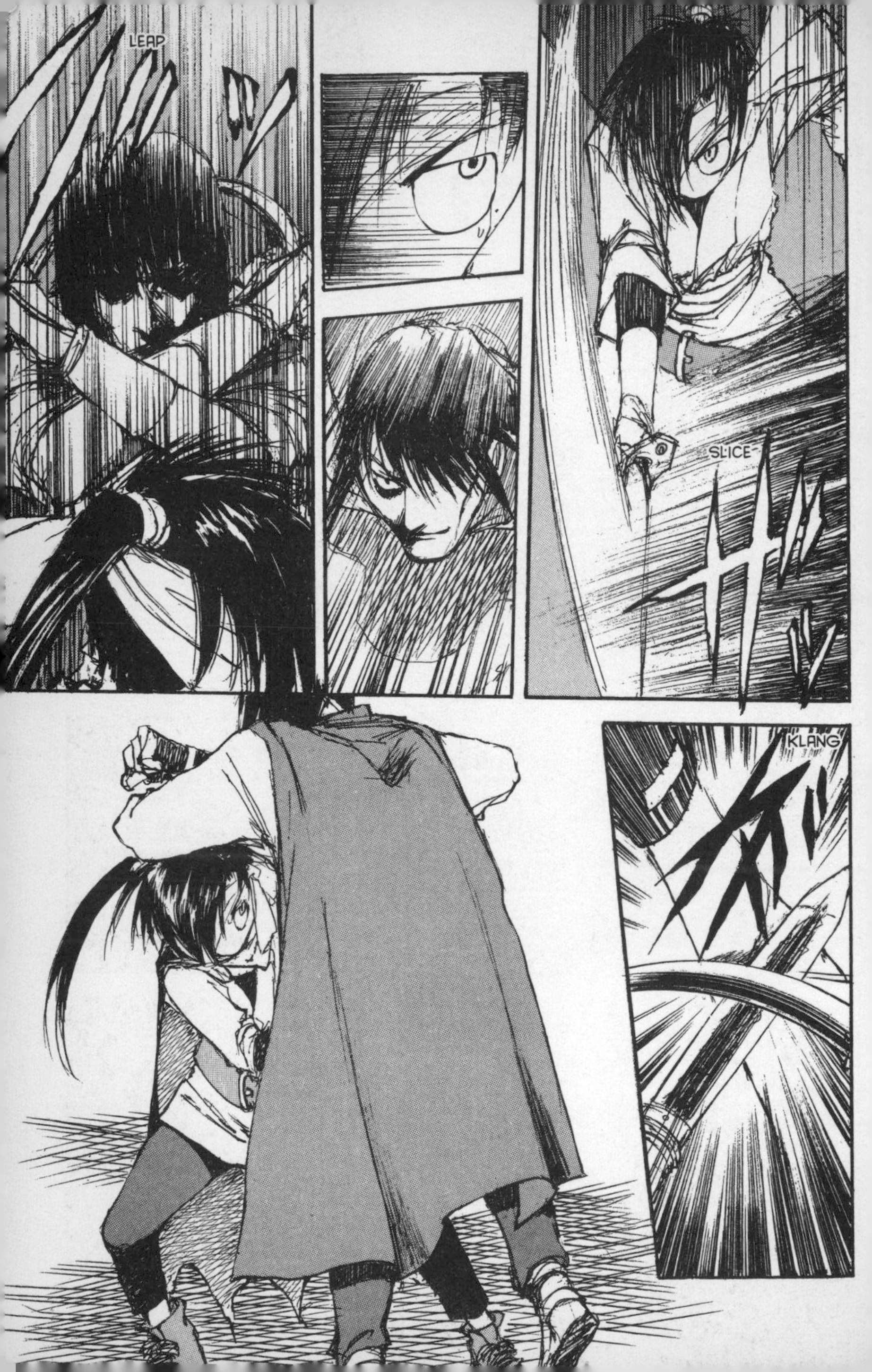
SLICE
LEAP
KLANG

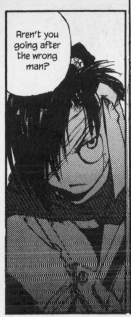

Aren't you going after the wrong man?

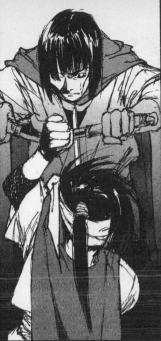

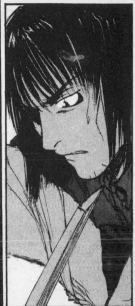

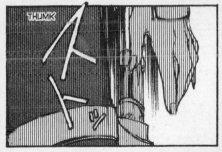

THUMK

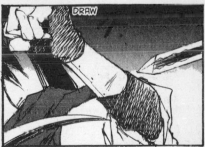

DRAW

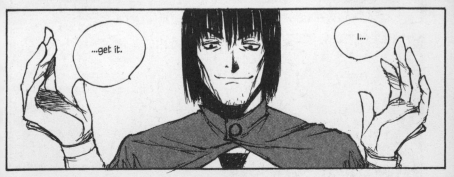

...get it.

I...

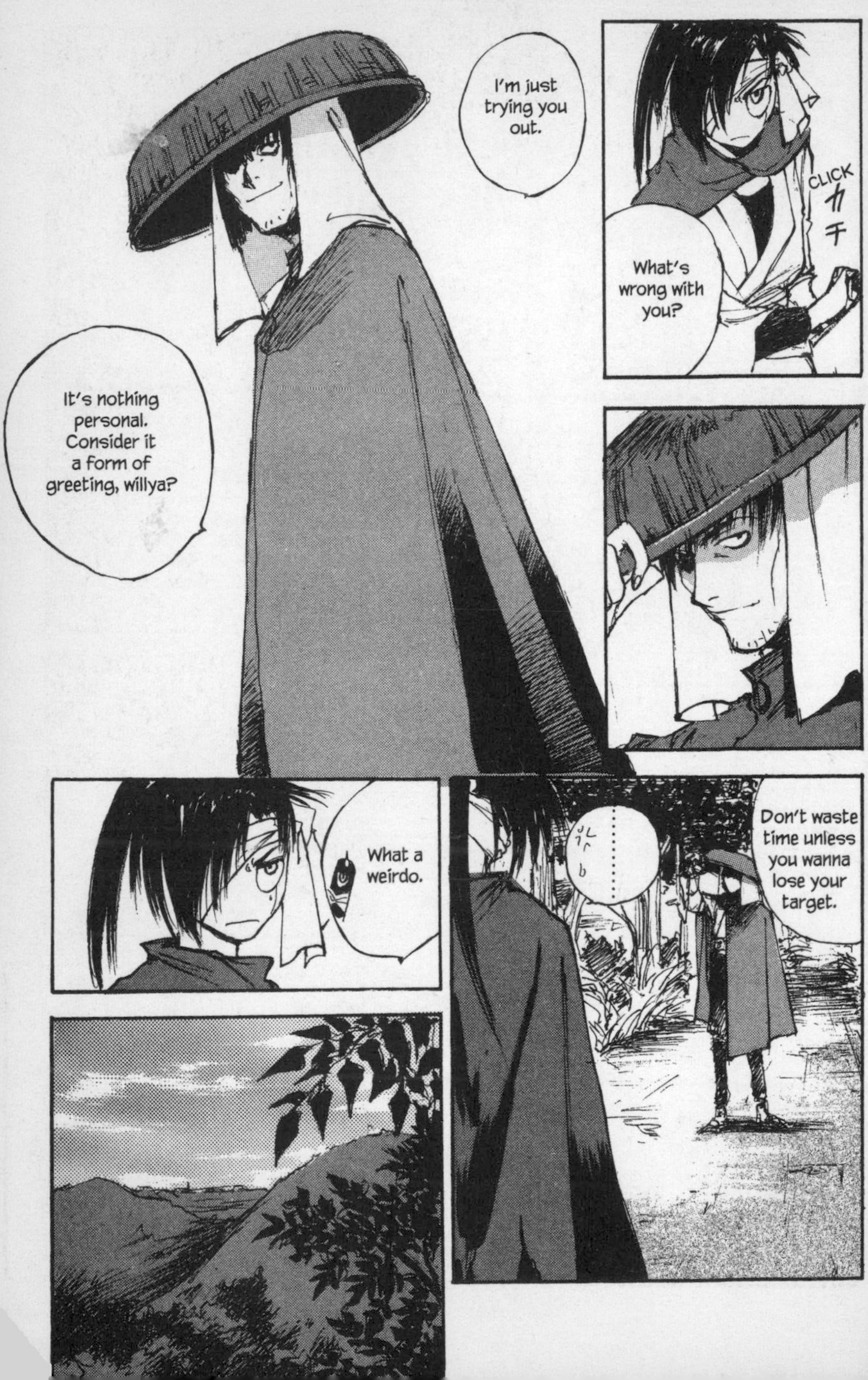
CLICK
カチ
What's wrong with you?
I'm just trying you out.
It's nothing personal. Consider it a form of greeting, willya?
Don't waste time unless you wanna lose your target.
What a weirdo.

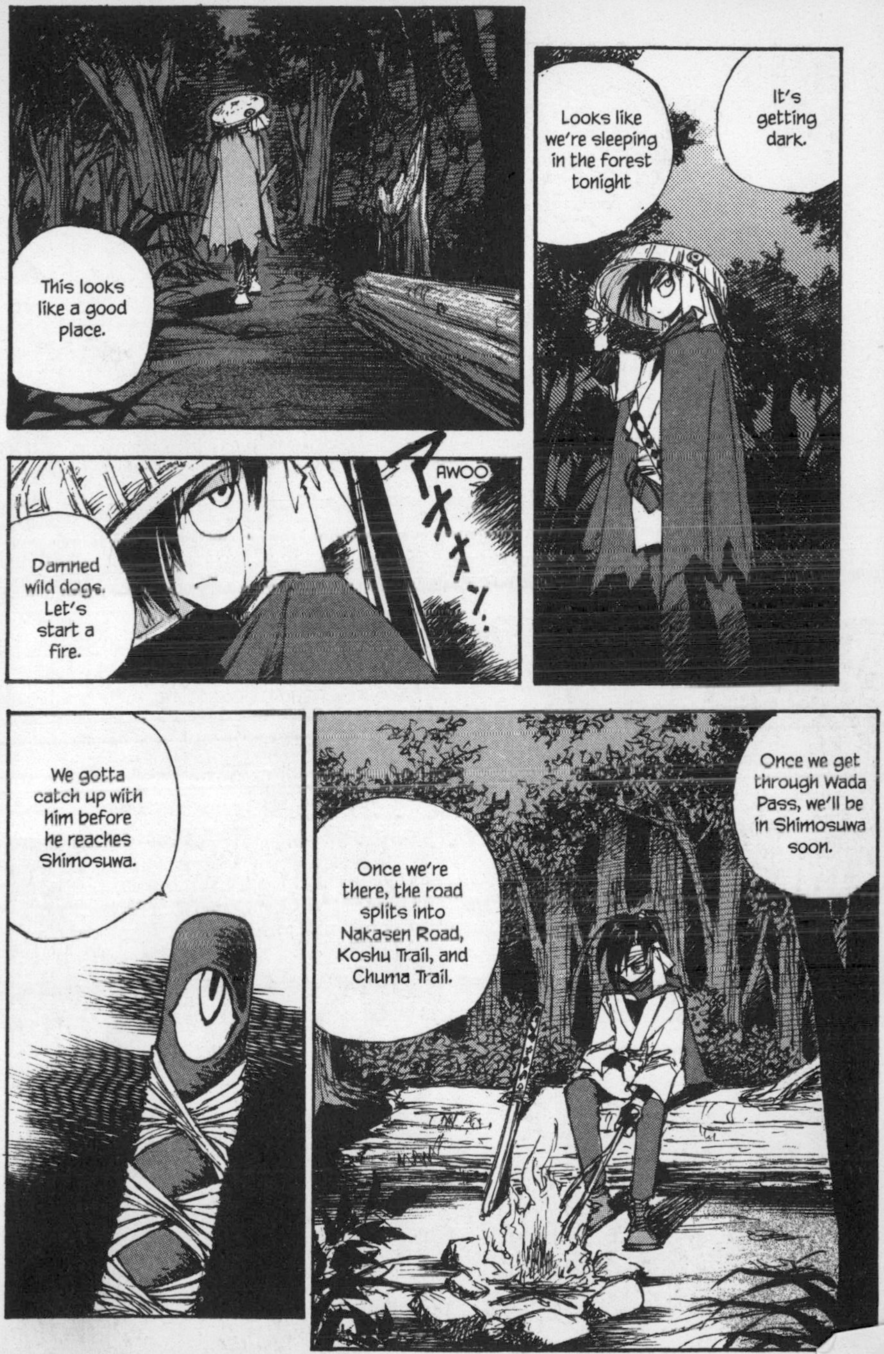
It's getting dark.
Looks like we're sleeping in the forest tonight
This looks like a good place.
AWOO
Damned wild dogs. Let's start a fire.
Once we get through Wada Pass, we'll be in Shimosuwa soon.
Once we're there, the road splits into Nakasen Road, Koshu Trail, and Chuma Trail.
We gotta catch up with him before he reaches Shimosuwa.

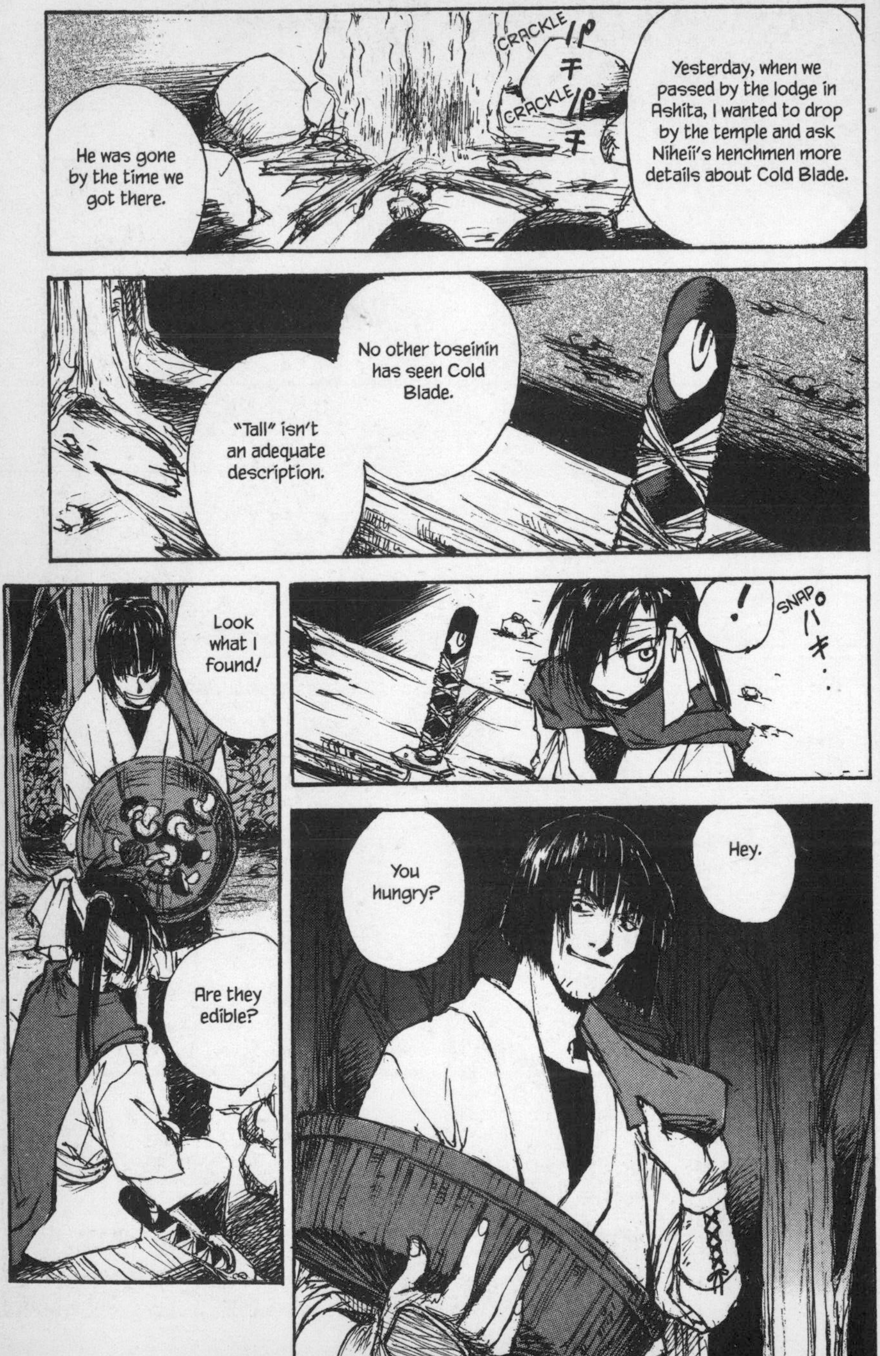
Yesterday, when we passed by the lodge in Ashita, I wanted to drop by the temple and ask Niheii's henchmen more details about Cold Blade.
CRACKLE パチ
CRACKLE パチ
He was gone by the time we got there.
No other toseinin has seen Cold Blade.
"Tall" isn't an adequate description.
SNAP パキ・・
!
Hey.
You hungry?
Look what I found!
Are they edible?

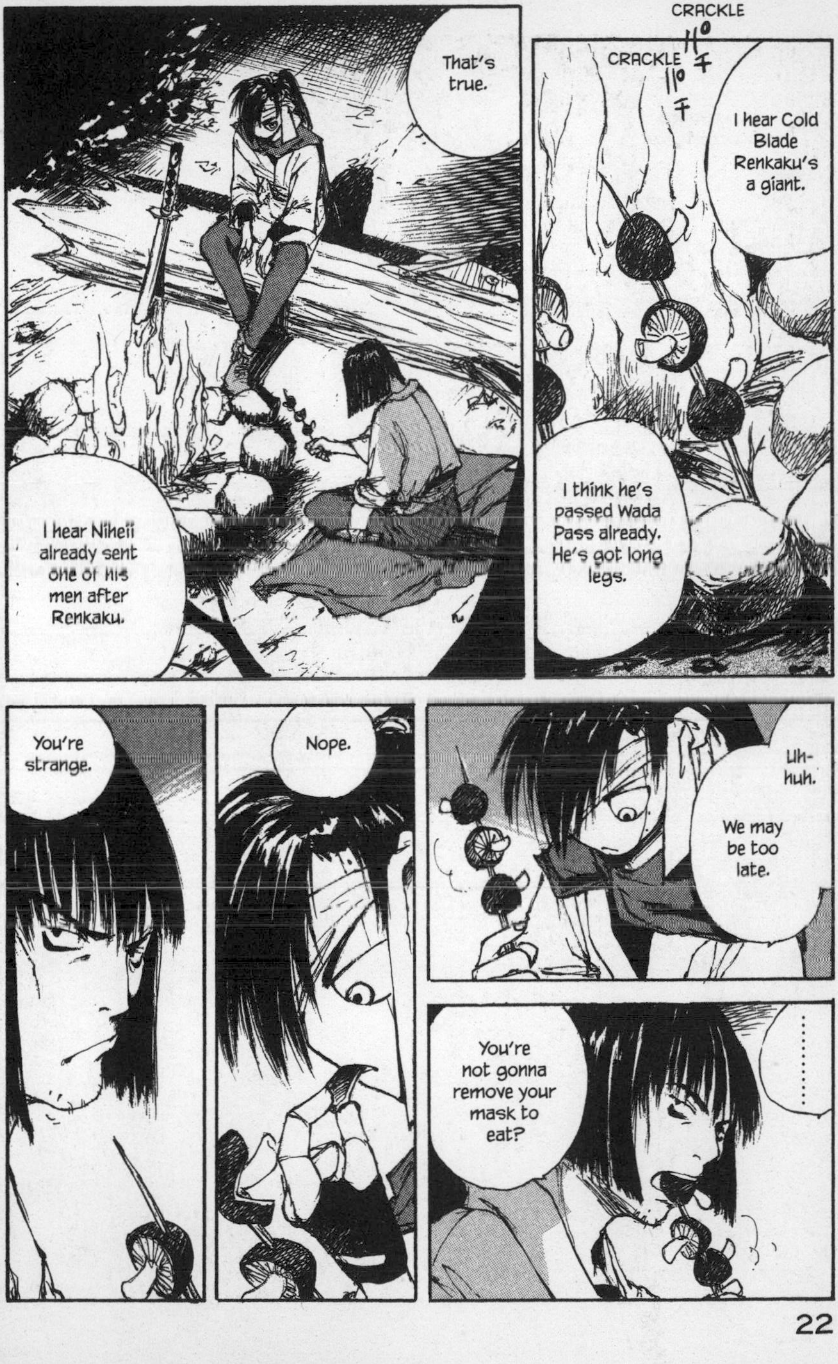
CRACKLE
CRACKLE
I hear Cold Blade Renkaku's a giant.
I think he's passed Wada Pass already. He's got long legs.
That's true.
I hear Niheii already sent one of his men after Renkaku.
Uh-huh.
We may be too late.
......
You're not gonna remove your mask to eat?
Nope.
You're strange.

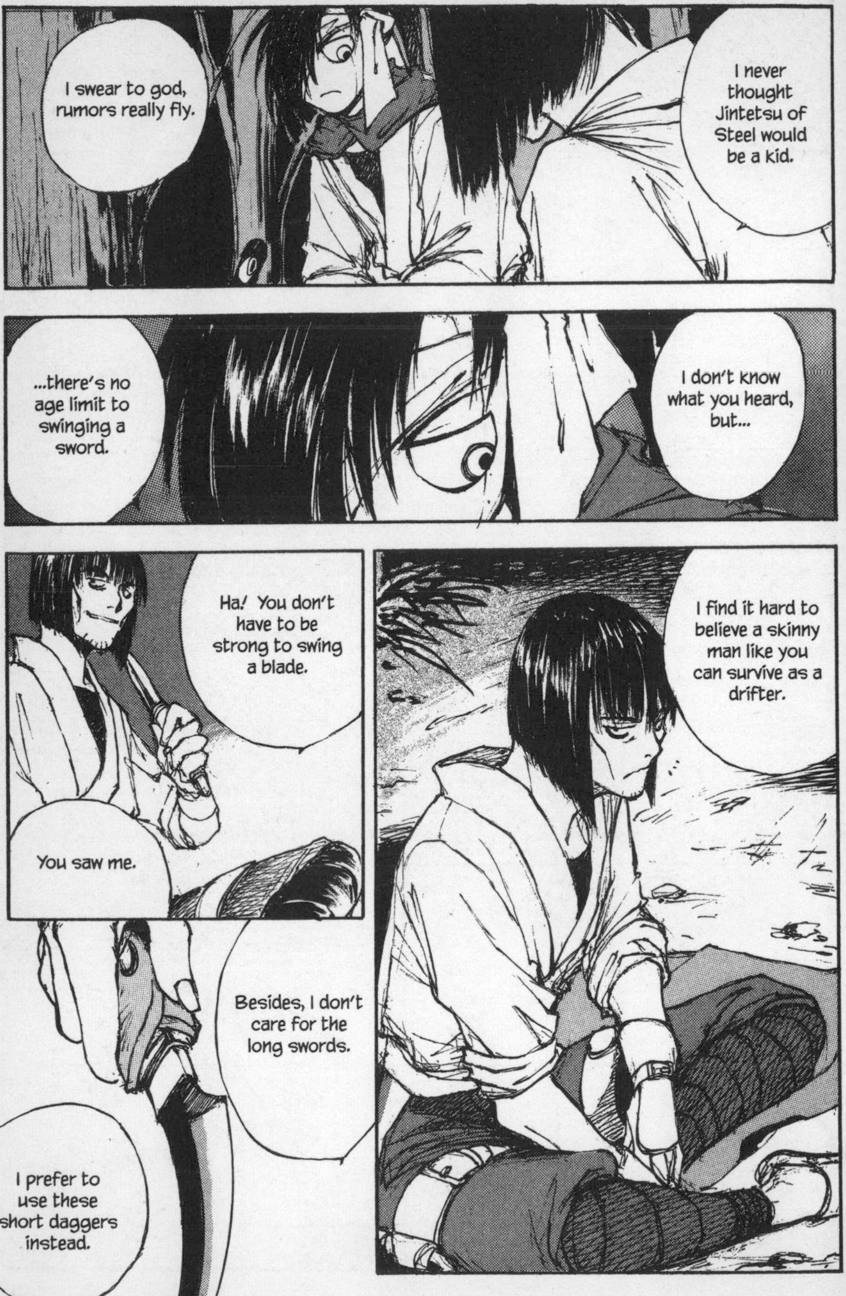
I never thought Jintetsu of Steel would be a kid.
I swear to god, rumors really fly.
I don't know what you heard, but...
...there's no age limit to swinging a sword.
I find it hard to believe a skinny man like you can survive as a drifter.
Ha! You don't have to be strong to swing a blade.
You saw me.
Besides, I don't care for the long swords.
I prefer to use these short daggers instead.

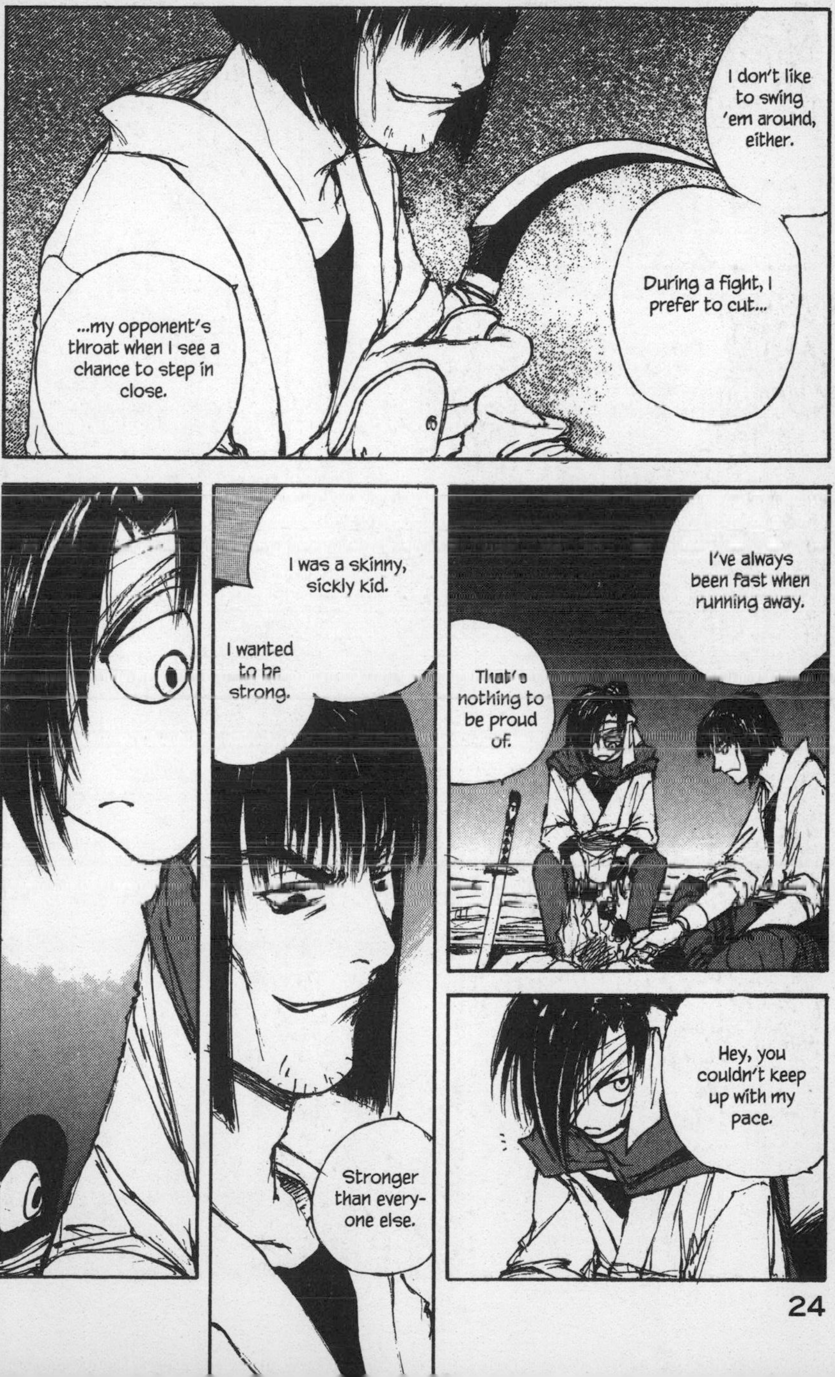

I don't like to swing 'em around, either.
During a fight, I prefer to cut...
...my opponent's throat when I see a chance to step in close.
I've always been fast when running away.
That's nothing to be proud of.
Hey, you couldn't keep up with my pace.
I was a skinny, sickly kid.
I wanted to be strong.
Stronger than every-one else.

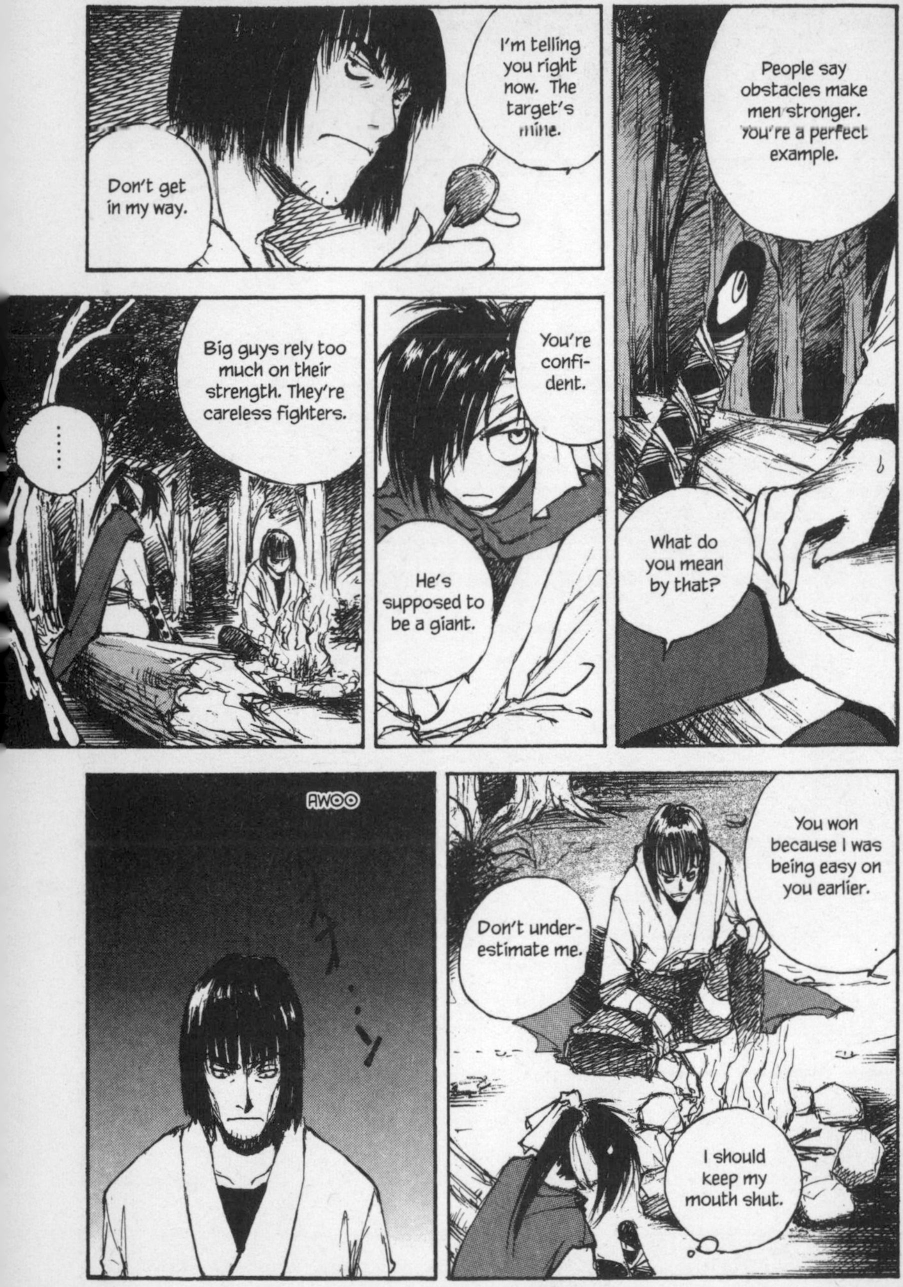
People say obstacles make men stronger. You're a perfect example.
What do you mean by that?
I'm telling you right now. The target's mine.
Don't get in my way.
You're confi-dent.
He's supposed to be a giant.
Big guys rely too much on their strength. They're careless fighters.
......
You won because I was being easy on you earlier.
Don't under-estimate me.
I should keep my mouth shut.
AWOO

It's getting chilly out here.
I'm gonna throw more sticks into the fire.
You're scared of wild dogs, huh?
Of course not!

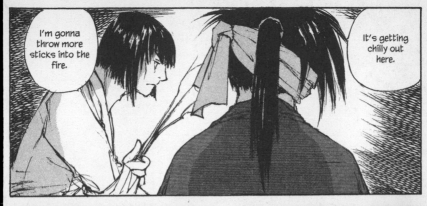

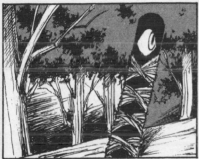

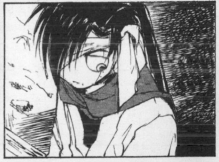

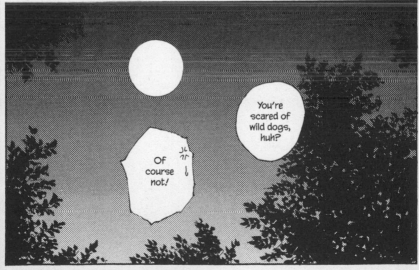

THE END OF CHAPTER 12 EPISODE 1

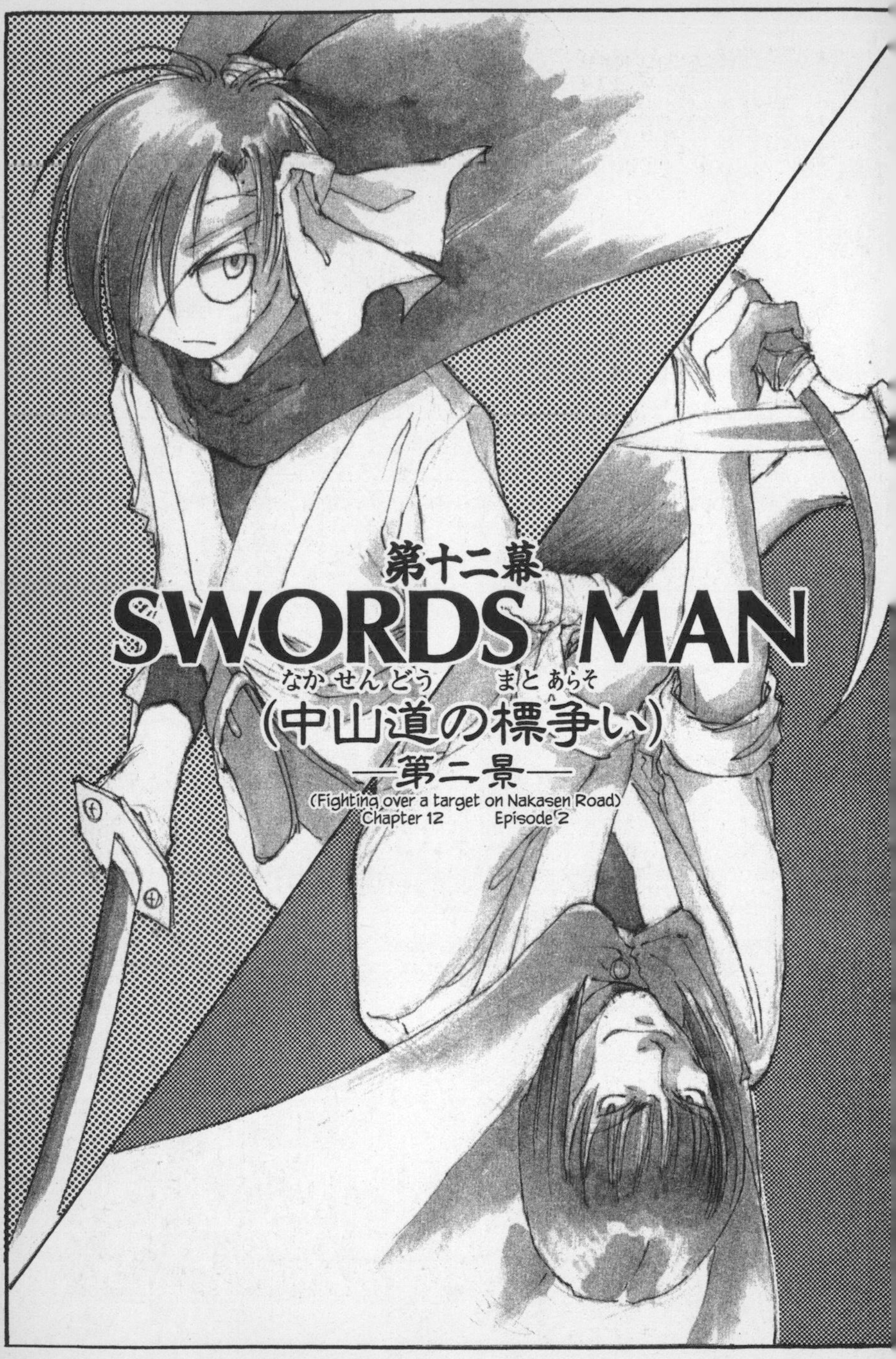
第十二幕
SWORDS MAN
なか せん どう まと あらそ
(中山道の標争い)
—第二景—
(Fighting over a target on Nakasen Road)
Chapter 12 Episode 2

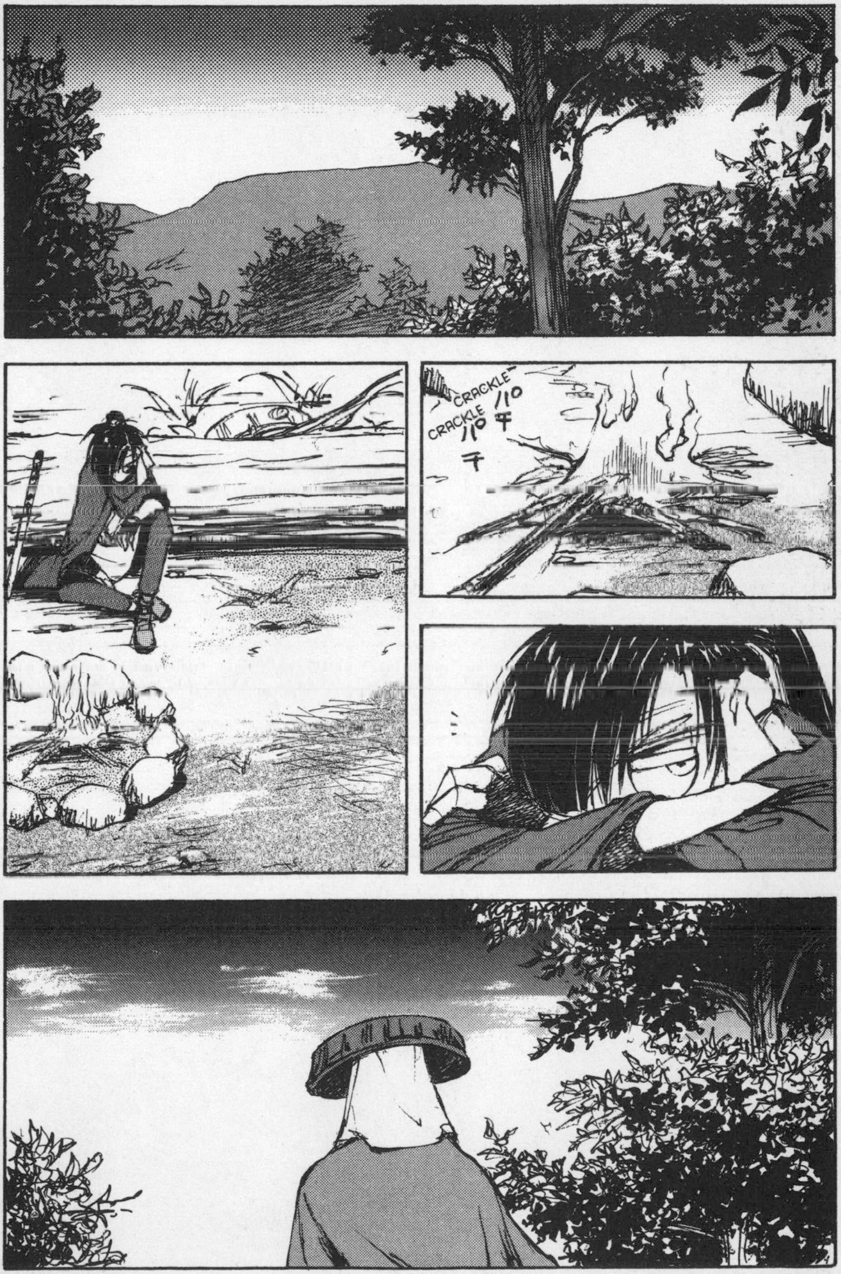
CRACKLE
CRACKLE
パチ
パチ

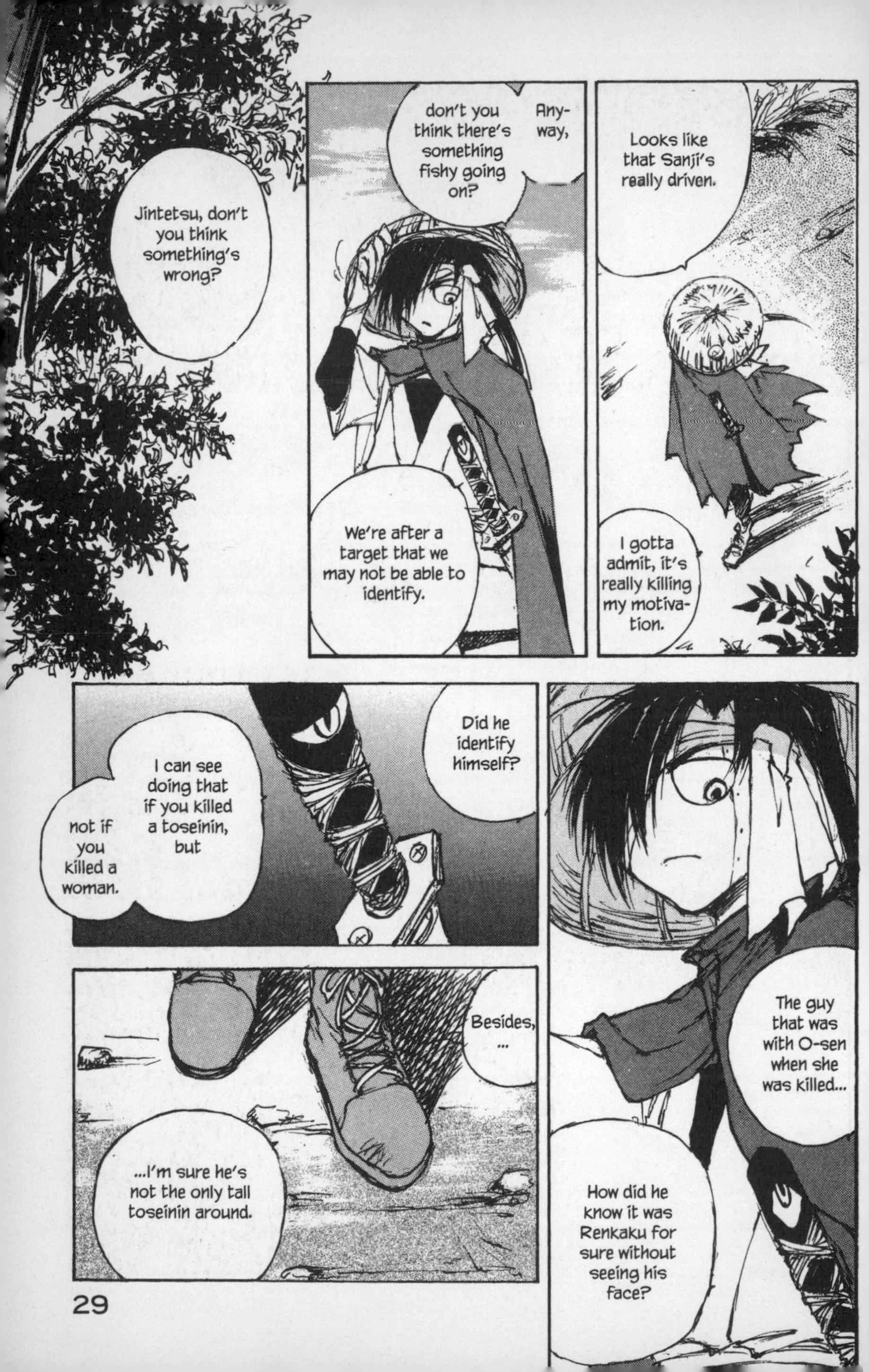
Looks like that Sanji's really driven.
I gotta admit, it's really killing my motivation.
Anyway,
don't you think there's something fishy going on?
We're after a target that we may not be able to identify.
Jintetsu, don't you think something's wrong?
The guy that was with O-sen when she was killed...
How did he know it was Renkaku for sure without seeing his face?
Did he identify himself?
I can see doing that if you killed a toseinin, but
not if you killed a woman.
Besides, ...
...I'm sure he's not the only tall toseinin around.

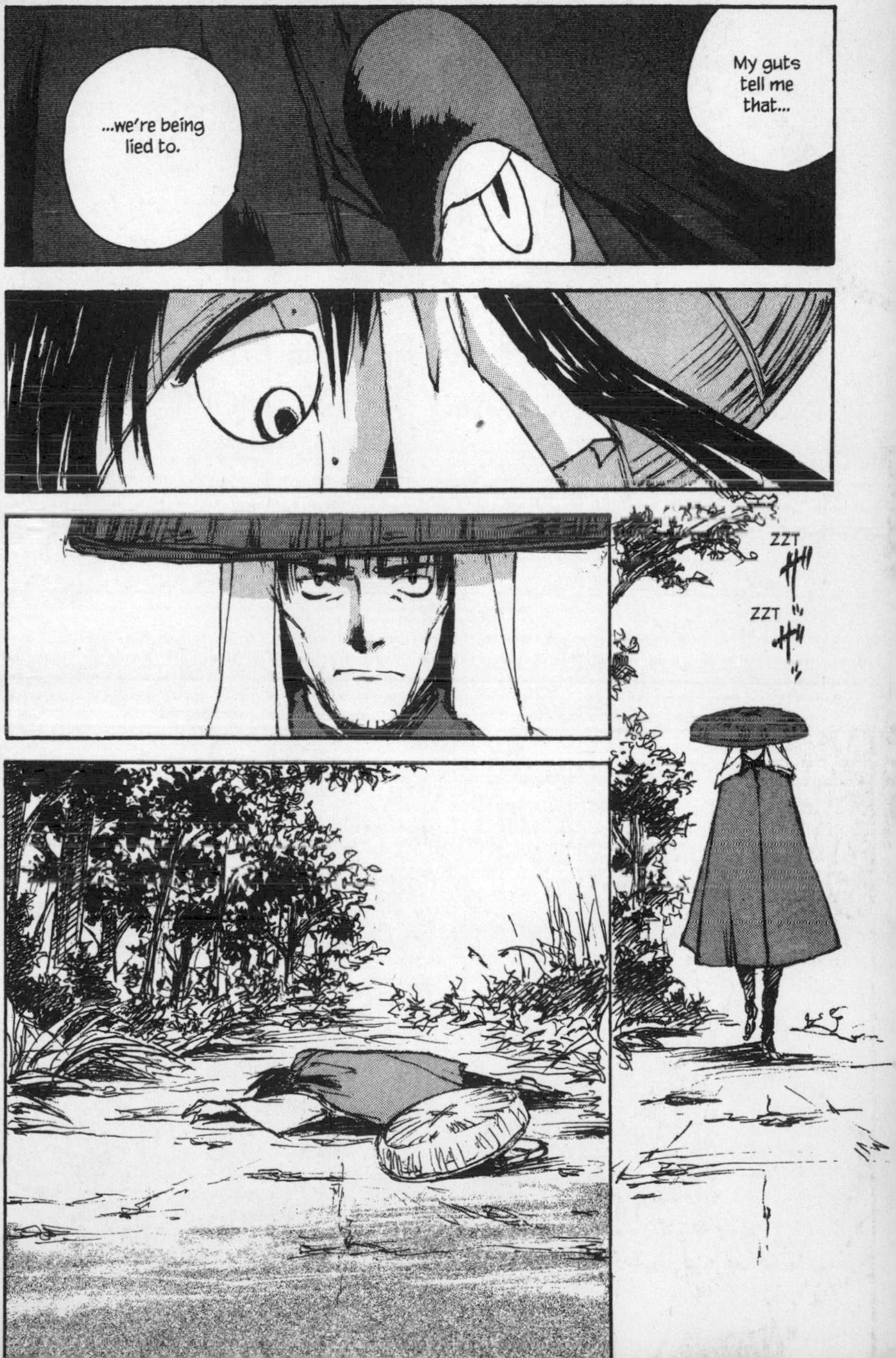
My guts tell me that...
...we're being lied to.
ZZT
ZZT

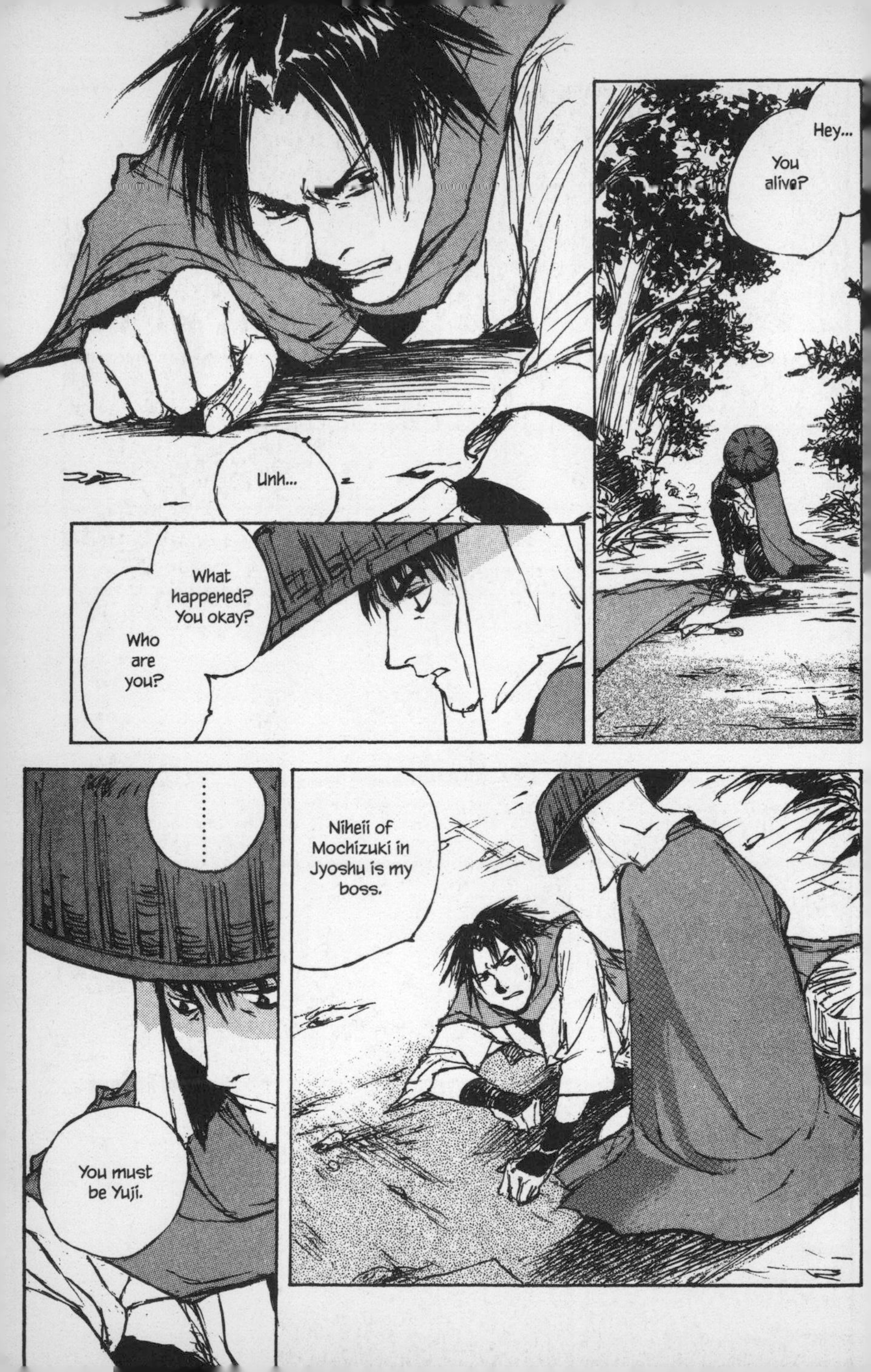
Hey...
You alive?
Unh...
What happened? You okay?
Who are you?
Niheii of Mochizuki in Jyoshu is my boss.
......
You must be Yuji.

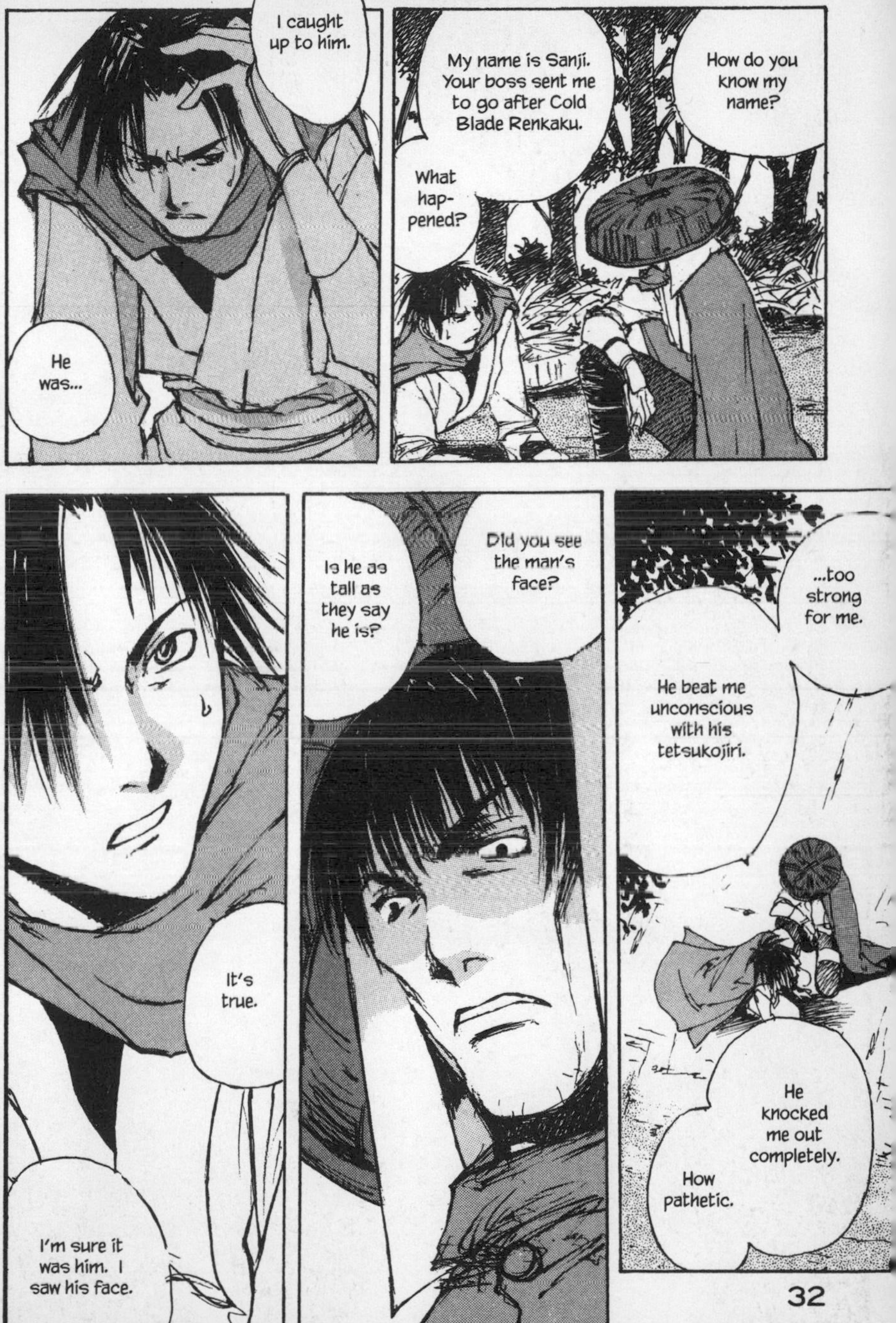
How do you know my name?
My name is Sanji. Your boss sent me to go after Cold Blade Renkaku.
What hap-pened?
I caught up to him.
He was...
...too strong for me.
He beat me unconscious with his tetsukojiri.
He knocked me out completely.
How pathetic.
Did you see the man's face?
Is he as tall as they say he is?
It's true.
I'm sure it was him. I saw his face.

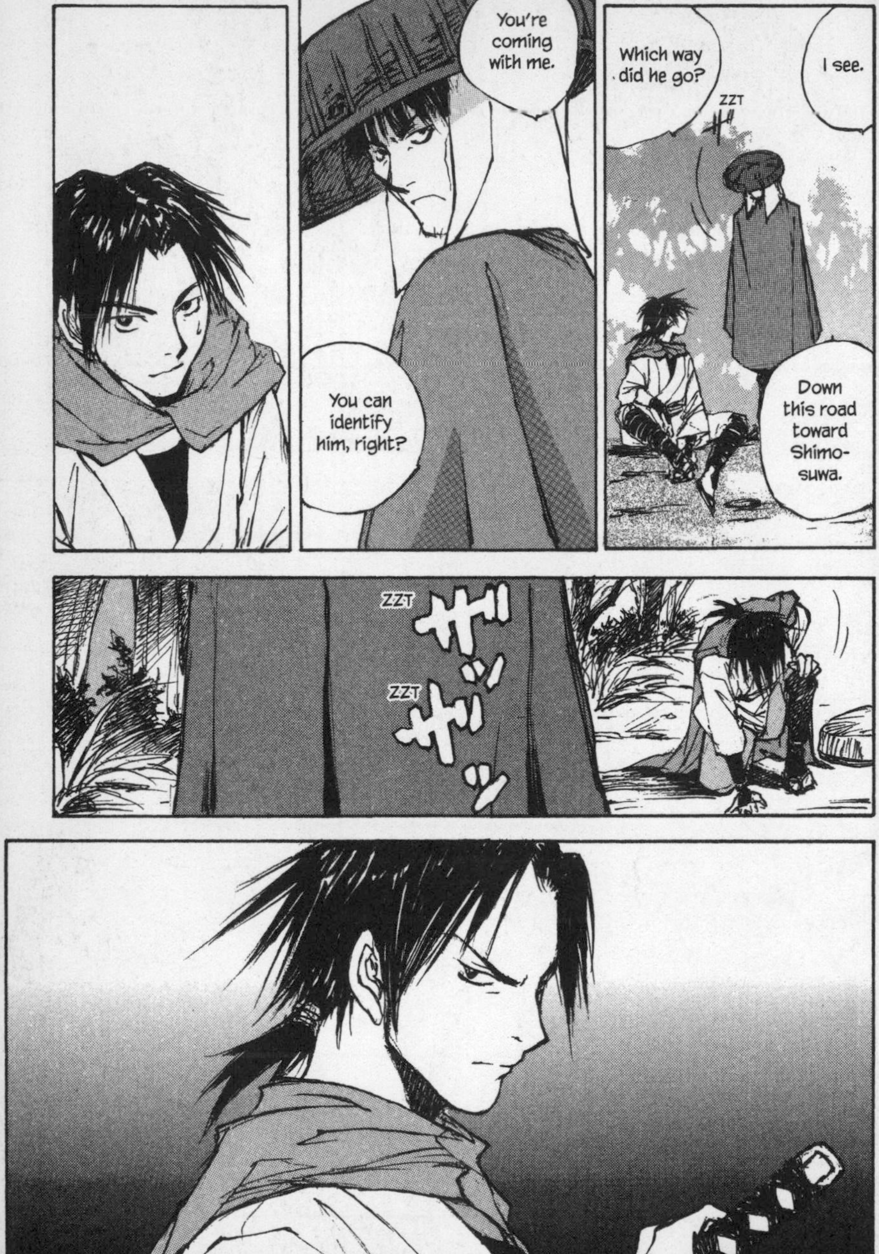
I see.
Which way did he go?
ZZT
Down this road toward Shimo-suwa.
You're coming with me.
You can identify him, right?
ZZT
ZZT

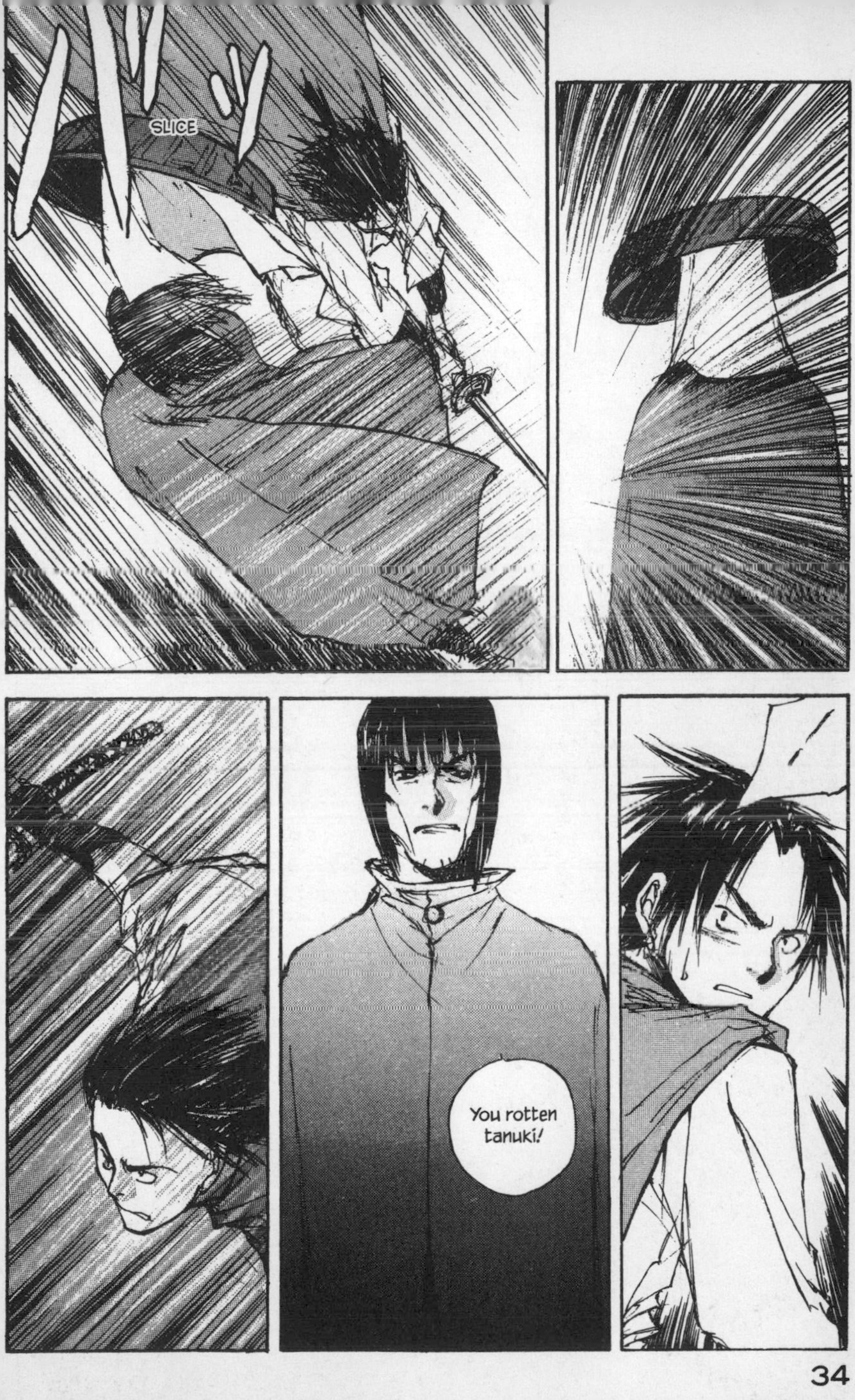
SLICE
You rotten tanuki!

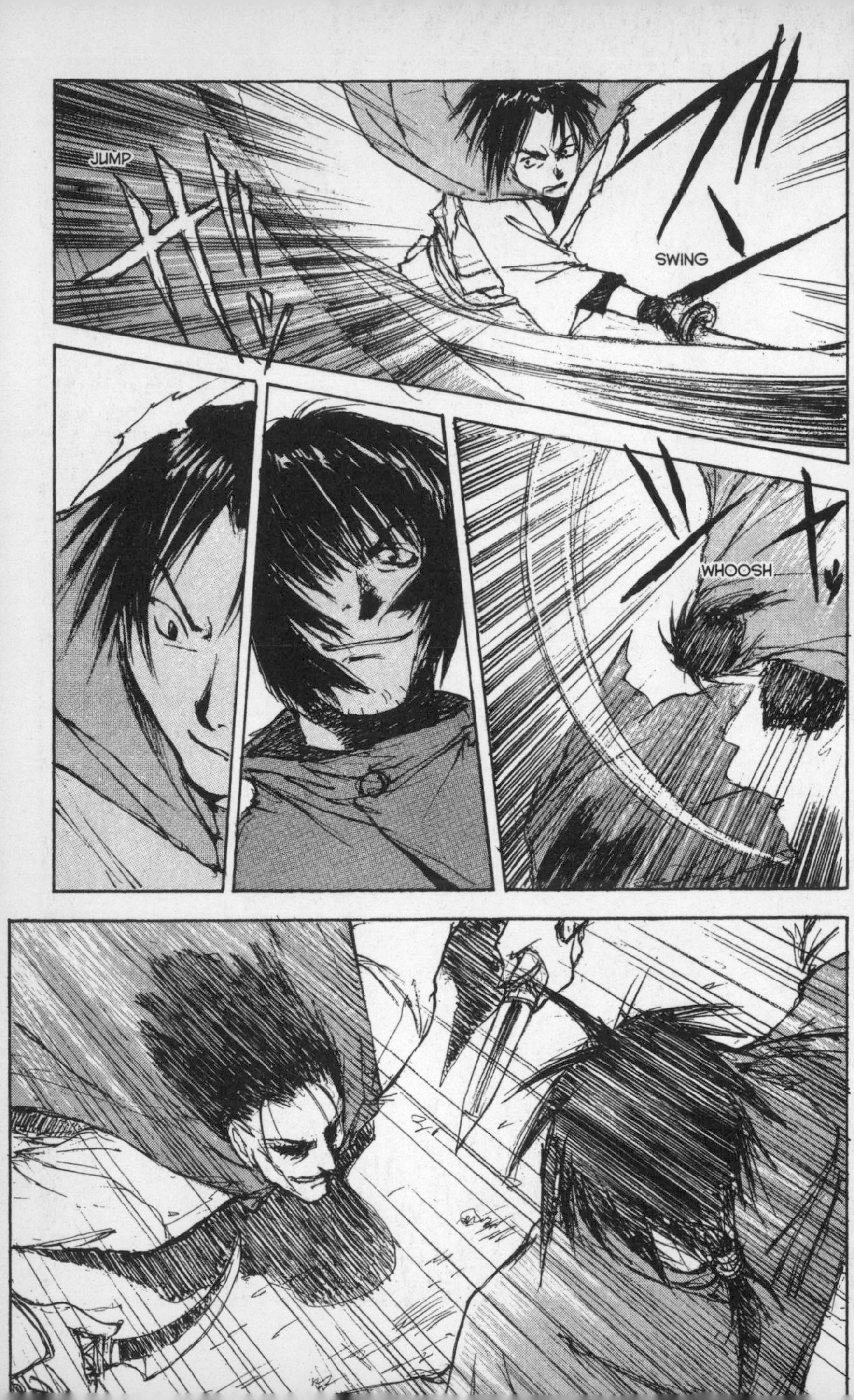
SWING
JUMP
WHOOSH

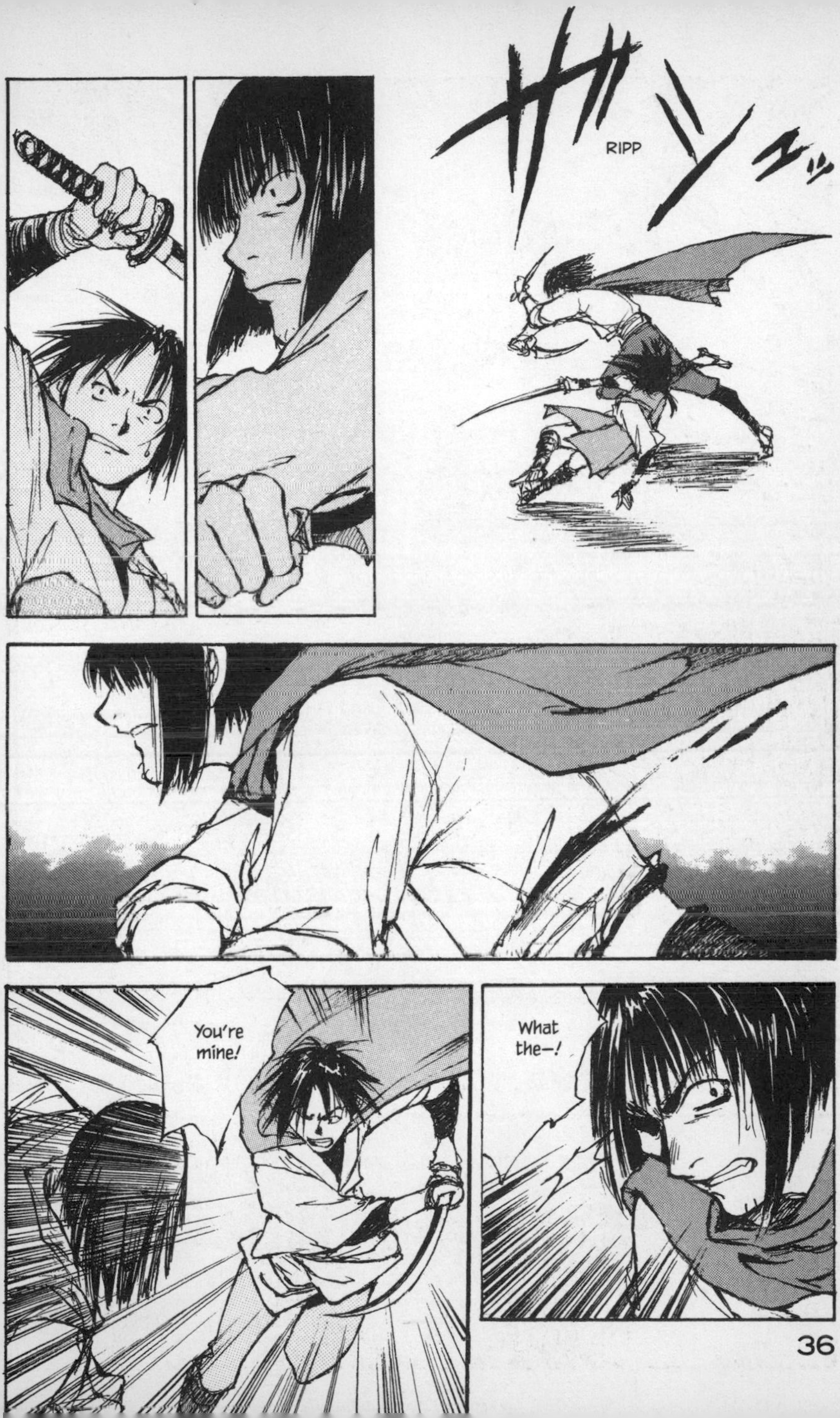
RIPP
What the–!
You're mine!

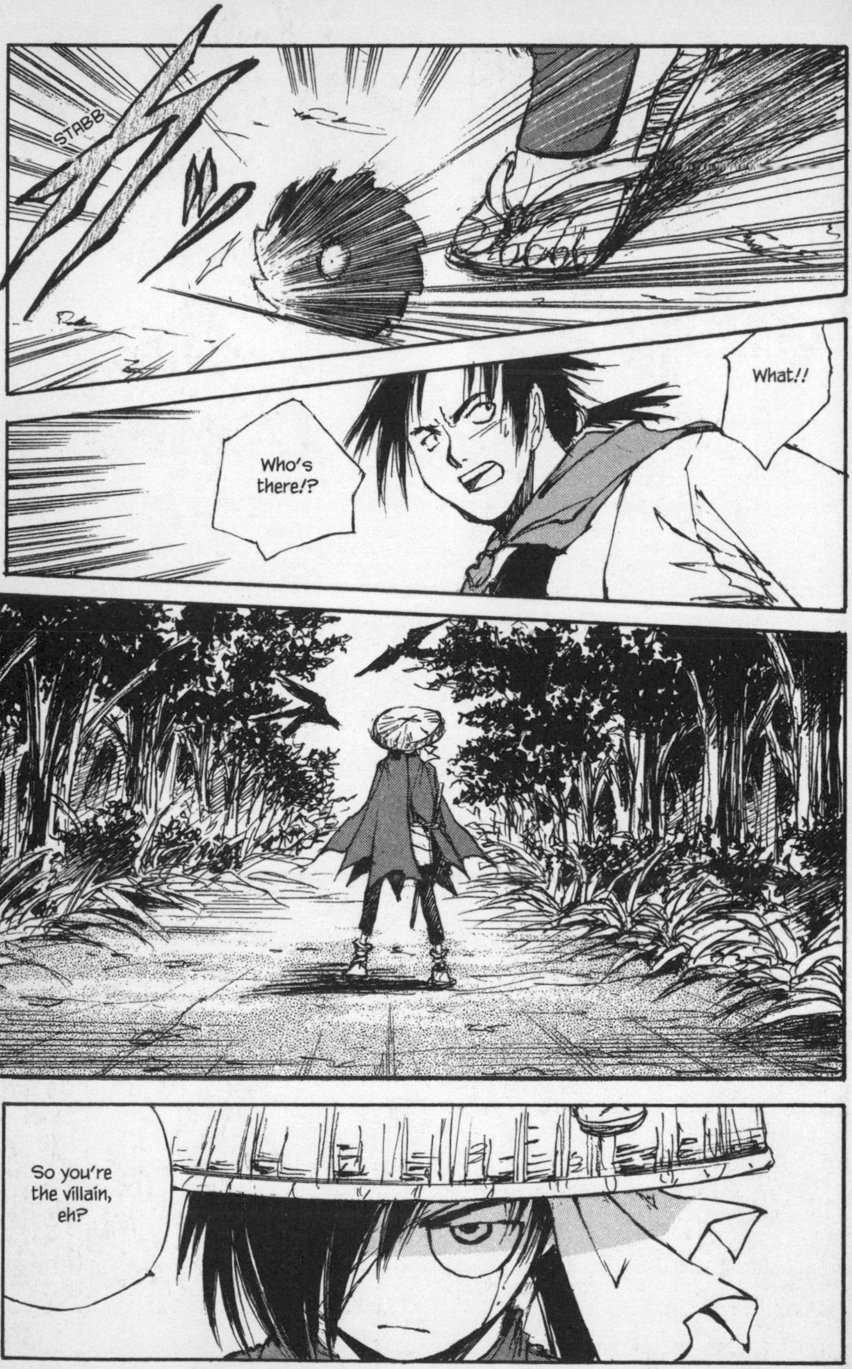
STABB
What!!
Who's there!?
So you're the villain, eh?

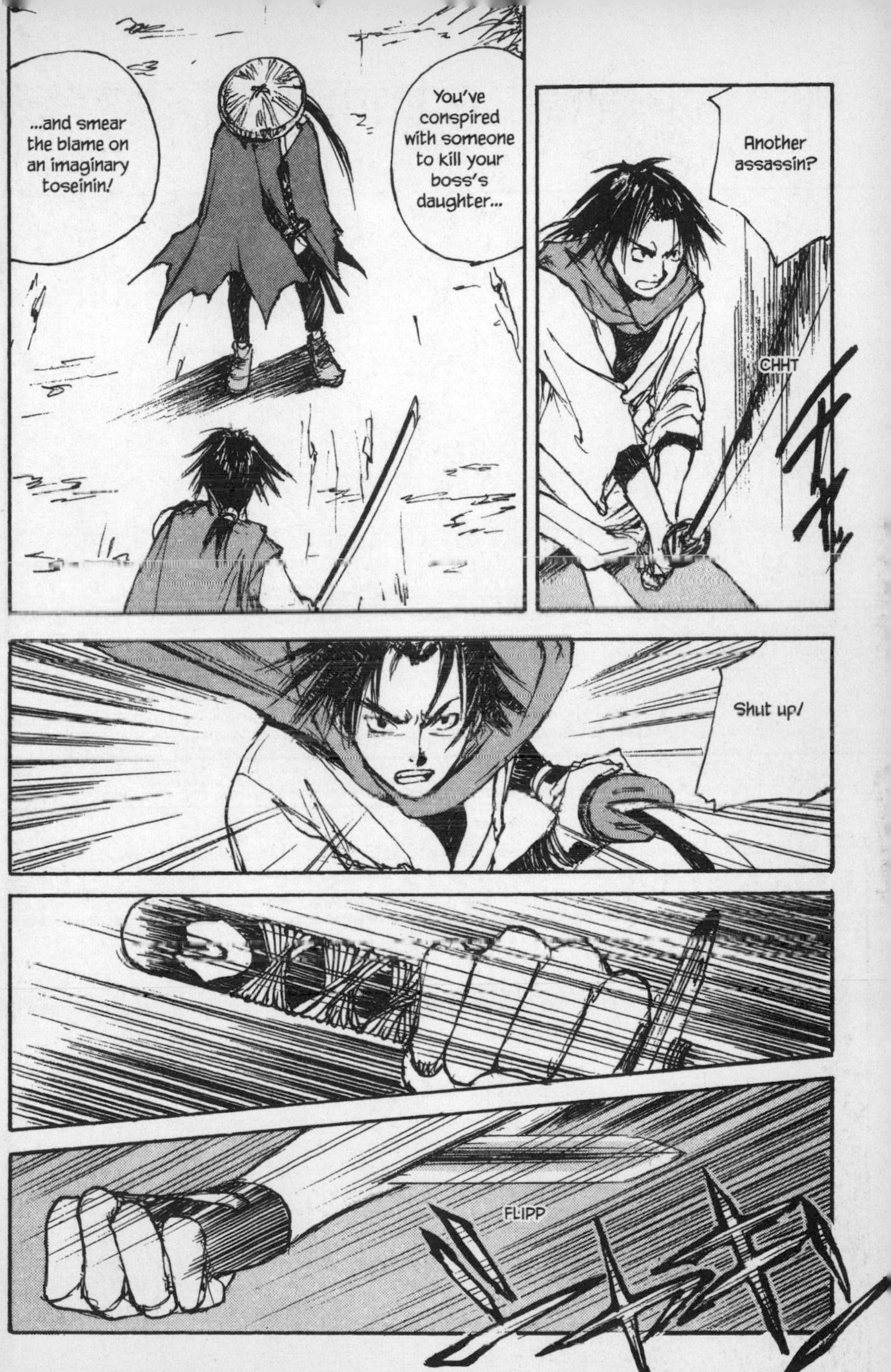
Another assassin?
CHHT
You've conspired with someone to kill your boss's daughter...
...and smear the blame on an imaginary toseinin!
Shut up!
FLIPP

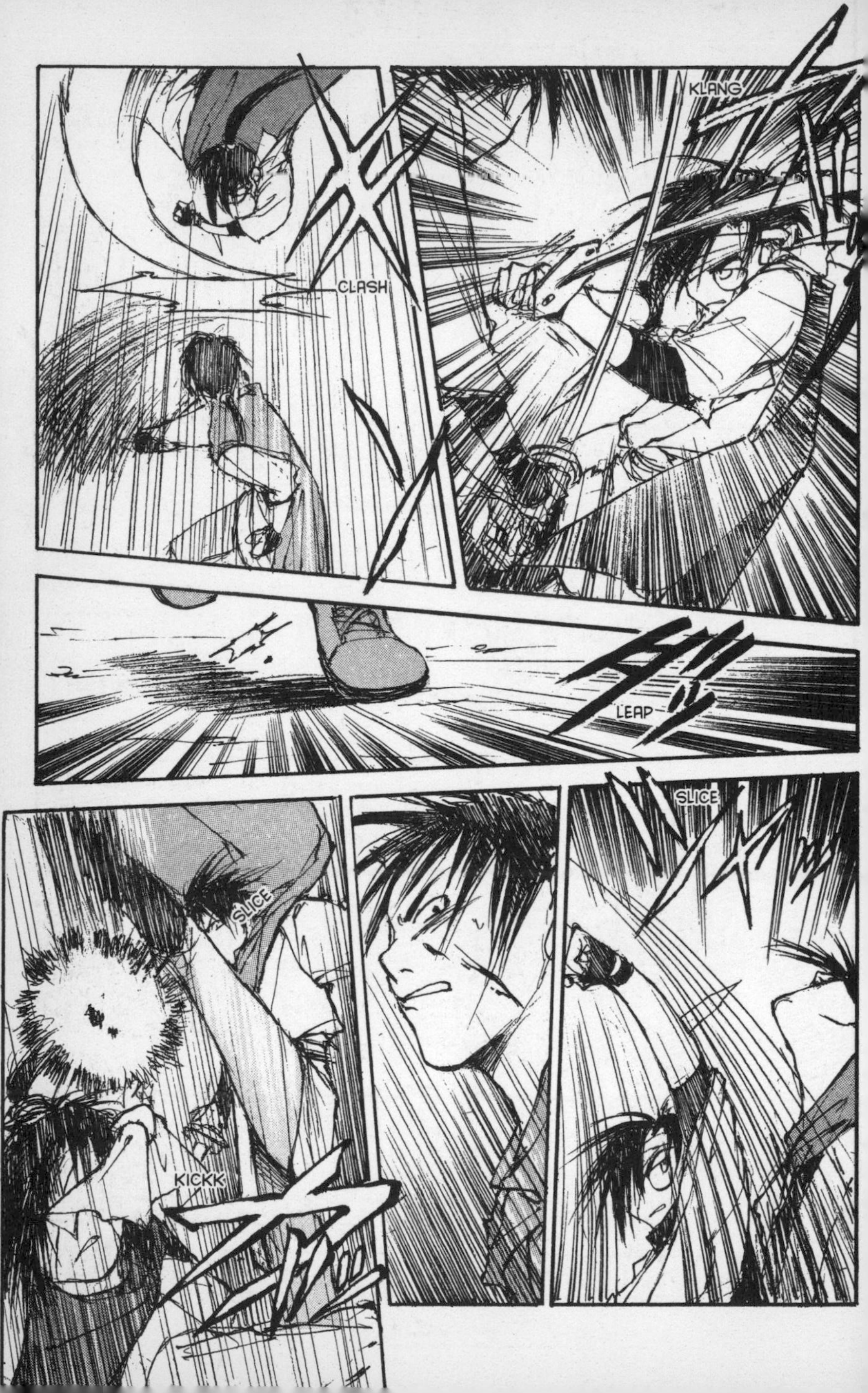
KLANG
CLASH
LEAP
SLICE
SLICE
KICKK

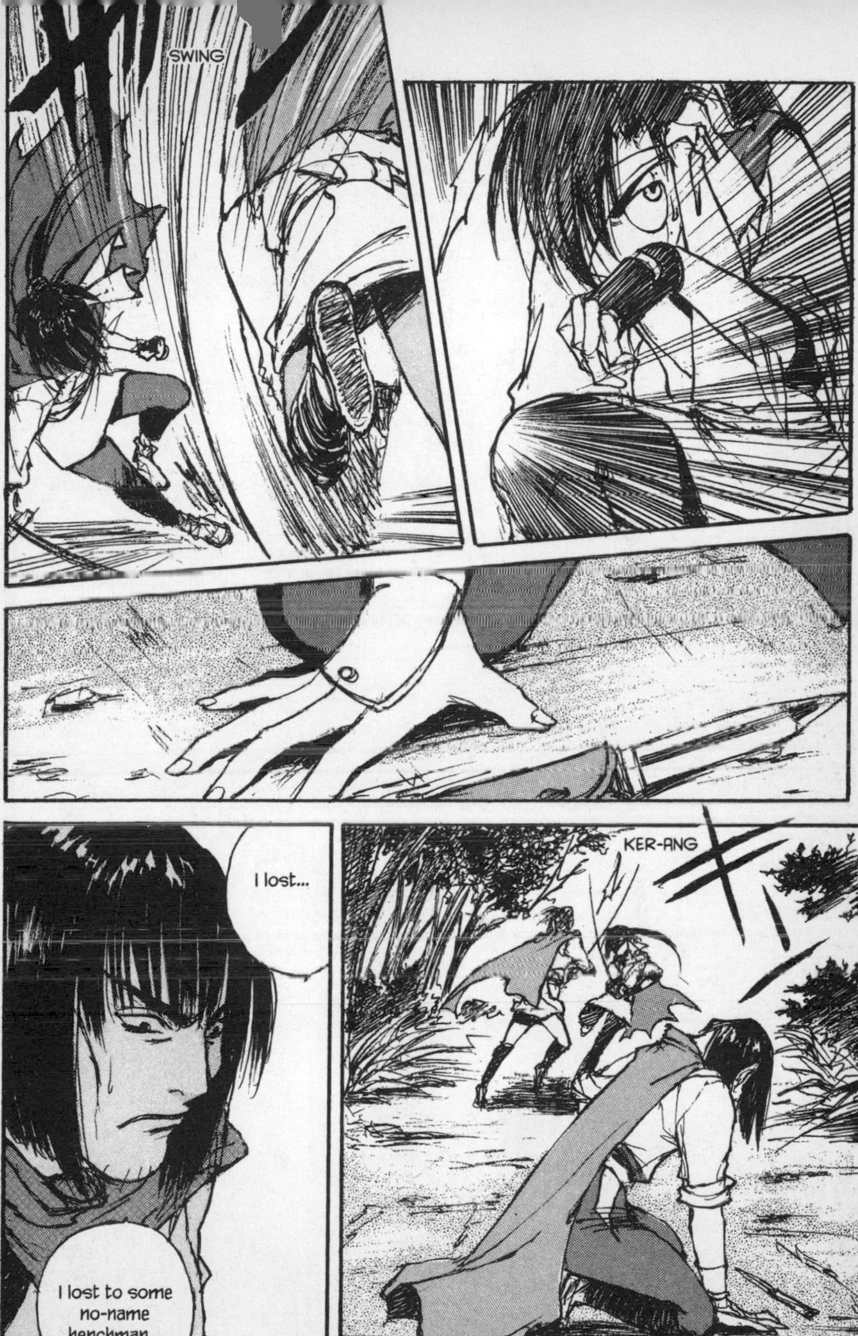
SWING
KER-ANG
I lost...
I lost to some no-name henchman...

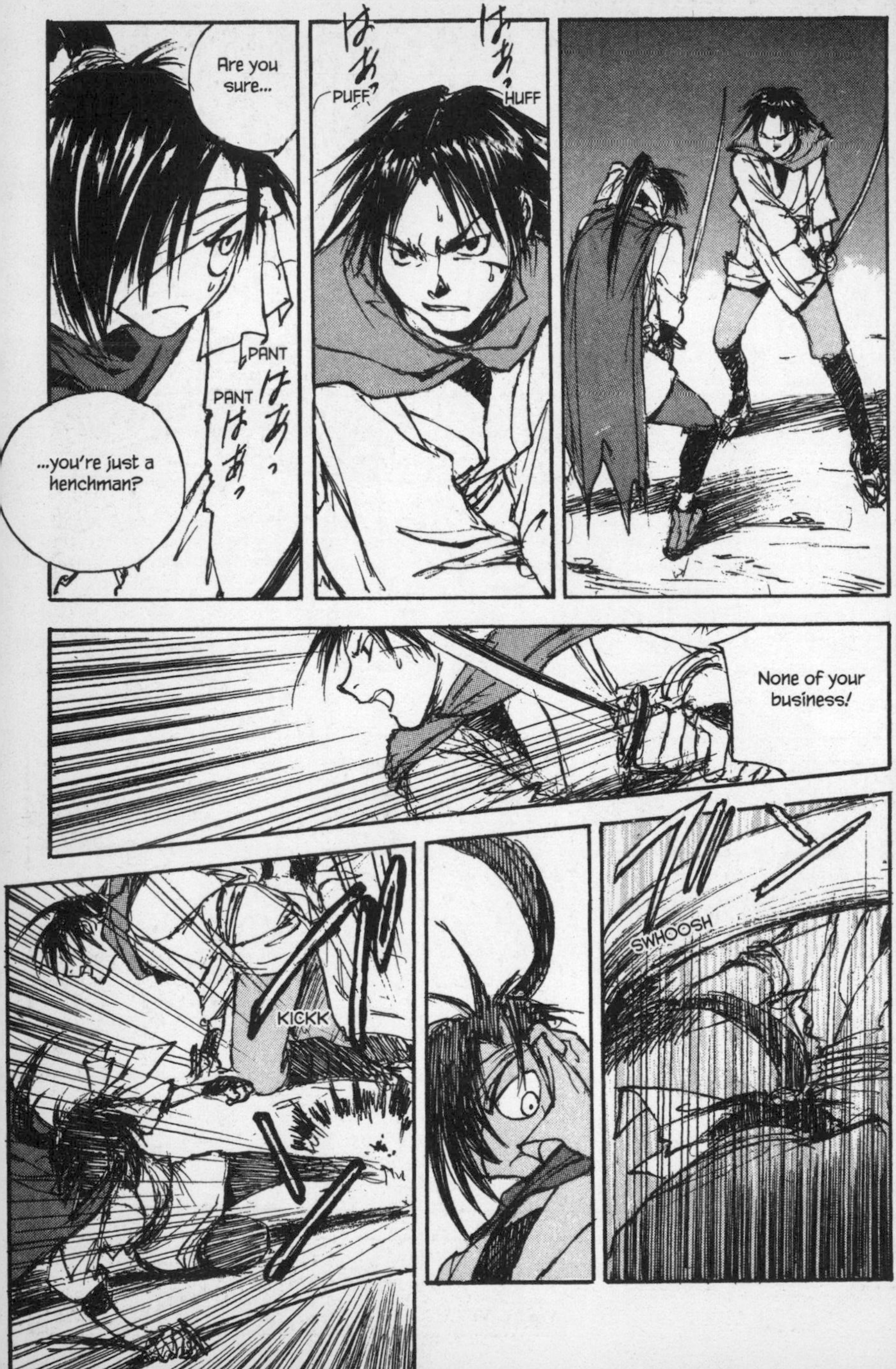
はあっ
HUFF
はあっ
PUFF
Are you sure...
PANT
はあっ
PANT
はあっ
...you're just a henchman?
None of your business!
SWHOOSH
KICKK

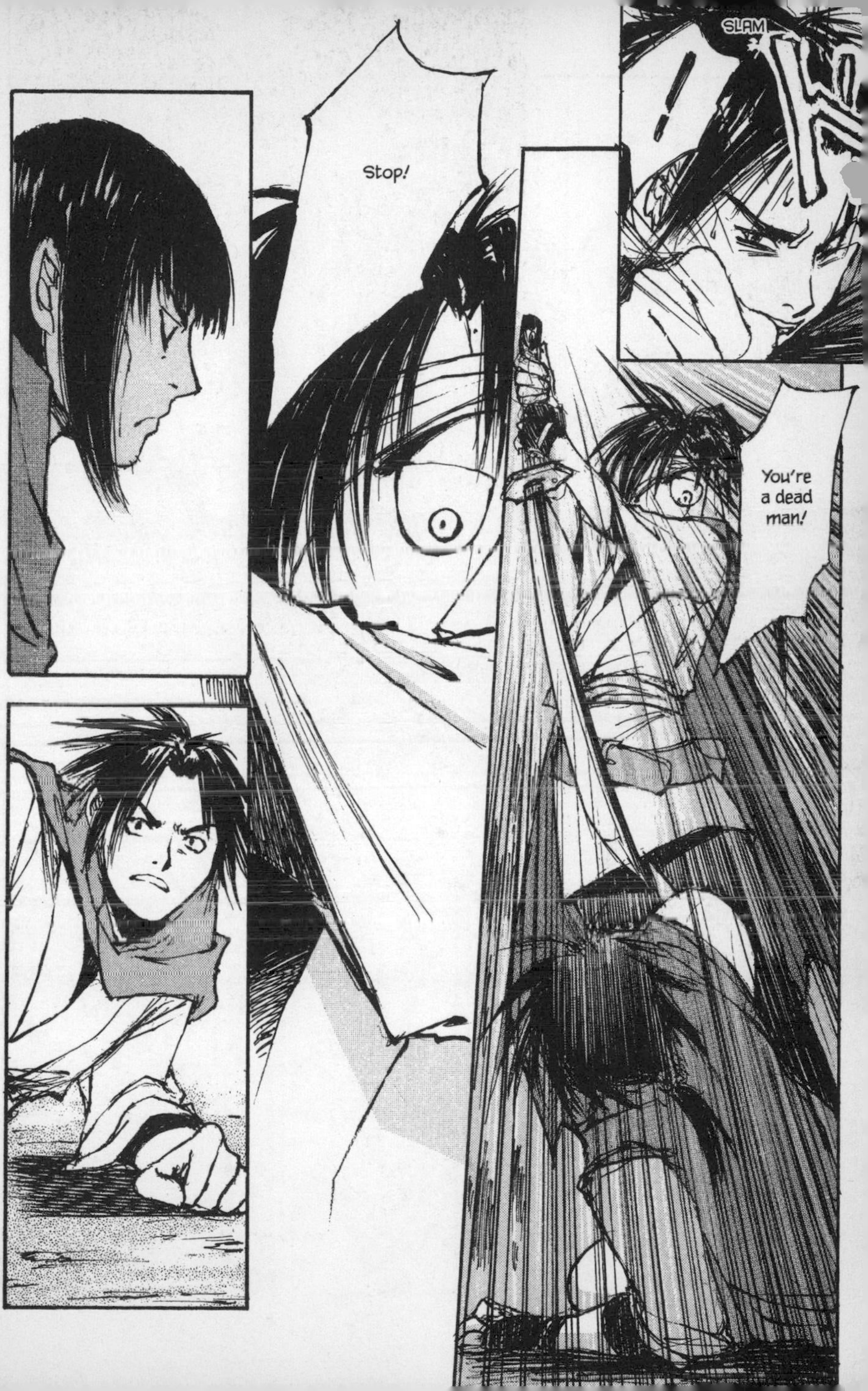
SLAM
!
You're a dead man!
Stop!

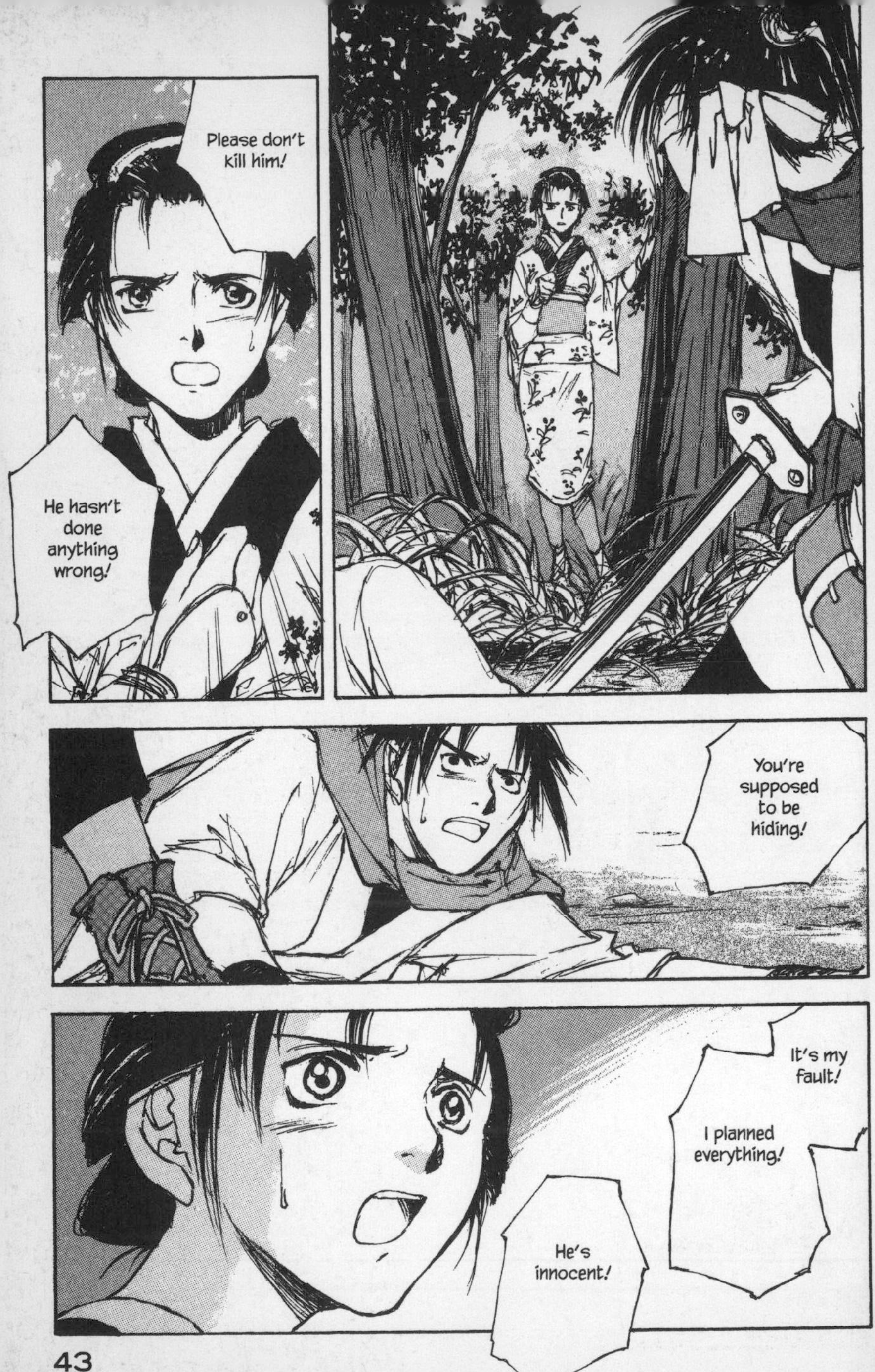
Please don't kill him!
He hasn't done anything wrong!
You're supposed to be hiding!
It's my fault!
I planned everything!
He's innocent!

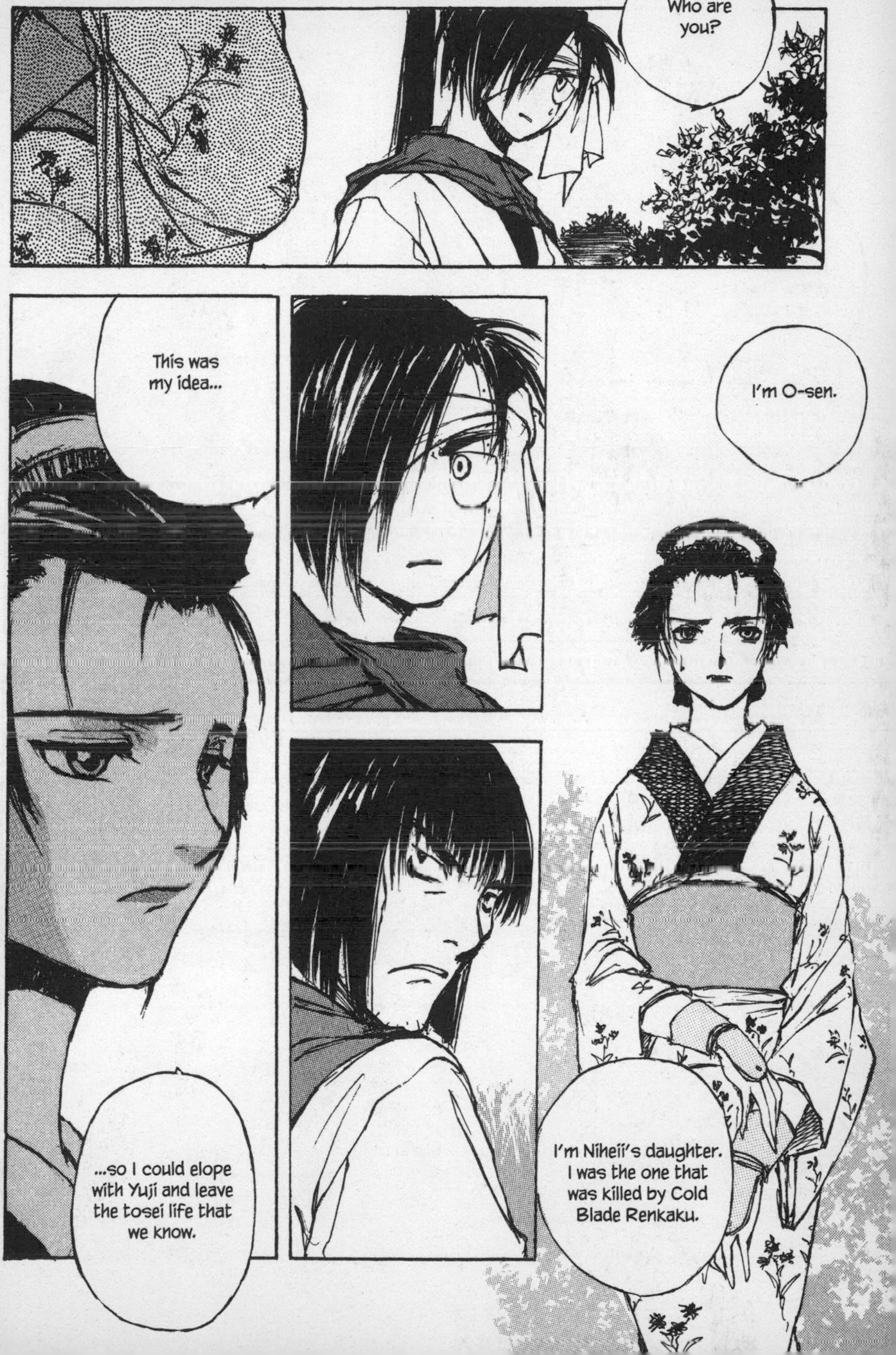

Who are you?
I'm O-sen.
I'm Niheii's daughter. I was the one that was killed by Cold Blade Renkaku.
This was my idea...
...so I could elope with Yuji and leave the tosei life that we know.

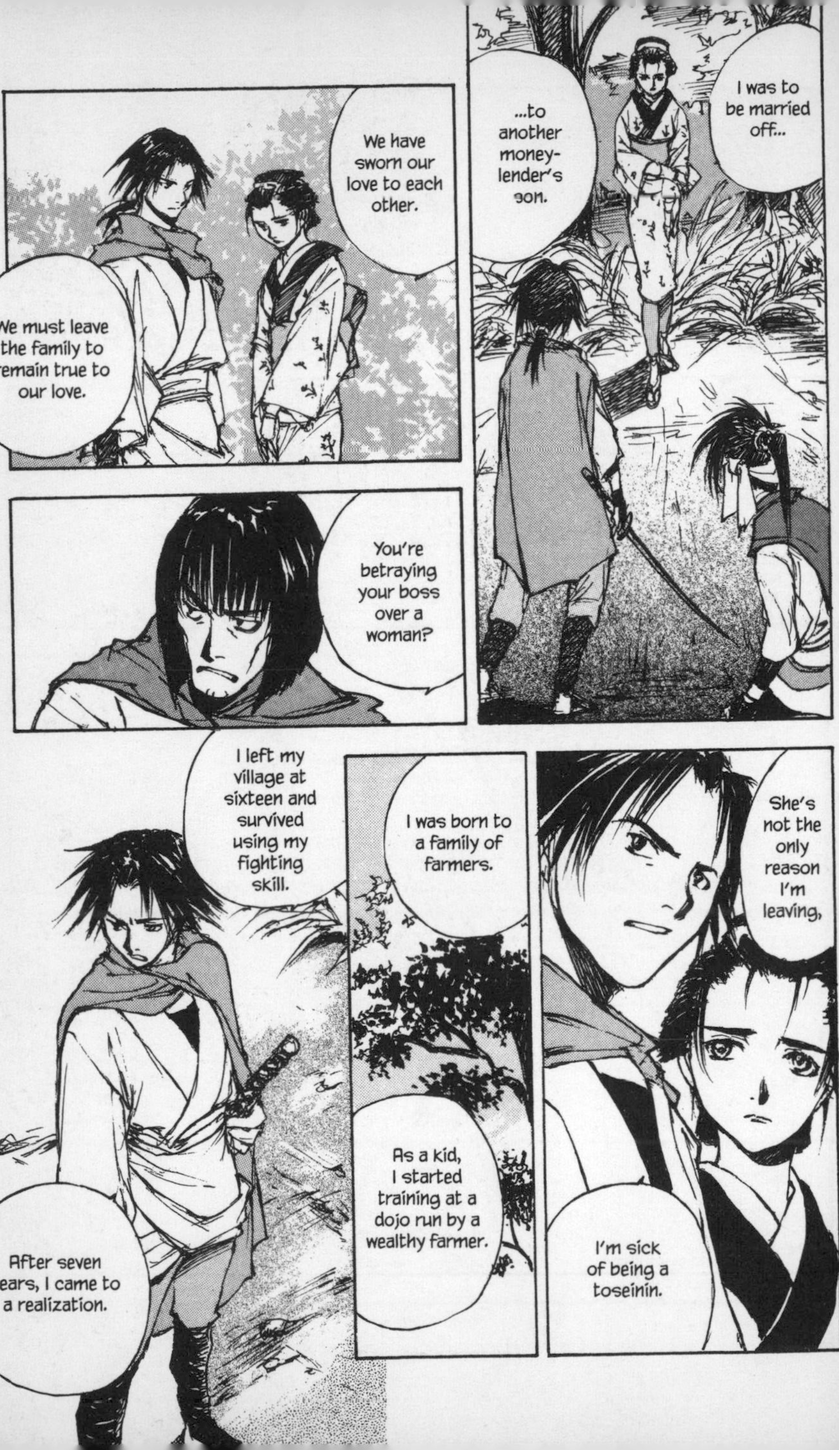
I was to be married off...
...to another money-lender's son.
We have sworn our love to each other.
We must leave the family to remain true to our love.
You're betraying your boss over a woman?
She's not the only reason I'm leaving,
I'm sick of being a toseinin.
I was born to a family of farmers.
As a kid, I started training at a dojo run by a wealthy farmer.
I left my village at sixteen and survived using my fighting skill.
After seven years, I came to a realization.

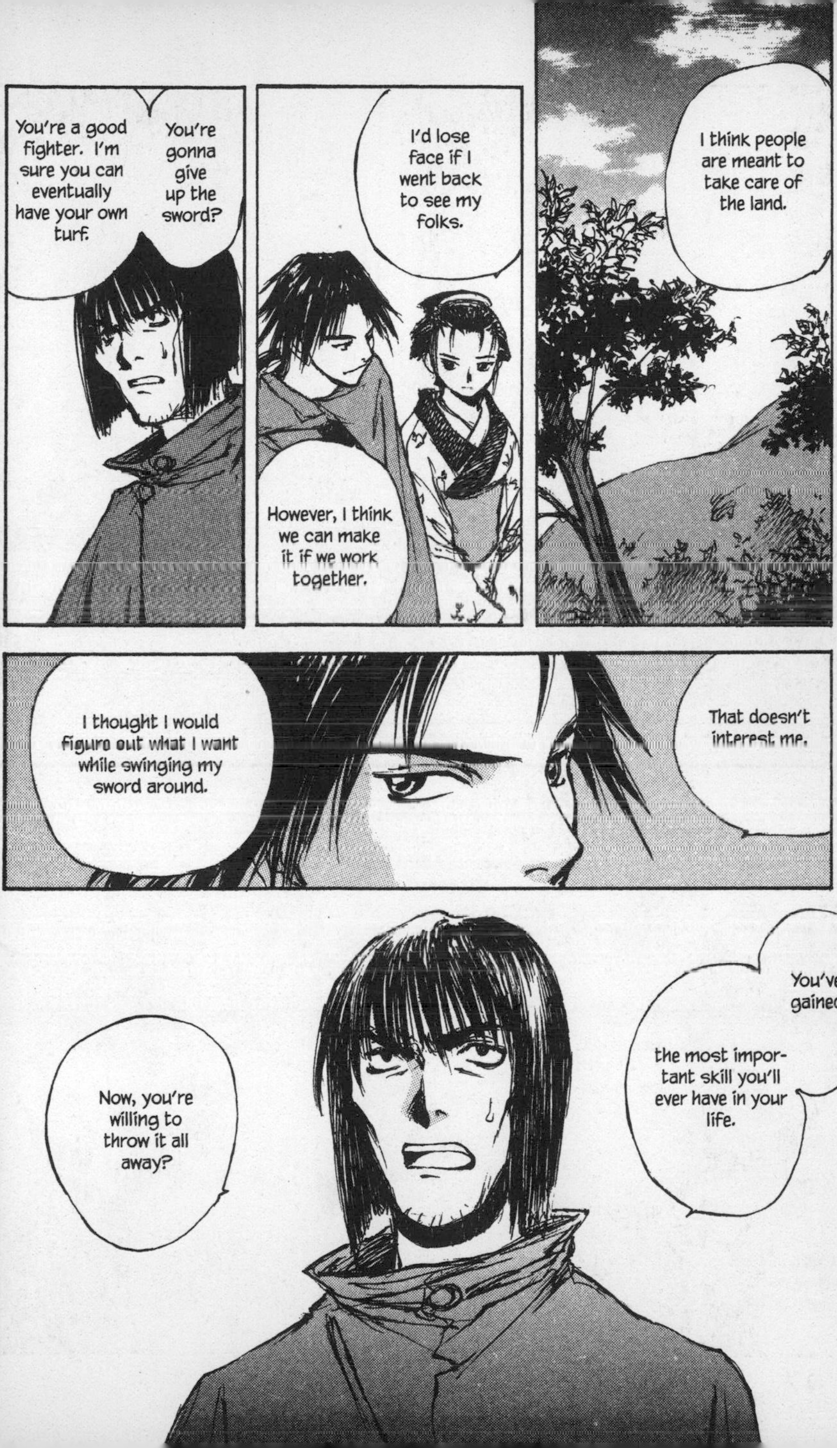
I think people are meant to take care of the land.
I'd lose face if I went back to see my folks.
However, I think we can make it if we work together.
You're gonna give up the sword?
You're a good fighter. I'm sure you can eventually have your own turf.
That doesn't interest me.
I thought I would figure out what I want while swinging my sword around.
You've gained
the most important skill you'll ever have in your life.
Now, you're willing to throw it all away?

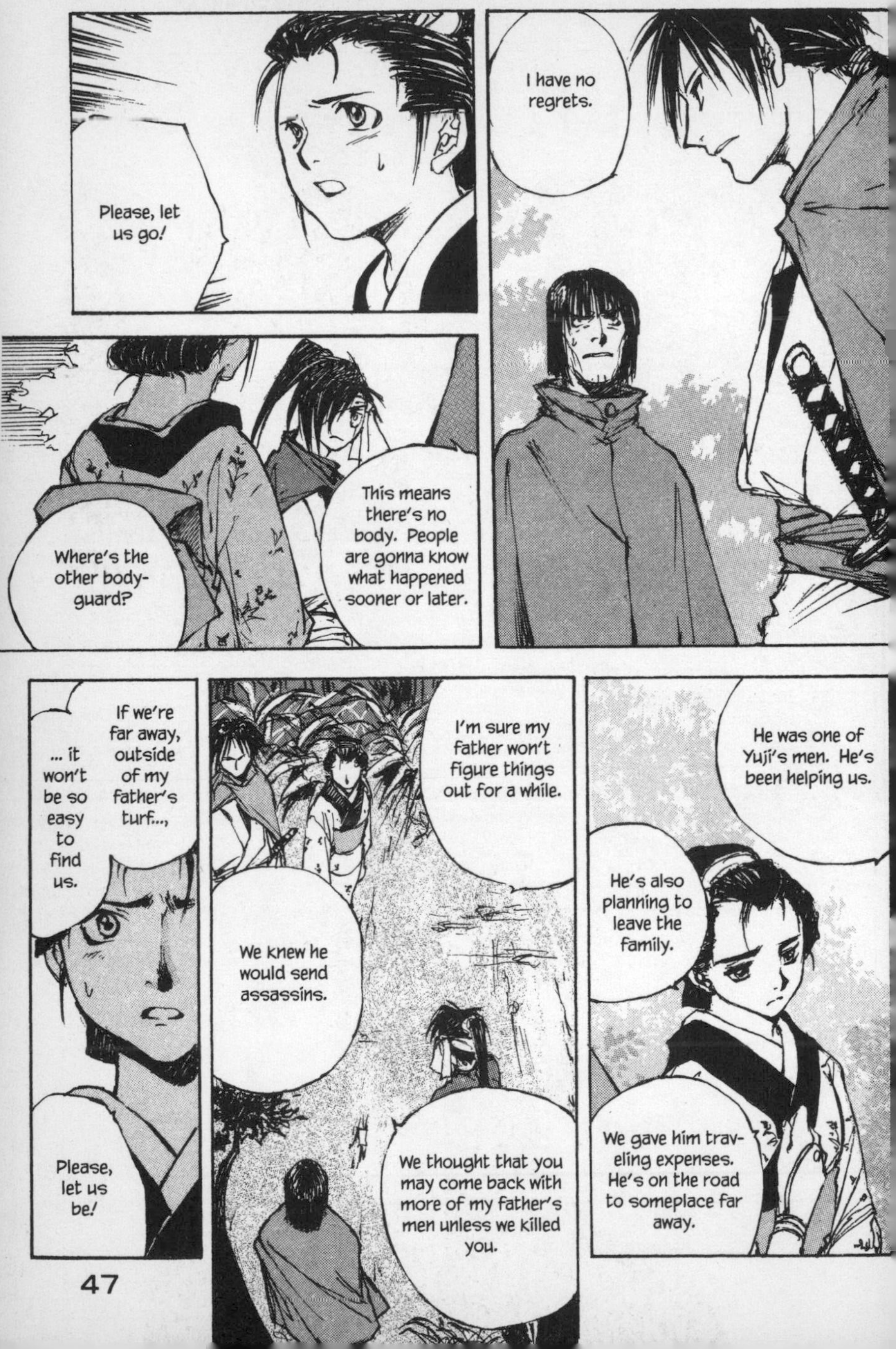
I have no regrets.
Please, let us go!
This means there's no body. People are gonna know what happened sooner or later.
Where's the other body-guard?
He was one of Yuji's men. He's been helping us.
He's also planning to leave the family.
We gave him trav-eling expenses. He's on the road to someplace far away.
I'm sure my father won't figure things out for a while.
We knew he would send assassins.
We thought that you may come back with more of my father's men unless we killed you.
If we're far away, outside of my father's turf...,
... it won't be so easy to find us.
Please, let us be!

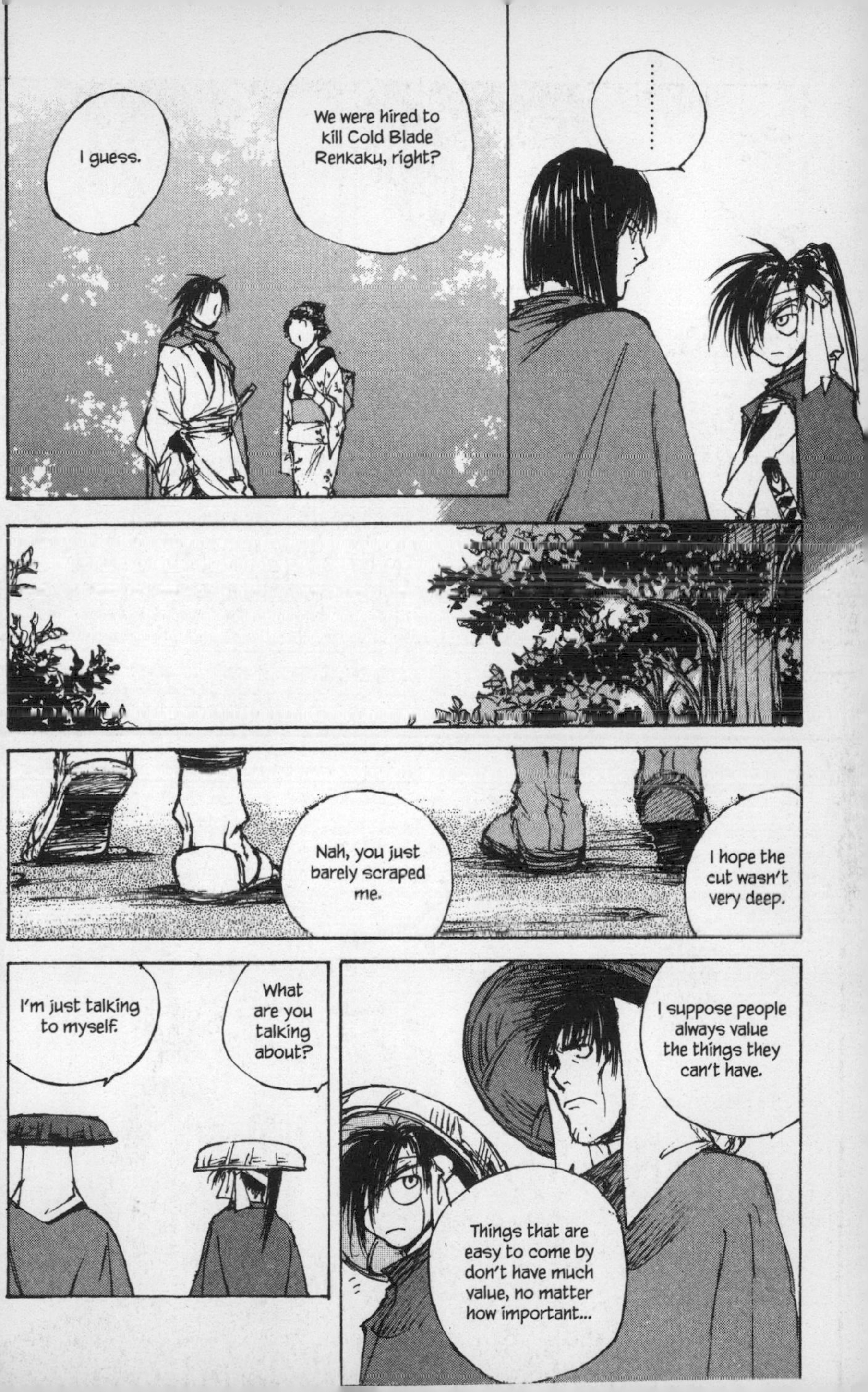
......
We were hired to kill Cold Blade Renkaku, right?
I guess.
I hope the cut wasn't very deep.
Nah, you just barely scraped me.
I suppose people always value the things they can't have.
Things that are easy to come by don't have much value, no matter how important...
What are you talking about?
I'm just talking to myself.

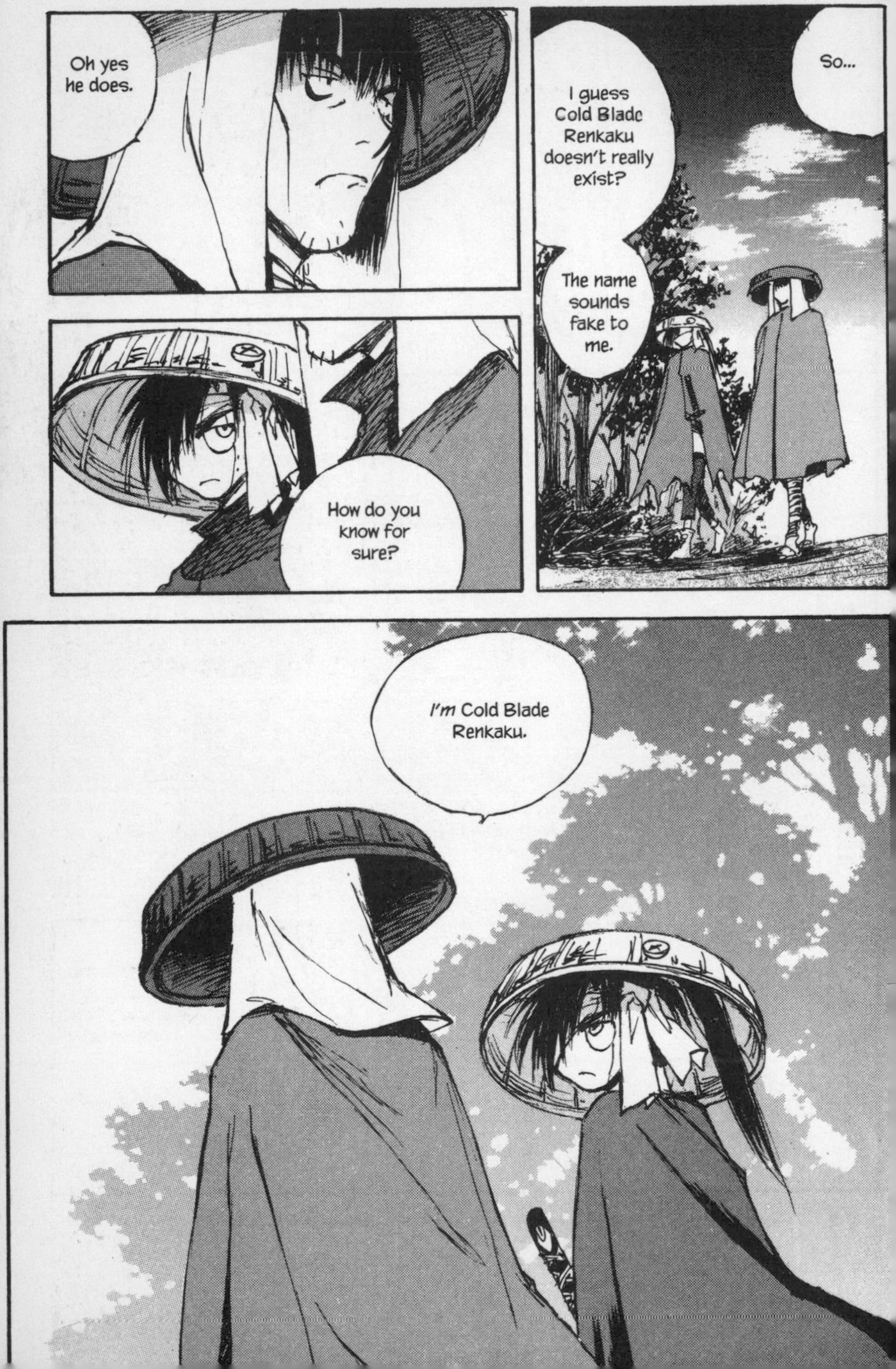
So...
I guess Cold Blade Renkaku doesn't really exist?
The name sounds fake to me.
Oh yes he does.
How do you know for sure?
I'm Cold Blade Renkaku.

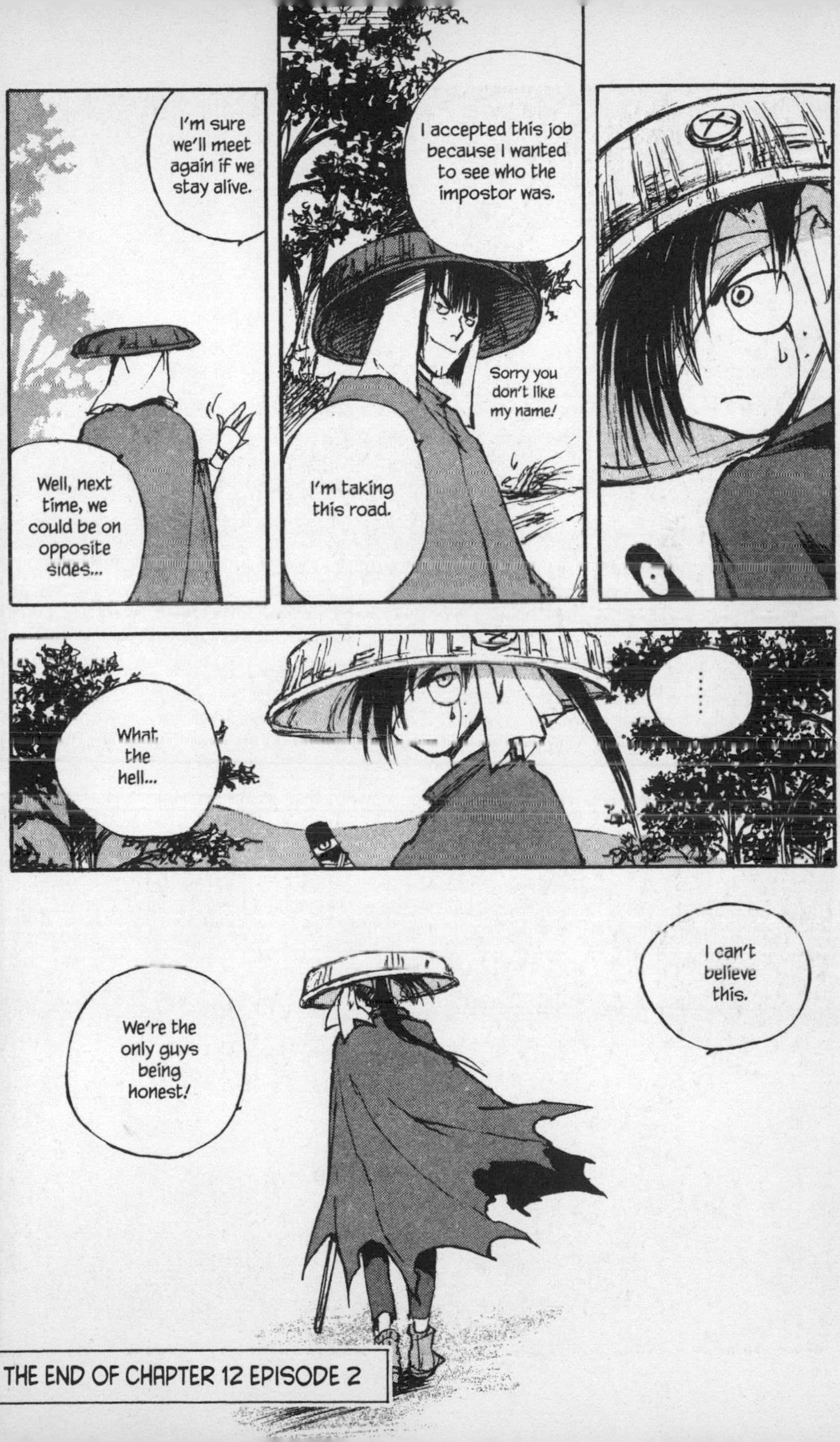
I accepted this job because I wanted to see who the impostor was.
Sorry you don't like my name!
I'm taking this road.
I'm sure we'll meet again if we stay alive.
Well, next time, we could be on opposite sides...
......
What the hell...
I can't believe this.
We're the only guys being honest!
THE END OF CHAPTER 12 EPISODE 2

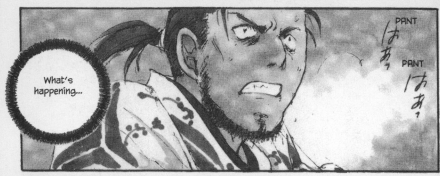

What's happening...

PANT

PANT

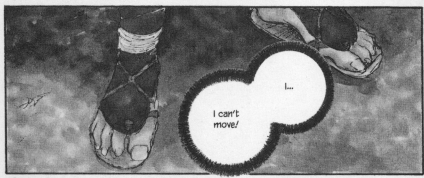

I...

I can't move!

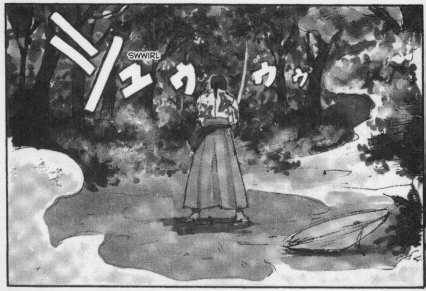

SWWIRL

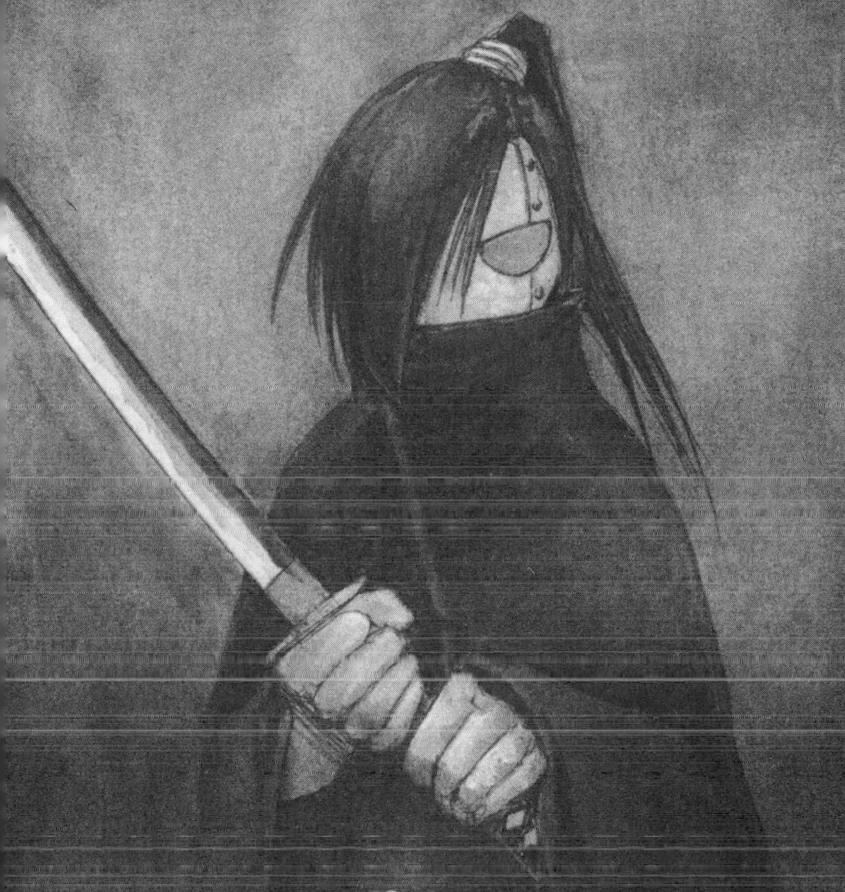

第十二幕

A DENSE FOG

（幽見峠の鐵）

—第一景—

(Kurogane of Kasumi Pass)

Chapter 13 Episode 1

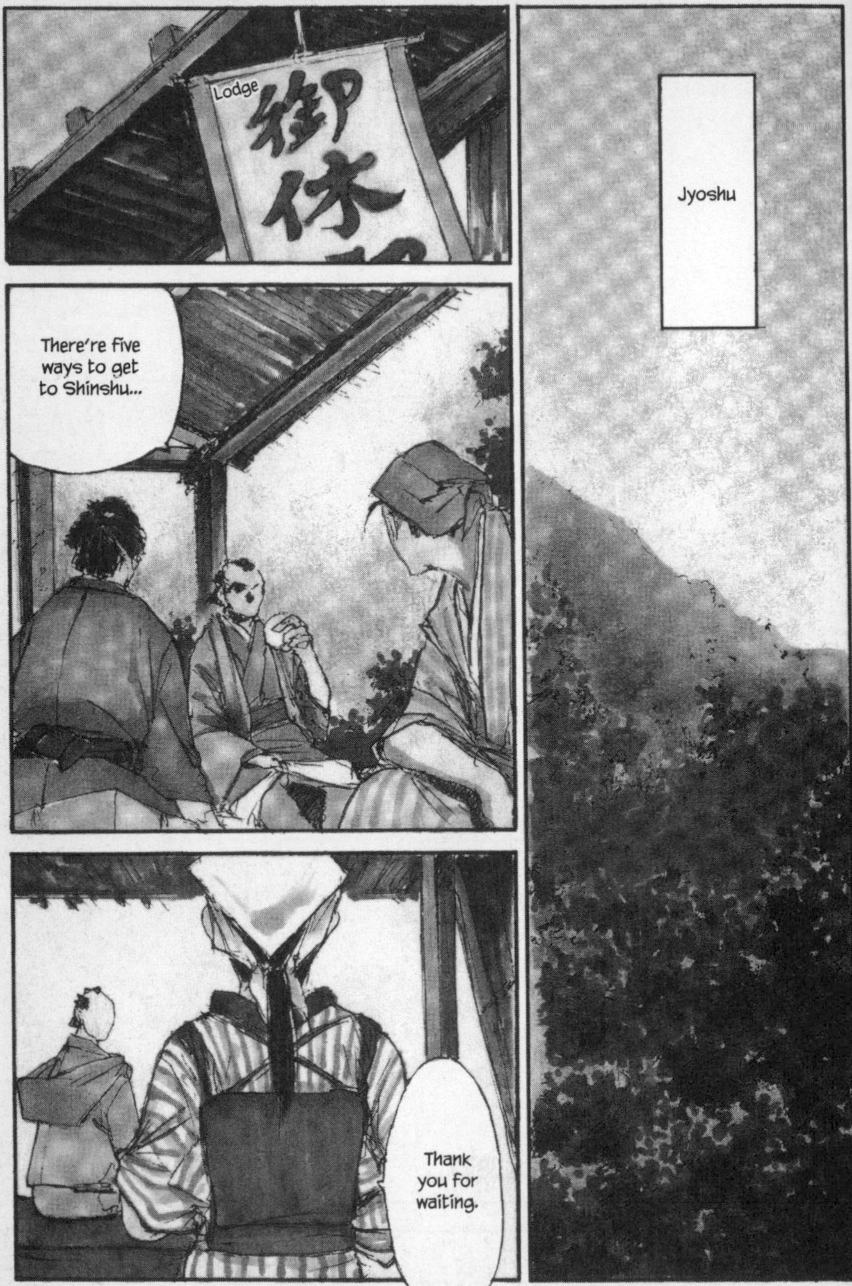
Jyoshu
Lodge
There're five ways to get to Shinshu...
Thank you for waiting.

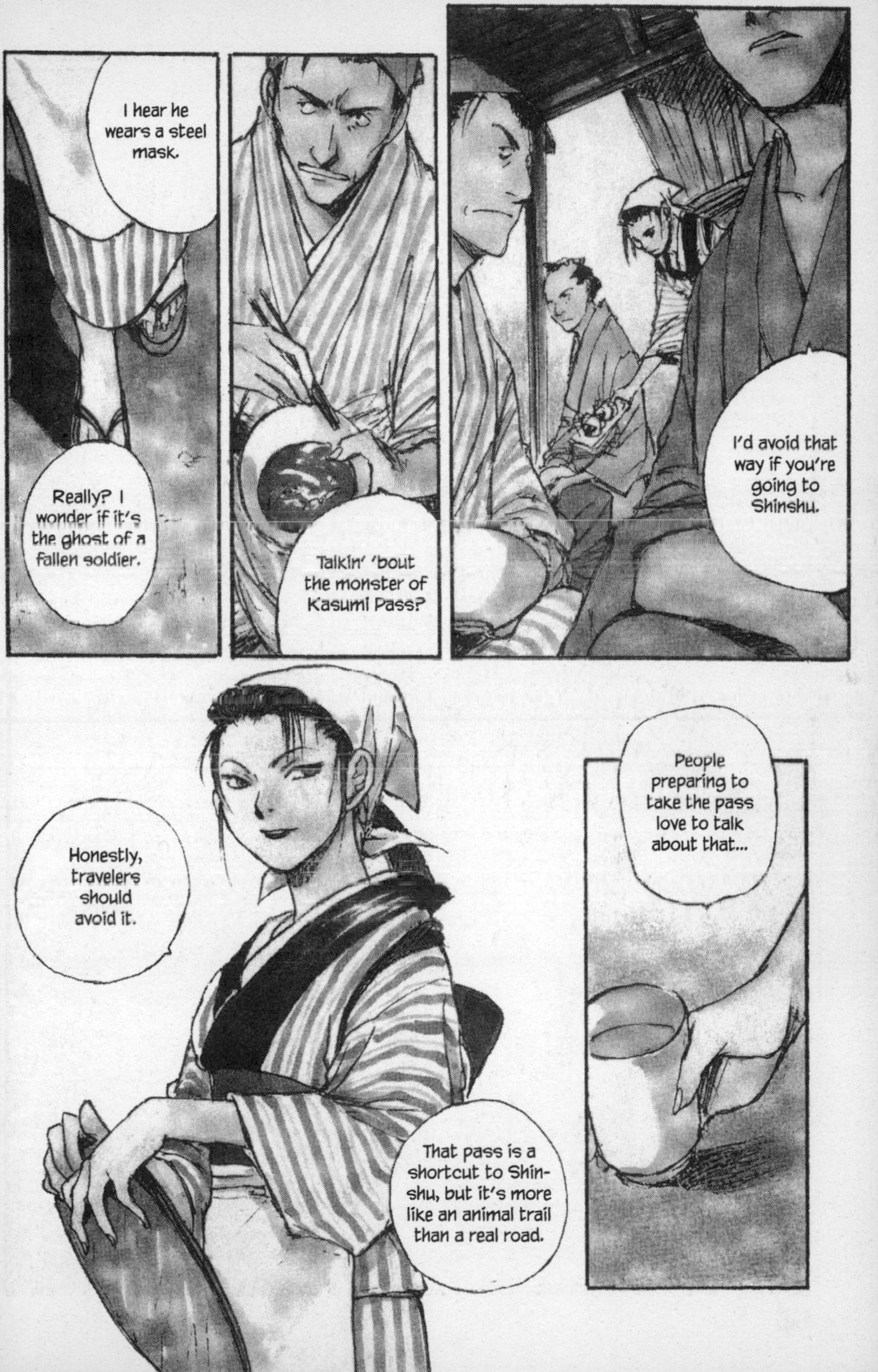
I'd avoid that way if you're going to Shinshu.
Talkin' 'bout the monster of Kasumi Pass?
I hear he wears a steel mask.
Really? I wonder if it's the ghost of a fallen soldier.
People preparing to take the pass love to talk about that...
That pass is a shortcut to Shin-shu, but it's more like an animal trail than a real road.
Honestly, travelers should avoid it.

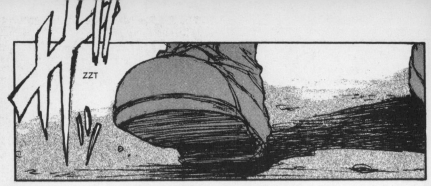

ZZT

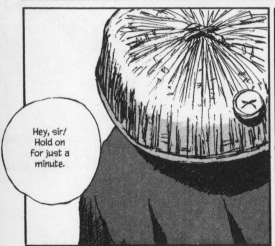

Hey, sir! Hold on for just a minute.

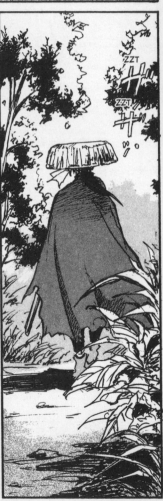

ZZT

ZZT

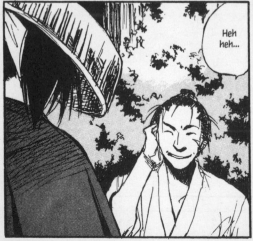

Heh heh...

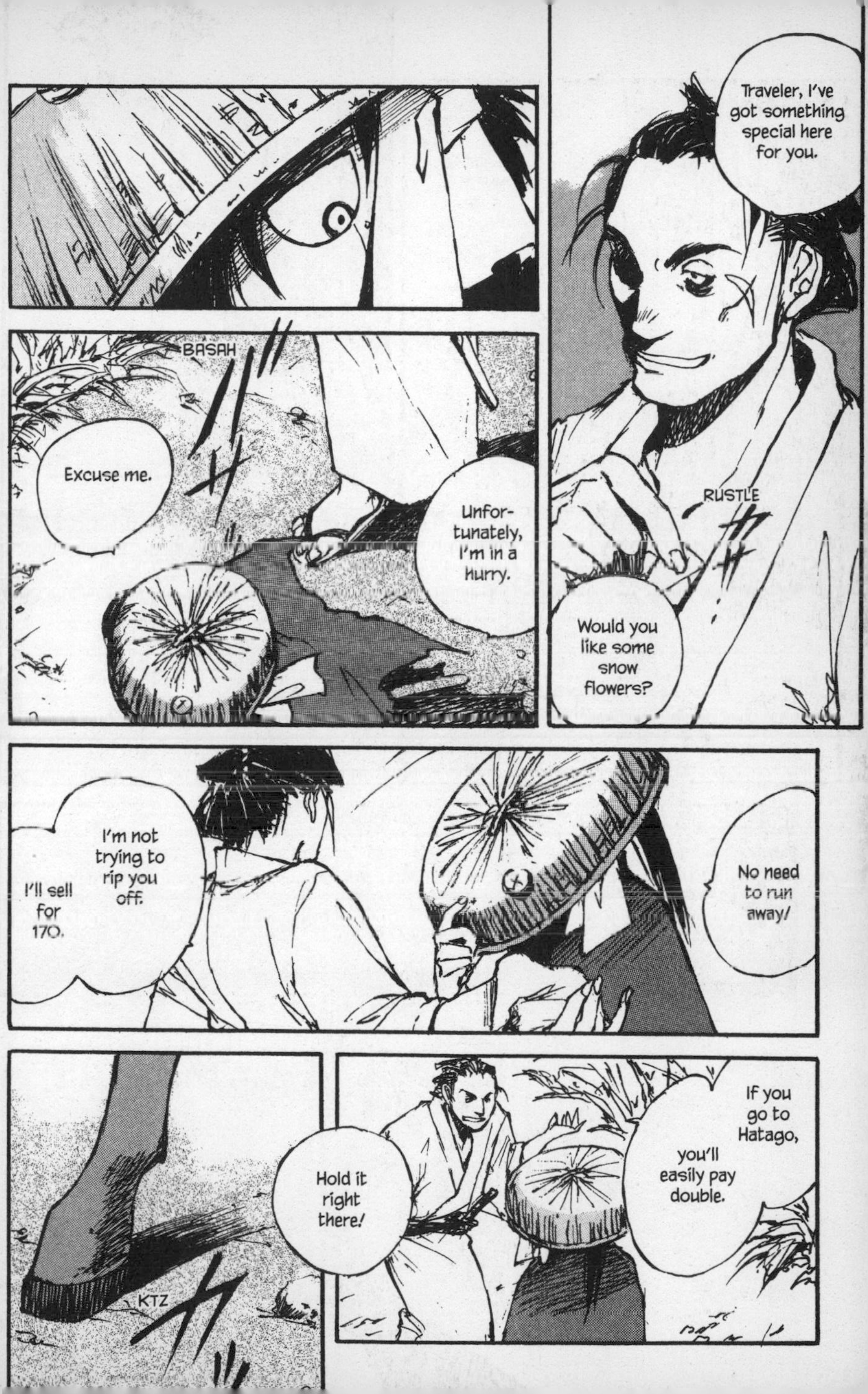
Traveler, I've got something special here for you.
RUSTLE
Would you like some snow flowers?
BASAH
Excuse me.
Unfortunately, I'm in a hurry.
No need to run away!
I'm not trying to rip you off.
I'll sell for 170.
If you go to Hatago,
you'll easily pay double.
Hold it right there!
KTZ

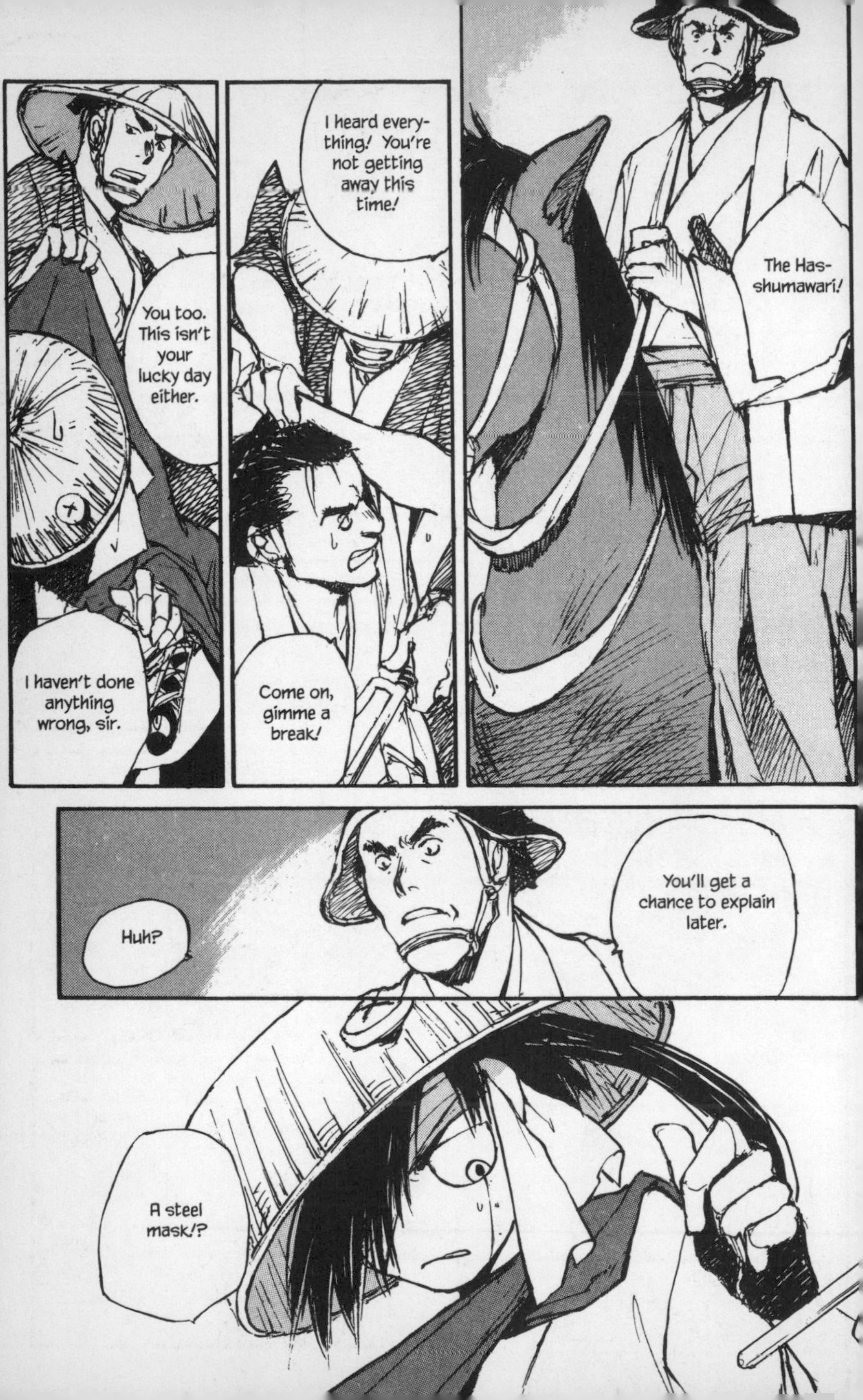
The Has-
shumawari!
I heard every-
thing! You're
not getting
away this
time!
Come on,
gimme a
break!
You too.
This isn't
your
lucky day
either.
I haven't done
anything
wrong, sir.
You'll get a
chance to explain
later.
Huh?
A steel
mask!?

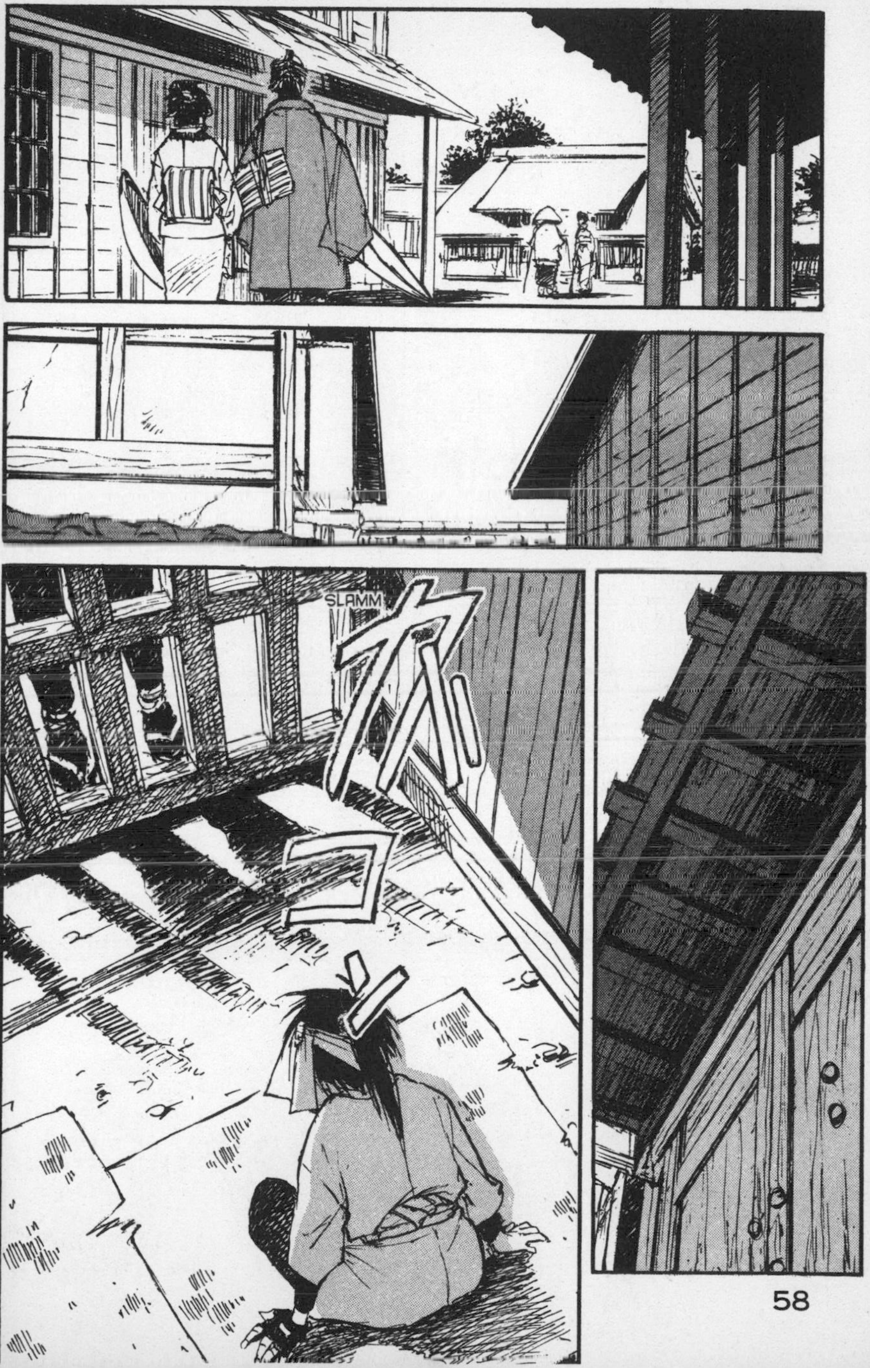
SLAMM

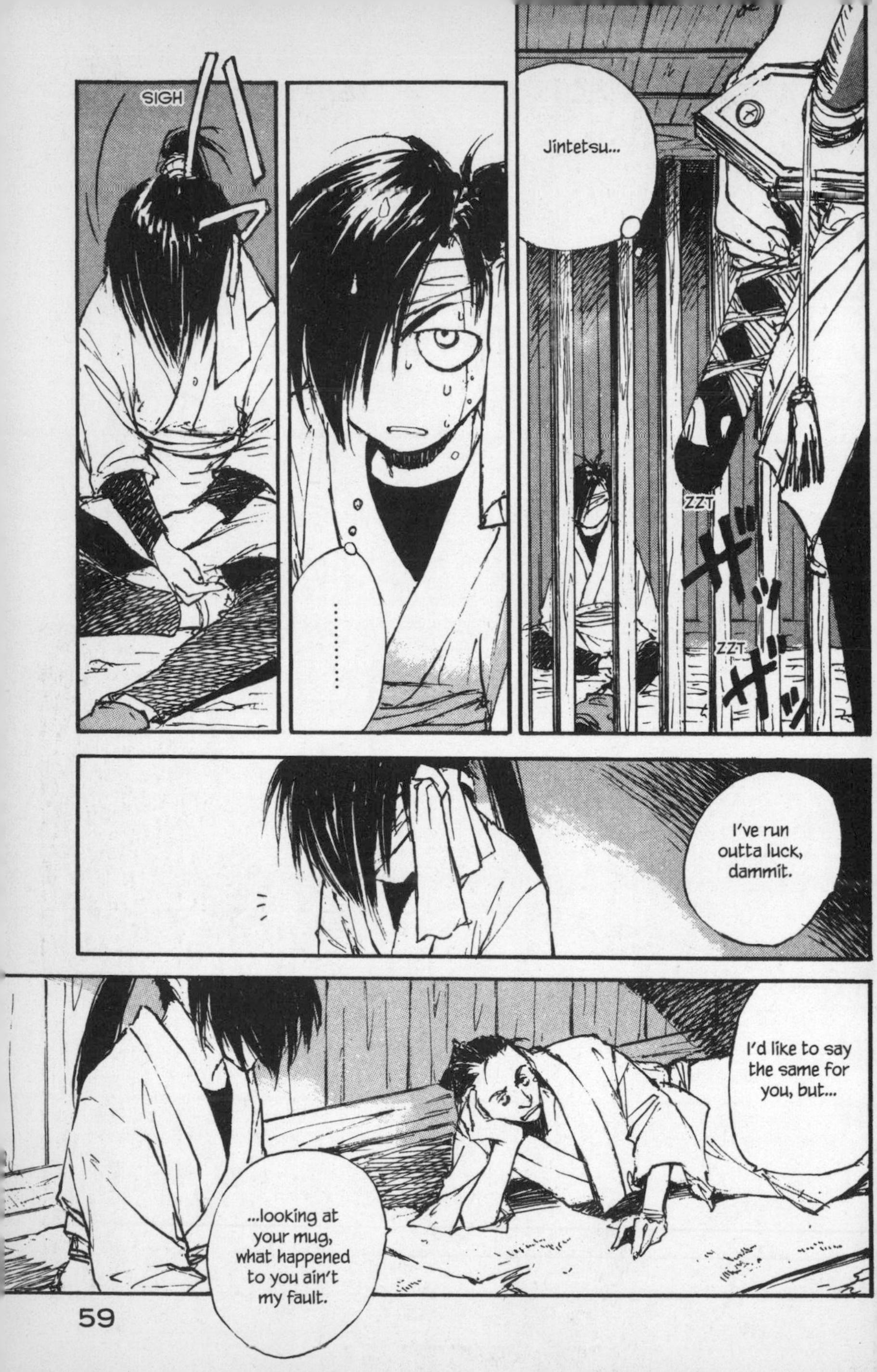
Jintetsu...
ZZT
ZZT
......
SIGH
I've run outta luck, dammit.
I'd like to say the same for you, but...
...looking at your mug, what happened to you ain't my fault.

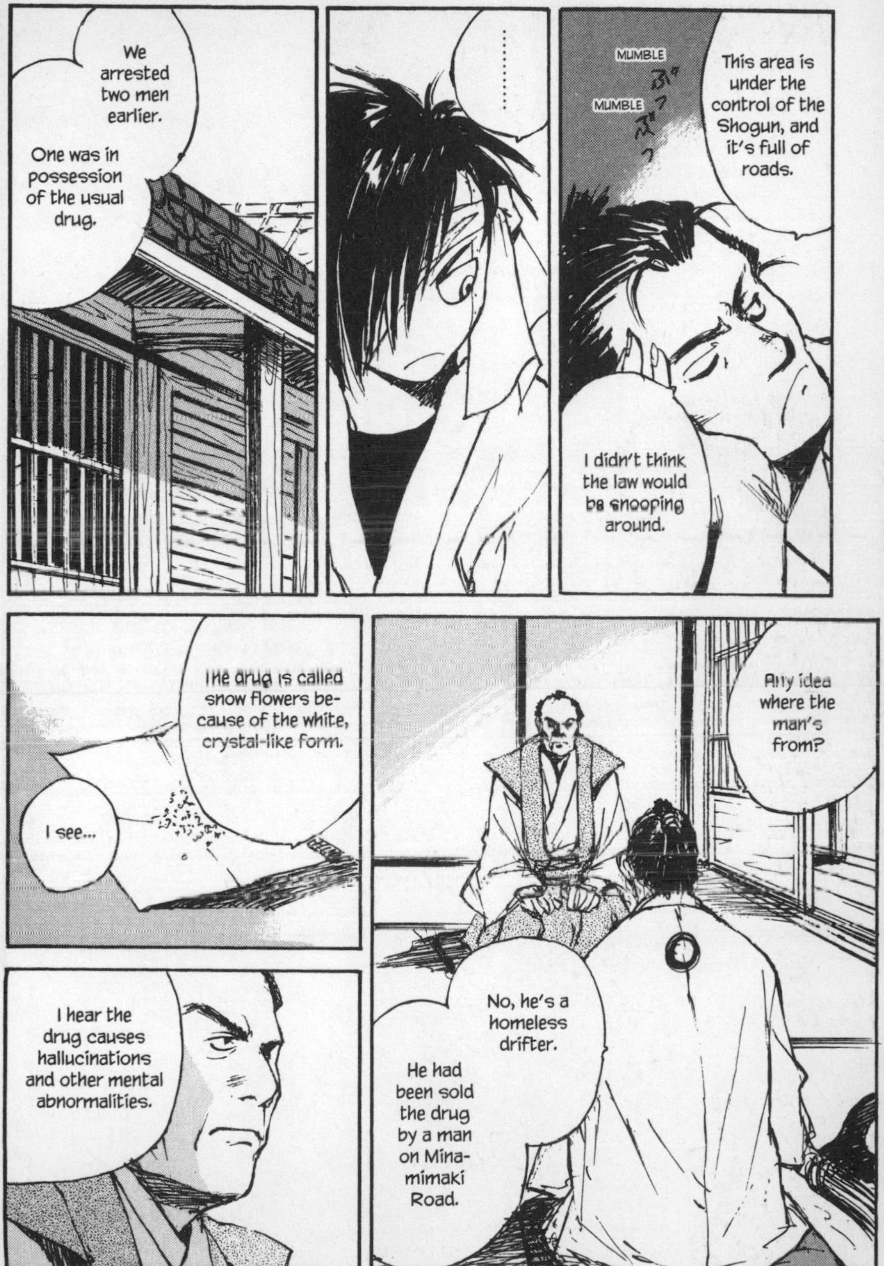
This area is under the control of the Shogun, and it's full of roads.
MUMBLE
ぶつぶつ
MUMBLE
I didn't think the law would be snooping around.
......
We arrested two men earlier.
One was in possession of the usual drug.
Any idea where the man's from?
No, he's a homeless drifter.
He had been sold the drug by a man on Mina-mimaki Road.
The drug is called snow flowers be-cause of the white, crystal-like form.
I see...
I hear the drug causes hallucinations and other mental abnormalities.

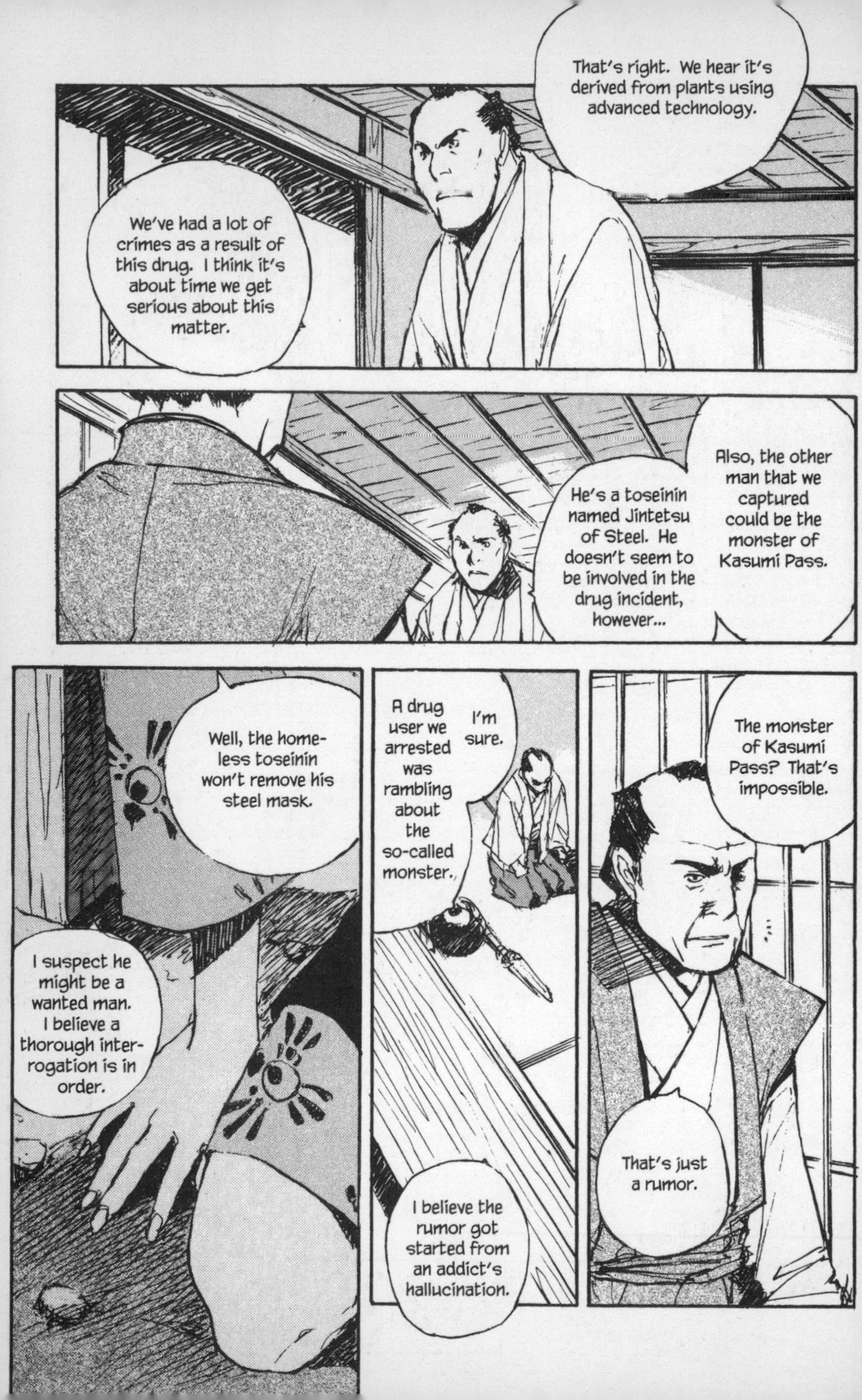
That's right. We hear it's derived from plants using advanced technology.
We've had a lot of crimes as a result of this drug. I think it's about time we get serious about this matter.
Also, the other man that we captured could be the monster of Kasumi Pass.
He's a toseinin named Jintetsu of Steel. He doesn't seem to be involved in the drug incident, however...
The monster of Kasumi Pass? That's impossible.
That's just a rumor.
I'm sure.
A drug user we arrested was rambling about the so-called monster.
I believe the rumor got started from an addict's hallucination.
Well, the home-less toseinin won't remove his steel mask.
I suspect he might be a wanted man. I believe a thorough inter-rogation is in order.

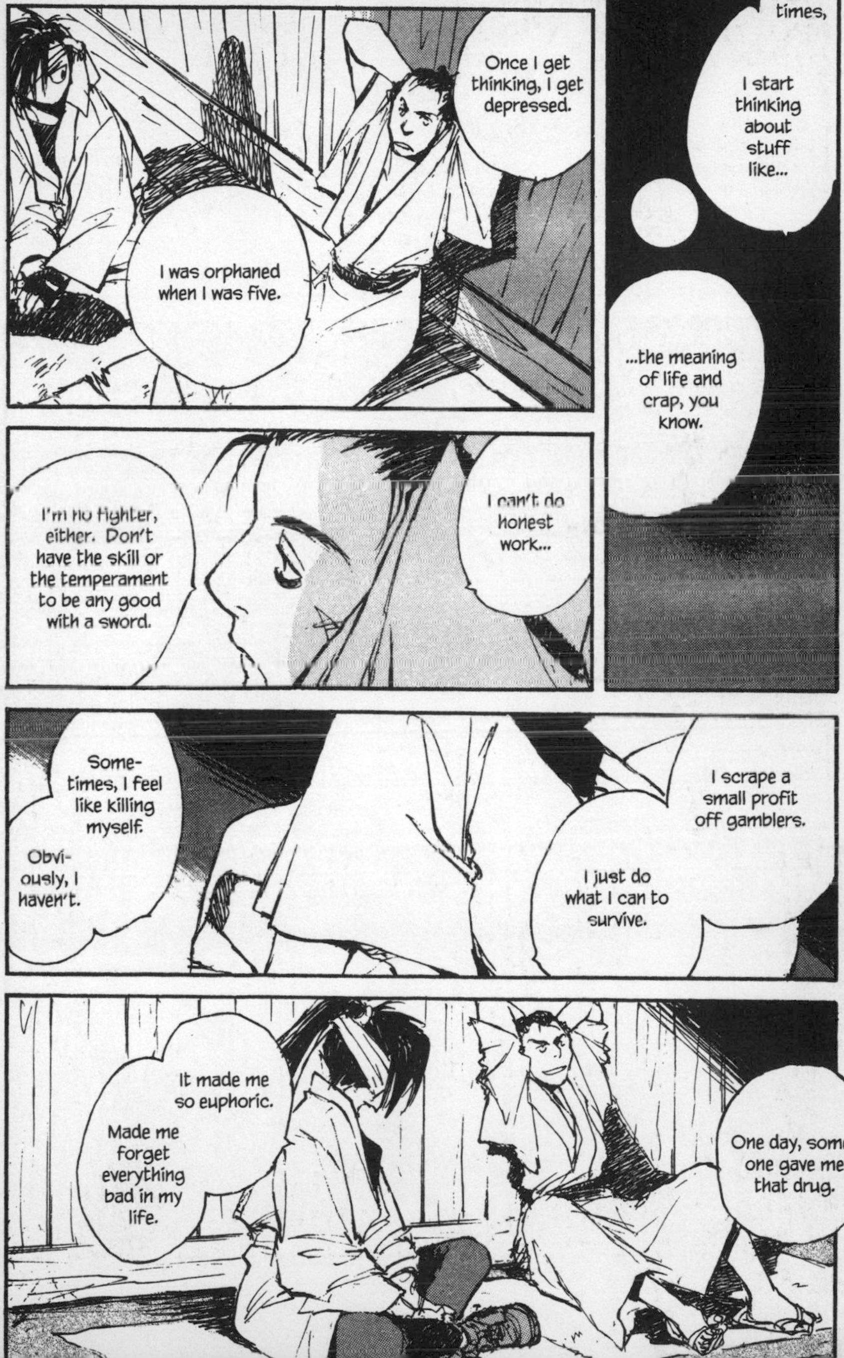
Some-times,
I start thinking about stuff like...
...the meaning of life and crap, you know.
Once I get thinking, I get depressed.
I was orphaned when I was five.
I can't do honest work...
I'm no fighter, either. Don't have the skill or the temperament to be any good with a sword.
I scrape a small profit off gamblers.
I just do what I can to survive.
Some-times, I feel like killing myself.
Obvi-ously, I haven't.
One day, some-one gave me that drug.
It made me so euphoric.
Made me forget everything bad in my life.

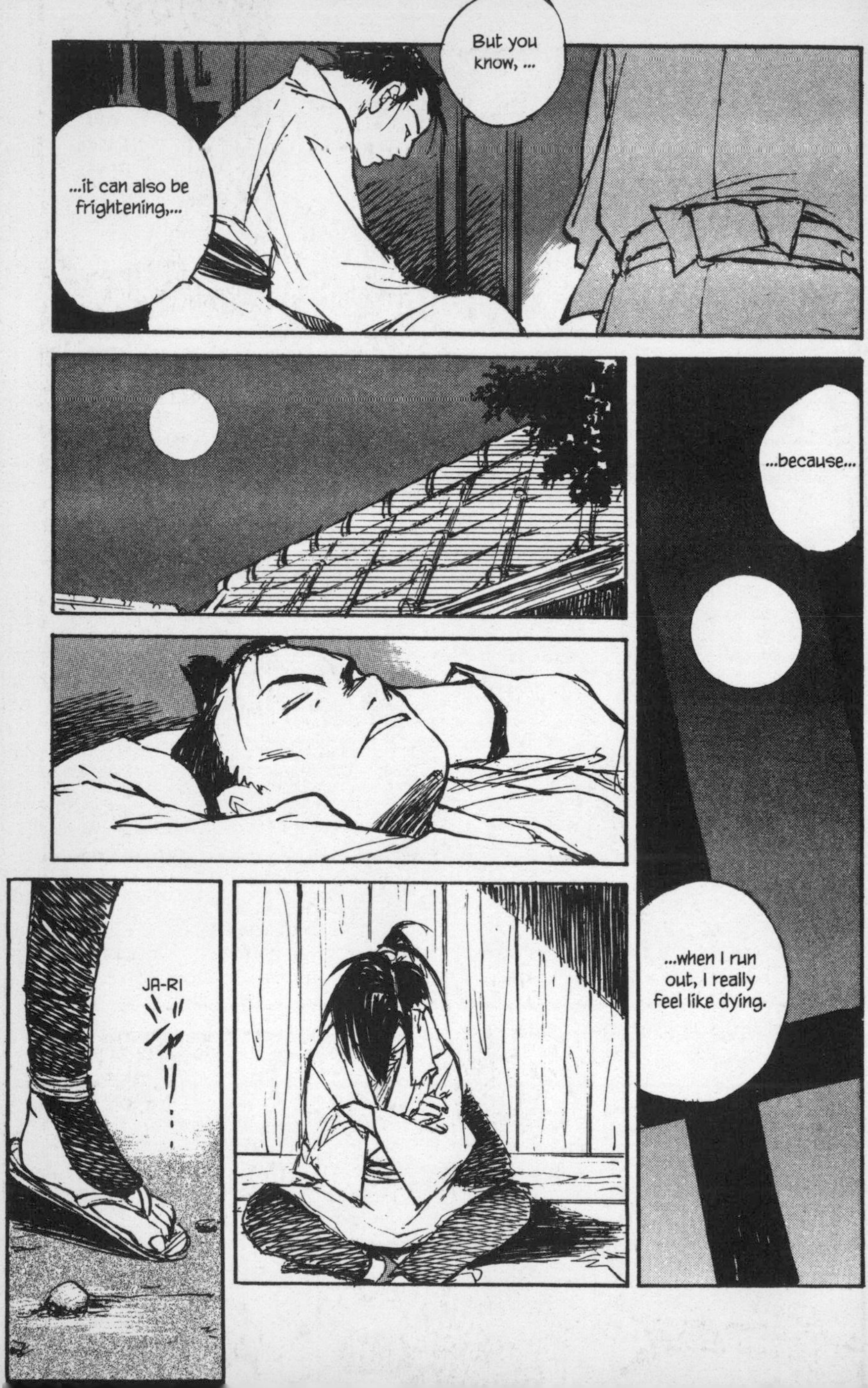
But you know, ...
...it can also be frightening,...
...because...
...when I run out, I really feel like dying.
JA-RI

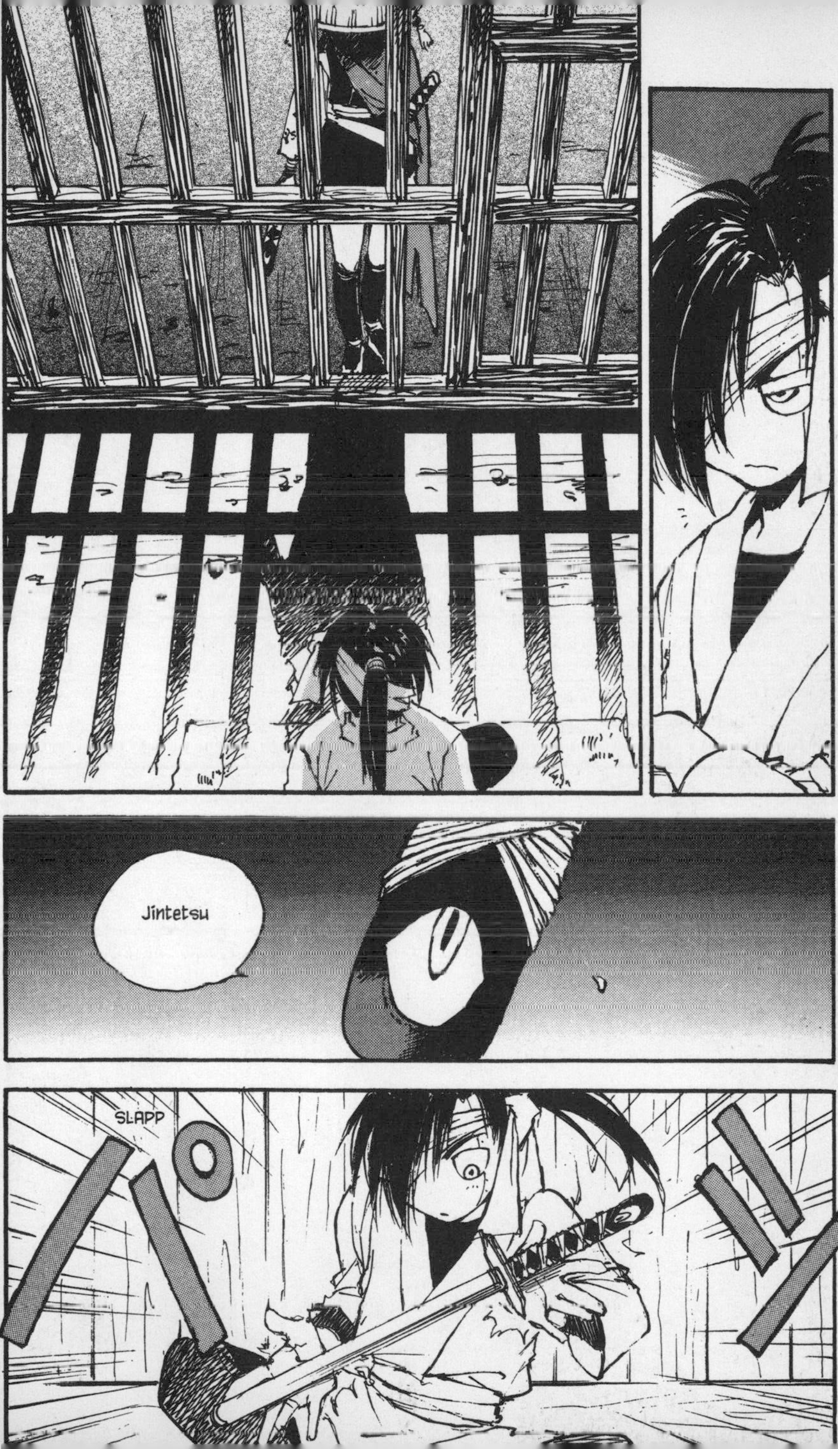
Jintetsu
SLAPP

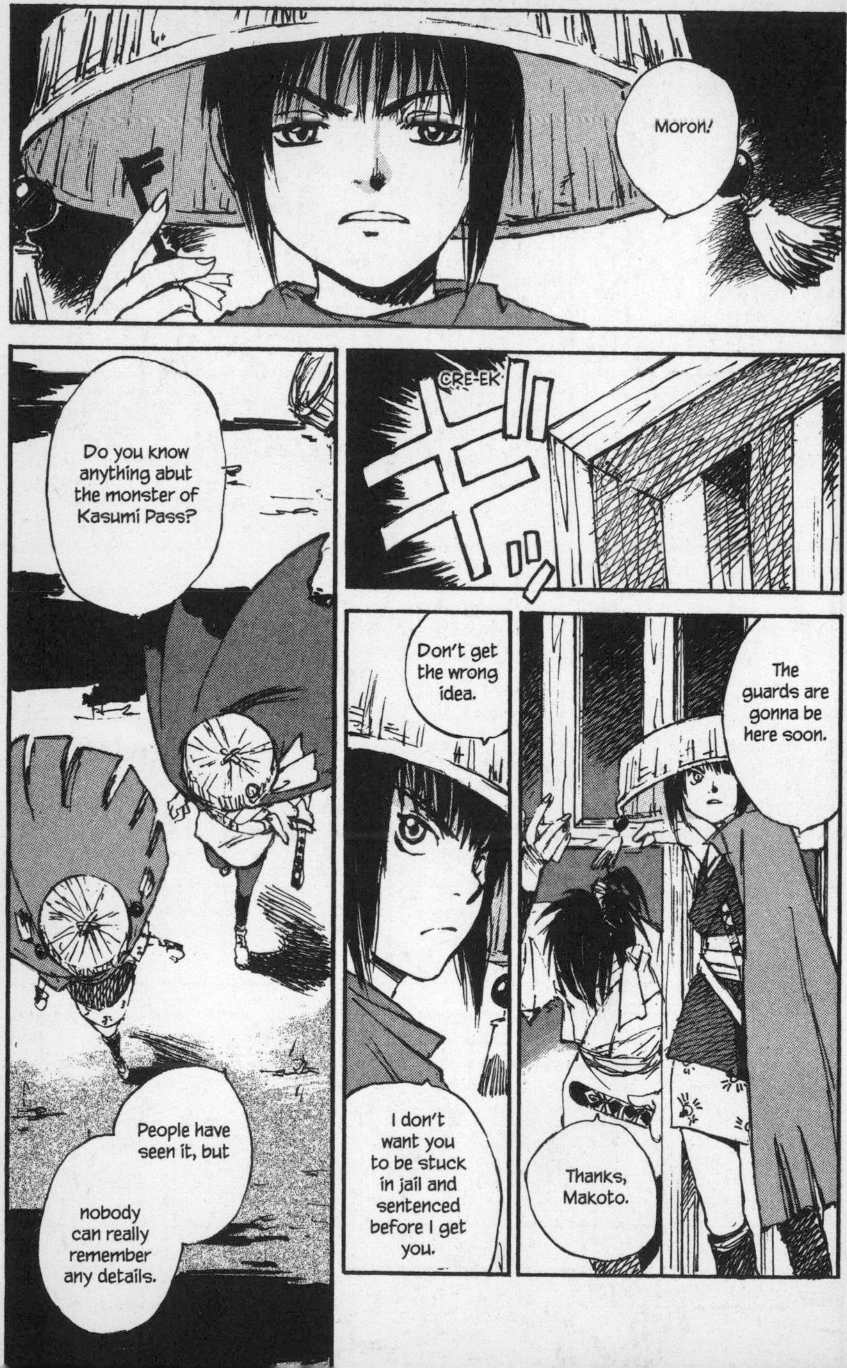
Moron!
CRE-EK
The guards are gonna be here soon.
Thanks, Makoto.
Don't get the wrong idea.
I don't want you to be stuck in jail and sentenced before I get you.
Do you know anything abut the monster of Kasumi Pass?
People have seen it, but
nobody can really remember any details.

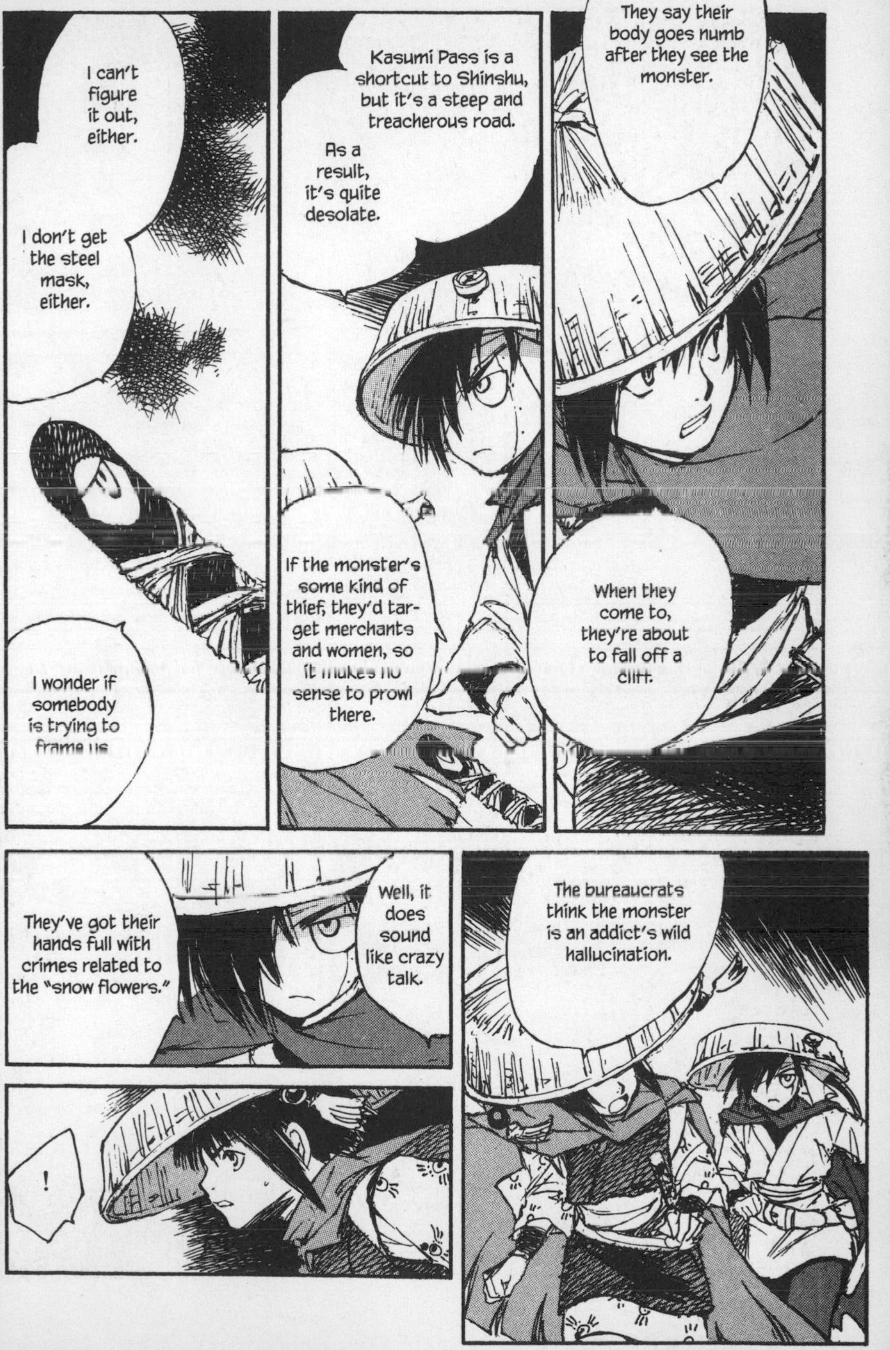

They say their body goes numb after they see the monster.
When they come to, they're about to fall off a cliff.
Kasumi Pass is a shortcut to Shinshu, but it's a steep and treacherous road.
As a result, it's quite desolate.
If the monster's some kind of thief, they'd target merchants and women, so it makes no sense to prowl there.
I can't figure it out, either.
I don't get the steel mask, either.
I wonder if somebody is trying to frame us.
The bureaucrats think the monster is an addict's wild hallucination.
Well, it does sound like crazy talk.
They've got their hands full with crimes related to the "snow flowers."
!

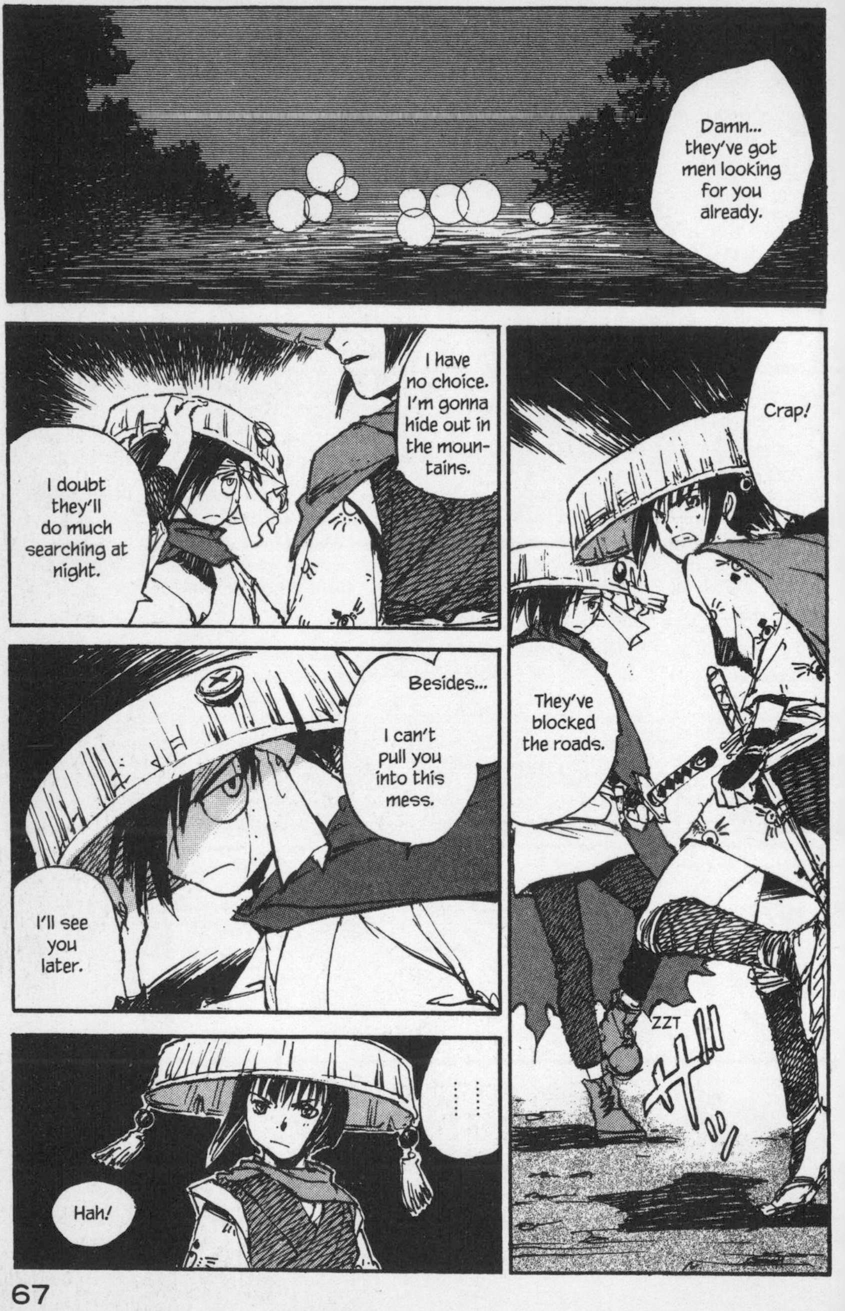
Damn... they've got men looking for you already.
Crap!
They've blocked the roads.
ZZT
I have no choice. I'm gonna hide out in the mountains.
I doubt they'll do much searching at night.
Besides...
I can't pull you into this mess.
I'll see you later.
......
Hah!

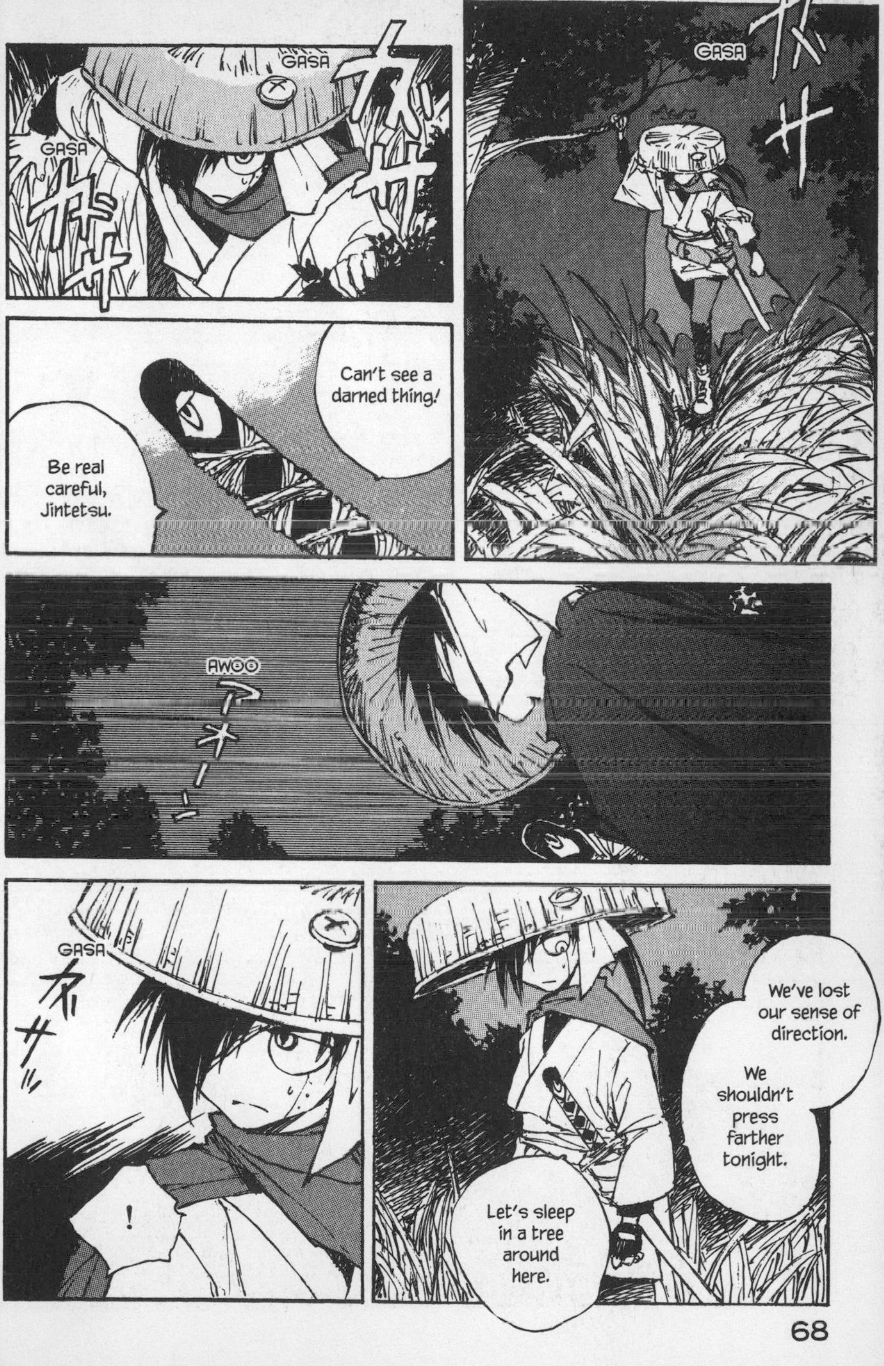
GASA
GASA
GASA
Can't see a darned thing!
Be real careful, Jintetsu.
AWOO
We've lost our sense of direction.
We shouldn't press farther tonight.
Let's sleep in a tree around here.
GASA
!

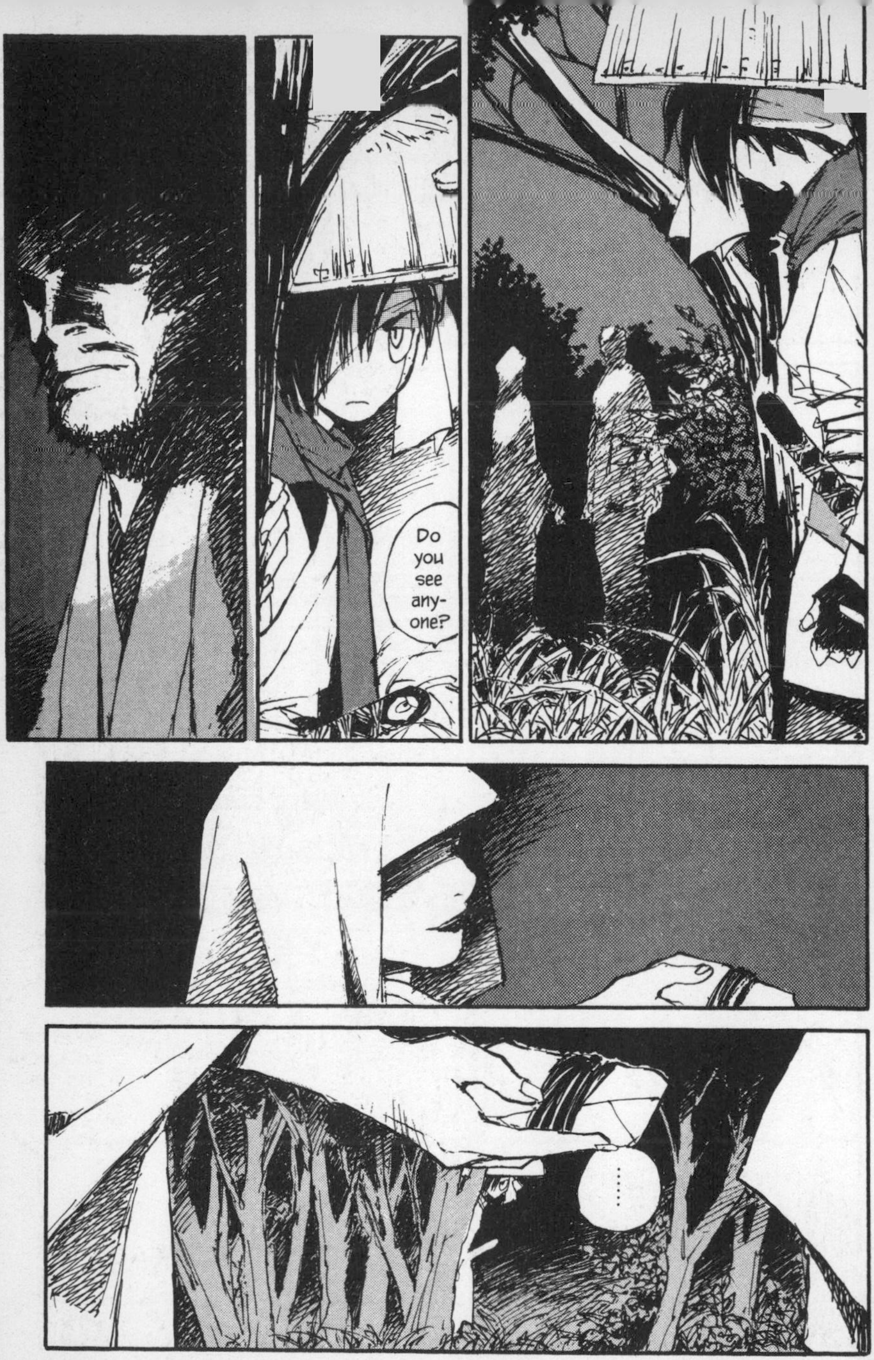
Do you see any-one?
……

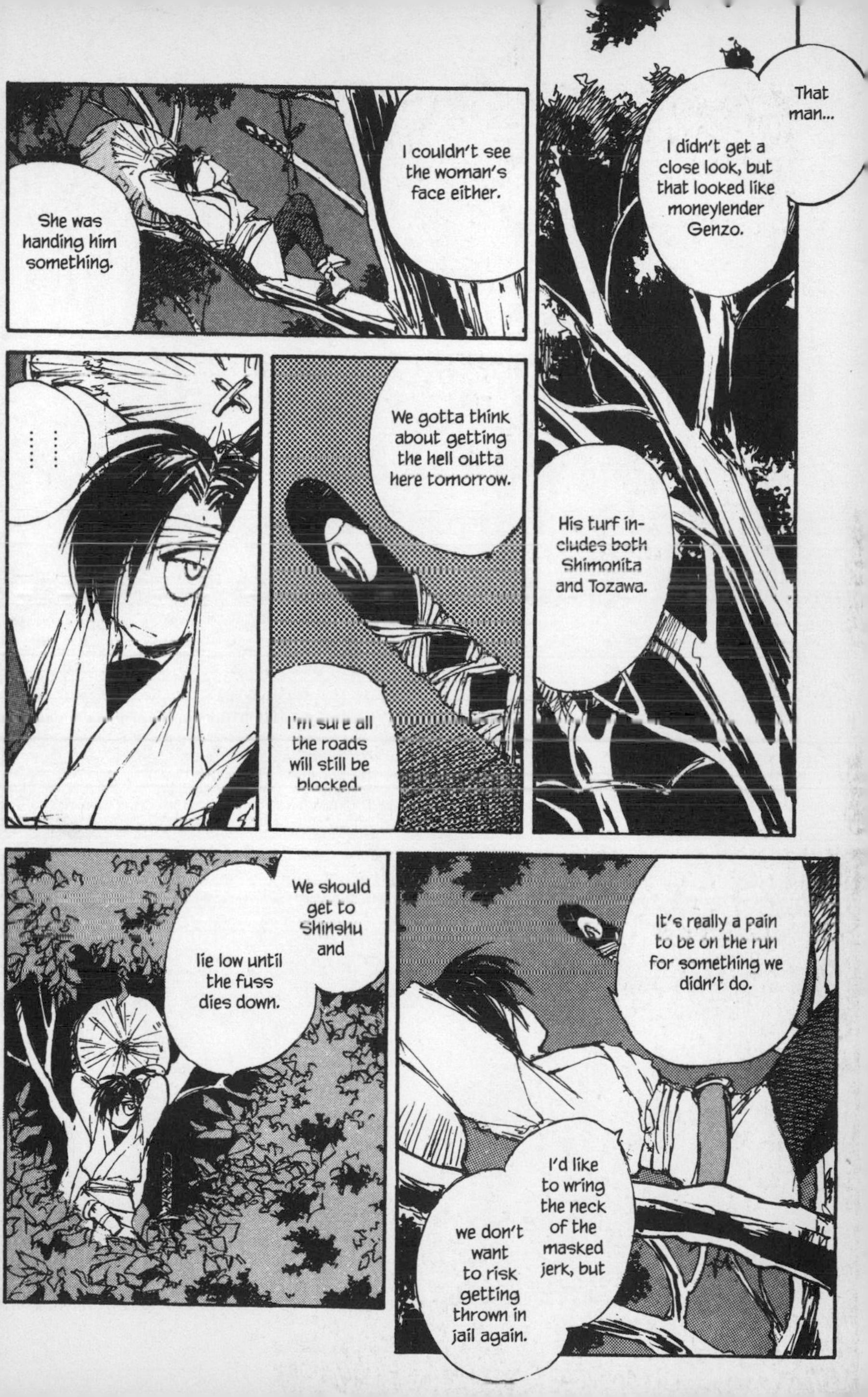
That man...
I didn't get a close look, but that looked like moneylender Genzo.
His turf includes both Shimonita and Tozawa.
I couldn't see the woman's face either.
She was handing him something.
We gotta think about getting the hell outta here tomorrow.
I'm sure all the roads will still be blocked.
......
It's really a pain to be on the run for something we didn't do.
I'd like to wring the neck of the masked jerk, but
we don't want to risk getting thrown in jail again.
We should get to Shinshu and
lie low until the fuss dies down.

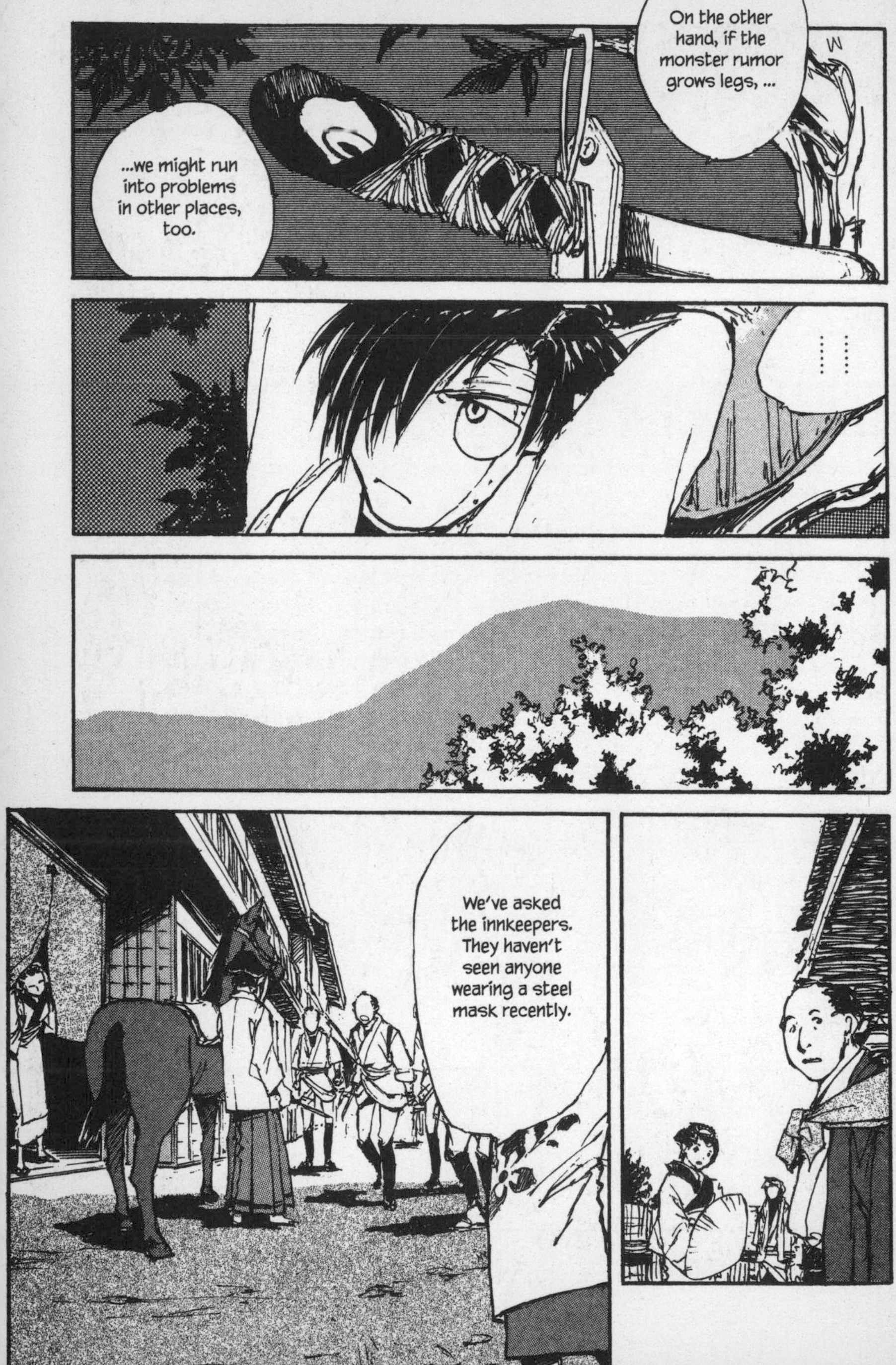
On the other hand, if the monster rumor grows legs, ...
...we might run into problems in other places, too.
We've asked the innkeepers. They haven't seen anyone wearing a steel mask recently.

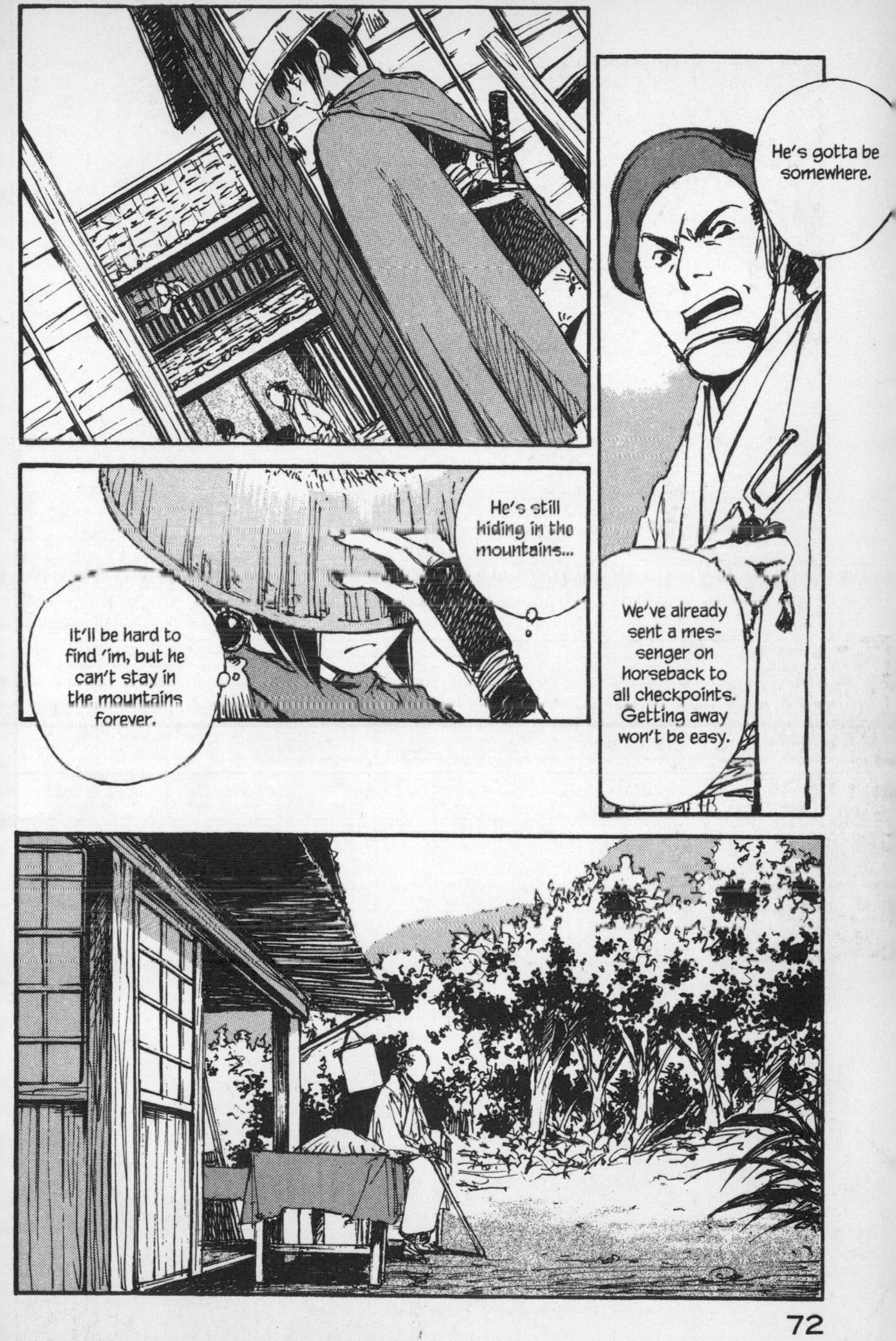
He's gotta be somewhere.
We've already sent a messenger on horseback to all checkpoints. Getting away won't be easy.
He's still hiding in the mountains...
It'll be hard to find 'im, but he can't stay in the mountains forever.

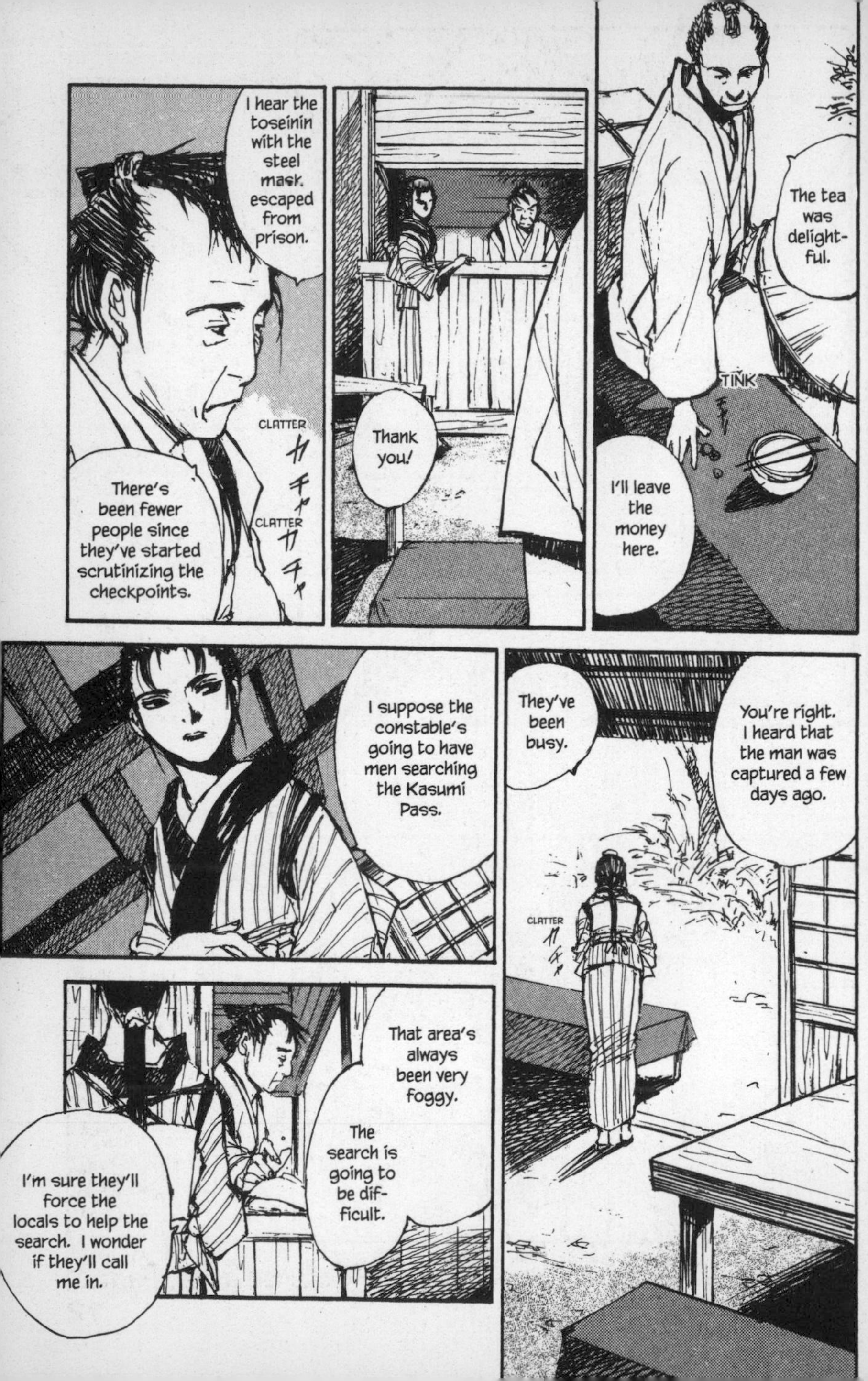
The tea was delight-ful.
TINK
I'll leave the money here.
Thank you!
I hear the toseinin with the steel mask escaped from prison.
CLATTER
CLATTER
There's been fewer people since they've started scrutinizing the checkpoints.
You're right. I heard that the man was captured a few days ago.
They've been busy.
CLATTER
I suppose the constable's going to have men searching the Kasumi Pass.
That area's always been very foggy.
The search is going to be dif-ficult.
I'm sure they'll force the locals to help the search. I wonder if they'll call me in.

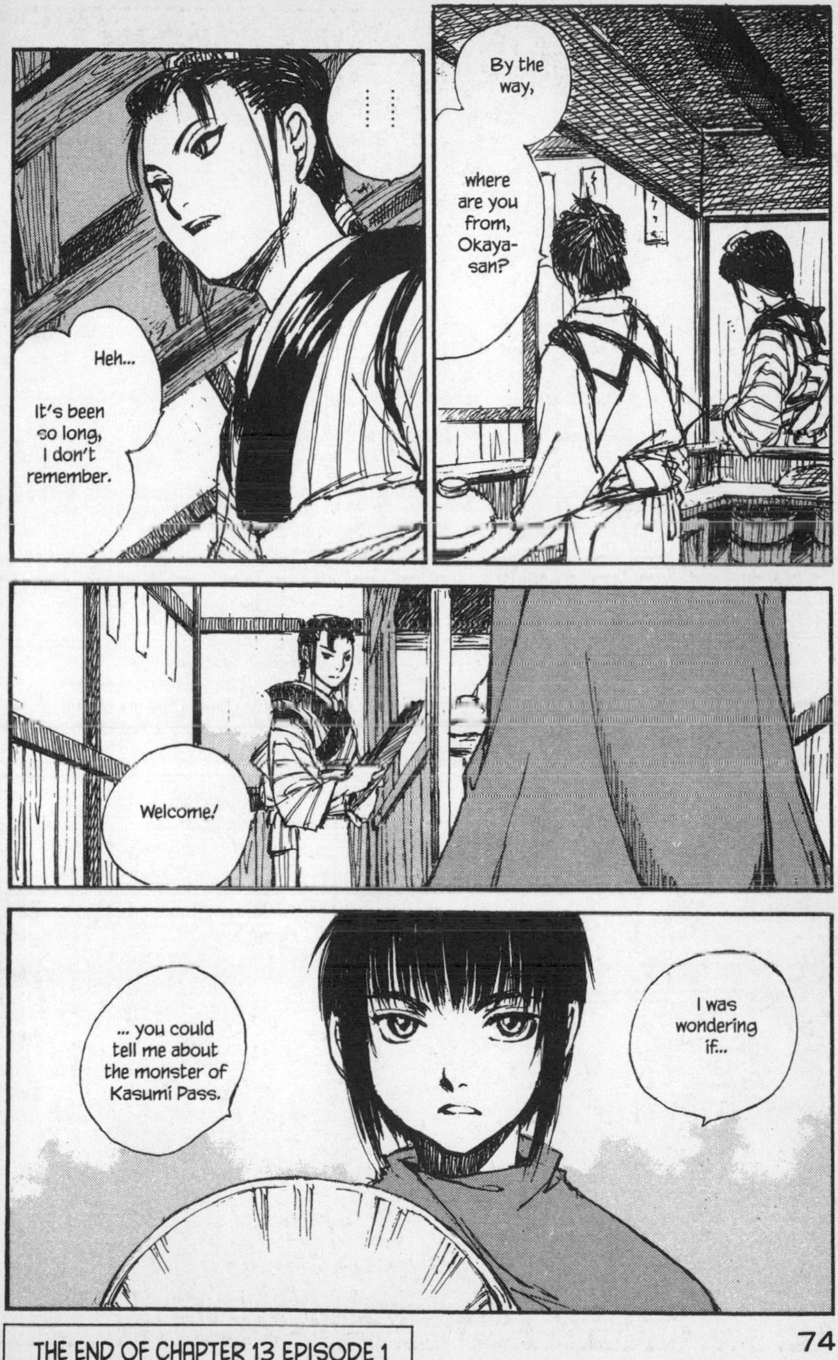
By the way,
where are you from, Okaya-san?
......
Heh...
It's been so long, I don't remember.
Welcome!
I was wondering if...
... you could tell me about the monster of Kasumi Pass.

THE END OF CHAPTER 13 EPISODE 1

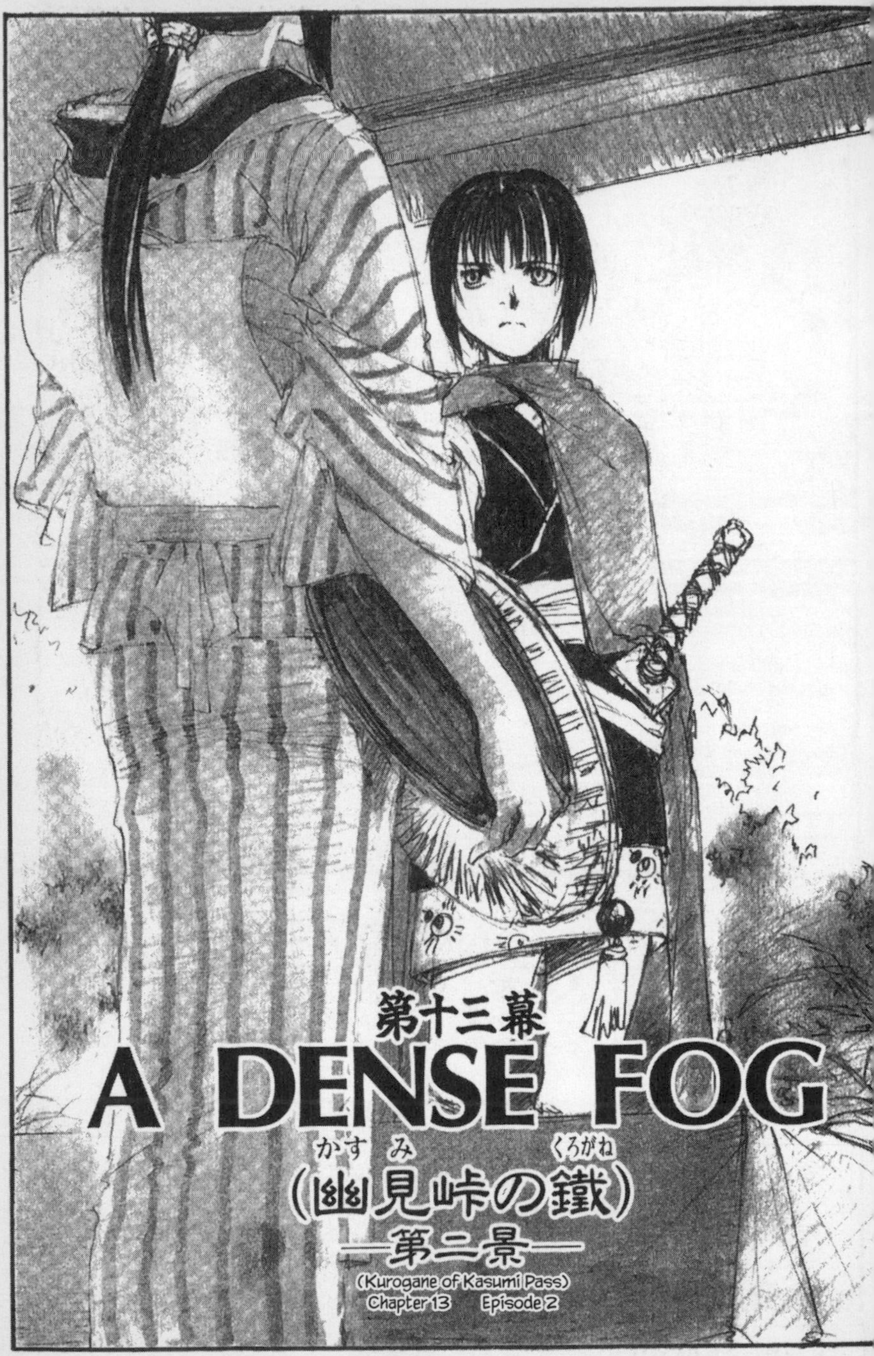
第十三幕
A DENSE FOG
かすみ くろがね
(幽見峠の鐵)
—第二景—
(Kurogane of Kasumi Pass)
Chapter 13 Episode 2

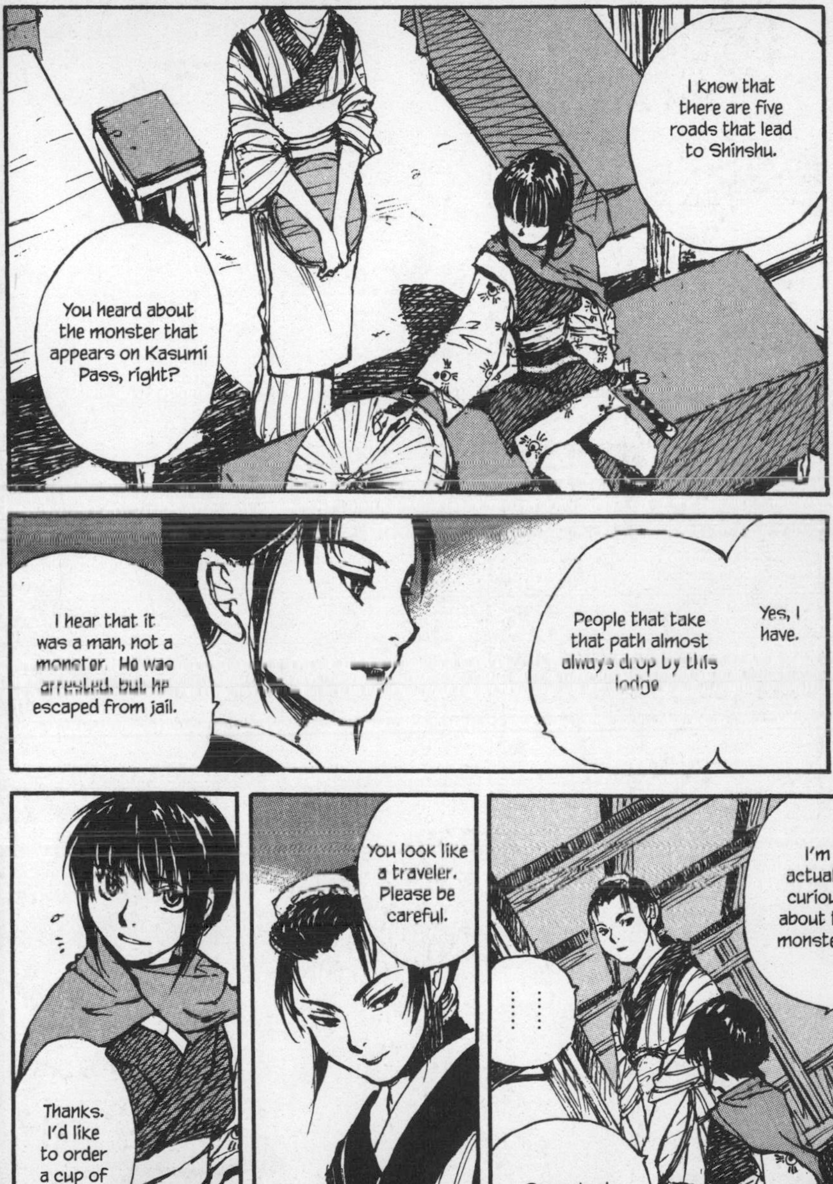
I know that there are five roads that lead to Shinshu.
You heard about the monster that appears on Kasumi Pass, right?
Yes, I have.
People that take that path almost always drop by this lodge
I hear that it was a man, not a monster. He was arrested, but he escaped from jail.
I'm actually curious about the monster...
......
So, nobody remembers much about it?
You look like a traveler. Please be careful.
Thanks. I'd like to order a cup of tea.

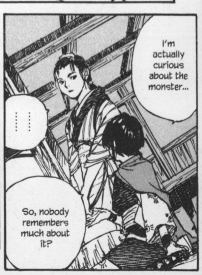

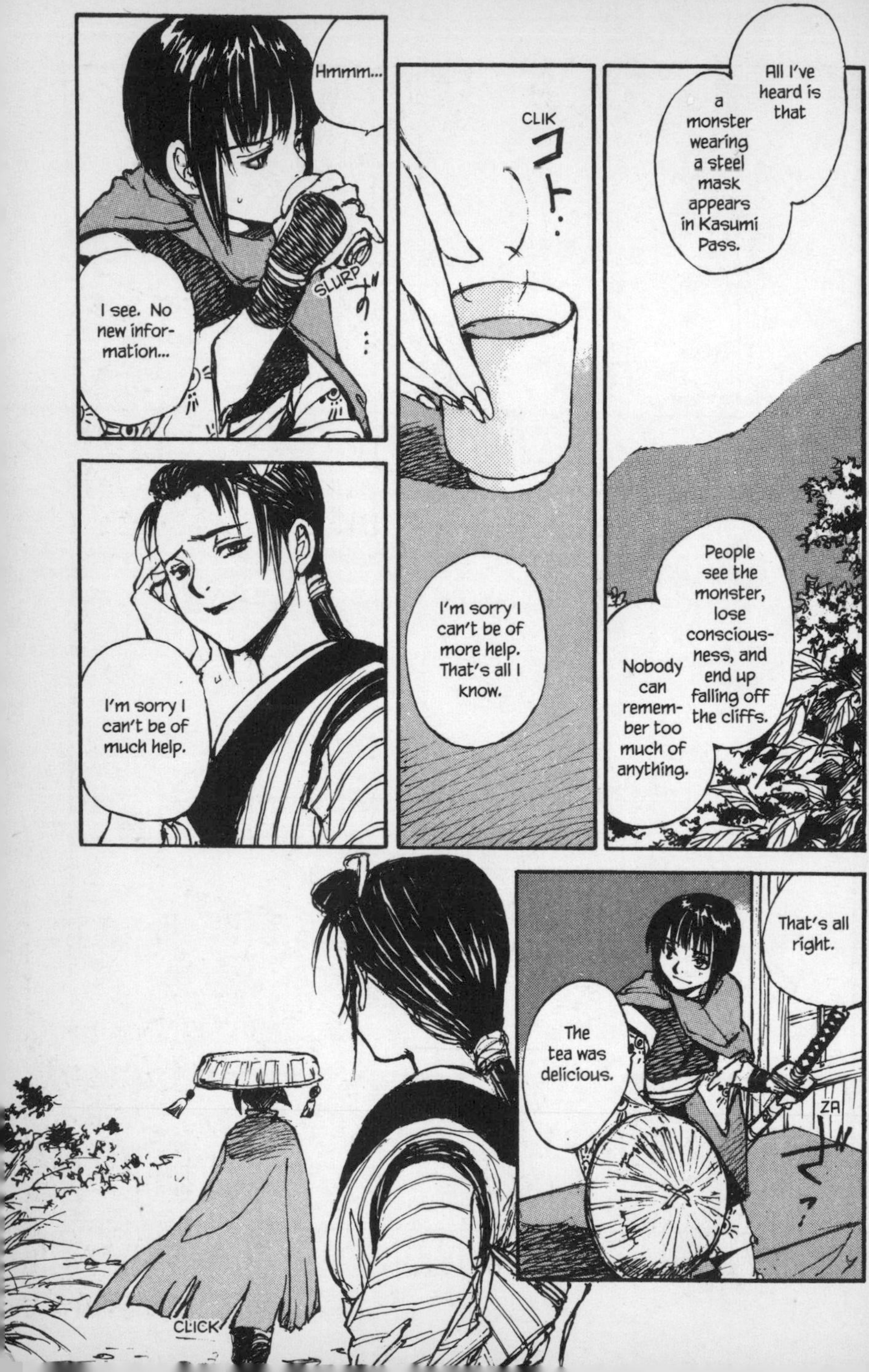
All I've heard is that
a monster wearing a steel mask appears in Kasumi Pass.
People see the monster, lose consciousness, and end up falling off the cliffs.
Nobody can remember too much of anything.
CLIK
コト
I'm sorry I can't be of more help. That's all I know.
Hmmm...
SLURP
I see. No new information...
I'm sorry I can't be of much help.
That's all right.
The tea was delicious.
ZA
CLICK

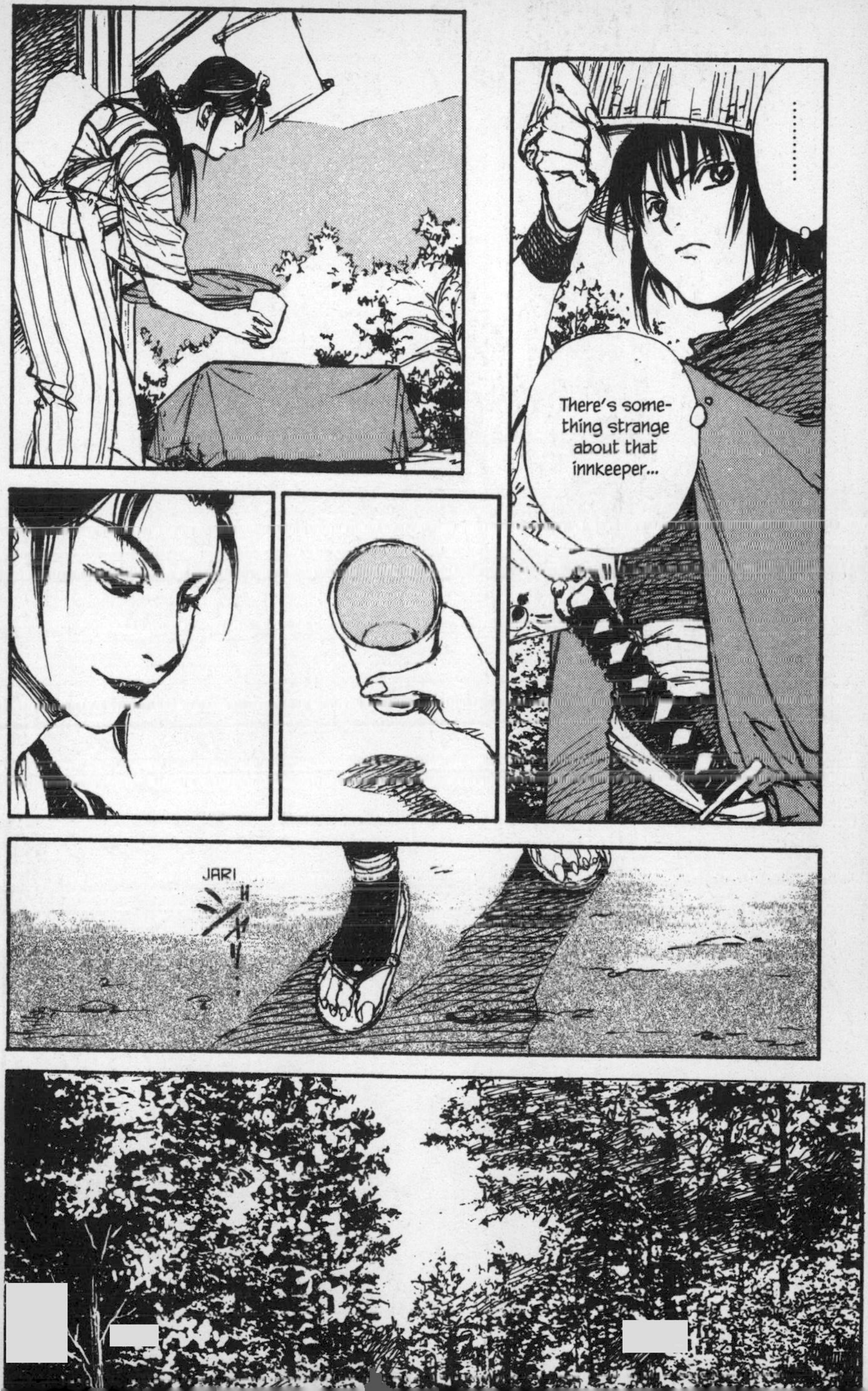
......
There's something strange about that innkeeper...
JARI

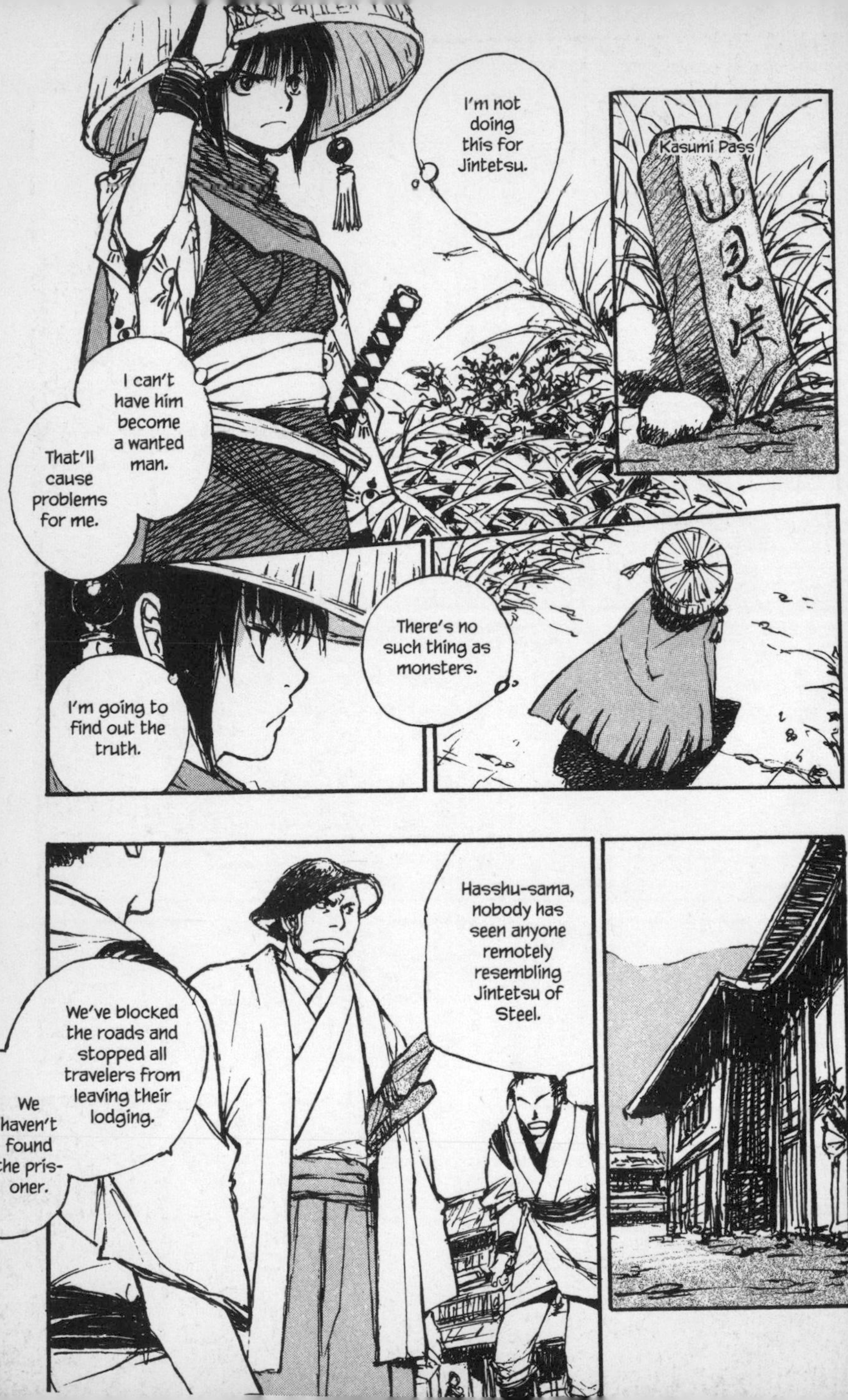
Kasumi Pass
I'm not doing this for Jintetsu.
I can't have him become a wanted man.
That'll cause problems for me.
There's no such thing as monsters.
I'm going to find out the truth.
Hasshu-sama, nobody has seen anyone remotely resembling Jintetsu of Steel.
We've blocked the roads and stopped all travelers from leaving their lodging.
We haven't found the pris-oner.

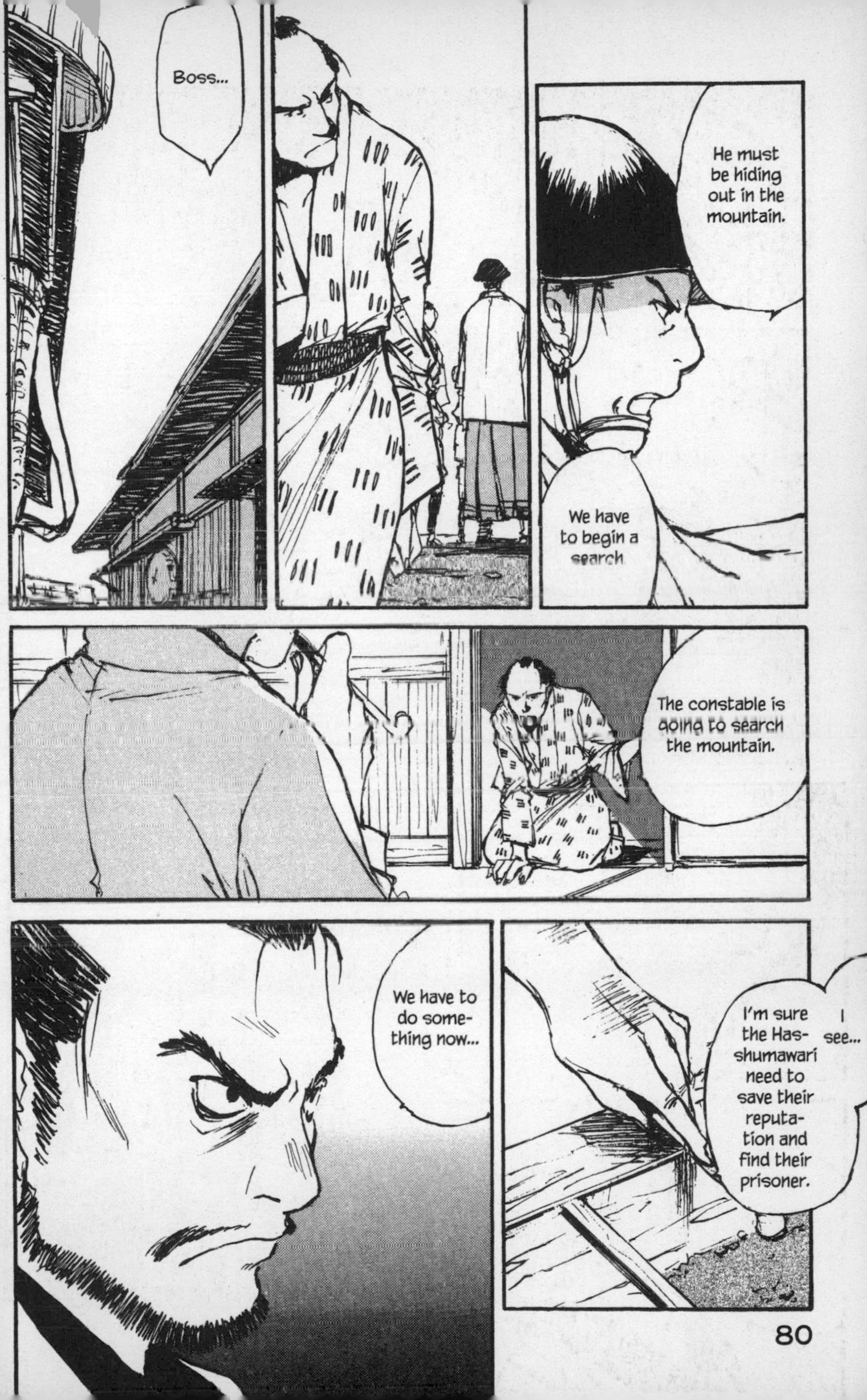
He must be hiding out in the mountain.
We have to begin a search.
Boss...
The constable is going to search the mountain.
I see...
I'm sure the Has-shumawari need to save their reputa-tion and find their prisoner.
We have to do some-thing now...

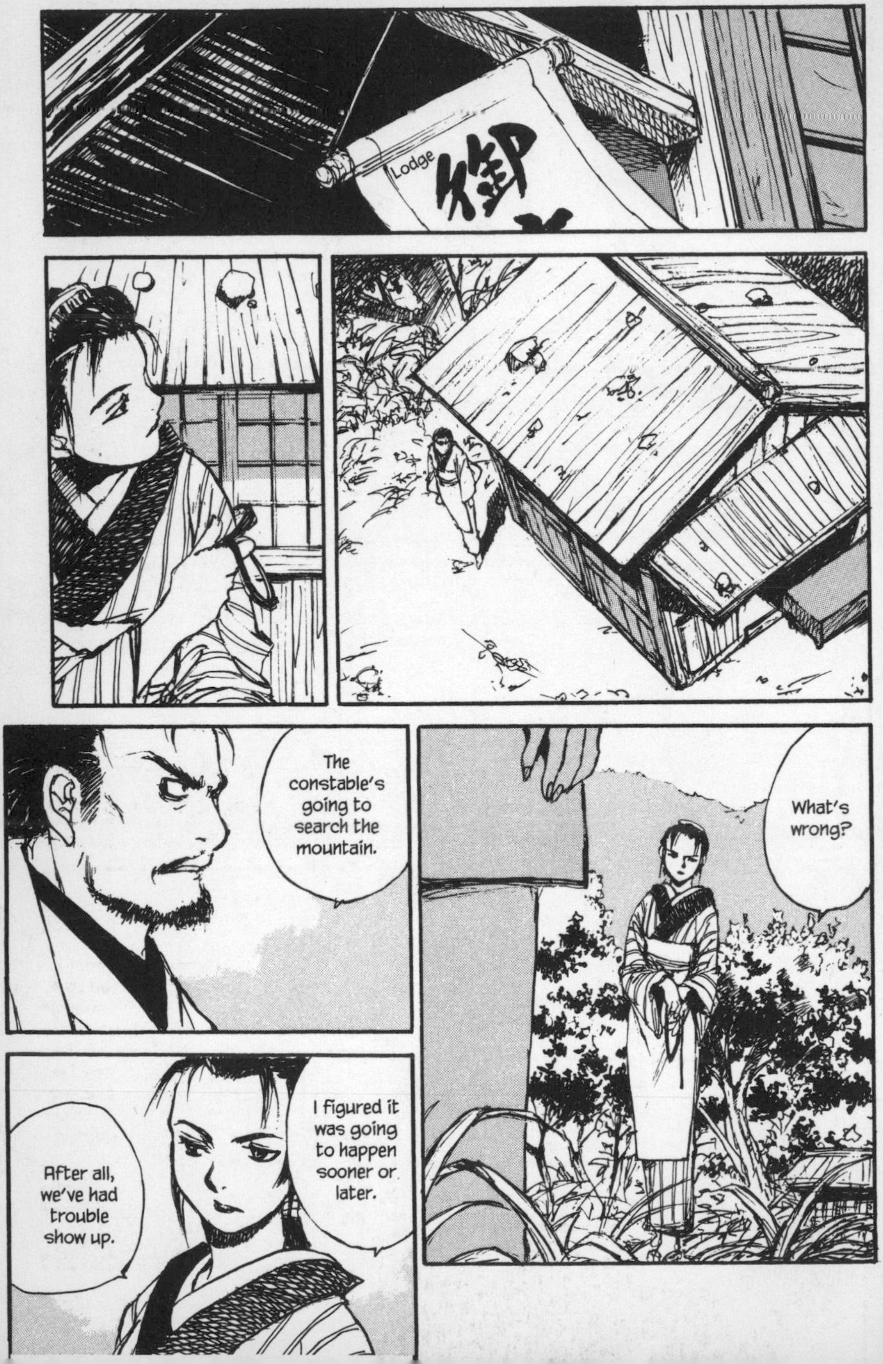
Lodge
What's wrong?
The constable's going to search the mountain.
I figured it was going to happen sooner or later.
After all, we've had trouble show up.

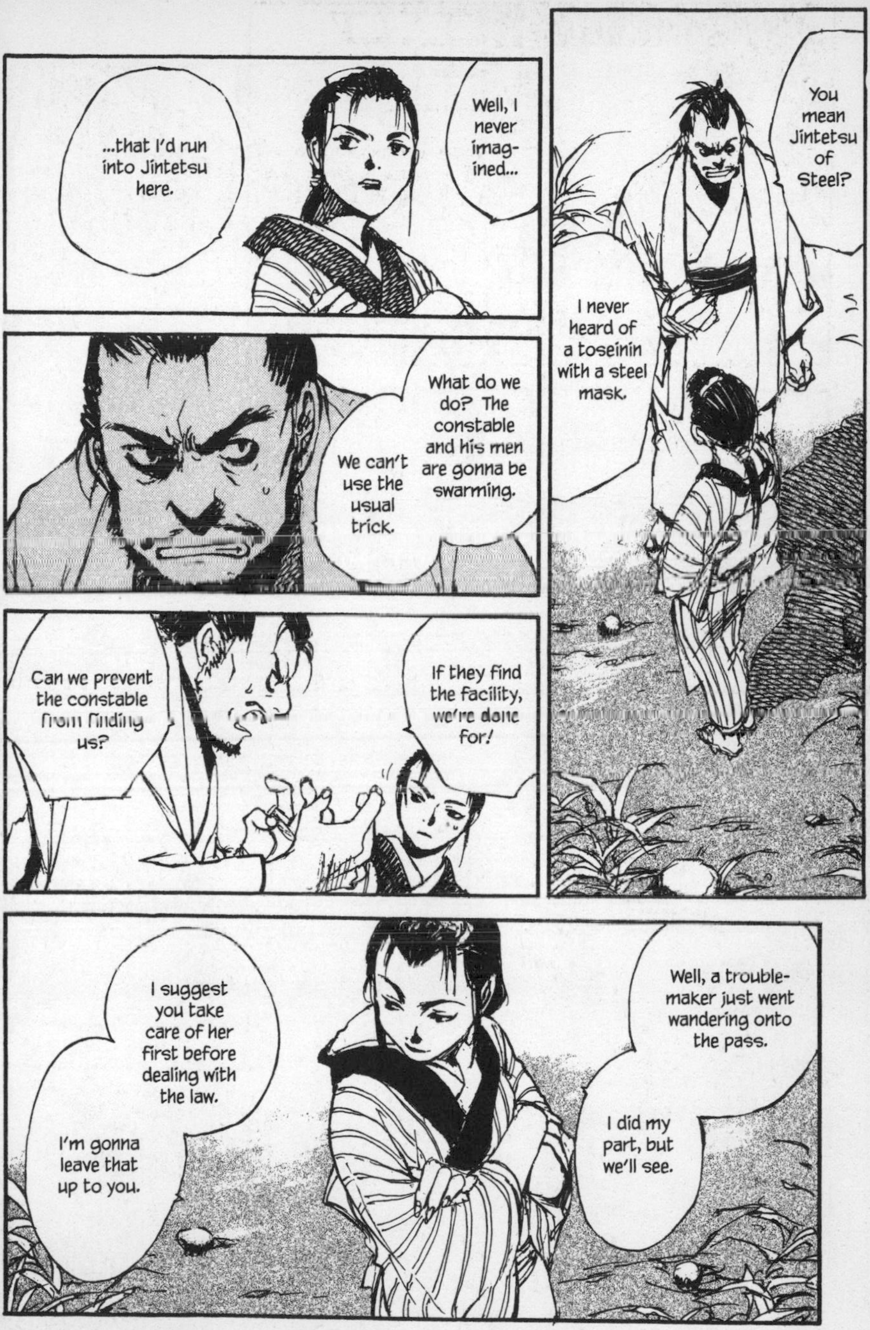
You mean Jintetsu of Steel?
I never heard of a toseinin with a steel mask.
Well, I never imagined...
...that I'd run into Jintetsu here.
What do we do? The constable and his men are gonna be swarming.
We can't use the usual trick.
If they find the facility, we're done for!
Can we prevent the constable from finding us?
Well, a trouble-maker just went wandering onto the pass.
I did my part, but we'll see.
I suggest you take care of her first before dealing with the law.
I'm gonna leave that up to you.

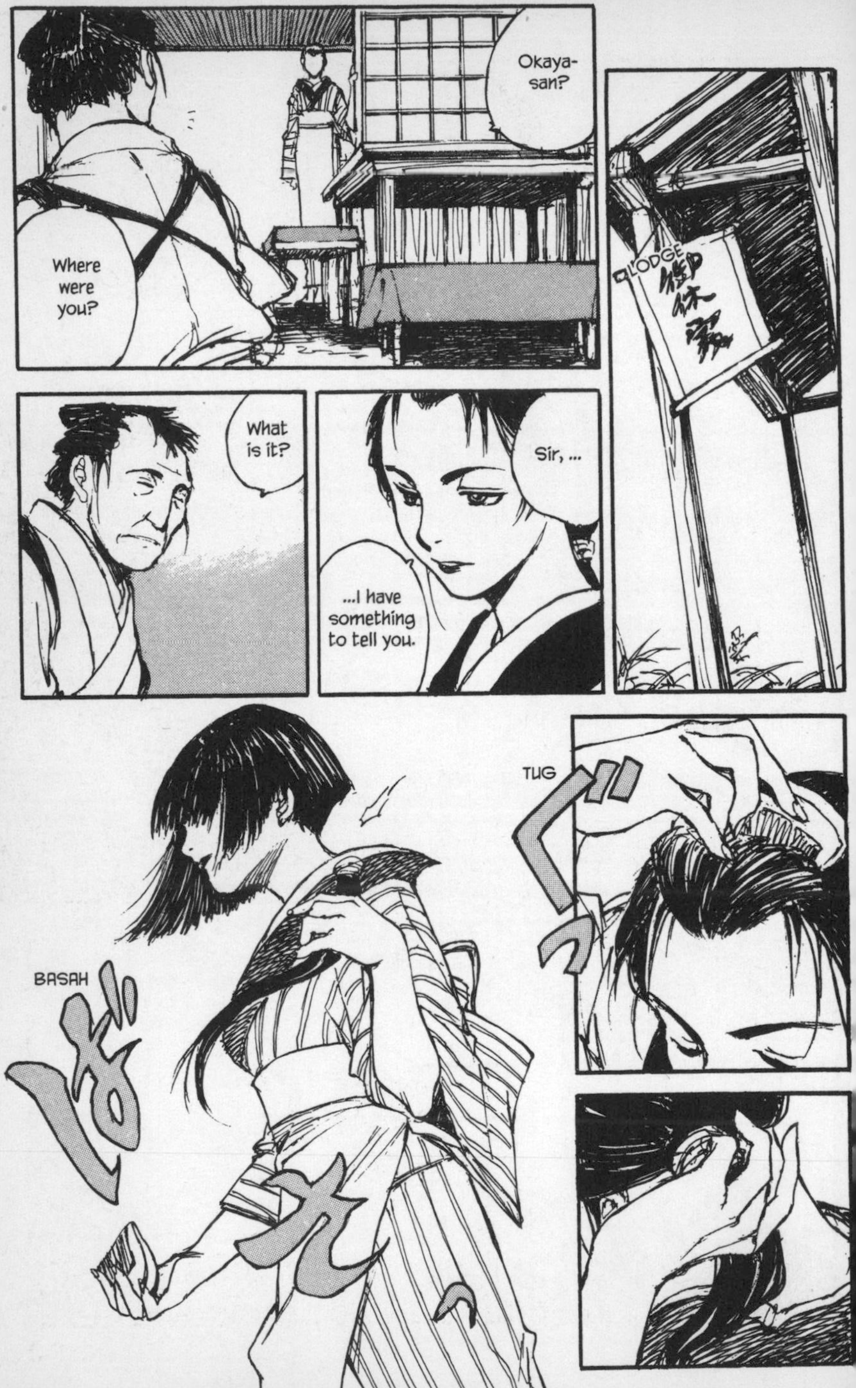
LODGE
Okaya-san?
Where were you?
Sir, ...
...I have something to tell you.
What is it?
TUG
BASAH

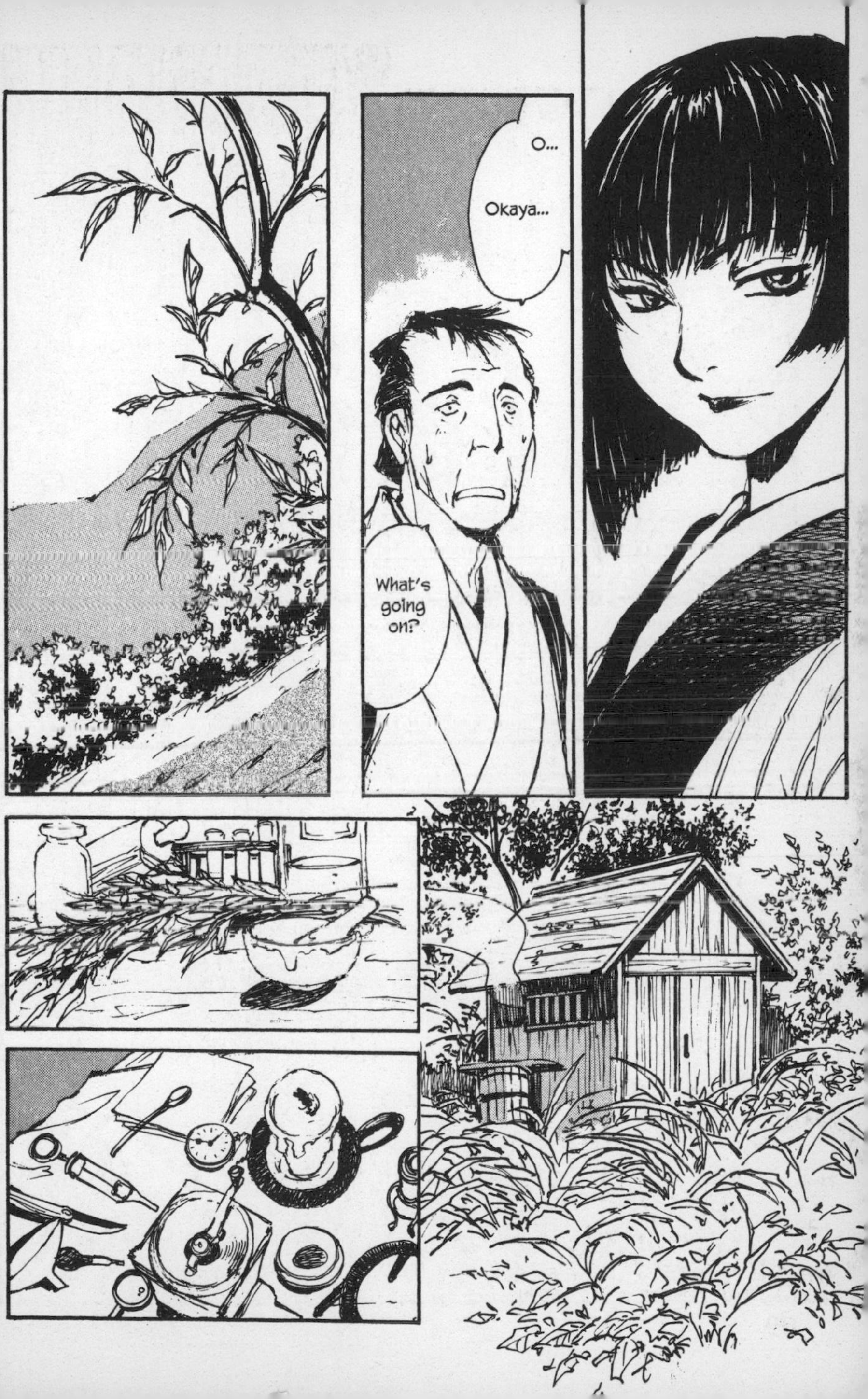
O...
Okaya...
What's going on?

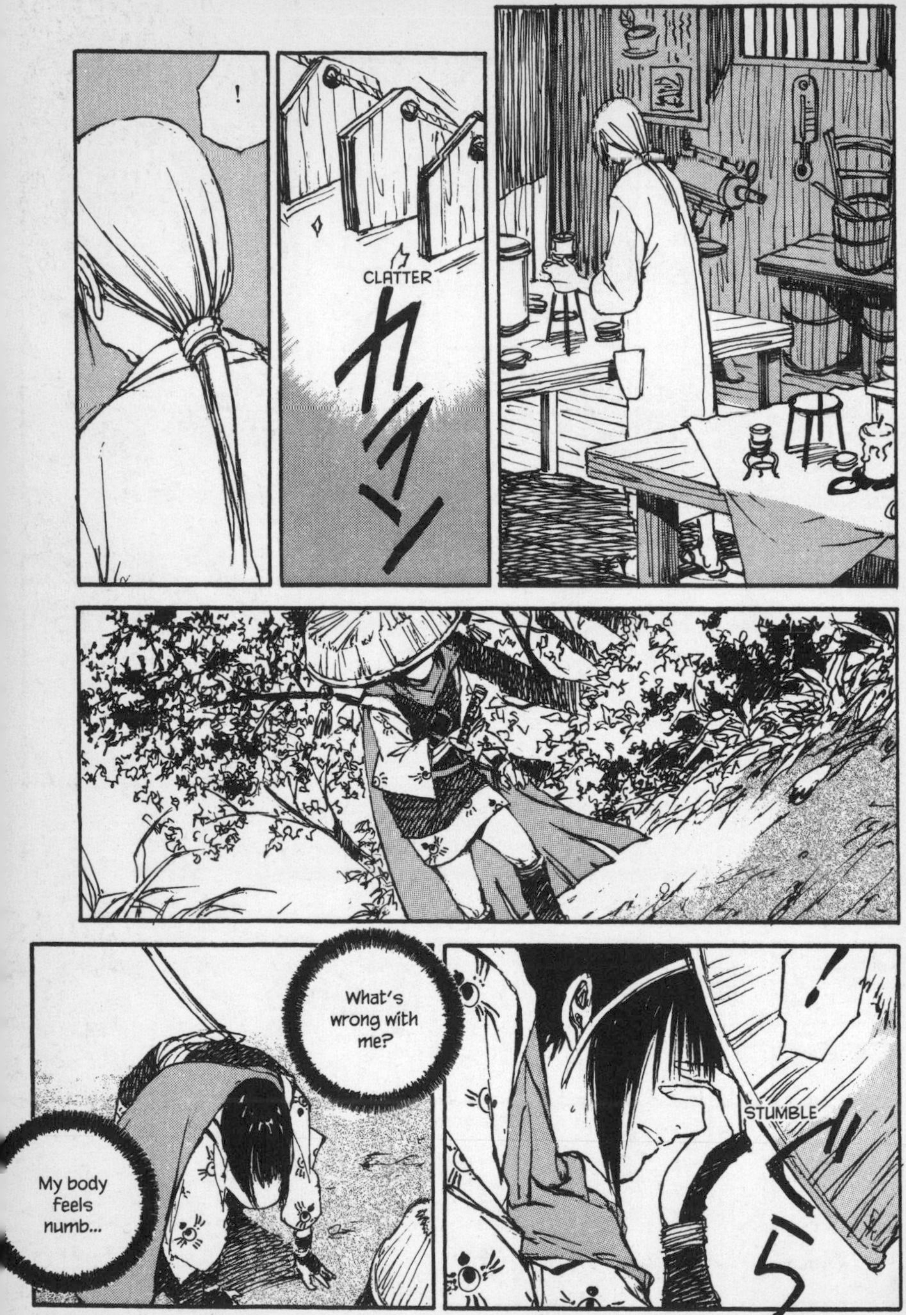
CLATTER
!
STUMBLE
What's wrong with me?
My body feels numb...

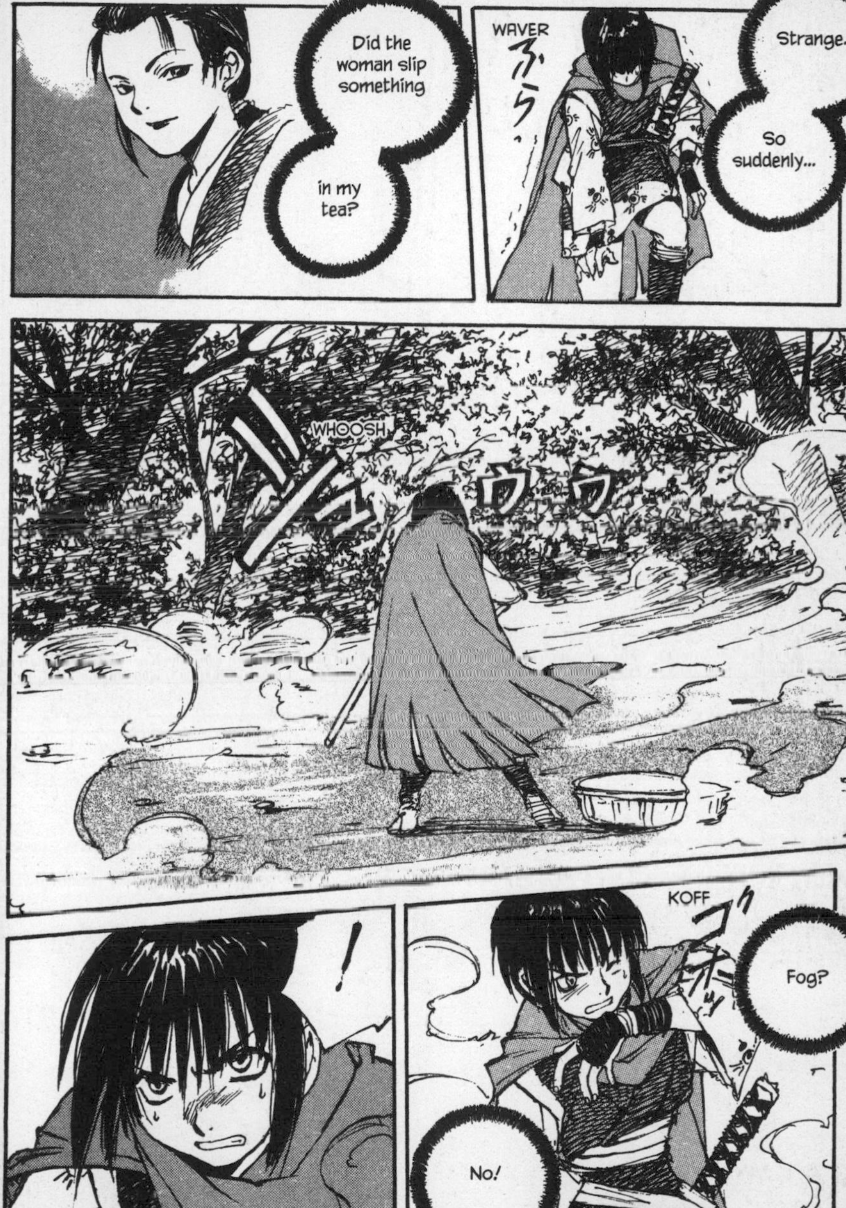
WAVER
Strange...
So suddenly...
Did the woman slip something
in my tea?
WHOOSH
KOFF
Fog?
No!
!

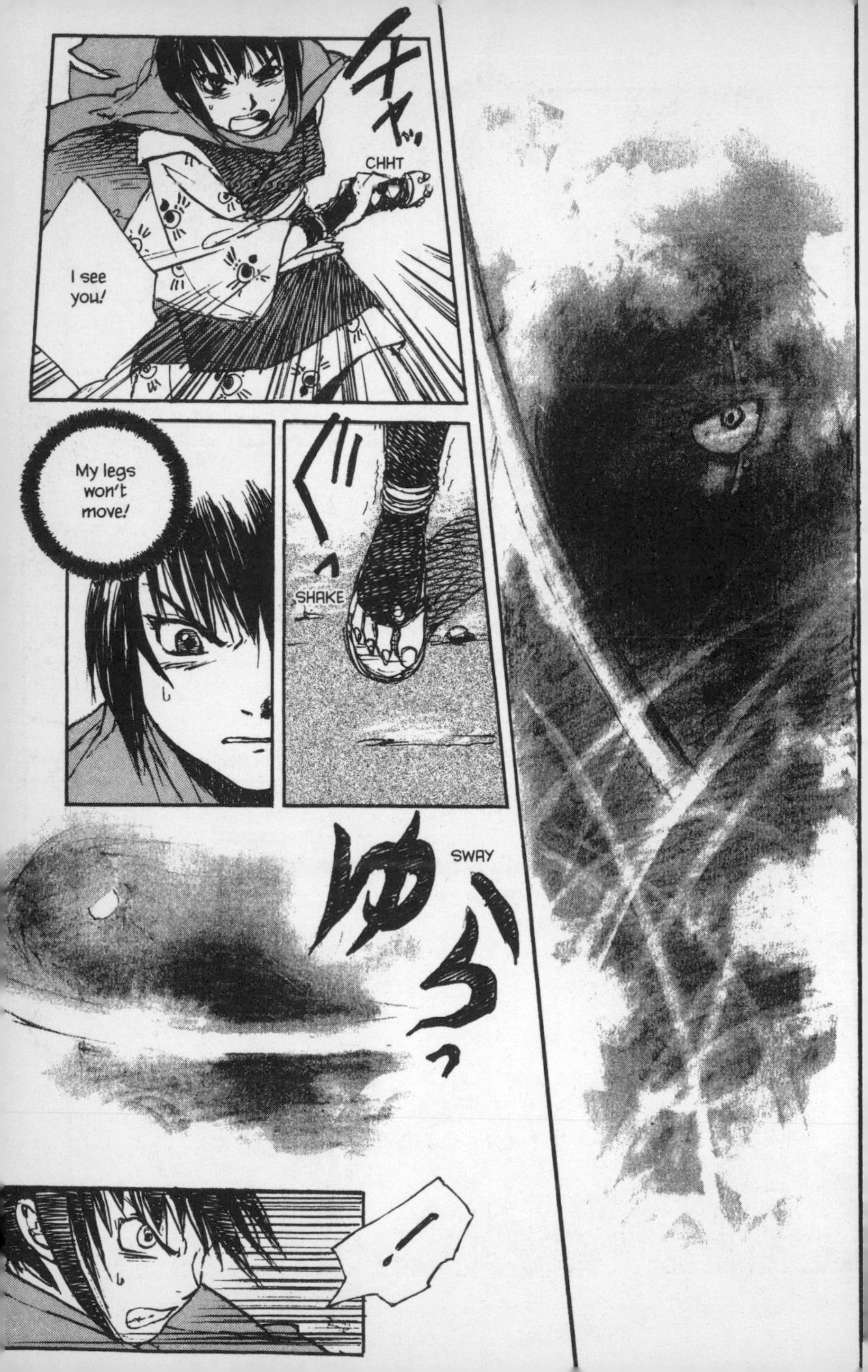
CHHT
I see you!
SHAKE
My legs won't move!
SWAY
!

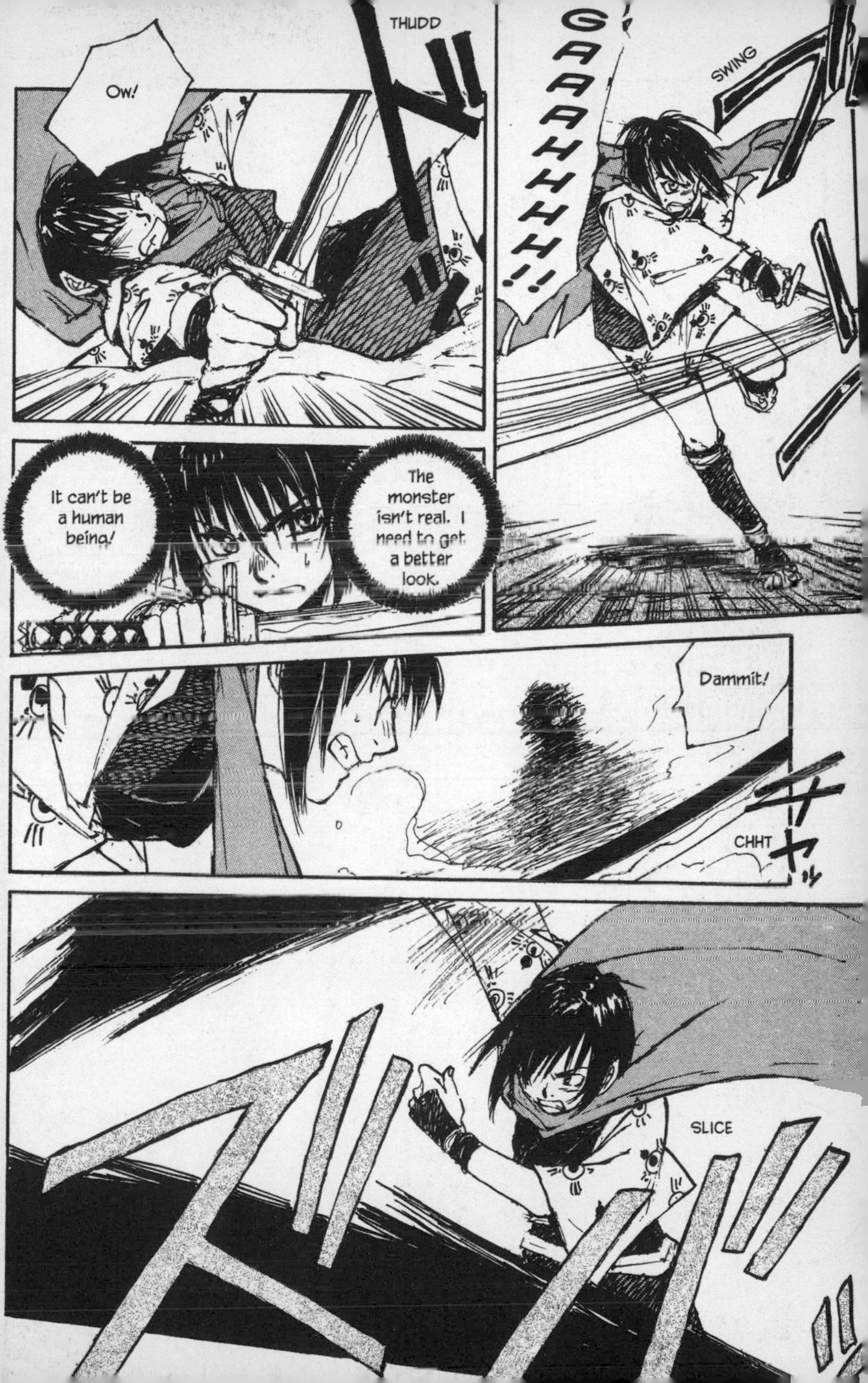
GAAAAHHHHH!!
SWING
THUDD
Ow!
The monster isn't real. I need to get a better look.
It can't be a human being!
Dammit!
CHHT
SLICE

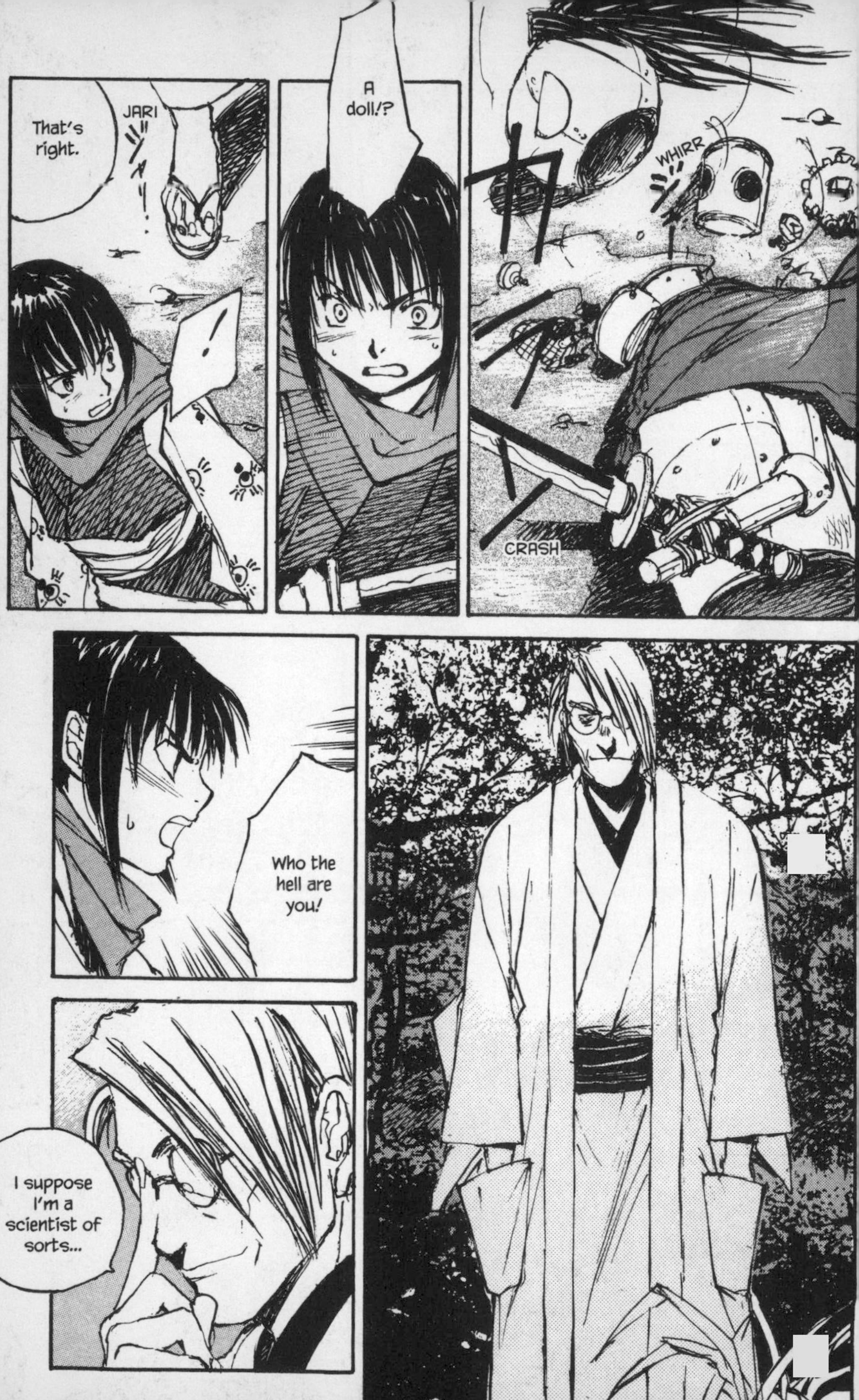
WHIRR
CRASH
A doll!?
JARI
That's right.
!
Who the hell are you!
I suppose I'm a scientist of sorts...

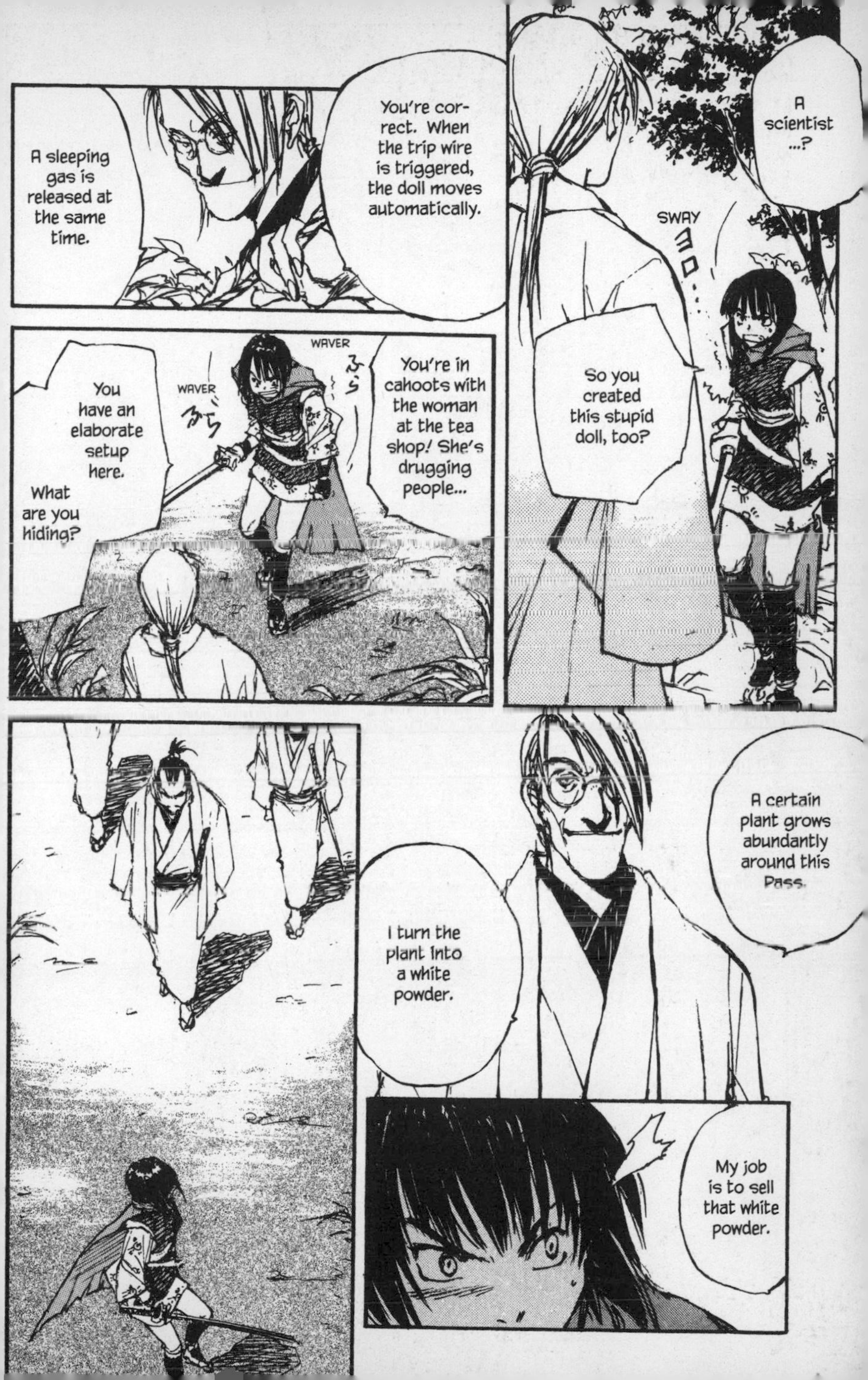
A scientist ...?
SWAY
ヨロ…
So you created this stupid doll, too?
You're correct. When the trip wire is triggered, the doll moves automatically.
A sleeping gas is released at the same time.
WAVER
ふら
You're in cahoots with the woman at the tea shop! She's drugging people...
WAVER
ふら
You have an elaborate setup here.
What are you hiding?
A certain plant grows abundantly around this Pass.
I turn the plant into a white powder.
My job is to sell that white powder.

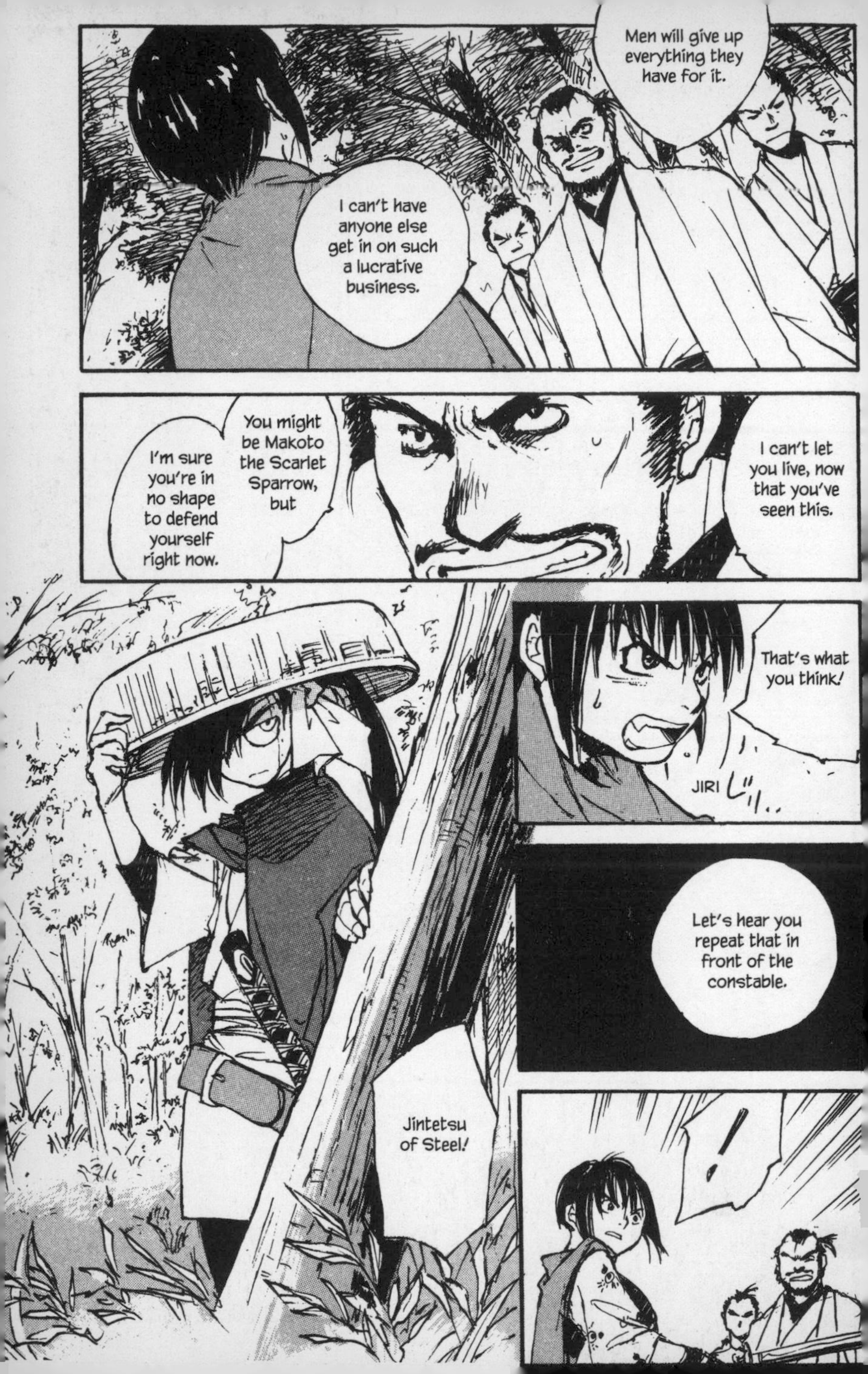
Men will give up everything they have for it.
I can't have anyone else get in on such a lucrative business.
I can't let you live, now that you've seen this.
You might be Makoto the Scarlet Sparrow, but
I'm sure you're in no shape to defend yourself right now.
That's what you think!
JIRI
Let's hear you repeat that in front of the constable.
!
Jintetsu of Steel!

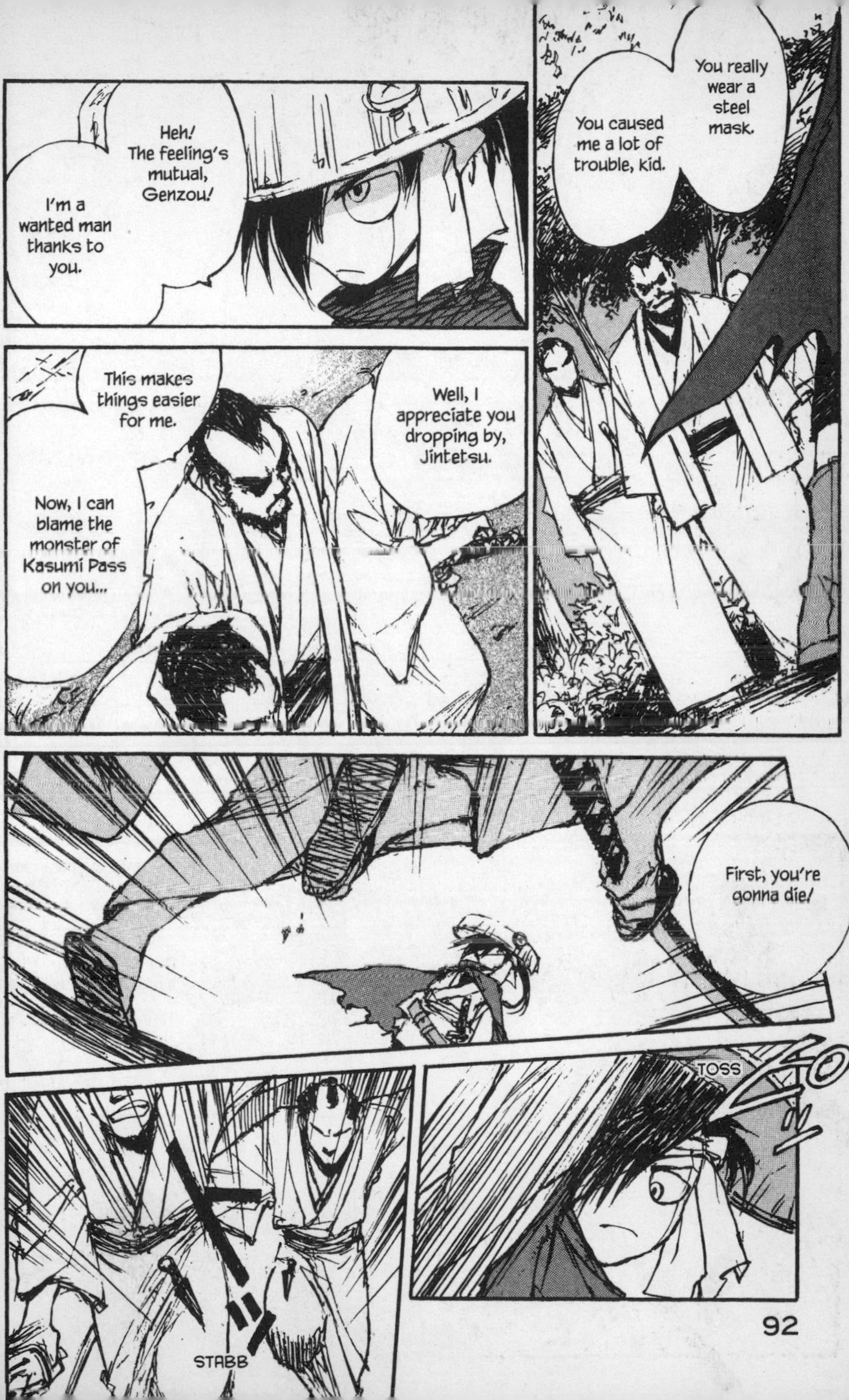
You really wear a steel mask.
You caused me a lot of trouble, kid.
Heh! The feeling's mutual, Genzou!
I'm a wanted man thanks to you.
Well, I appreciate you dropping by, Jintetsu.
This makes things easier for me.
Now, I can blame the monster of Kasumi Pass on you...
First, you're gonna die!
TOSS
STABB

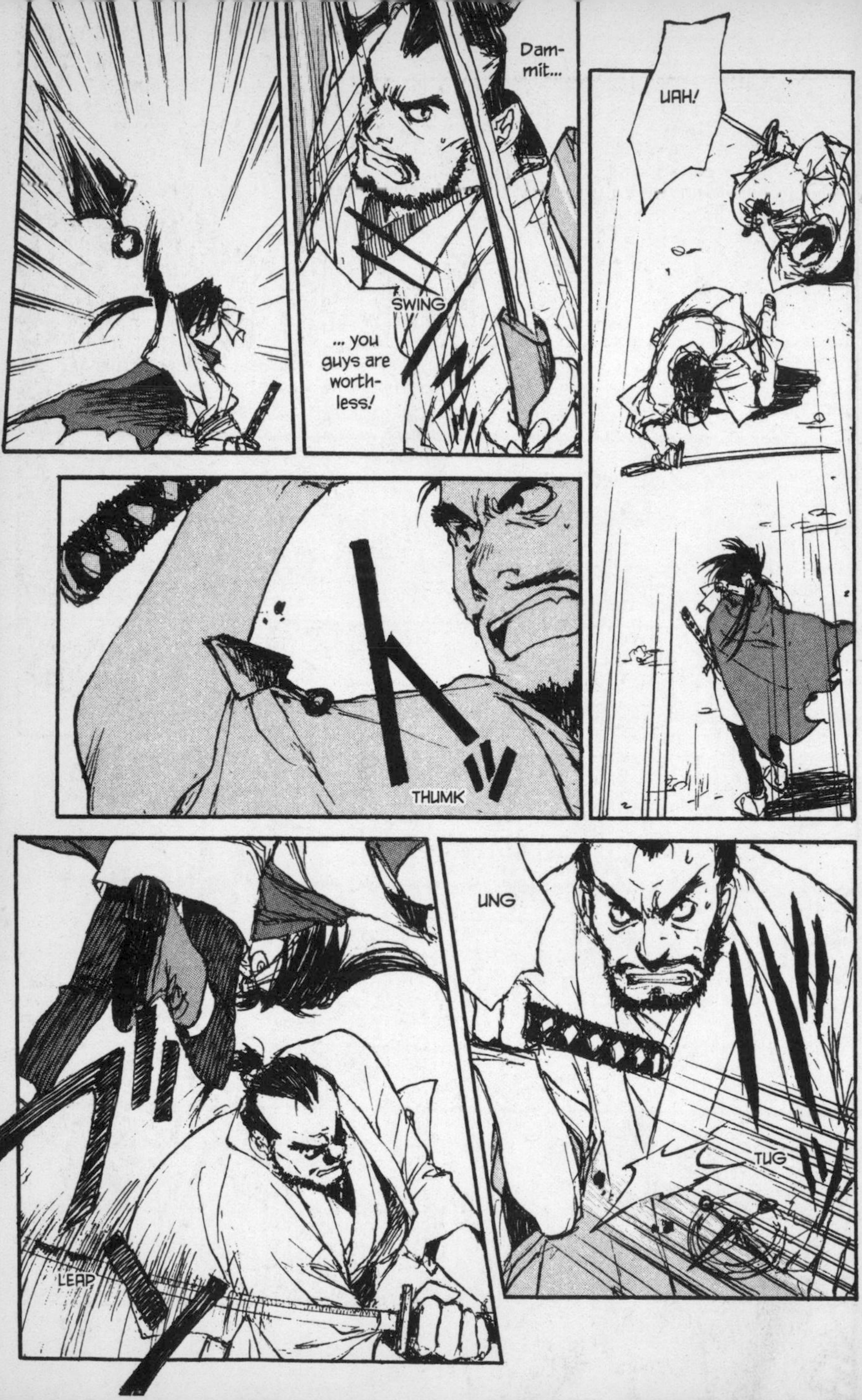
UAH!
Dam-mit...
SWING
... you guys are worthless!
THUMK
UNG
TUG
LEAP

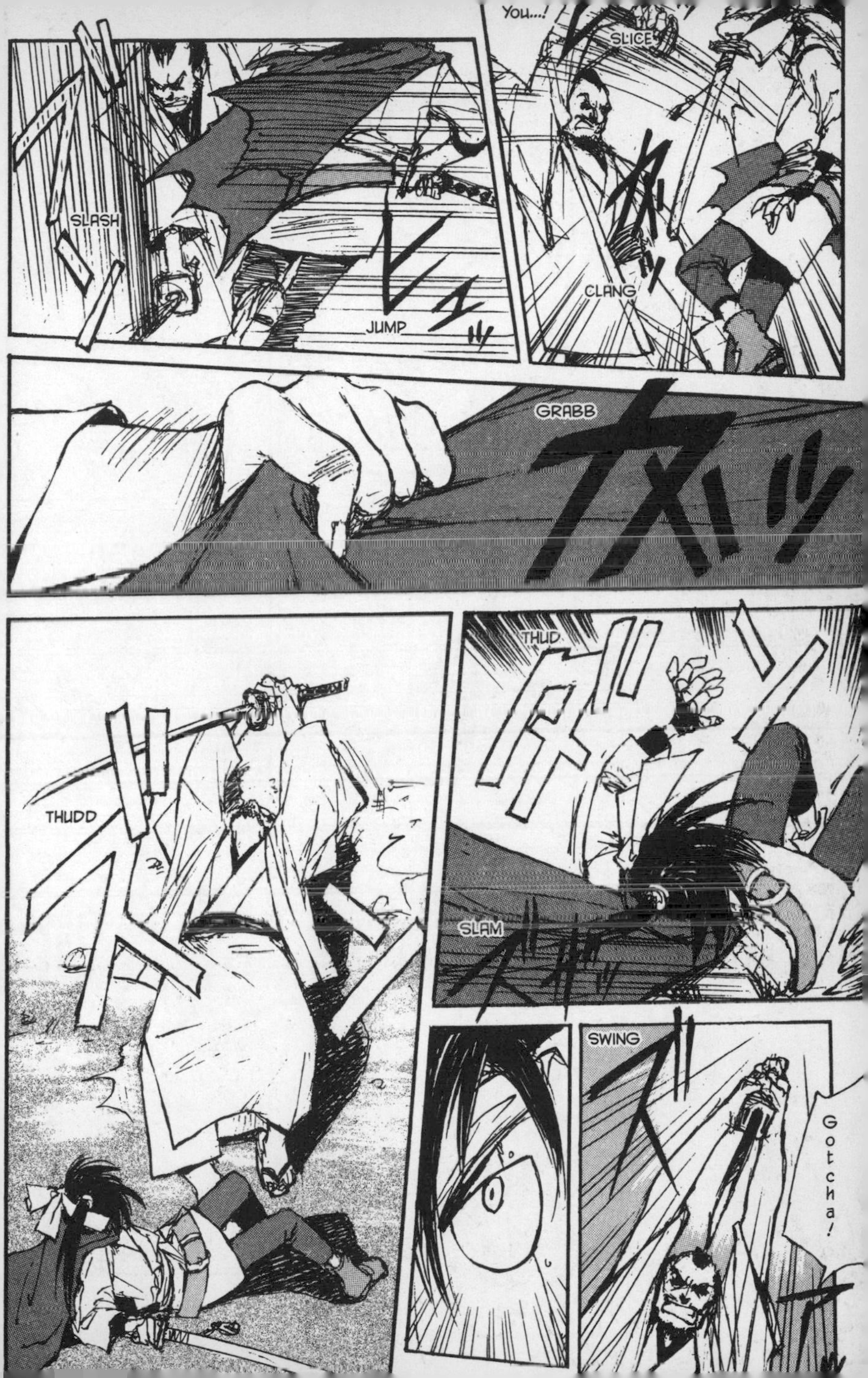
You...!
SLICE
CLANG
SLASH
JUMP
GRABB
THUD
SLAM
SWING
Gotcha!
THUDD

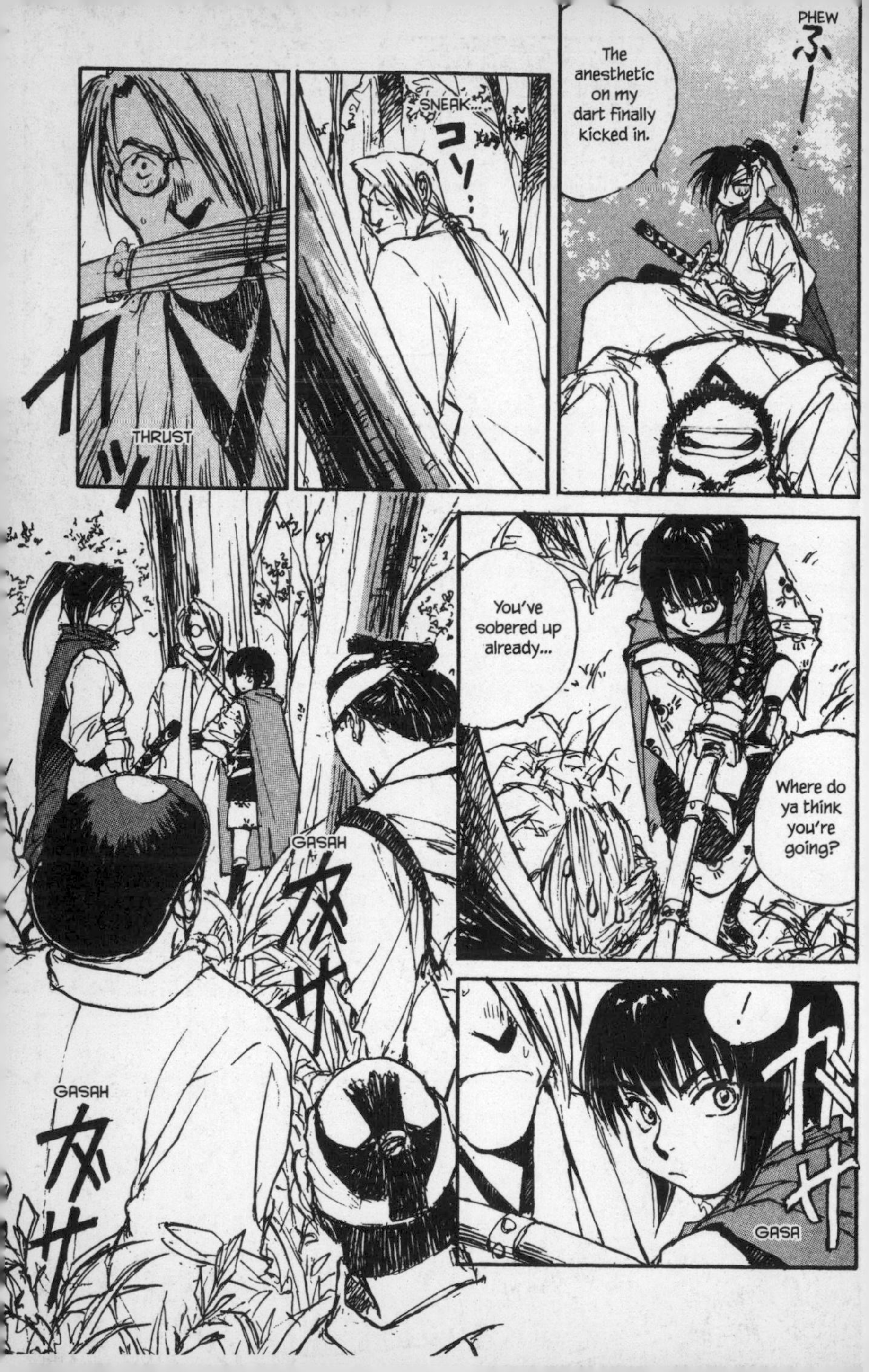
PHEW
The anesthetic on my dart finally kicked in.
SNEAK...
THRUST
You've sobered up already...
Where do ya think you're going?
GASAH
!
GASA
GASAH

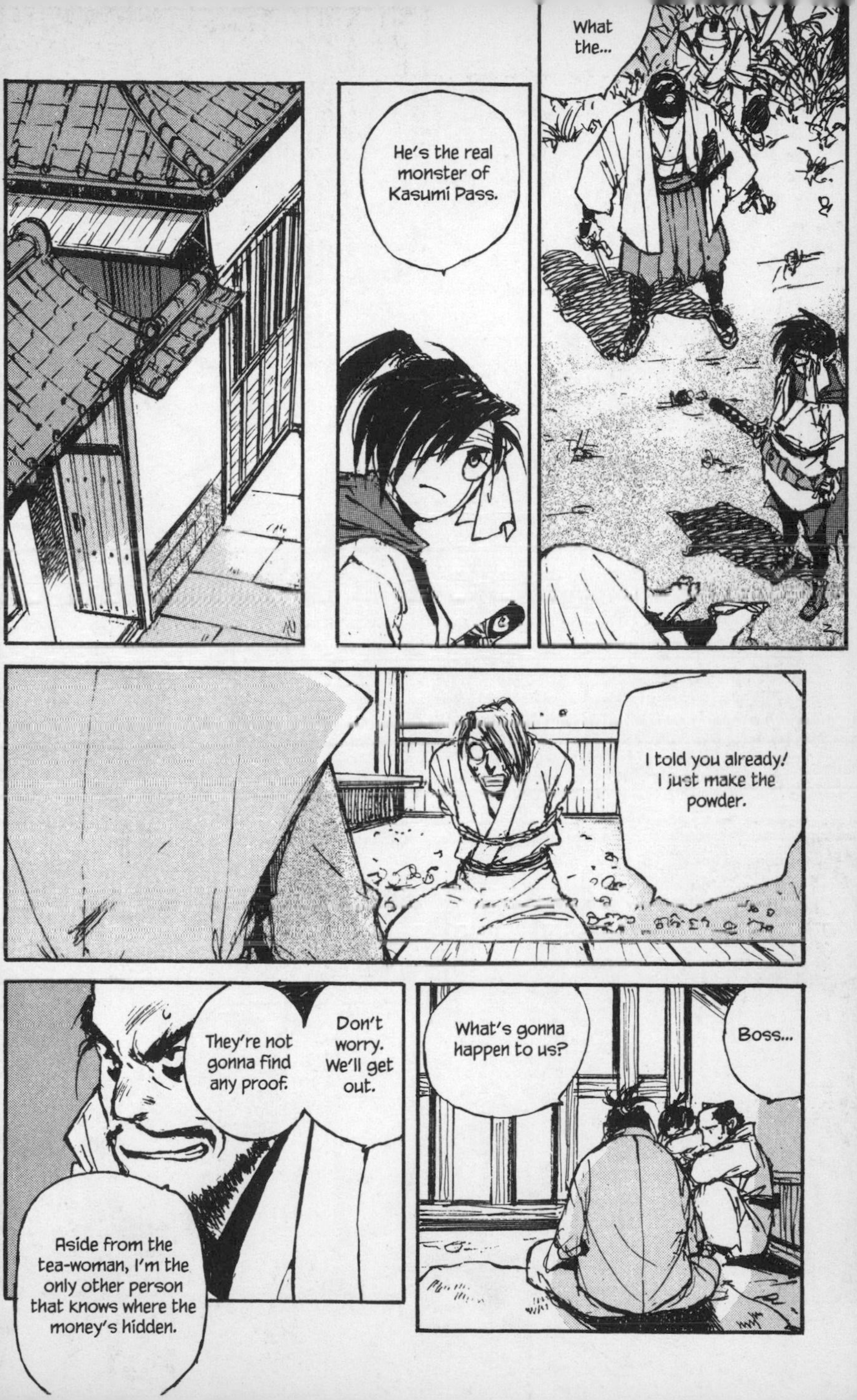

What the...
He's the real monster of Kasumi Pass.
I told you already! I just make the powder.
Boss...
What's gonna happen to us?
Don't worry. We'll get out.
They're not gonna find any proof.
Aside from the tea-woman, I'm the only other person that knows where the money's hidden.

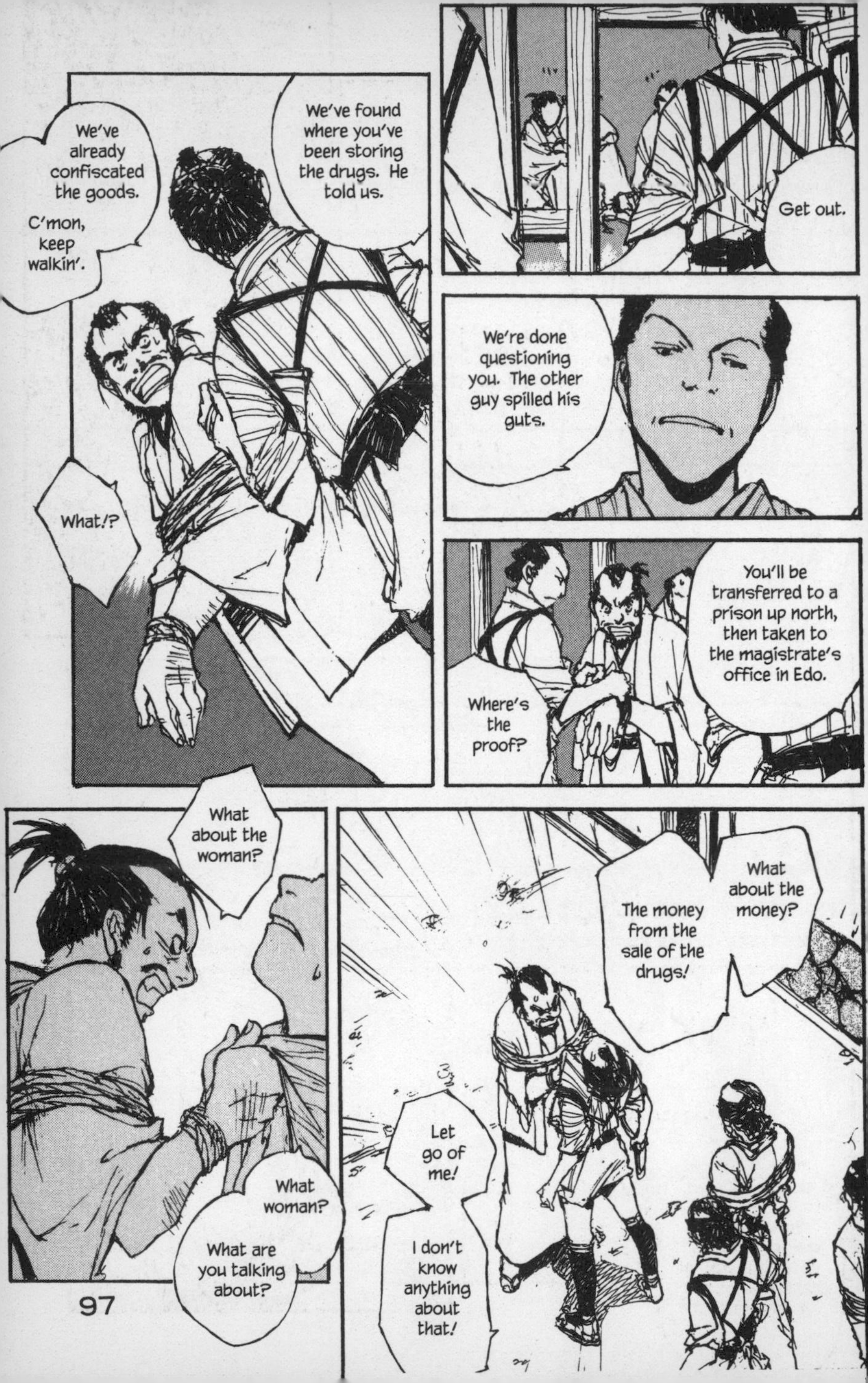
Get out.
We're done questioning you. The other guy spilled his guts.
You'll be transferred to a prison up north, then taken to the magistrate's office in Edo.
Where's the proof?
We've found where you've been storing the drugs. He told us.
We've already confiscated the goods.
C'mon, keep walkin'.
What!?
What about the money?
The money from the sale of the drugs!
Let go of me!
I don't know anything about that!
What about the woman?
What woman?
What are you talking about?

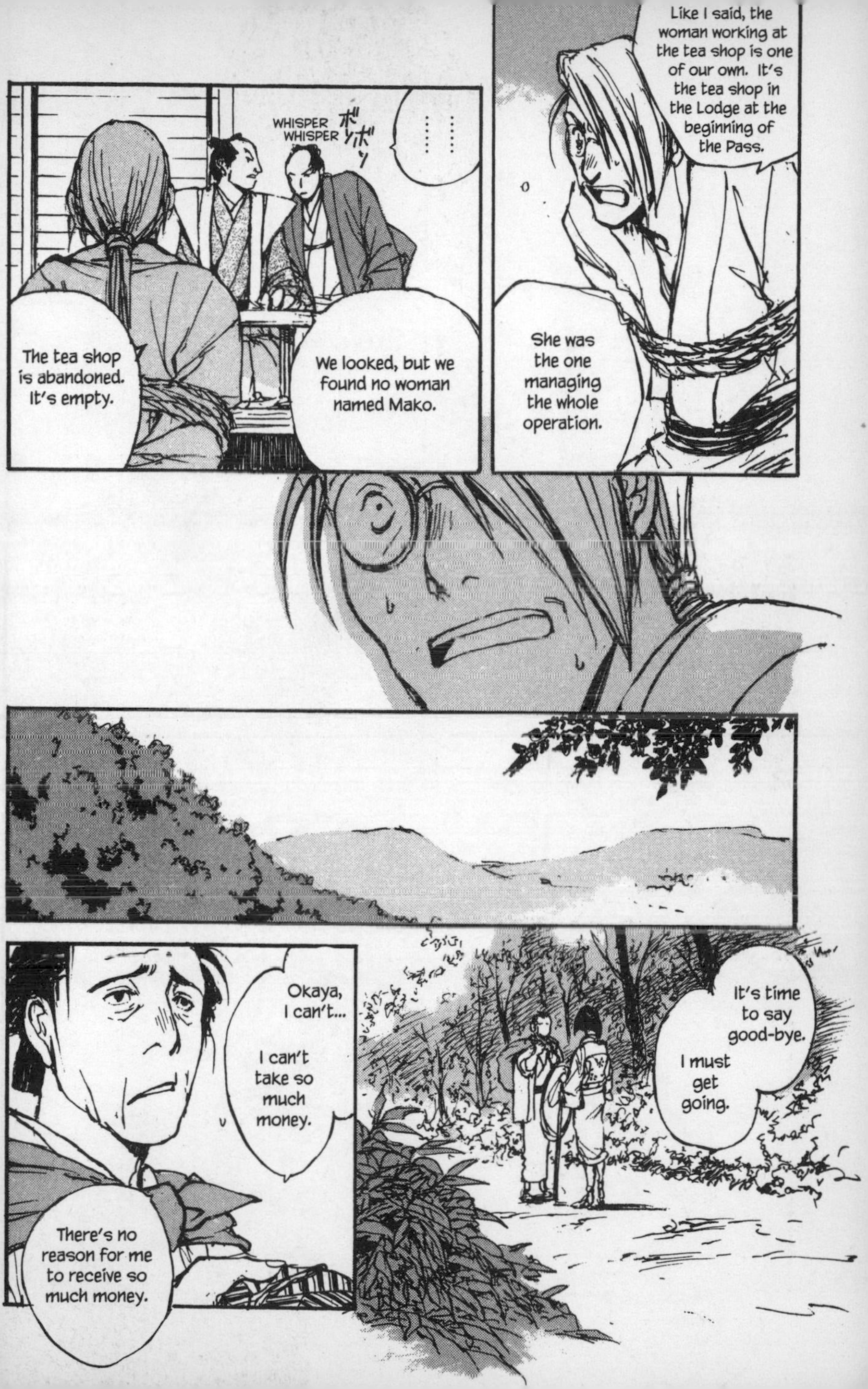
Like I said, the woman working at the tea shop is one of our own. It's the tea shop in the Lodge at the beginning of the Pass.
She was the one managing the whole operation.
......
WHISPER WHISPER
ボソボソ
We looked, but we found no woman named Mako.
The tea shop is abandoned. It's empty.
It's time to say good-bye.
I must get going.
Okaya, I can't...
I can't take so much money.
There's no reason for me to receive so much money.

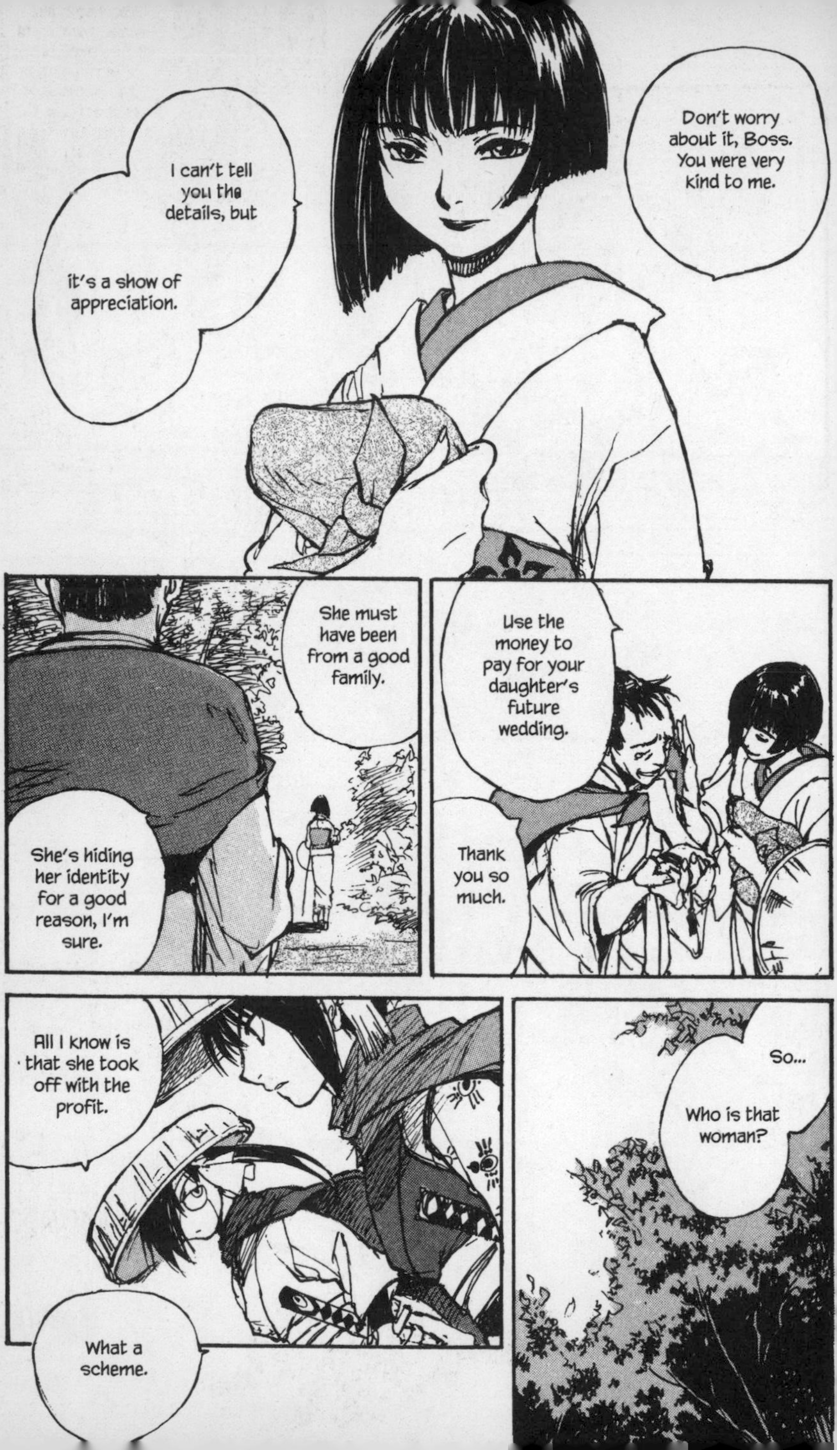
Don't worry about it, Boss. You were very kind to me.
I can't tell you the details, but
it's a show of appreciation.
Use the money to pay for your daughter's future wedding.
Thank you so much.
She must have been from a good family.
She's hiding her identity for a good reason, I'm sure.
So...
Who is that woman?
All I know is that she took off with the profit.
What a scheme.

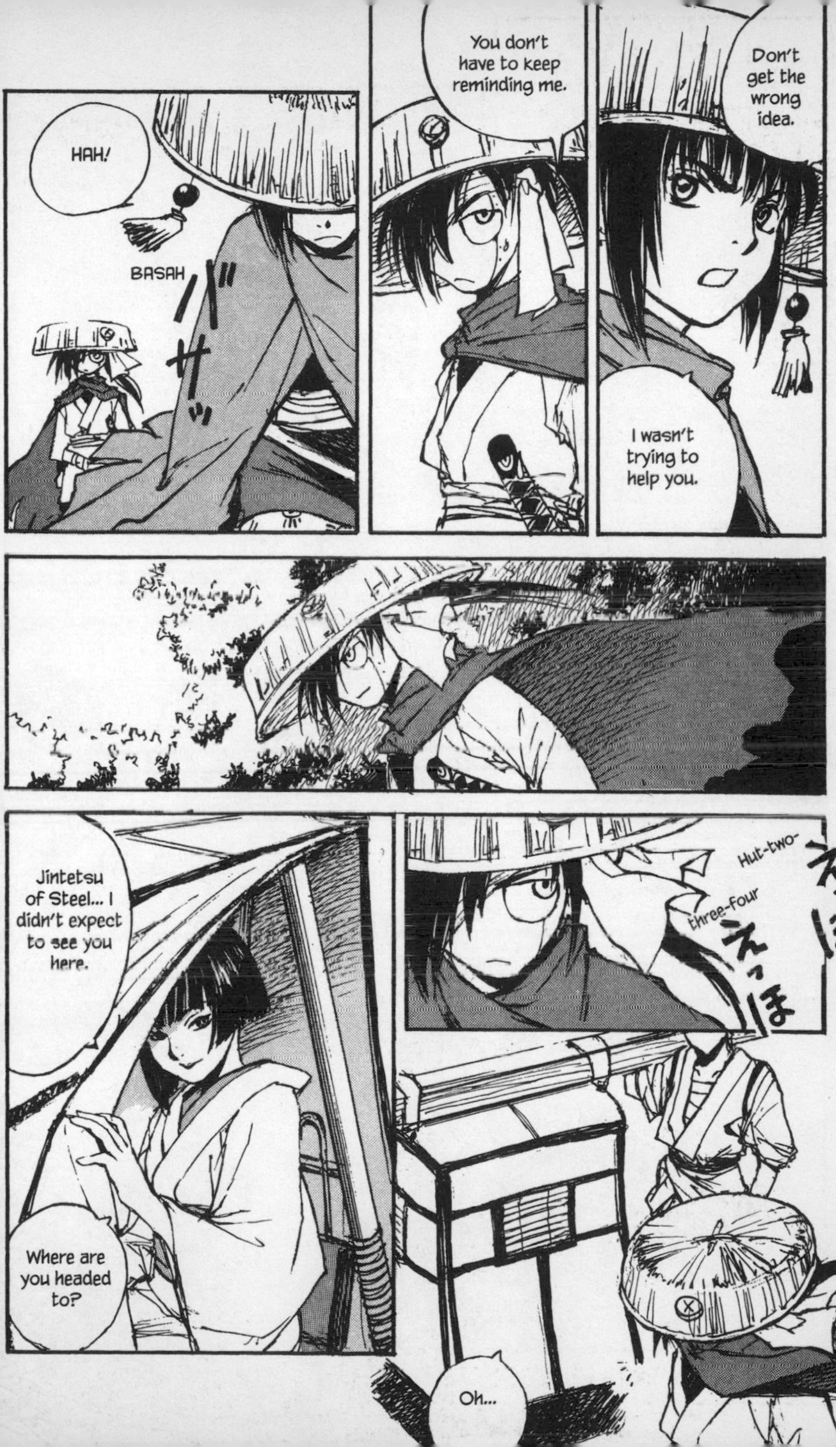
Don't get the wrong idea.
I wasn't trying to help you.
You don't have to keep reminding me.
HAH!
BASAH
バサッ
Hut-two-
えっほ
three-four
えっほ
Jintetsu of Steel... I didn't expect to see you here.
Where are you headed to?
Oh...

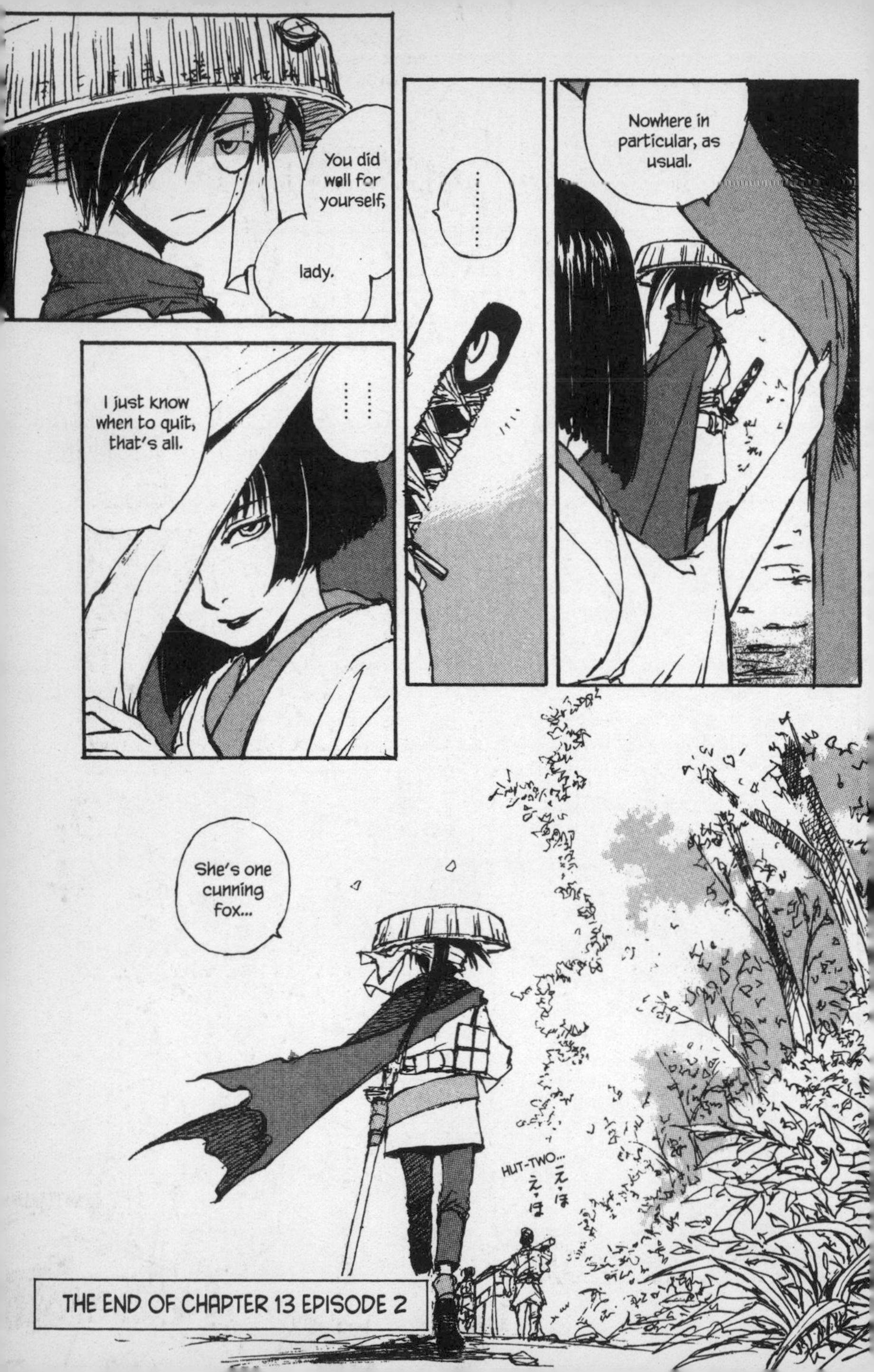
Nowhere in particular, as usual.
......
You did well for yourself,
lady.
......
I just know when to quit, that's all.
She's one cunning fox...
HUT-TWO...
THE END OF CHAPTER 13 EPISODE 2

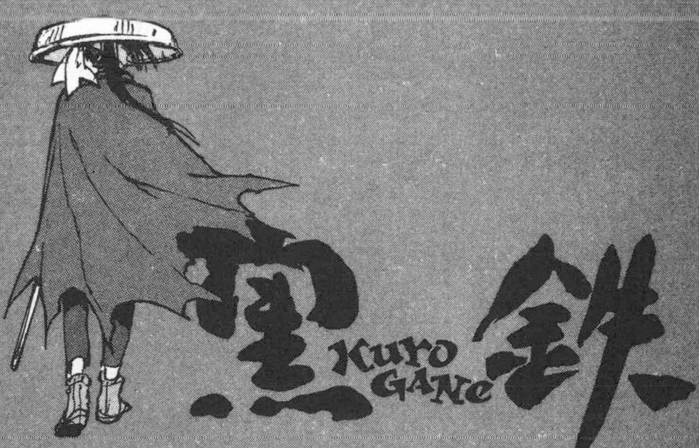
黒鉄
KURO GANE

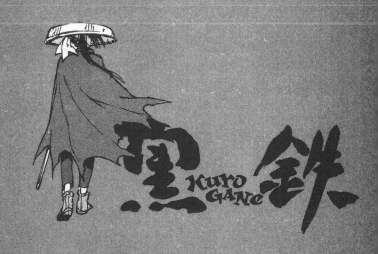

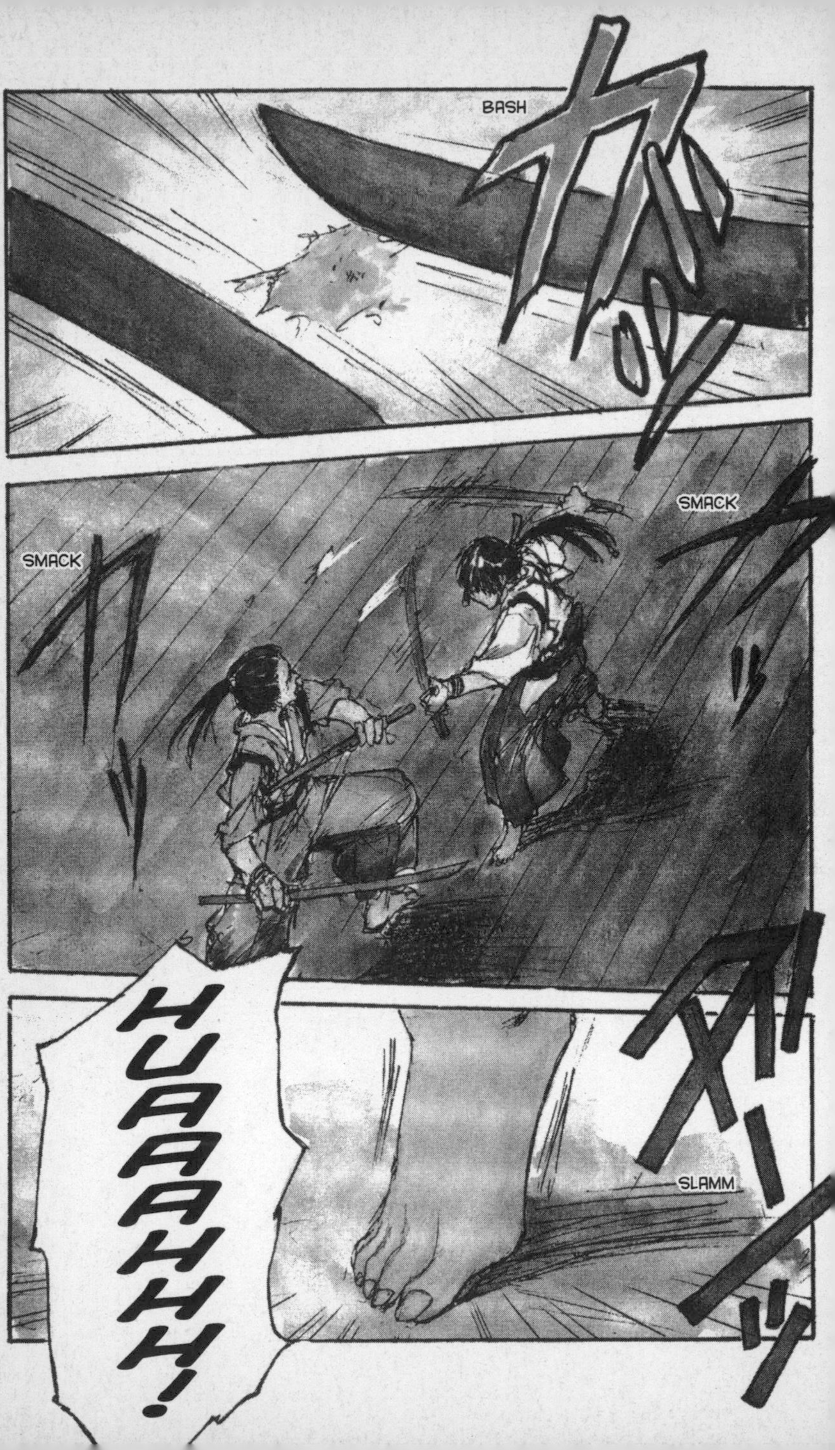
BASH
SMACK
SMACK
SLAMM
HUAAAHHH!

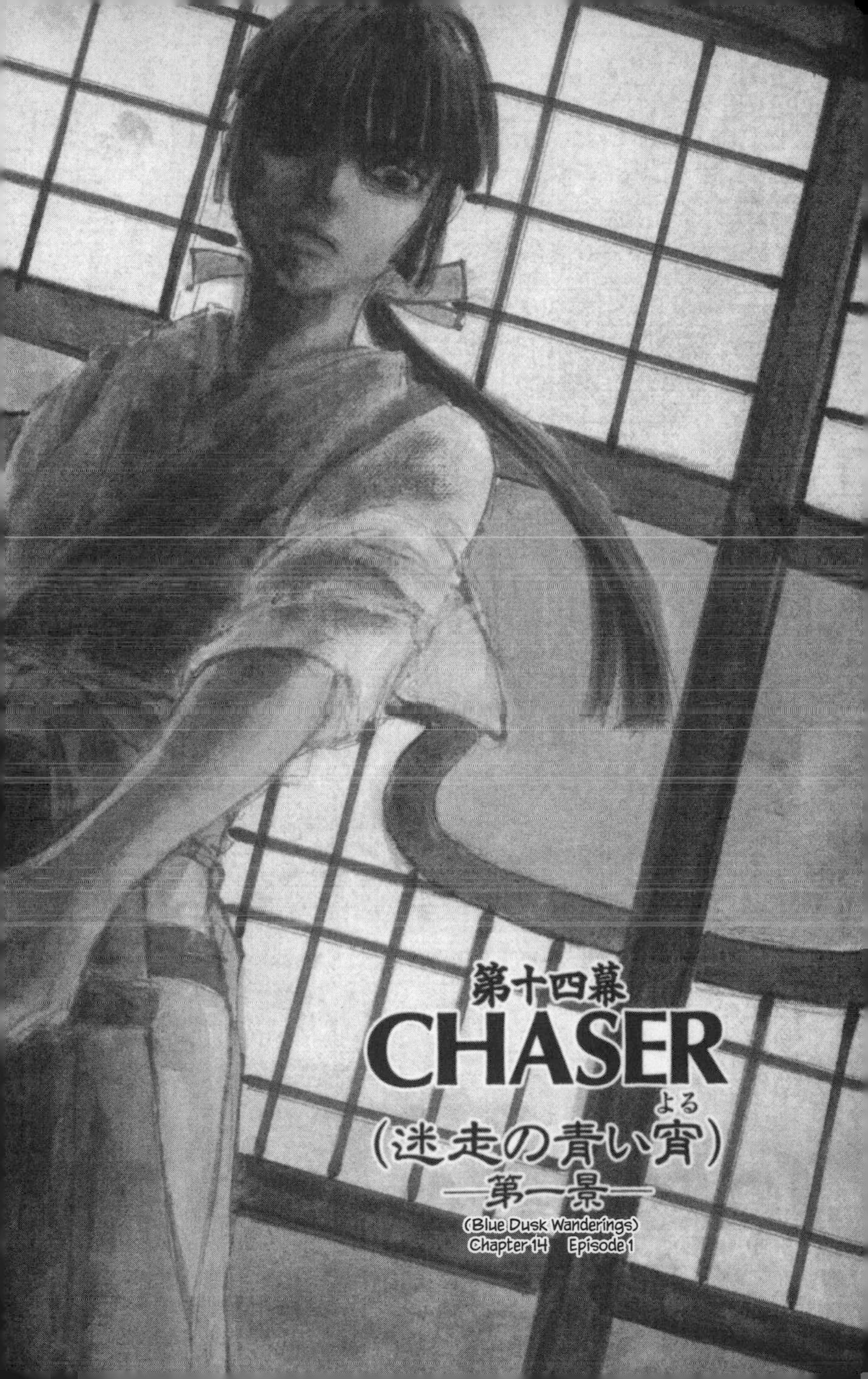
第十四幕
CHASER
よる
(迷走の青い宵)
—第一景—
(Blue Dusk Wanderings)
Chapter 14 Episode 1

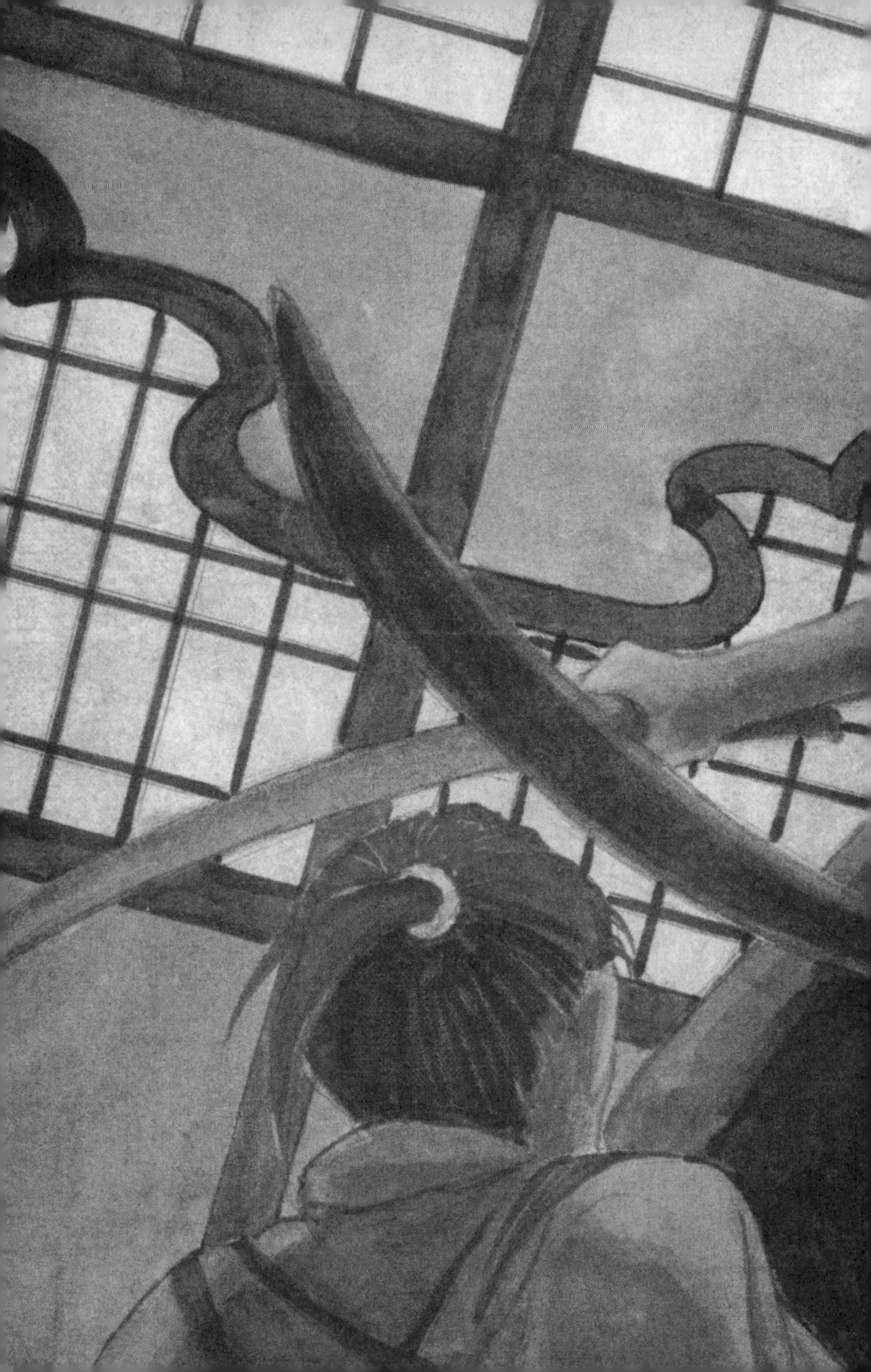

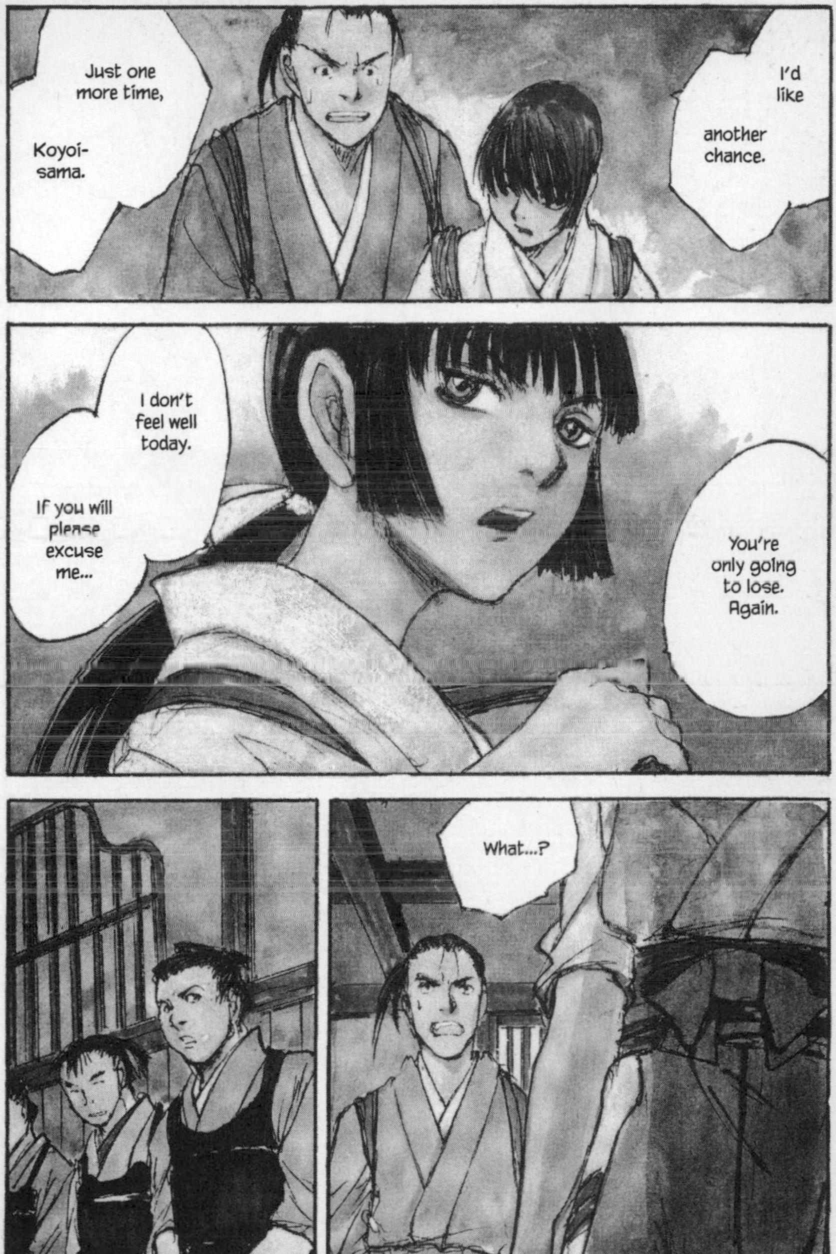
I'd like another chance.
Just one more time, Koyoi-sama.
I don't feel well today. If you will please excuse me...
You're only going to lose. Again.
What...?

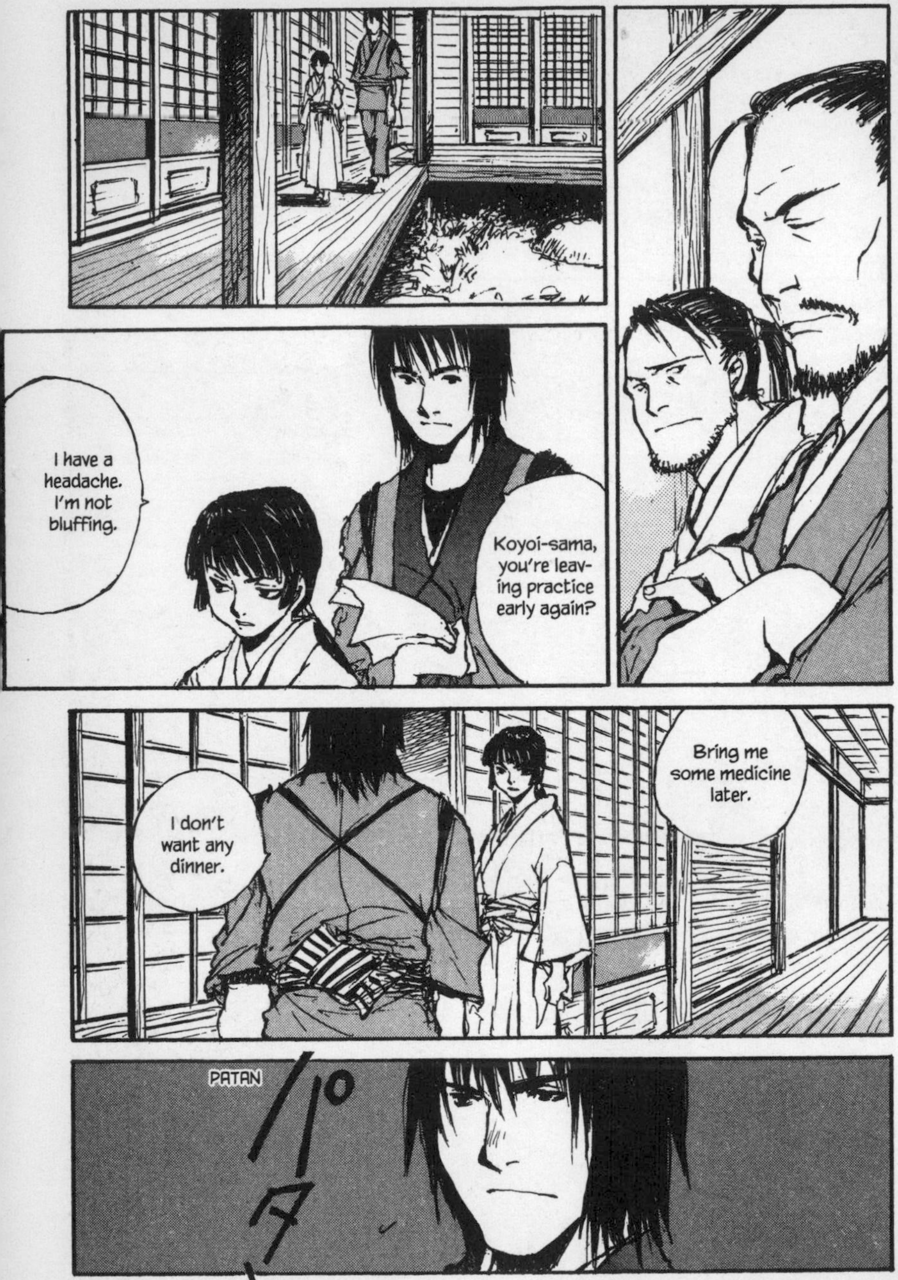
Koyoi-sama, you're leaving practice early again?
I have a headache. I'm not bluffing.
Bring me some medicine later.
I don't want any dinner.
PATAN

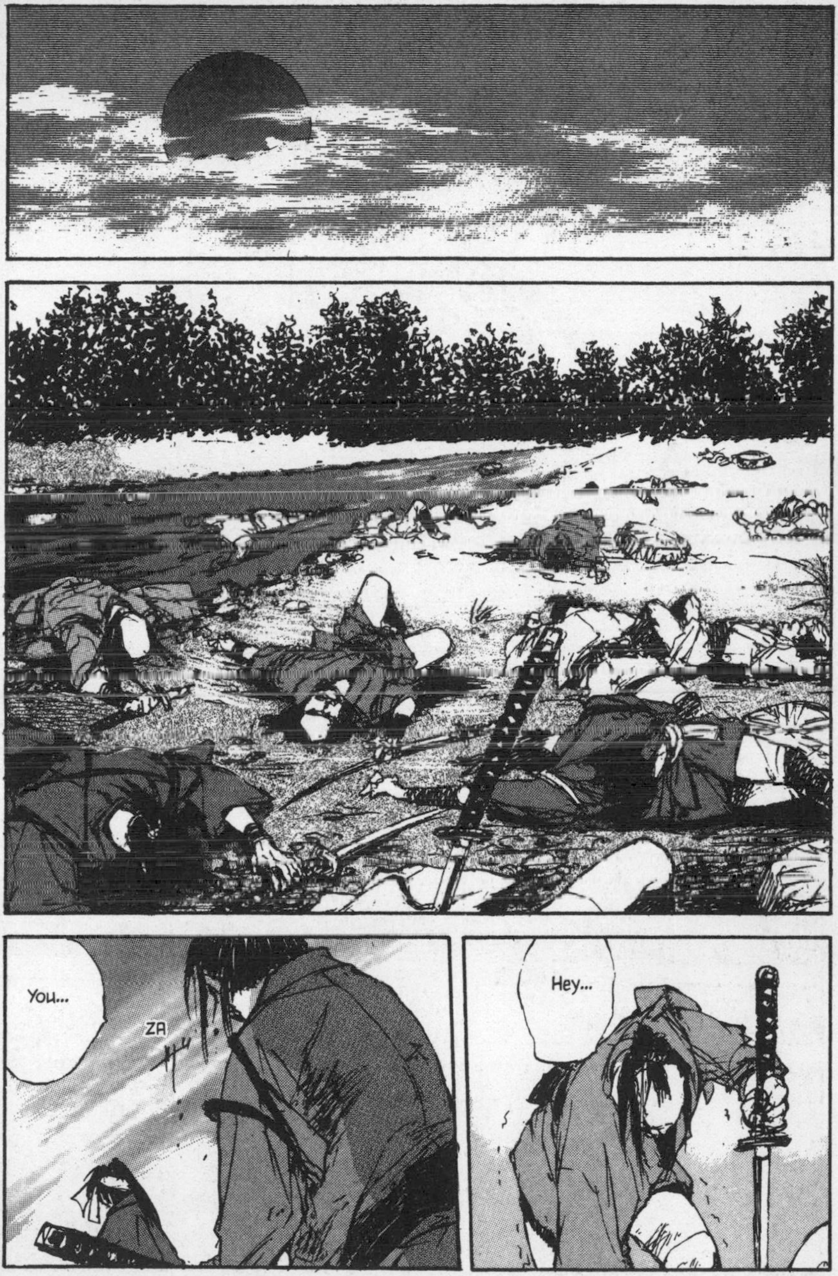
Hey...
You...
ZA

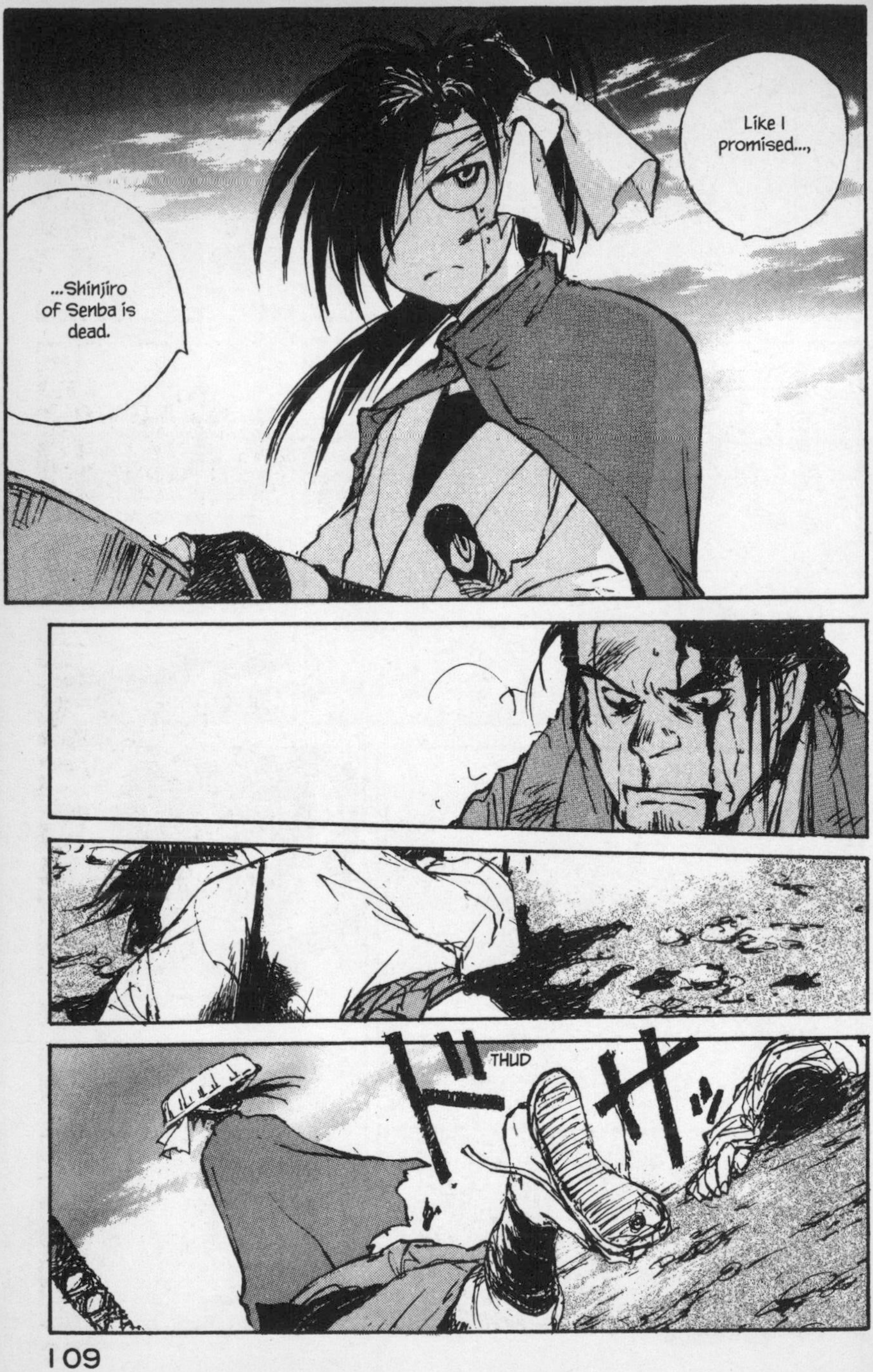
Like I promised...,
...Shinjiro of Senba is dead.
THUD

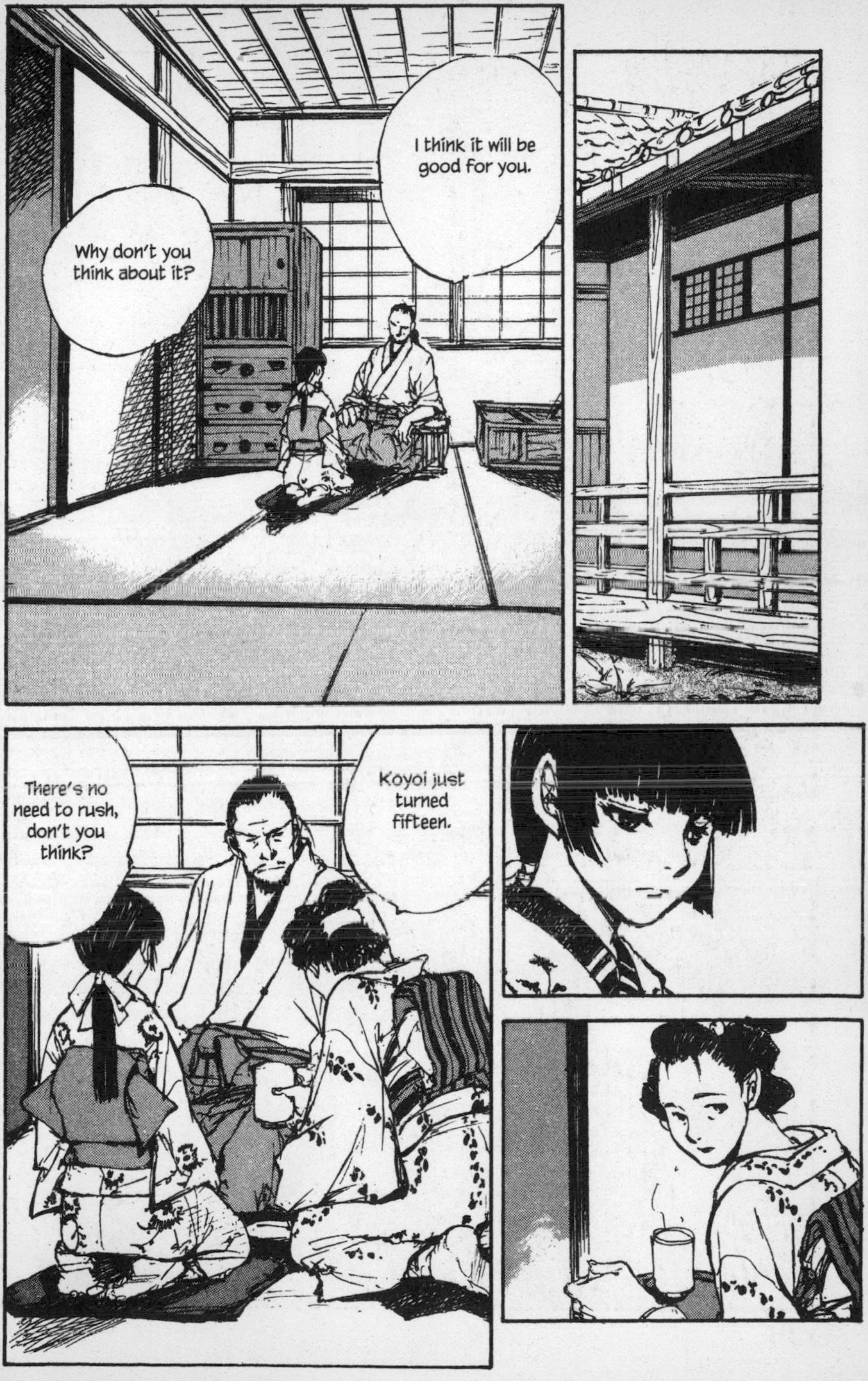
I think it will be good for you.
Why don't you think about it?
Koyoi just turned fifteen.
There's no need to rush, don't you think?

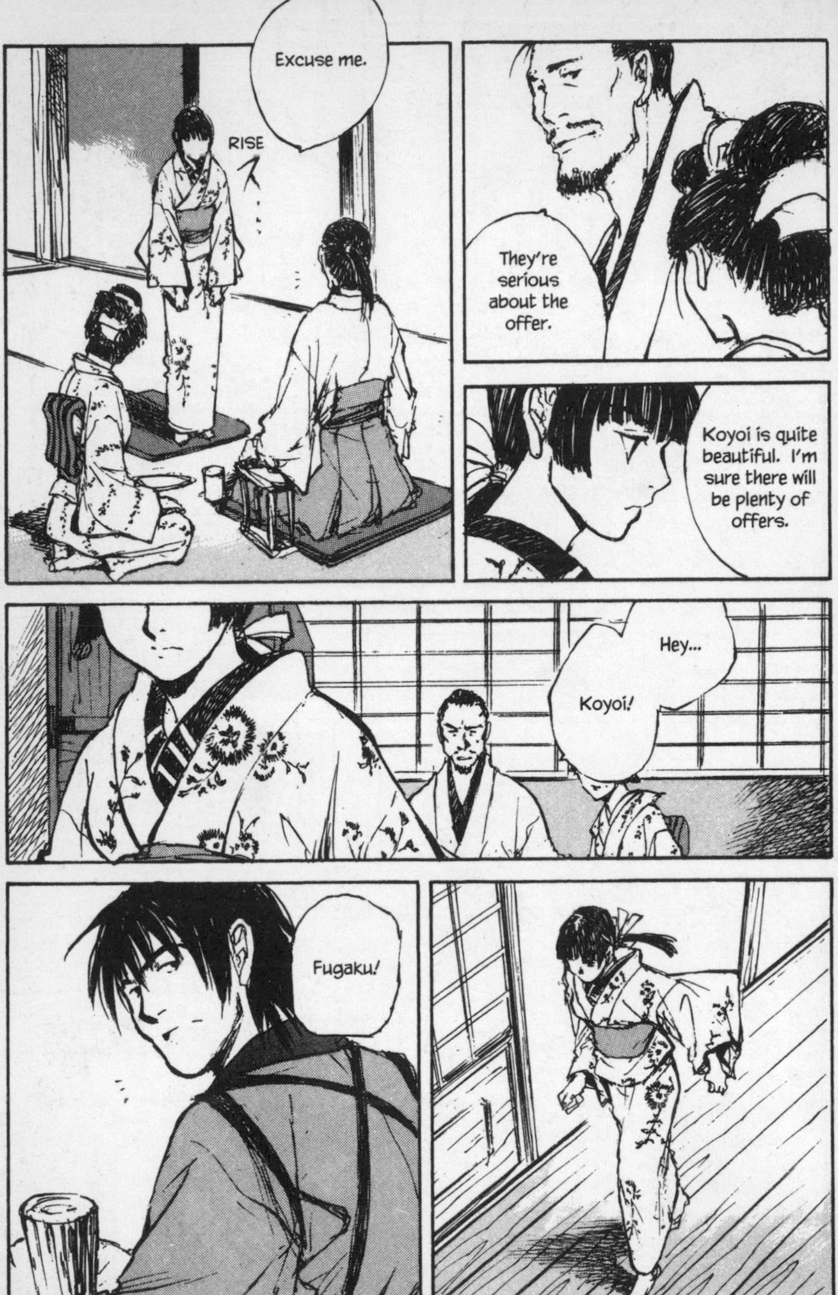
They're serious about the offer.
Koyoi is quite beautiful. I'm sure there will be plenty of offers.
Excuse me.
RISE
Hey...
Koyoi!
Fugaku!

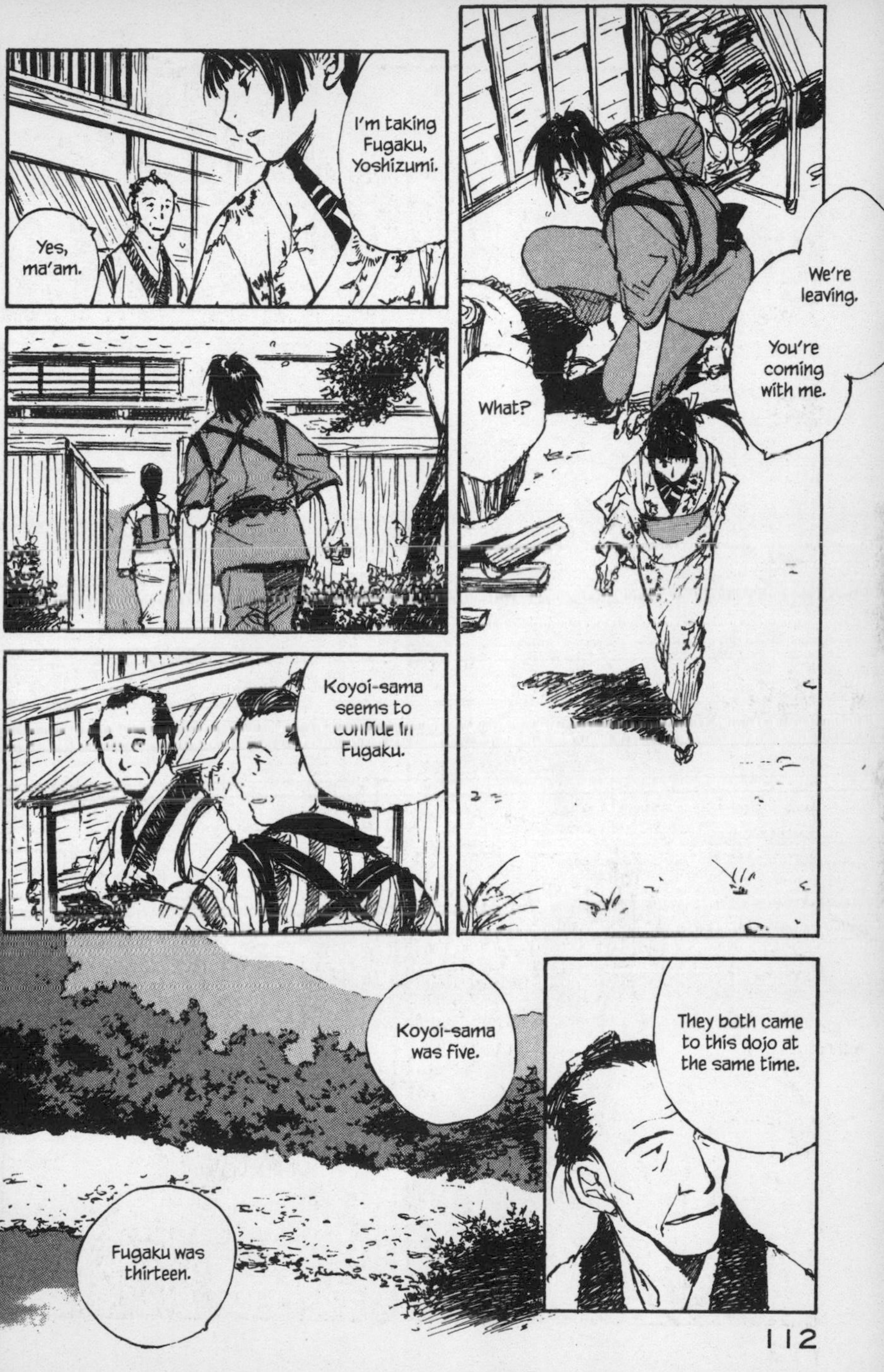
We're leaving.
You're coming with me.
What?
I'm taking Fugaku, Yoshizumi.
Yes, ma'am.
Koyoi-sama seems to confide in Fugaku.
They both came to this dojo at the same time.
Koyoi-sama was five.
Fugaku was thirteen.

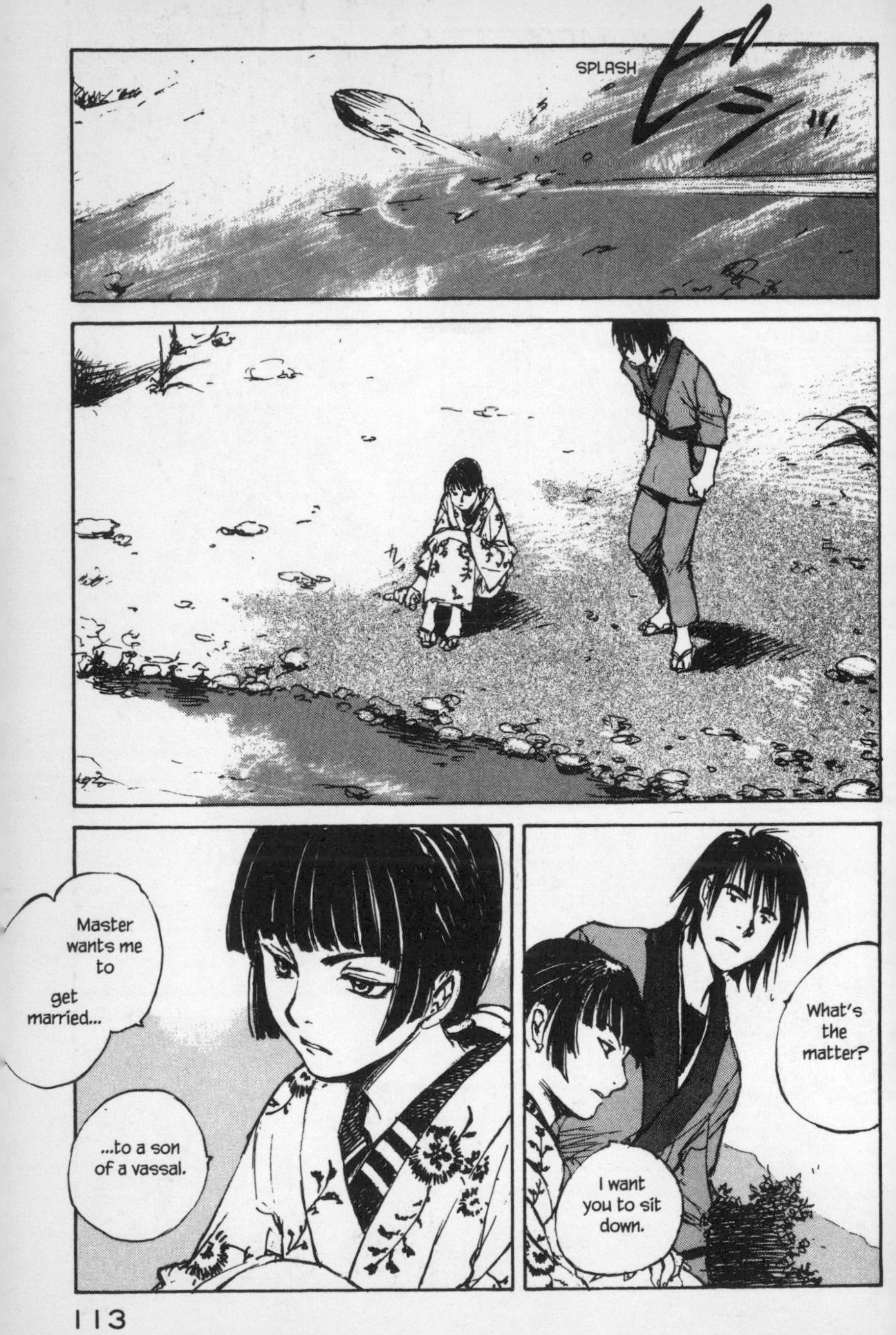
SPLASH
What's the matter?
I want you to sit down.
Master wants me to get married...
...to a son of a vassal.

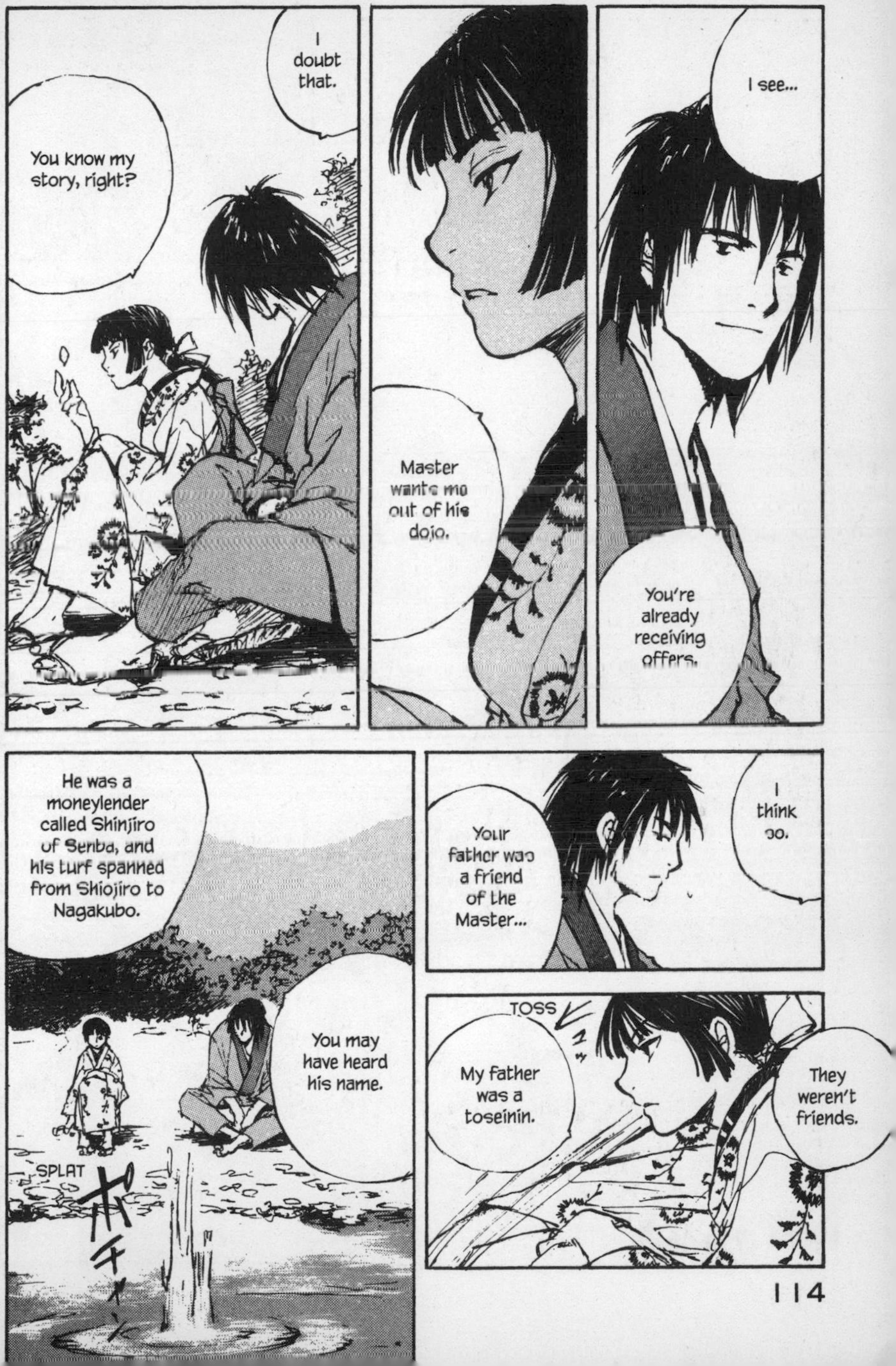
I see...
You're already receiving offers.
Master wants me out of his dojo.
I doubt that.
You know my story, right?
I think so.
Your father was a friend of the Master...
They weren't friends.
TOSS
My father was a toseinin.
He was a moneylender called Shinjiro of Senba, and his turf spanned from Shiojiro to Nagakubo.
You may have heard his name.
SPLAT

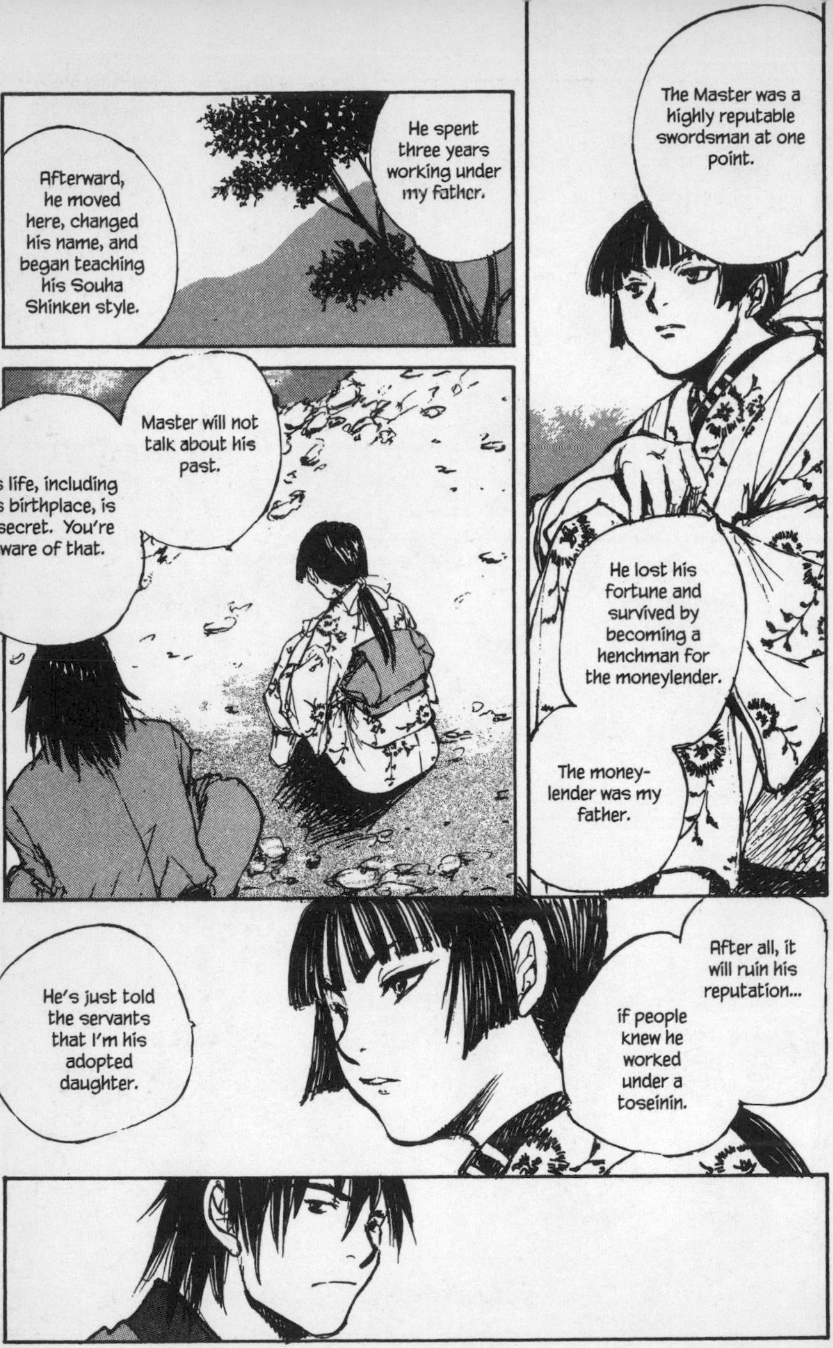
The Master was a highly reputable swordsman at one point.
He lost his fortune and survived by becoming a henchman for the moneylender.
The money-lender was my father.
He spent three years working under my father.
Afterward, he moved here, changed his name, and began teaching his Souha Shinken style.
Master will not talk about his past.
His life, including his birthplace, is a secret. You're aware of that.
After all, it will ruin his reputation...
if people knew he worked under a toseinin.
He's just told the servants that I'm his adopted daughter.

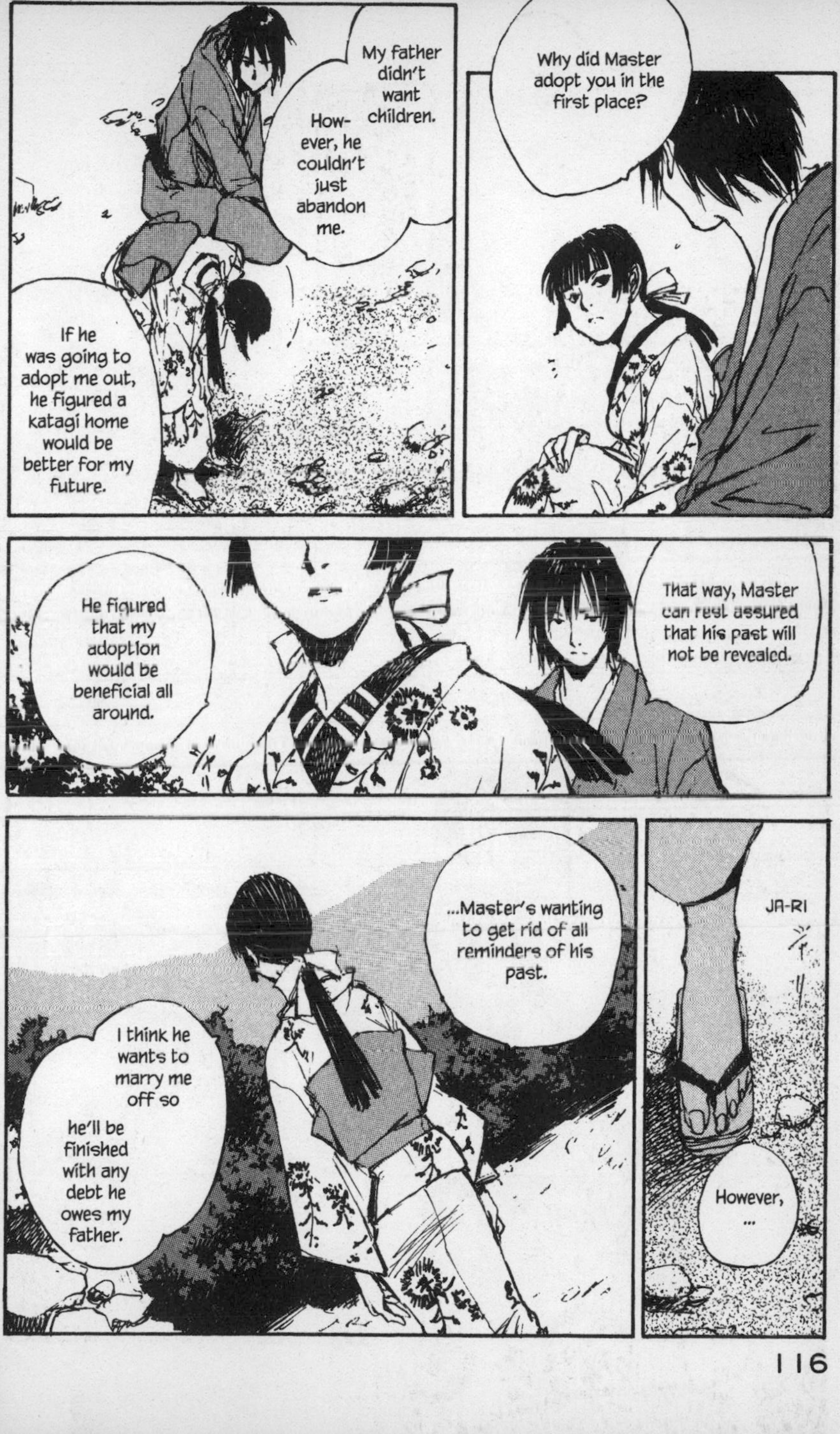
Why did Master adopt you in the first place?
My father didn't want children.
How-ever, he couldn't just abandon me.
If he was going to adopt me out, he figured a katagi home would be better for my future.
That way, Master can rest assured that his past will not be revealed.
He figured that my adoption would be beneficial all around.
JA-RI
However, ...
...Master's wanting to get rid of all reminders of his past.
I think he wants to marry me off so
he'll be finished with any debt he owes my father.

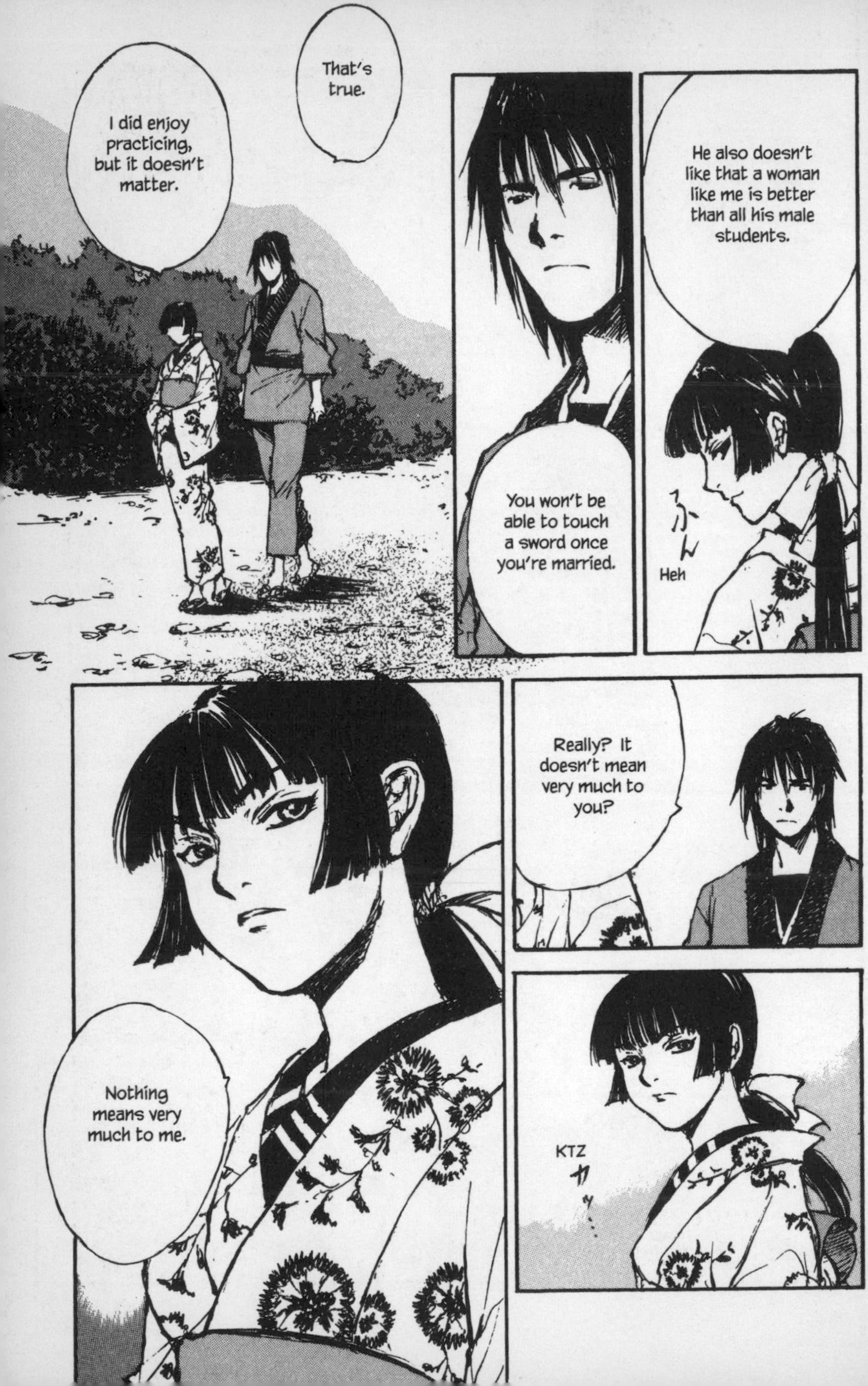
He also doesn't like that a woman like me is better than all his male students.
ふん
Heh
You won't be able to touch a sword once you're married.
That's true.
I did enjoy practicing, but it doesn't matter.
Really? It doesn't mean very much to you?
KTZ
カッ
Nothing means very much to me.

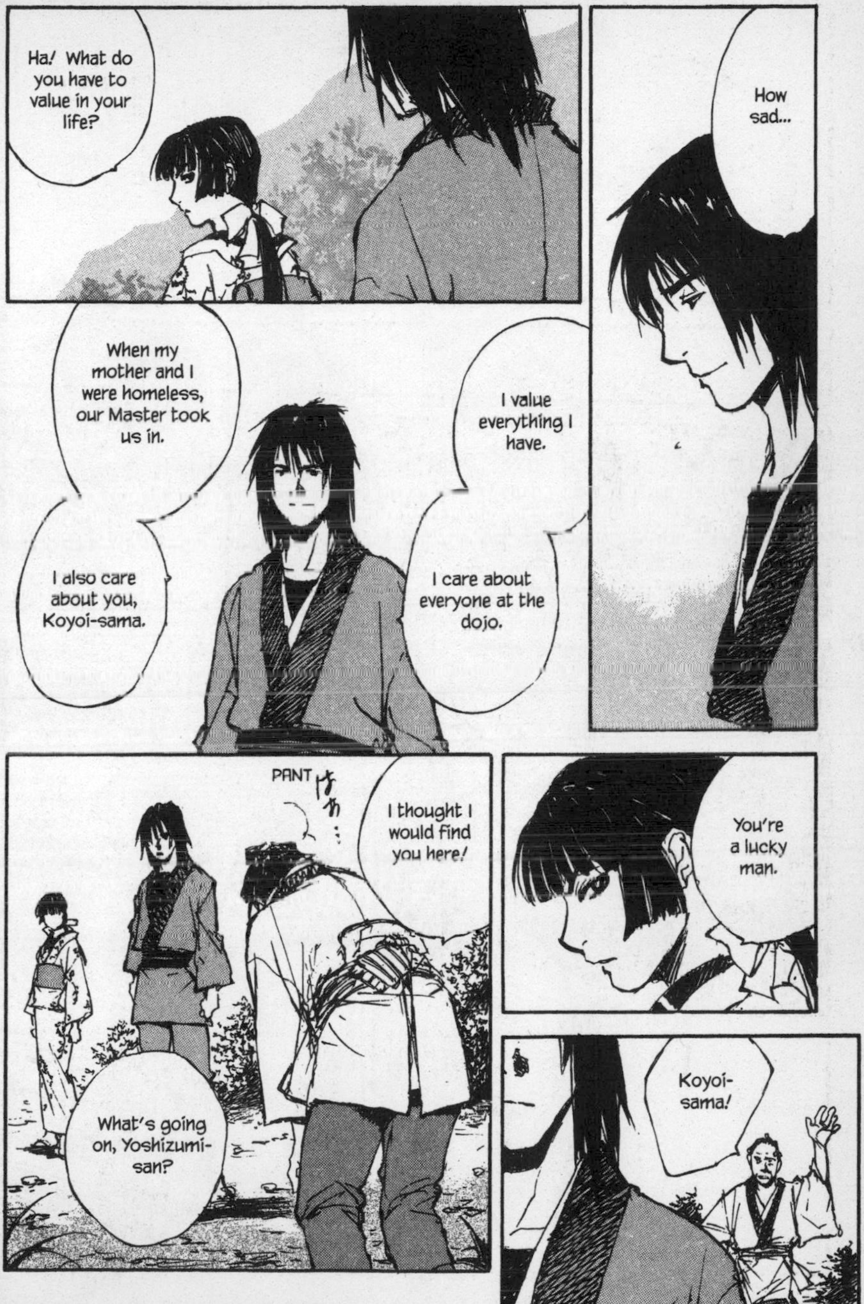
How sad...
Ha! What do you have to value in your life?
I value everything I have.
I care about everyone at the dojo.
When my mother and I were homeless, our Master took us in.
I also care about you, Koyoi-sama.
You're a lucky man.
Koyoi-sama!
I thought I would find you here!
PANT
What's going on, Yoshizumi-san?

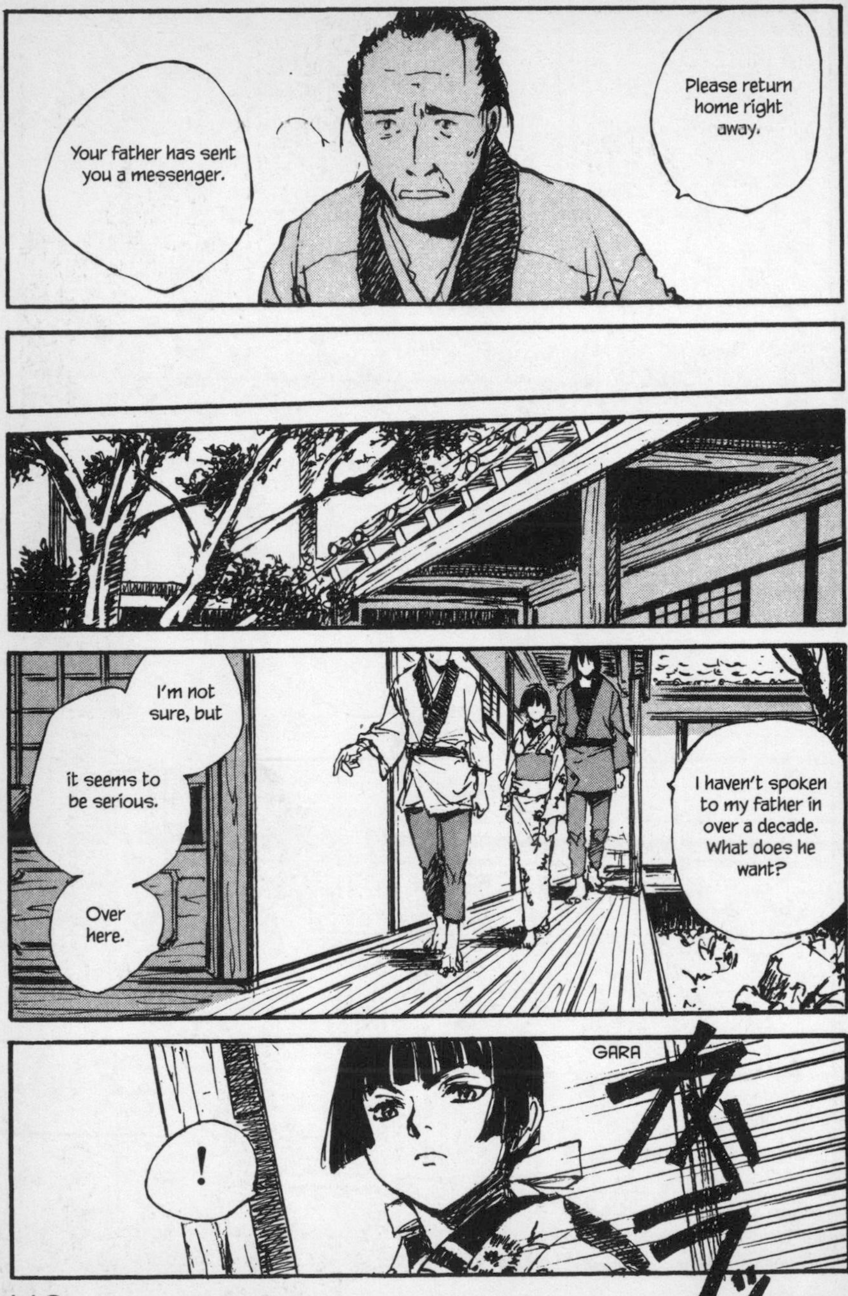
Please return home right away.
Your father has sent you a messenger.
I haven't spoken to my father in over a decade. What does he want?
I'm not sure, but
it seems to be serious.
Over here.
GARA
!

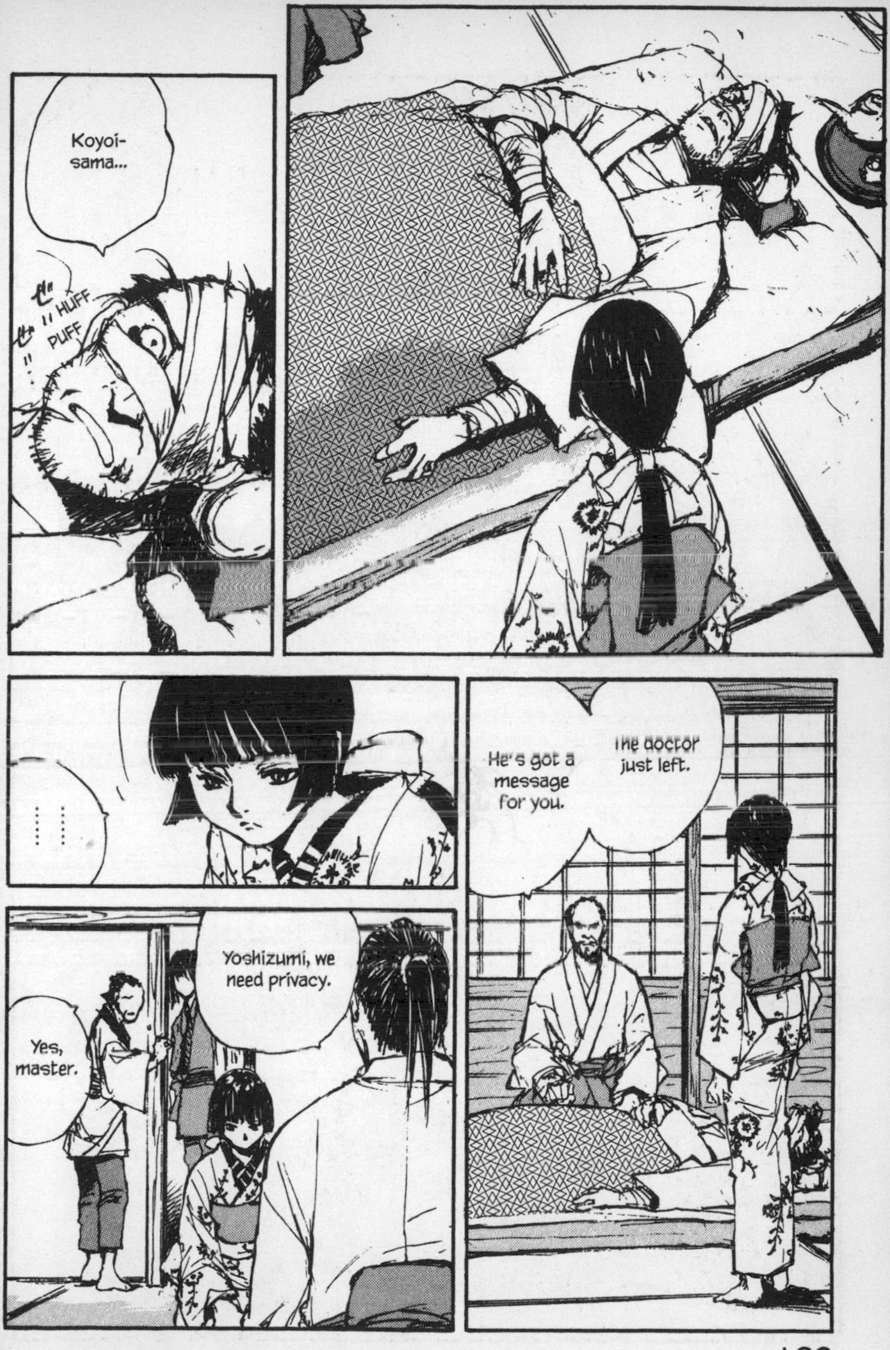
Koyoi-sama...
HUFF
PUFF
The doctor just left.
He's got a message for you.
......
Yoshizumi, we need privacy.
Yes, master.

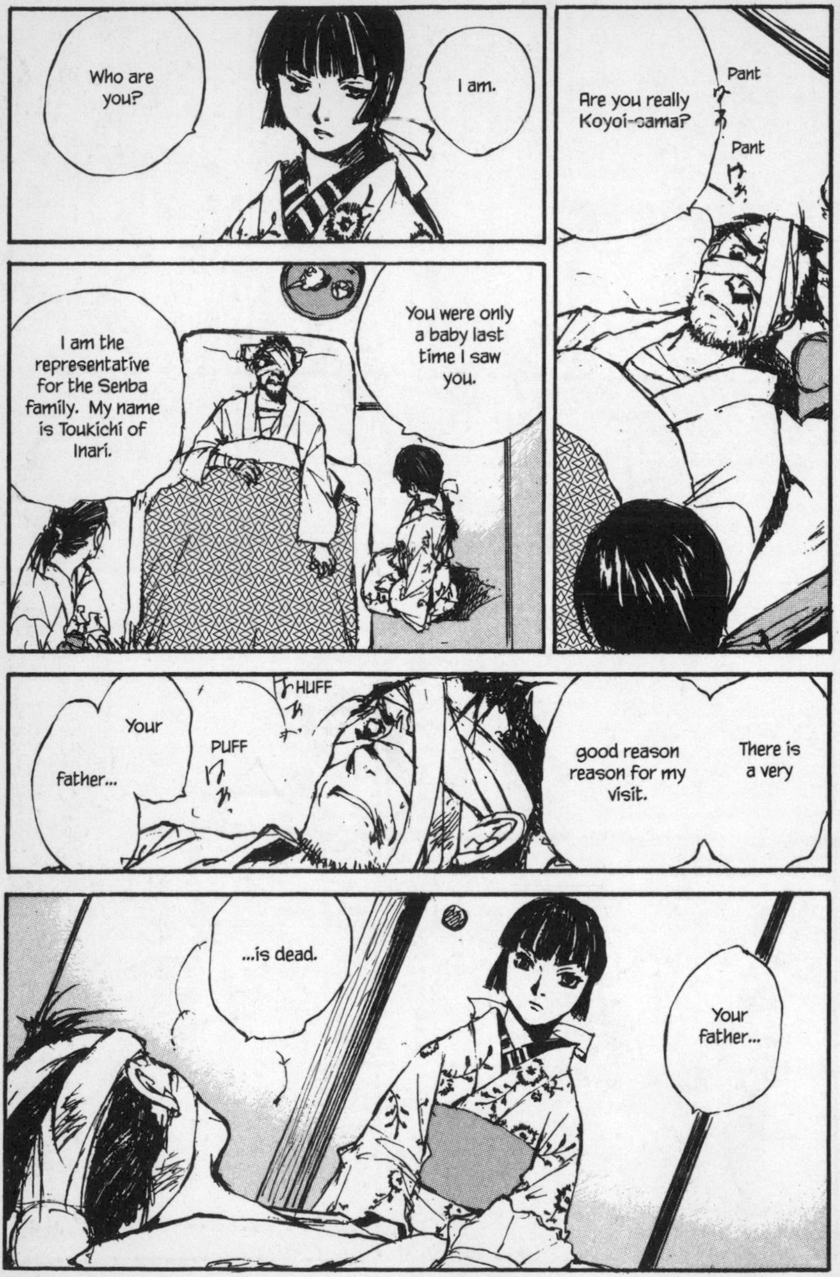
Are you really Koyoi-sama?
Pant
Pant
I am.
Who are you?
You were only a baby last time I saw you.
I am the representative for the Senba family. My name is Toukichi of Inari.
There is a very
good reason reason for my visit.
HUFF
PUFF
Your father...
Your father...
...is dead.

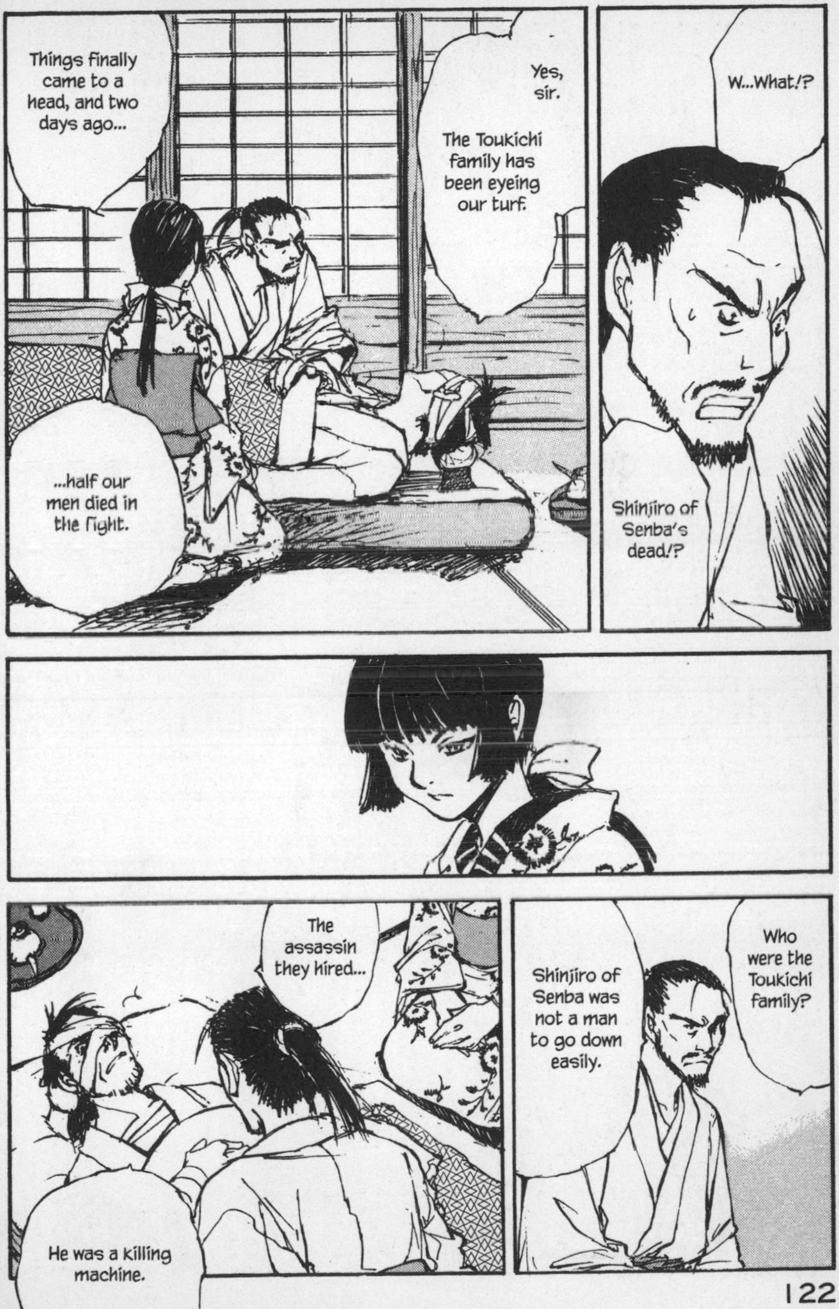
W...What!?
Shinjiro of Senba's dead!?
Yes, sir.
The Toukichi family has been eyeing our turf.
Things finally came to a head, and two days ago...
...half our men died in the fight.
Who were the Toukichi family?
Shinjiro of Senba was not a man to go down easily.
The assassin they hired...
He was a killing machine.

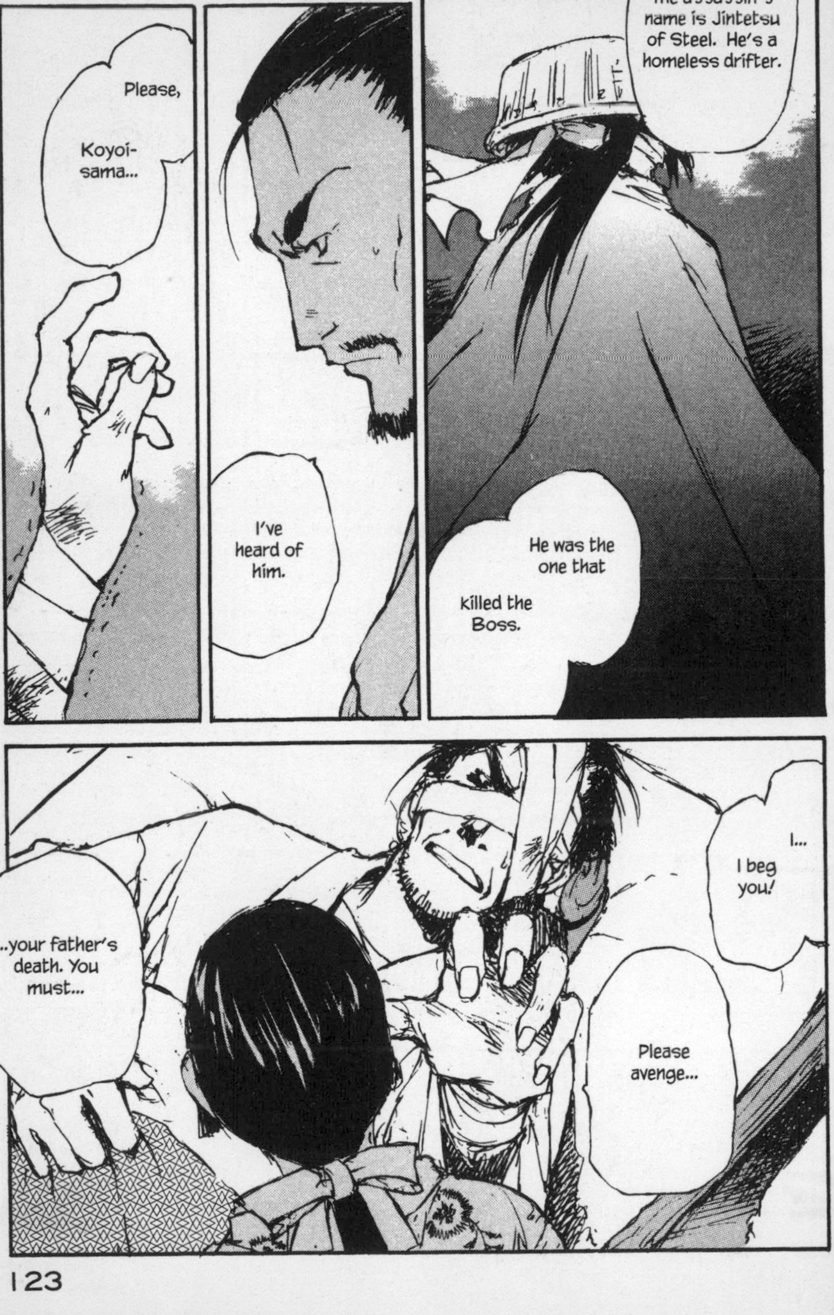
The assassin's name is Jintetsu of Steel. He's a homeless drifter.
He was the one that
killed the Boss.
I've heard of him.
Please,
Koyoi-sama...
I...
I beg you!
Please avenge...
...your father's death. You must...

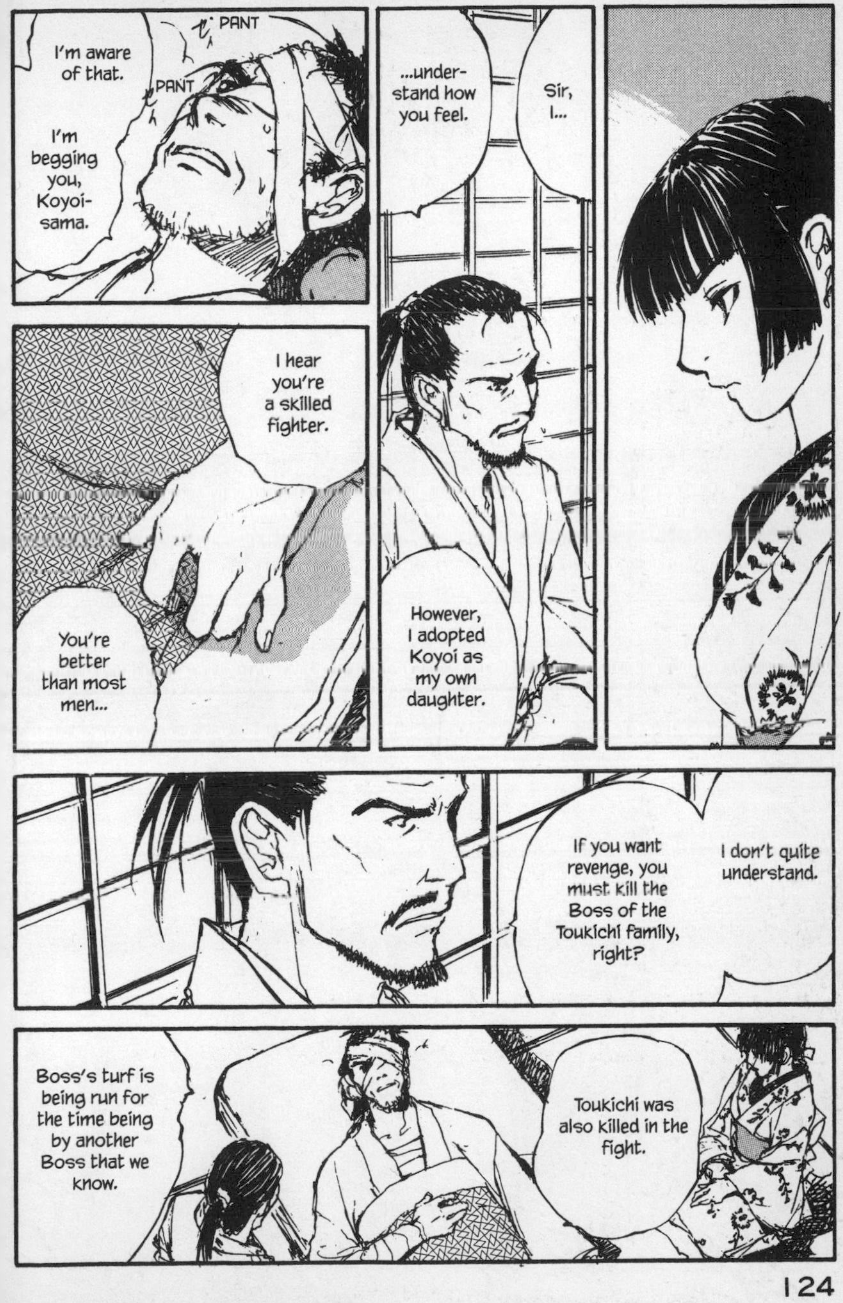
Sir, I...
...under-stand how you feel.
However, I adopted Koyoi as my own daughter.
PANT
PANT
I'm aware of that.
I'm begging you, Koyoi-sama.
I hear you're a skilled fighter.
You're better than most men...
I don't quite understand.
If you want revenge, you must kill the Boss of the Toukichi family, right?
Toukichi was also killed in the fight.
Boss's turf is being run for the time being by another Boss that we know.

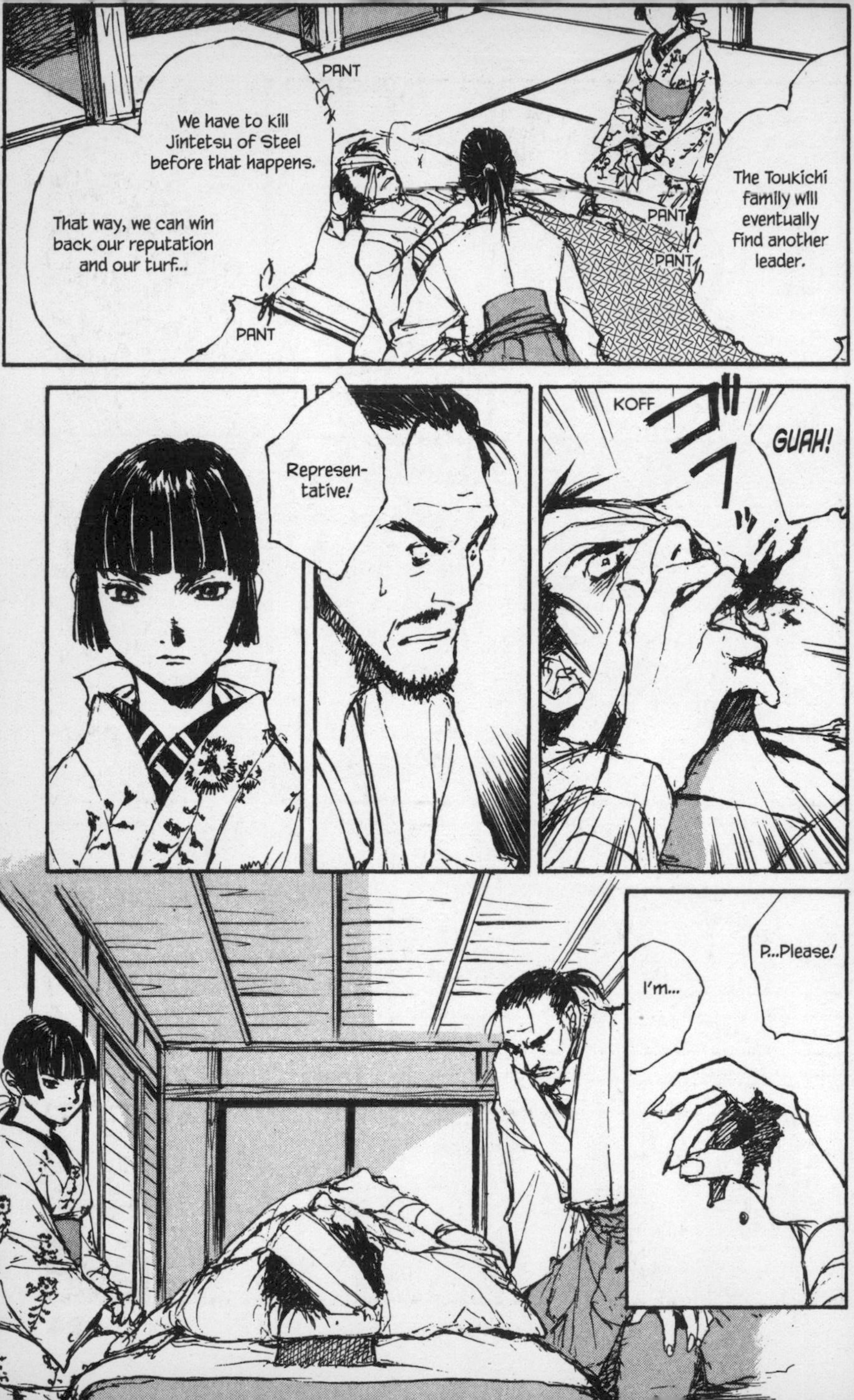
The Toukichi family will eventually find another leader.
PANT
PANT
PANT
We have to kill Jintetsu of Steel before that happens.
That way, we can win back our reputation and our turf...
PANT
GUAH!
KOFF
Represen-tative!
P...Please!
I'm...

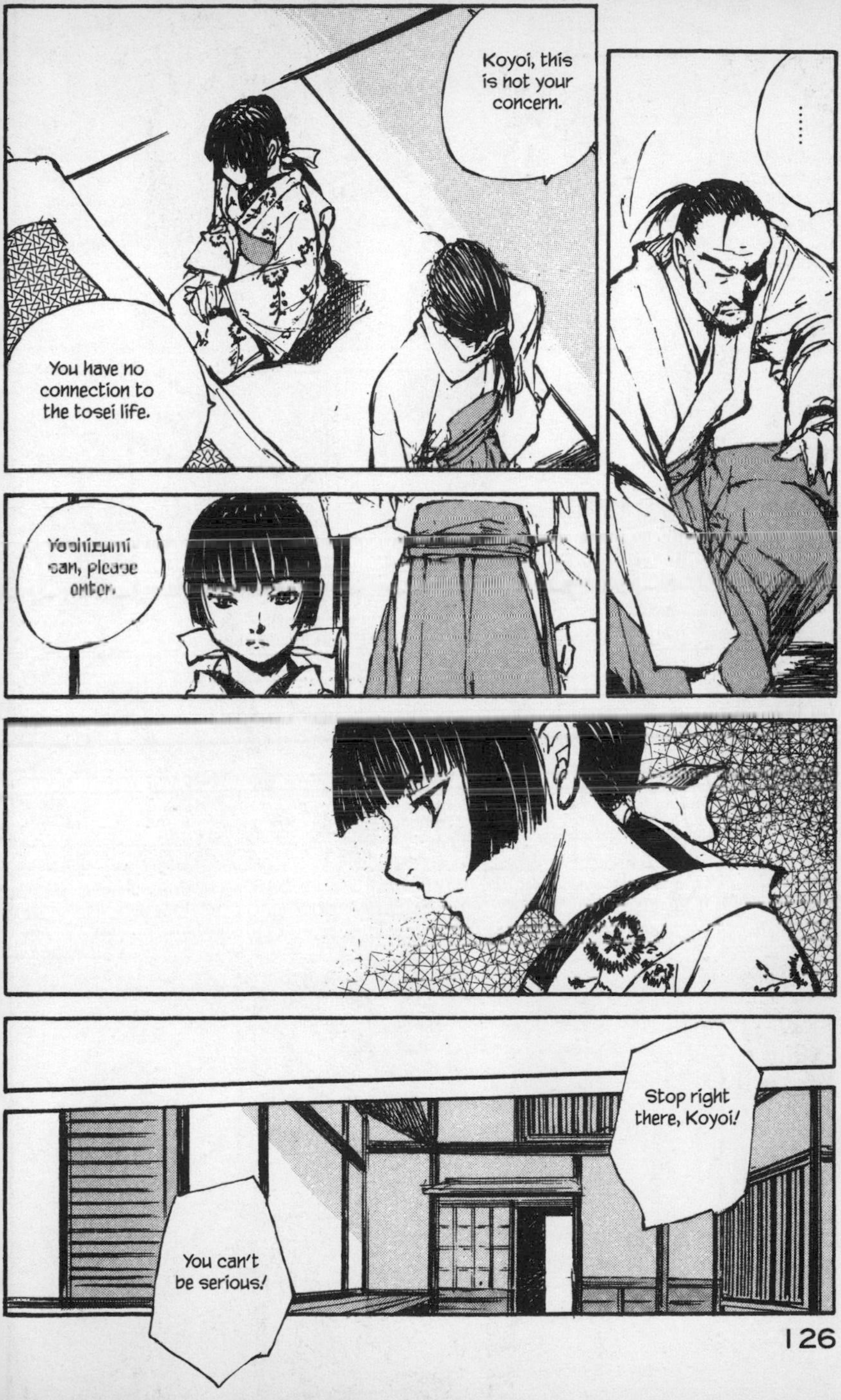
……
Koyoi, this is not your concern.
You have no connection to the tosei life.
Yoshizumi san, please enter.
Stop right there, Koyoi!
You can't be serious!

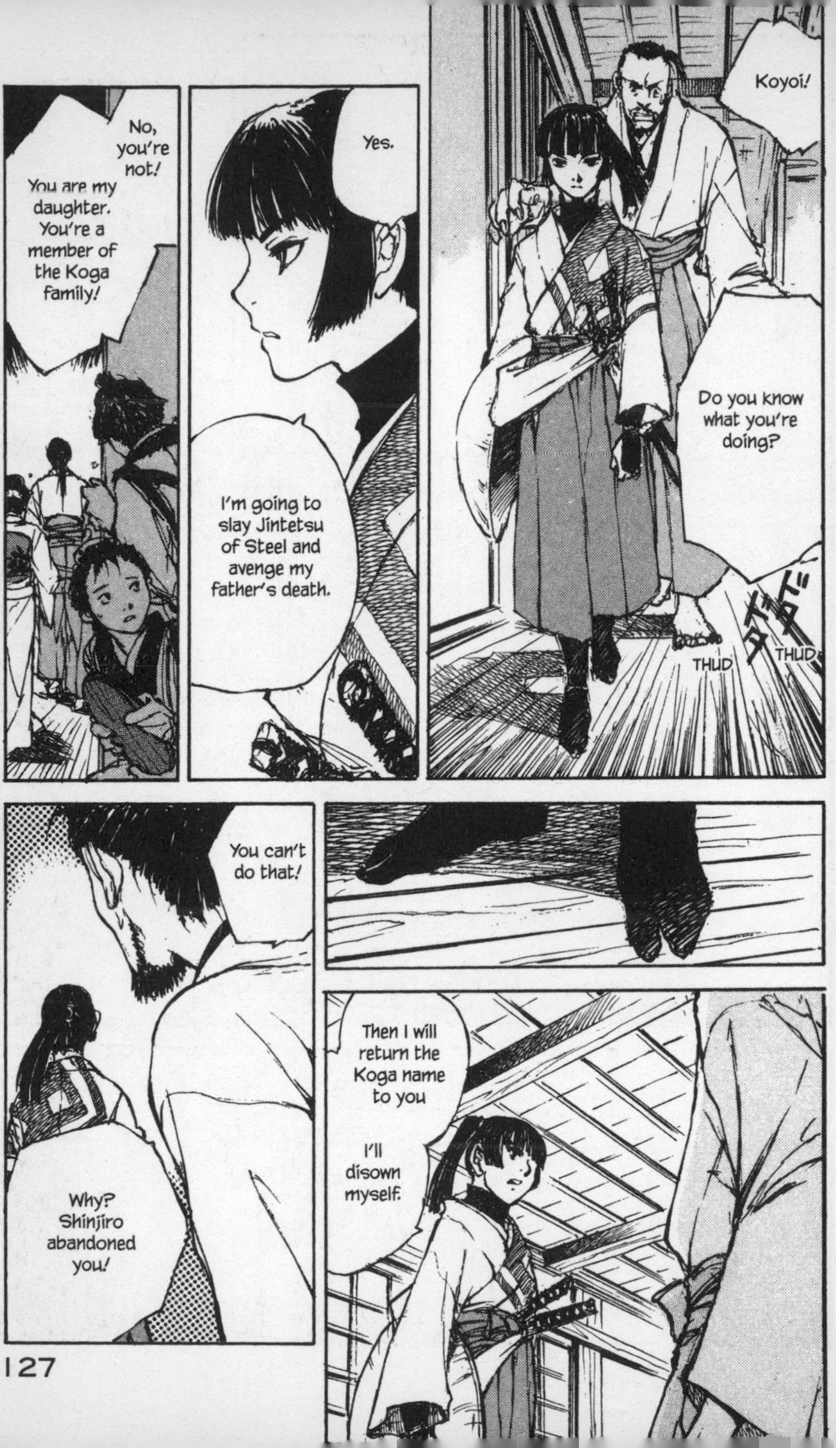
Koyoi!
Do you know what you're doing?
THUD
THUD
Yes.
I'm going to slay Jintetsu of Steel and avenge my father's death.
No, you're not!
You are my daughter. You're a member of the Koga family!
Then I will return the Koga name to you
I'll disown myself.
You can't do that!
Why? Shinjiro abandoned you!

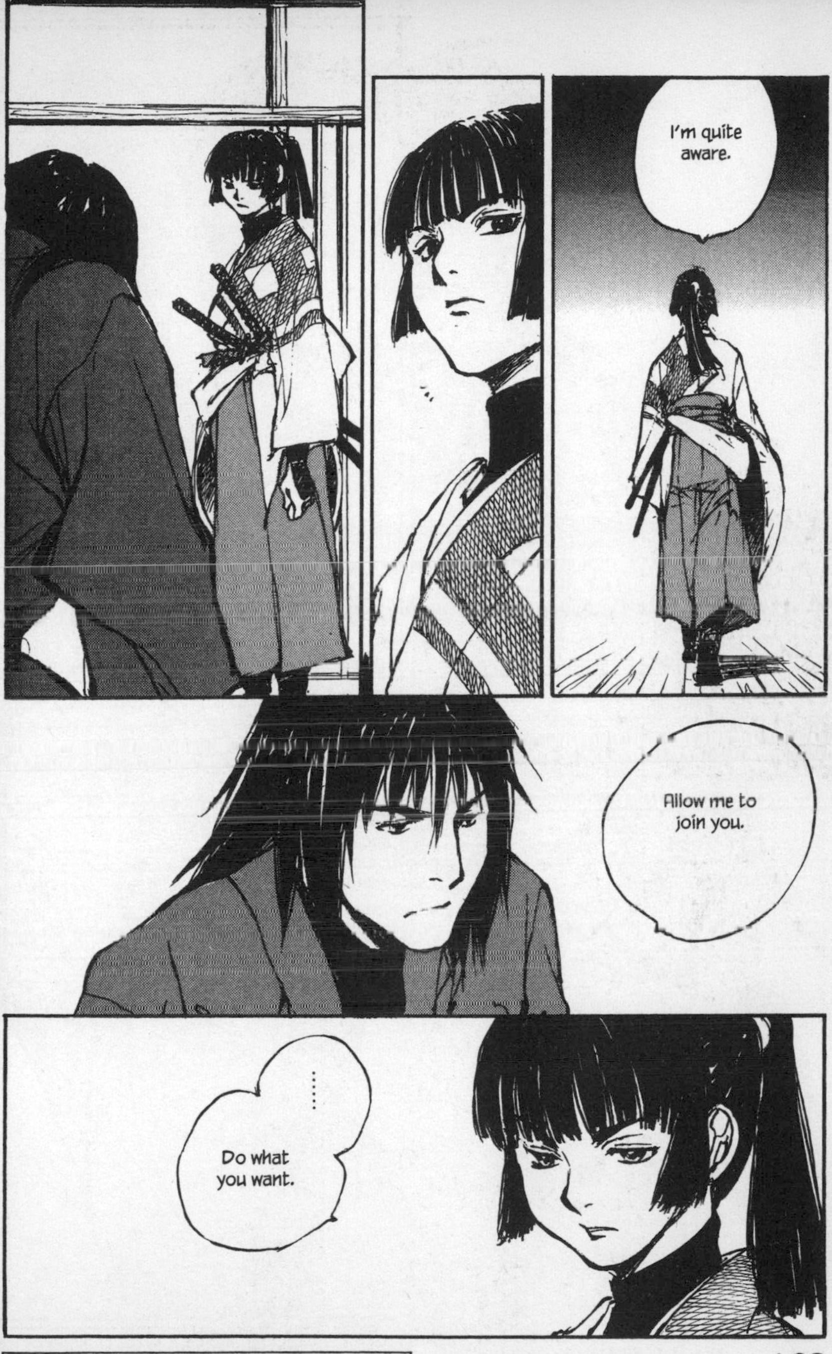
I'm quite aware.
Allow me to join you.
……
Do what you want.

THE END OF CHAPTER 14 EPISODE 1

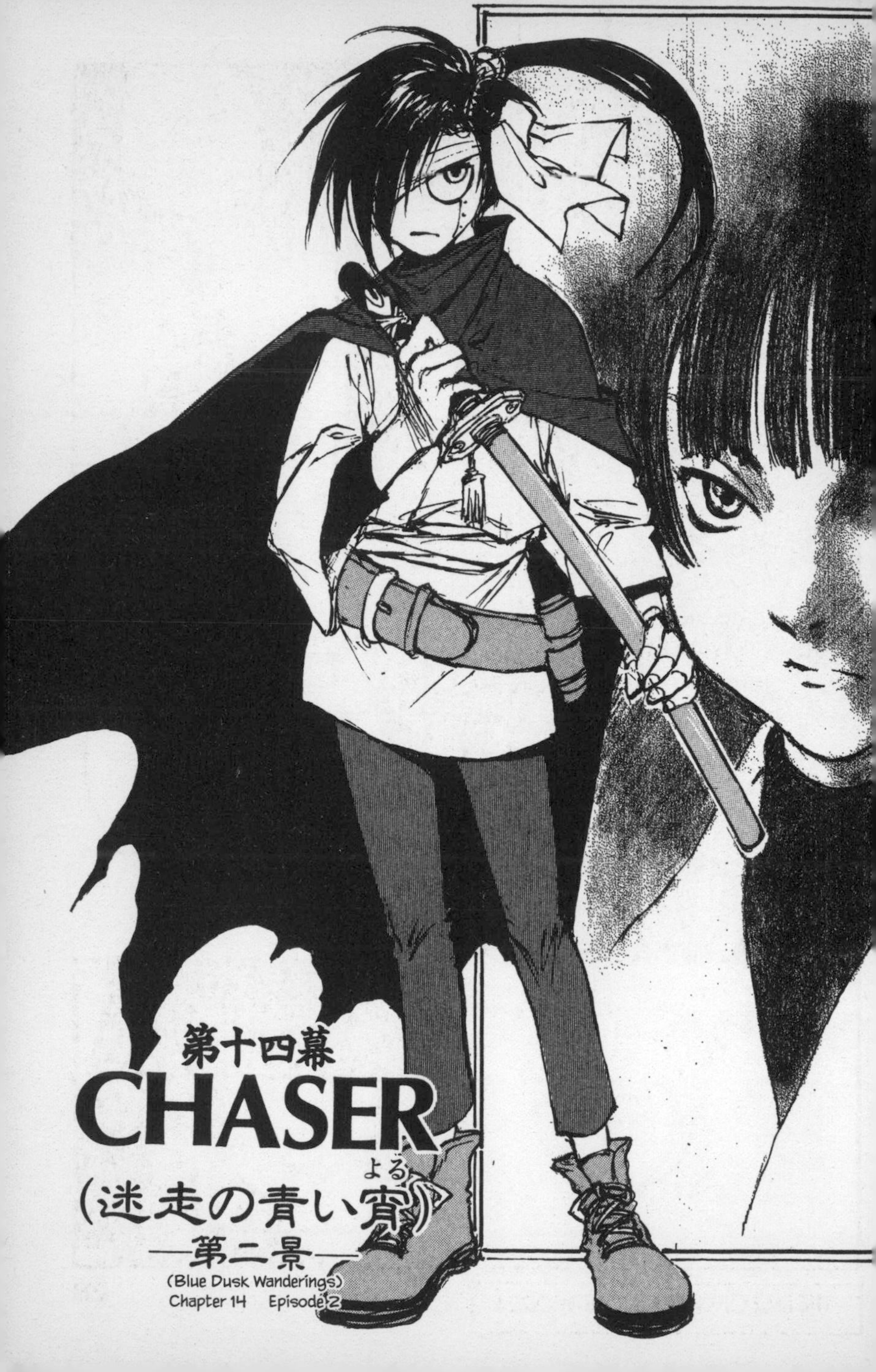
第十四幕
CHASER
(迷走の青い宵)
よる
—第二景—
(Blue Dusk Wanderings)
Chapter 14 Episode 2

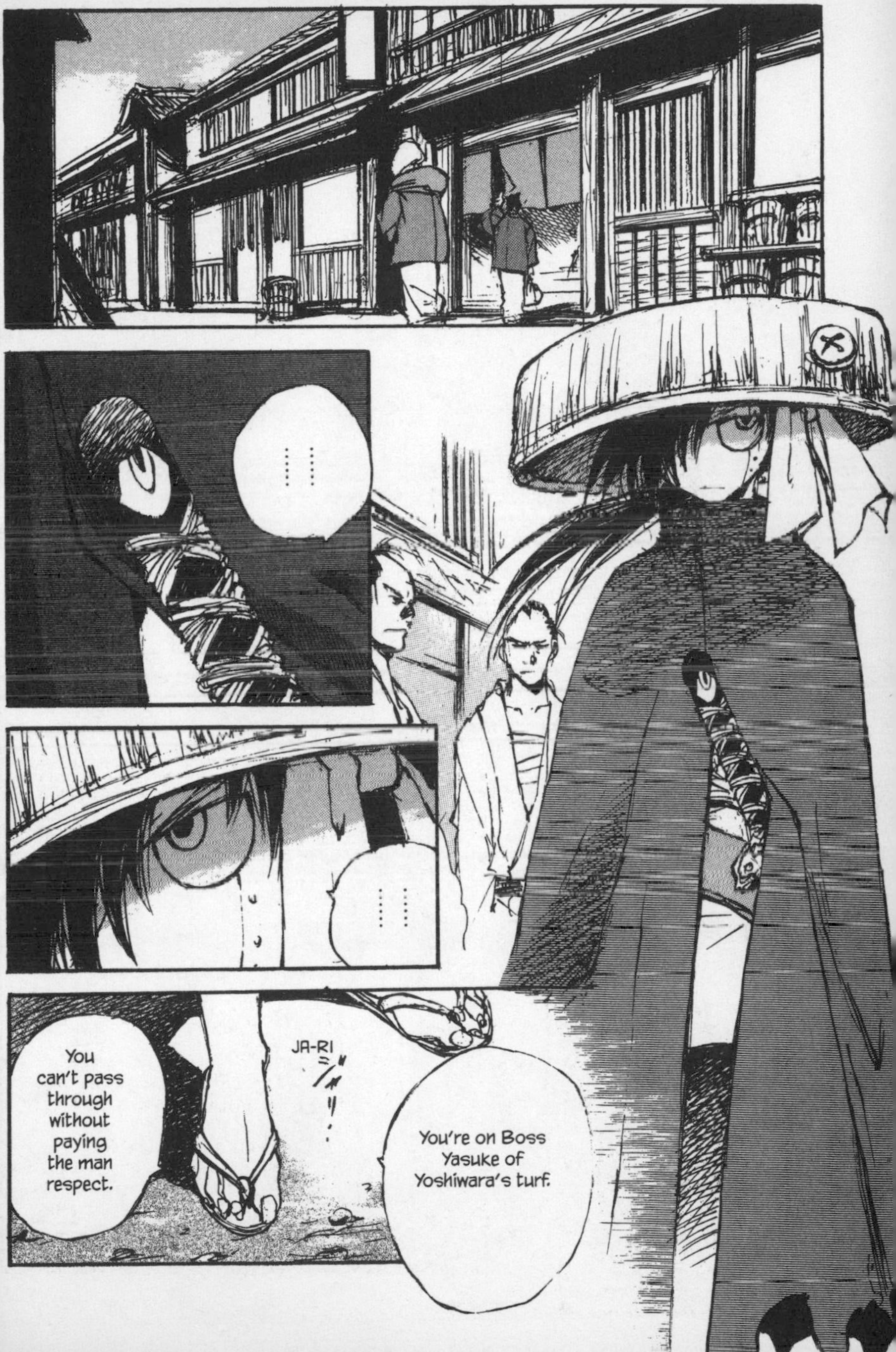
......
......
You're on Boss Yasuke of Yoshiwara's turf.
JA-RI
You can't pass through without paying the man respect.

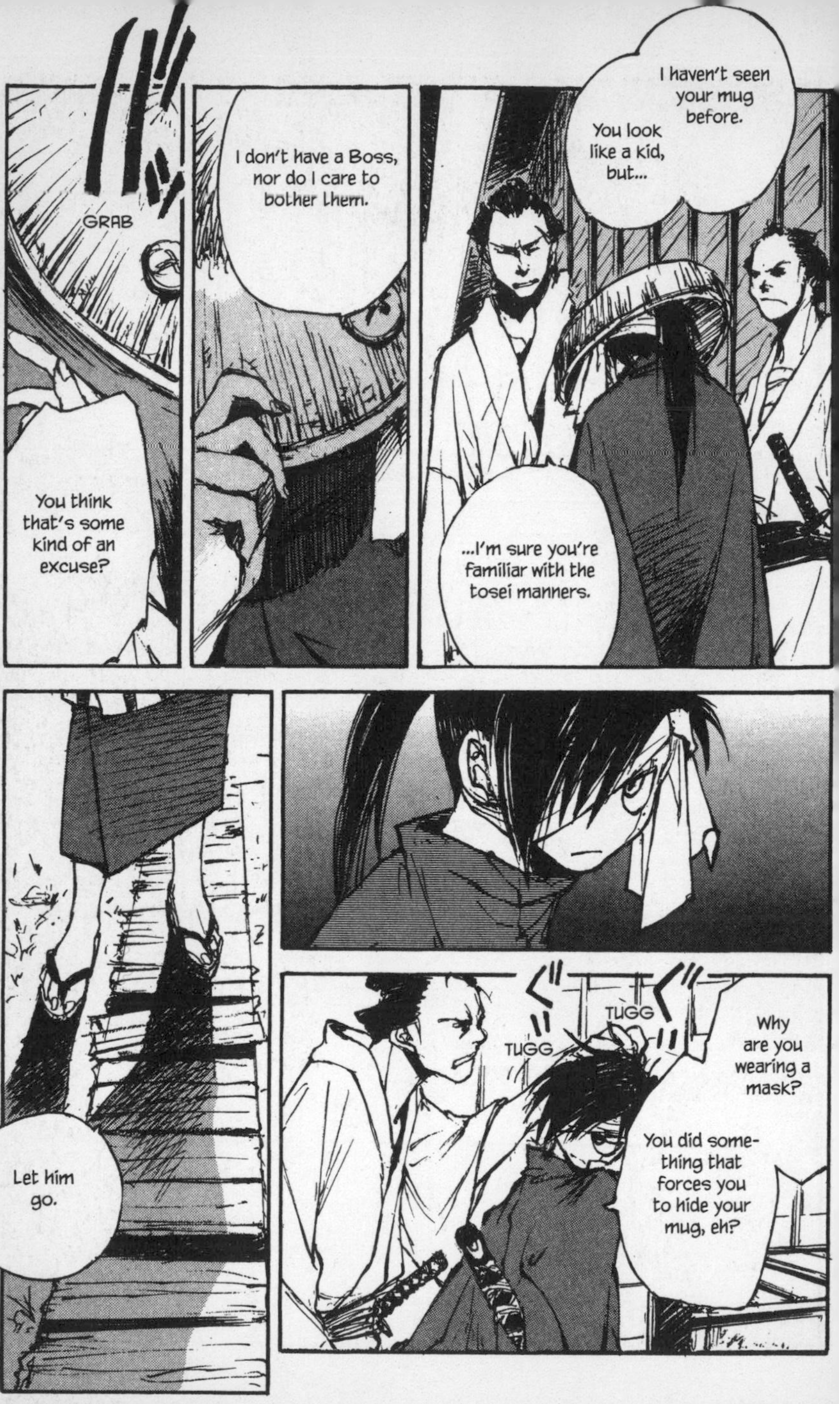
I haven't seen your mug before.
You look like a kid, but...
...I'm sure you're familiar with the tosei manners.
I don't have a Boss, nor do I care to bother them.
GRAB
You think that's some kind of an excuse?
TUGG
TUGG
Why are you wearing a mask?
You did something that forces you to hide your mug, eh?
Let him go.

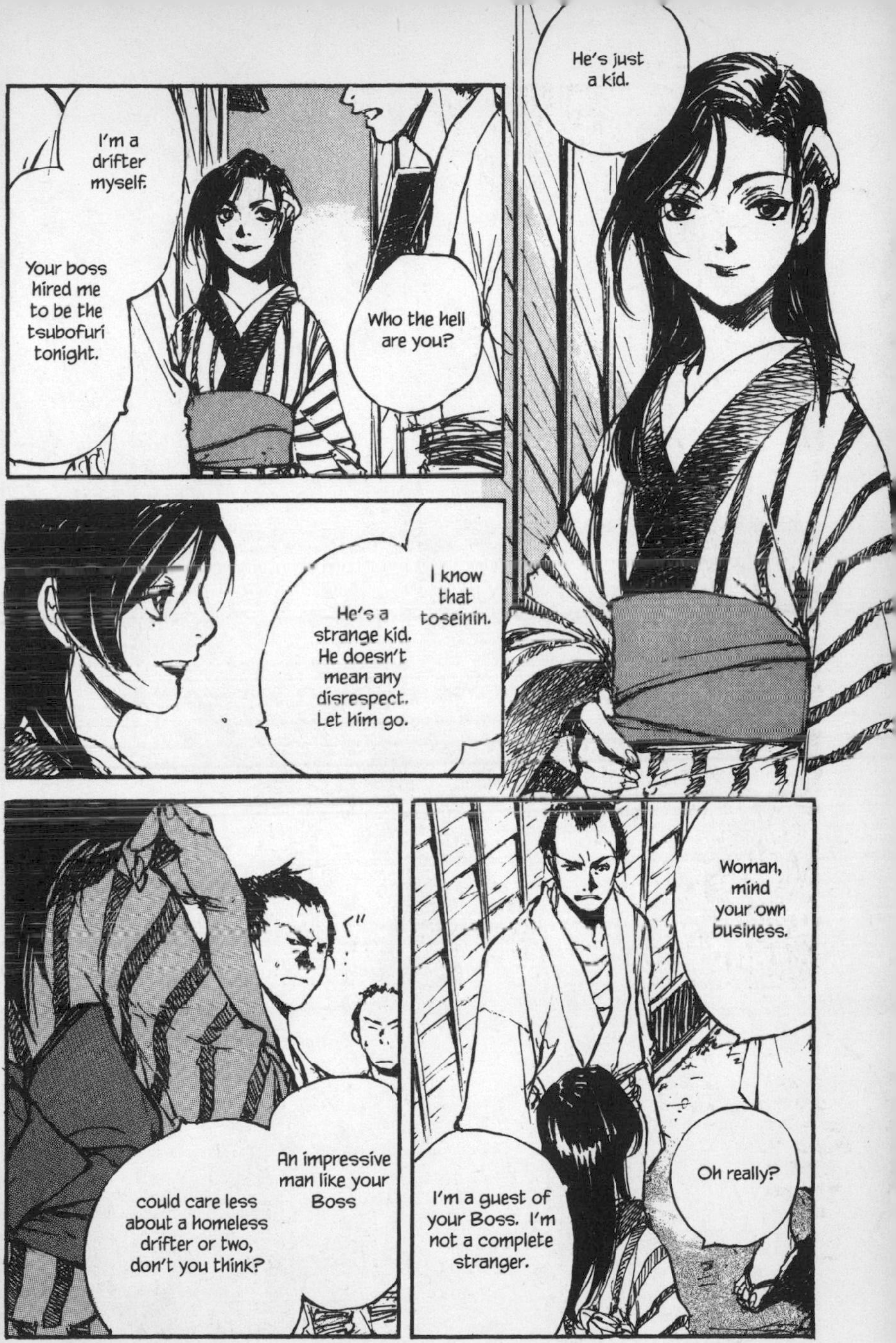
He's just a kid.
Who the hell are you?
I'm a drifter myself.
Your boss hired me to be the tsubofuri tonight.
I know that toseinin.
He's a strange kid. He doesn't mean any disrespect. Let him go.
Woman, mind your own business.
Oh really?
I'm a guest of your Boss. I'm not a complete stranger.
An impressive man like your Boss
could care less about a homeless drifter or two, don't you think?

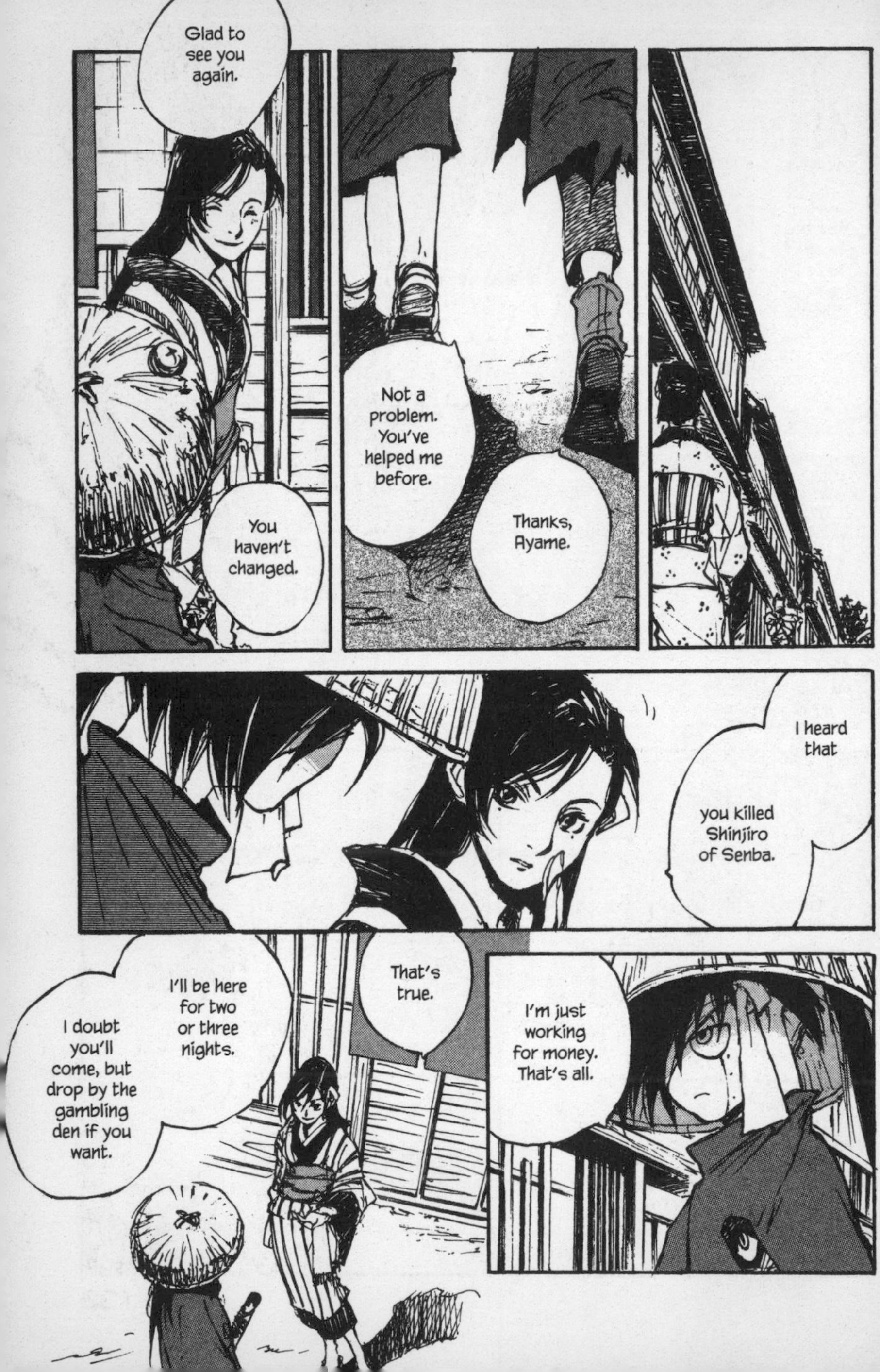
Thanks, Ayame.
Not a problem. You've helped me before.
Glad to see you again.
You haven't changed.
I heard that
you killed Shinjiro of Senba.
I'm just working for money. That's all.
That's true.
I'll be here for two or three nights.
I doubt you'll come, but drop by the gambling den if you want.

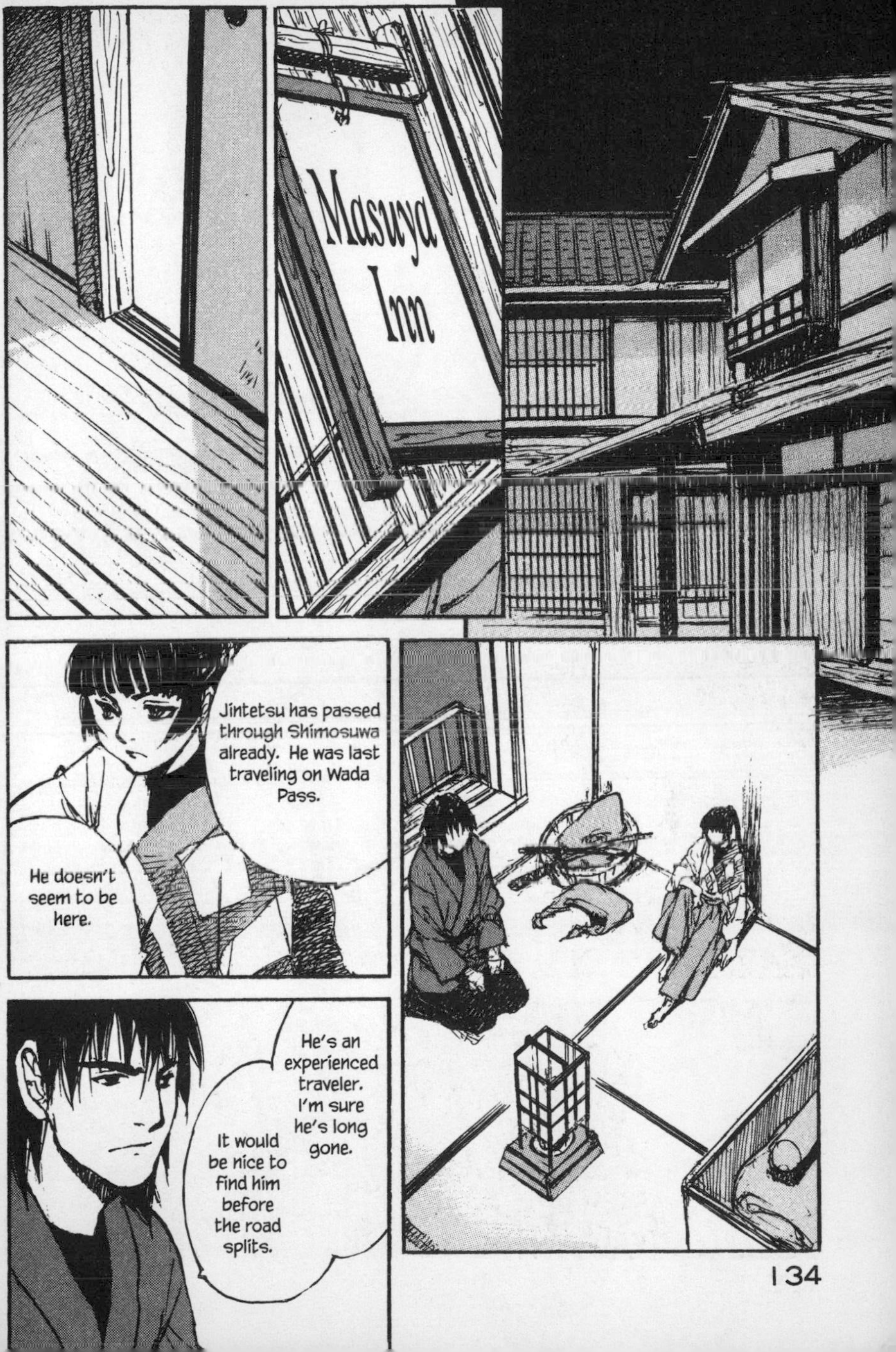
Masuya Inn
Jintetsu has passed through Shimosuwa already. He was last traveling on Wada Pass.
He doesn't seem to be here.
He's an experienced traveler. I'm sure he's long gone.
It would be nice to find him before the road splits.

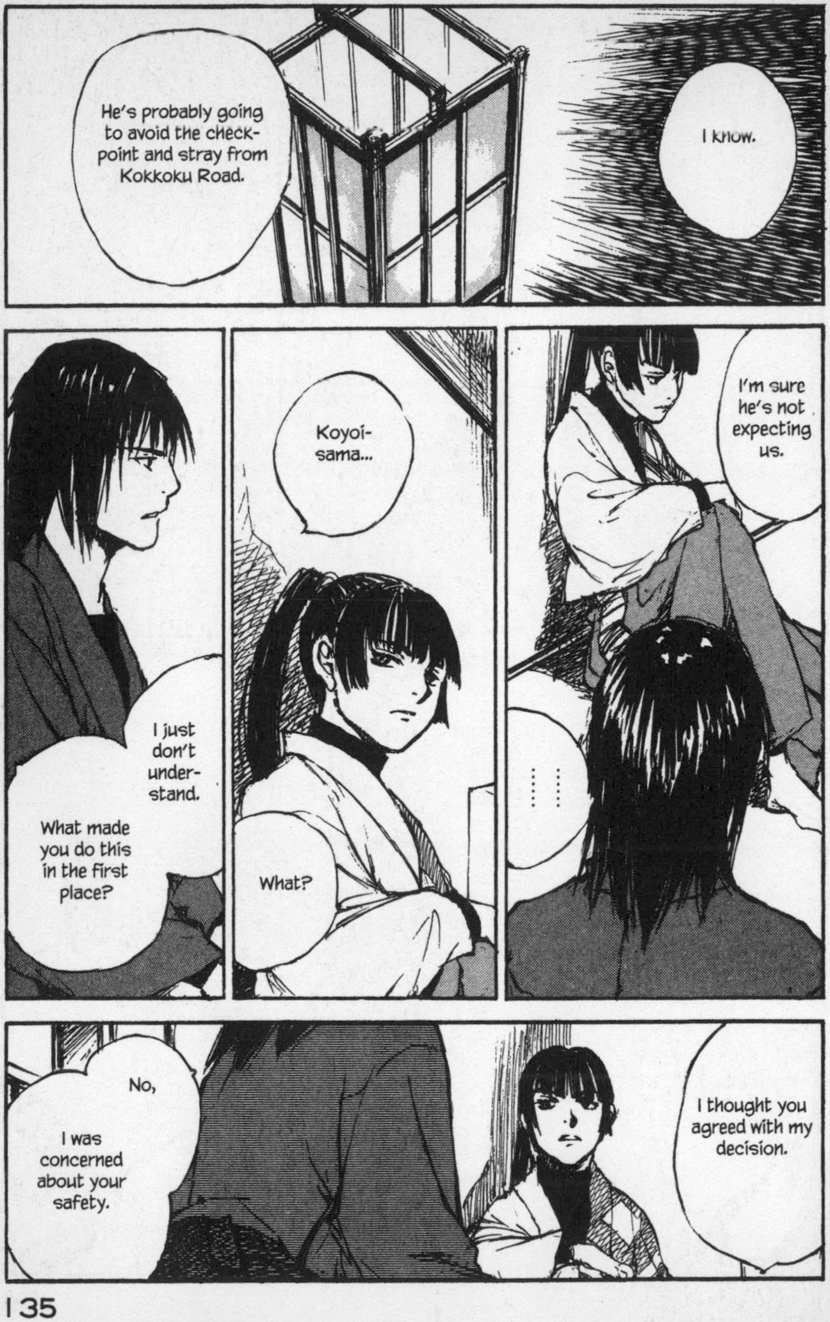

I know.
He's probably going to avoid the check-point and stray from Kokkoku Road.
I'm sure he's not expecting us.
……
Koyoi-sama...
What?
I just don't under-stand.
What made you do this in the first place?
I thought you agreed with my decision.
No,
I was concerned about your safety.

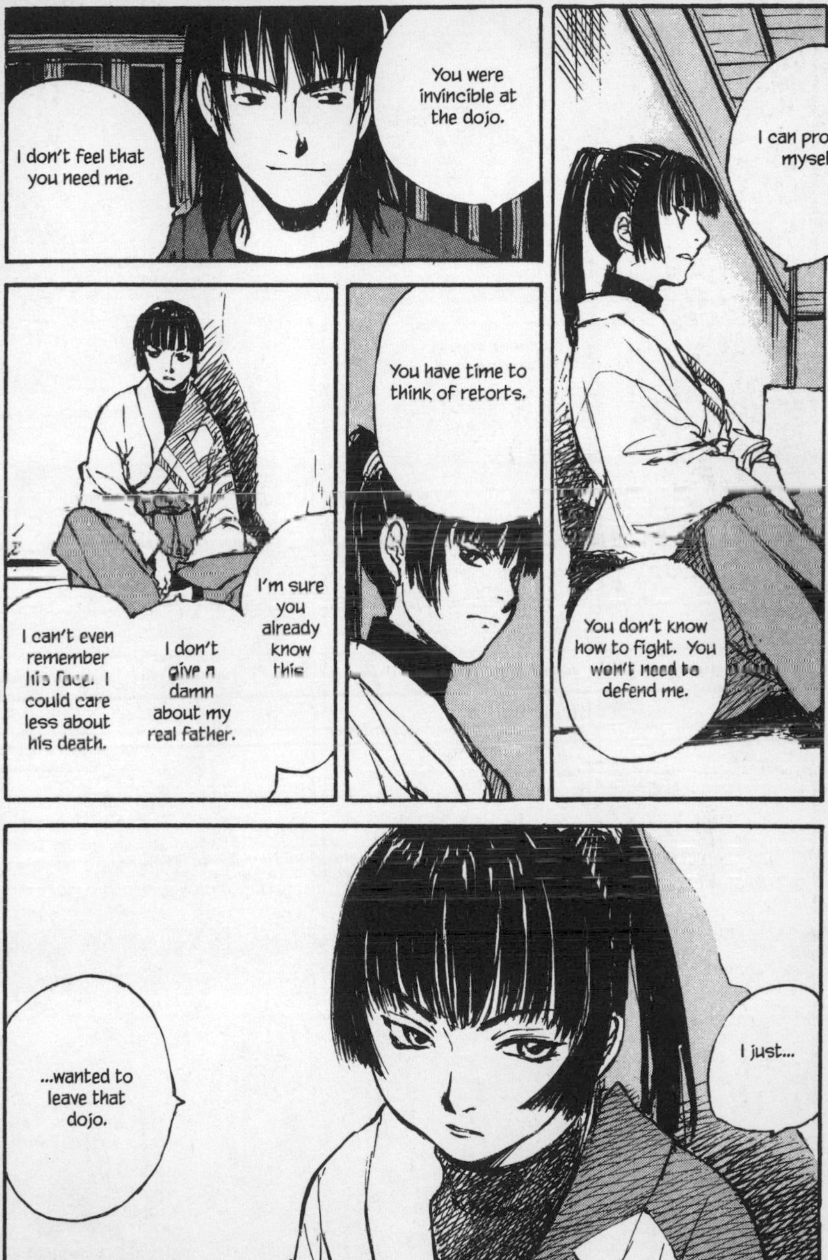
I can protect myself.
You don't know how to fight. You won't need to defend me.
You were invincible at the dojo.
I don't feel that you need me.
You have time to think of retorts.
I'm sure you already know this
I don't give a damn about my real father.
I can't even remember his face. I could care less about his death.
I just...
...wanted to leave that dojo.

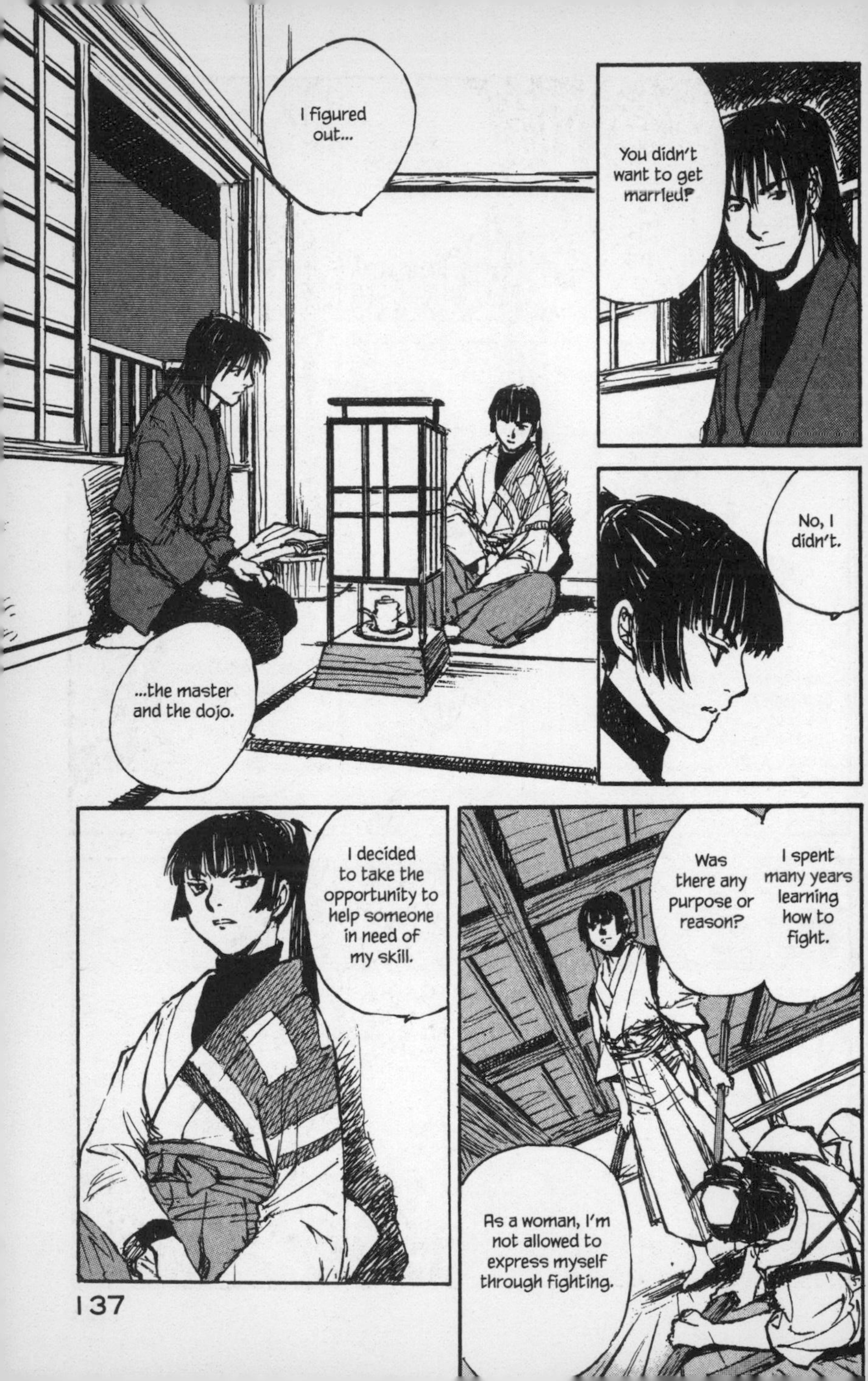
You didn't want to get married?
No, I didn't.
I figured out...
...the master and the dojo.
I spent many years learning how to fight.
Was there any purpose or reason?
As a woman, I'm not allowed to express myself through fighting.
I decided to take the opportunity to help someone in need of my skill.

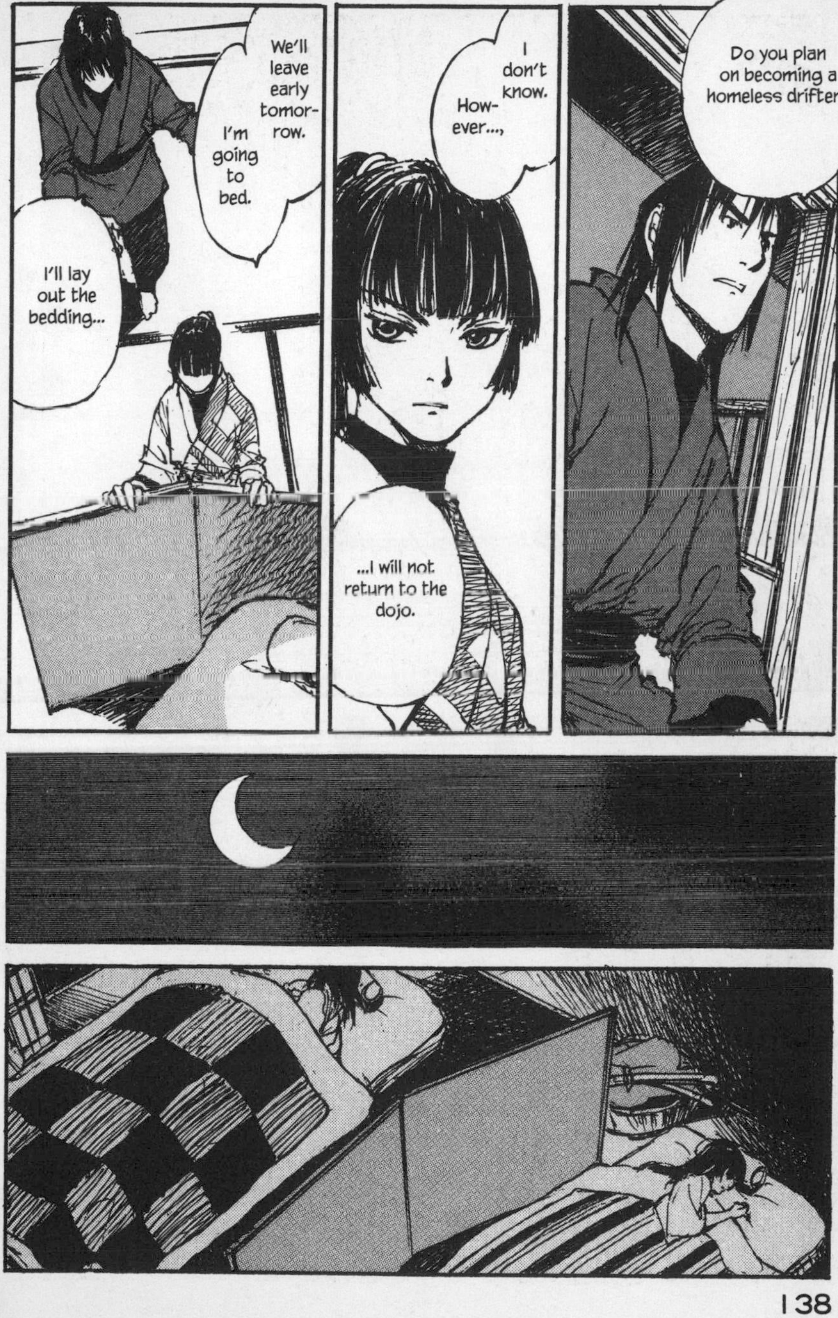
Do you plan on becoming a homeless drifter?
I don't know.
How-ever...,
...I will not return to the dojo.
We'll leave early tomor-row.
I'm going to bed.
I'll lay out the bedding...

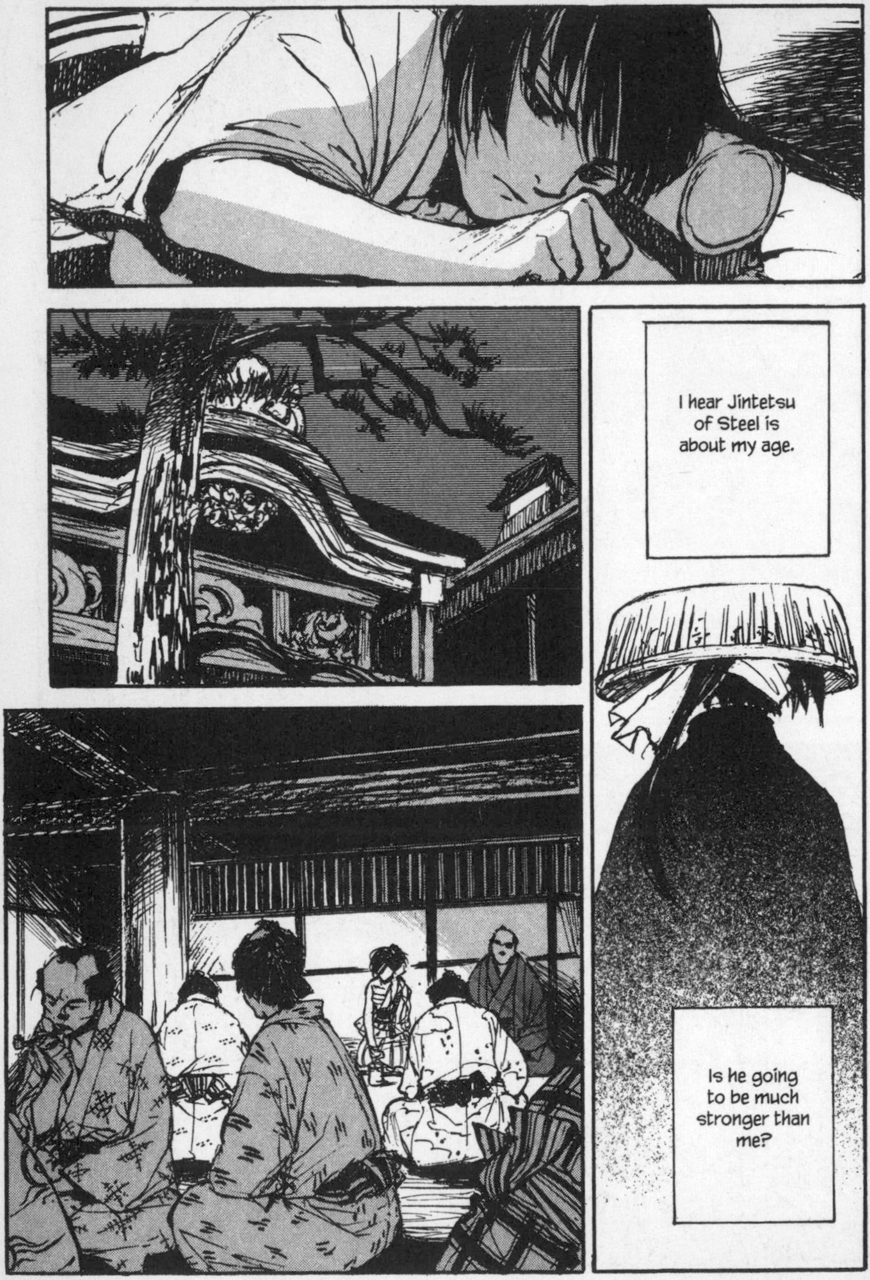
I hear Jintetsu of Steel is about my age.
Is he going to be much stronger than me?

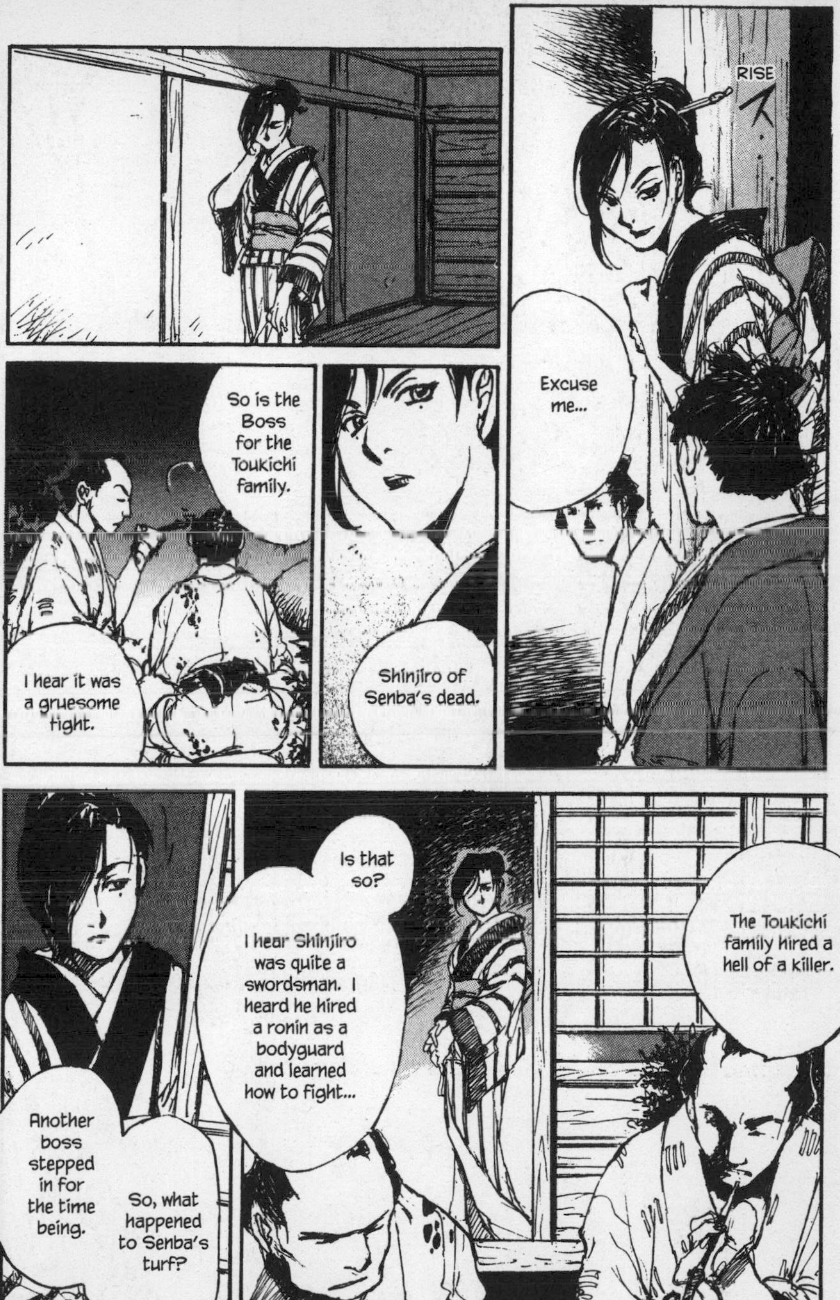
RISE
Excuse me...
Shinjiro of Senba's dead.
So is the Boss for the Toukichi family.
I hear it was a gruesome fight.
The Toukichi family hired a hell of a killer.
Is that so?
I hear Shinjiro was quite a swordsman. I heard he hired a ronin as a bodyguard and learned how to fight...
So, what happened to Senba's turf?
Another boss stepped in for the time being.

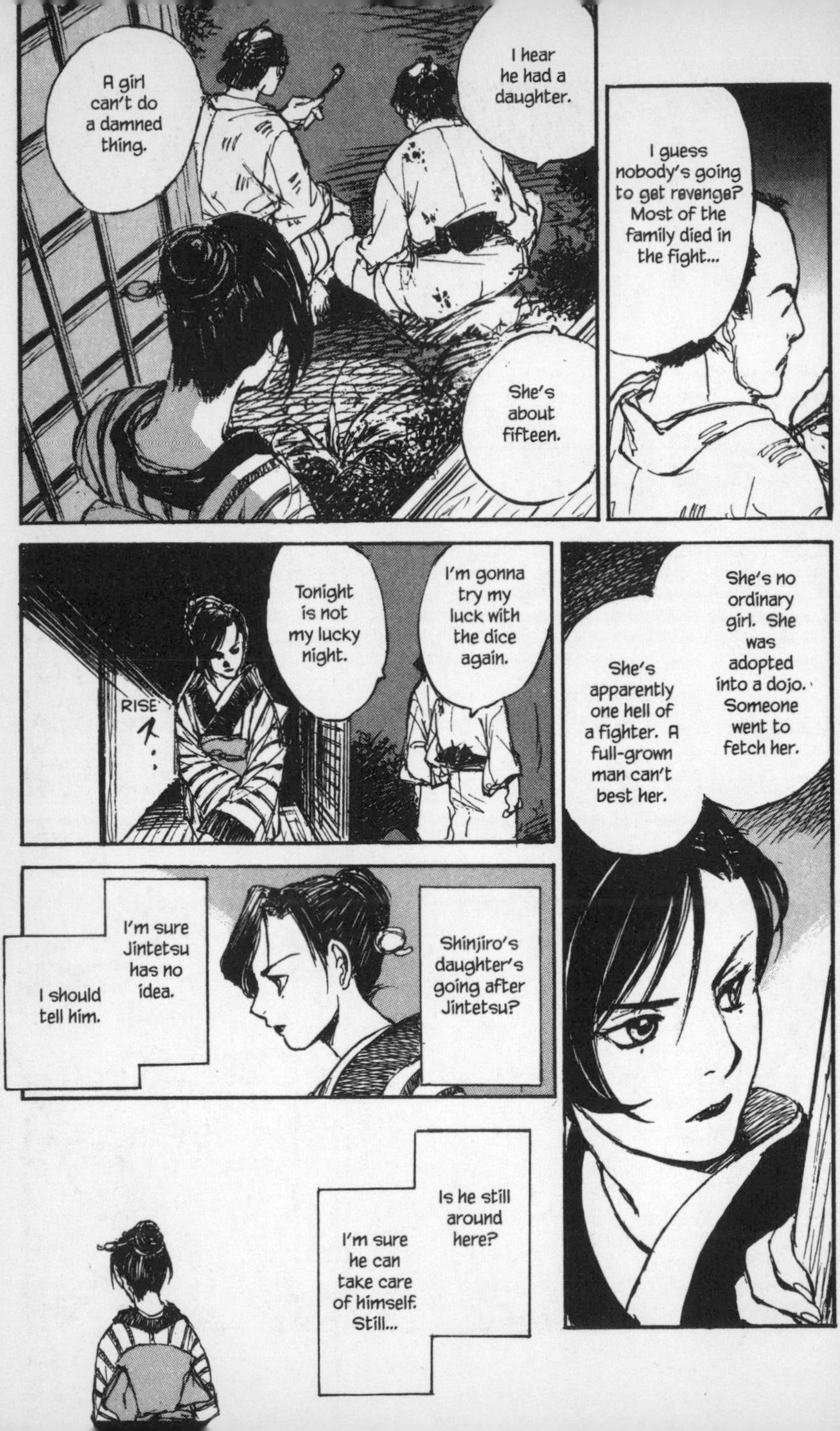
I guess nobody's going to get revenge? Most of the family died in the fight...
I hear he had a daughter.
She's about fifteen.
A girl can't do a damned thing.
She's no ordinary girl. She was adopted into a dojo. Someone went to fetch her.
She's apparently one hell of a fighter. A full-grown man can't best her.
I'm gonna try my luck with the dice again.
Tonight is not my lucky night.
RISE
Shinjiro's daughter's going after Jintetsu?
I'm sure Jintetsu has no idea.
I should tell him.
Is he still around here?
I'm sure he can take care of himself. Still...

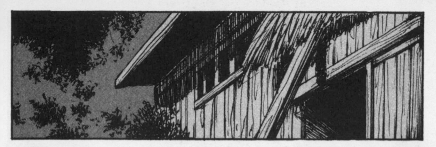

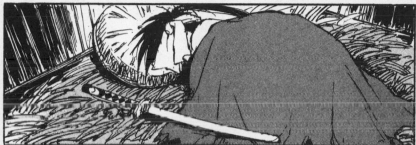

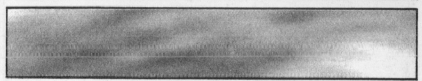

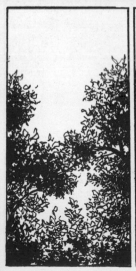

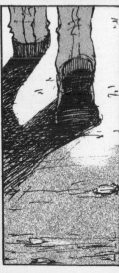

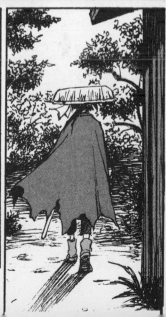

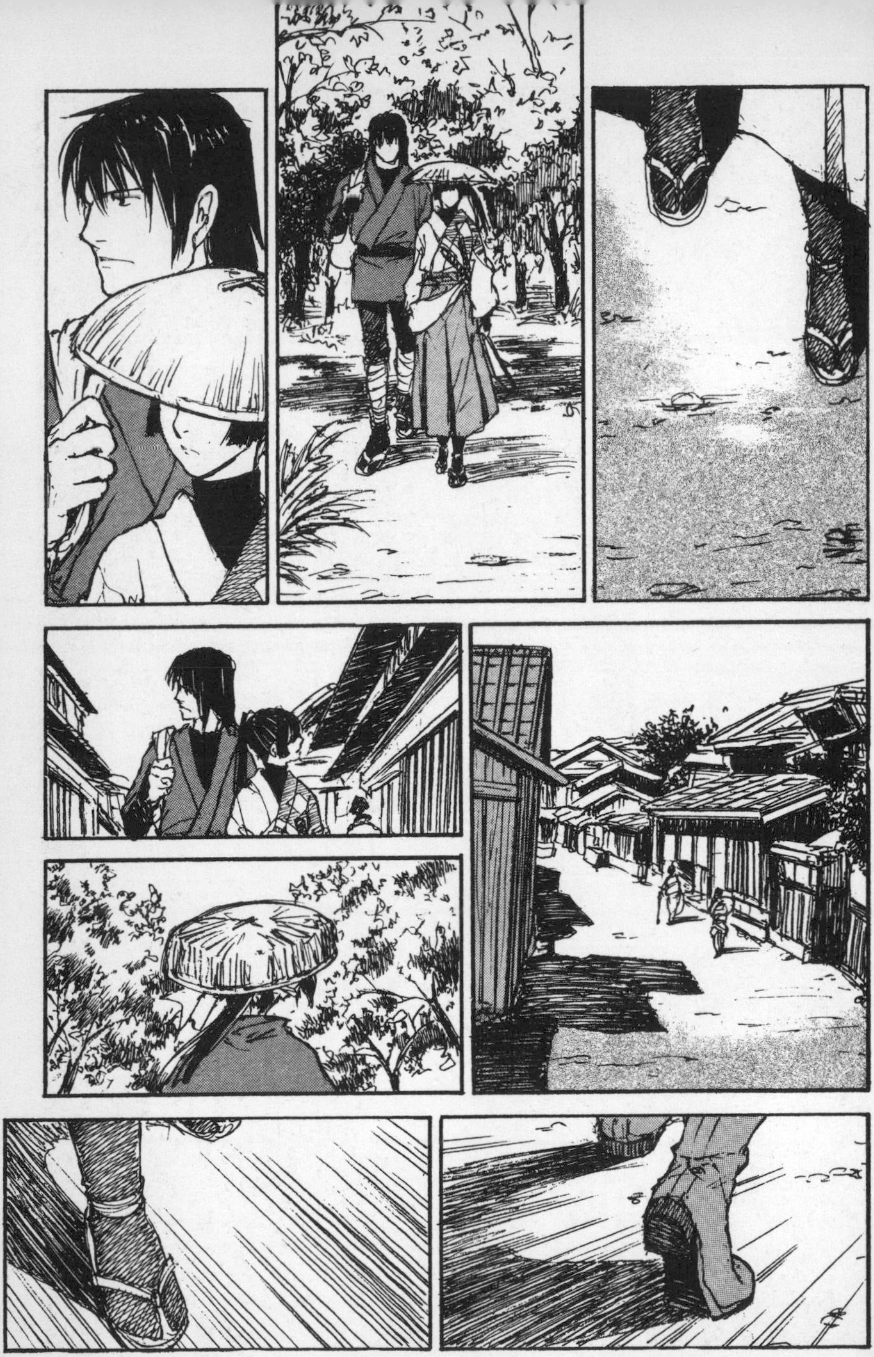

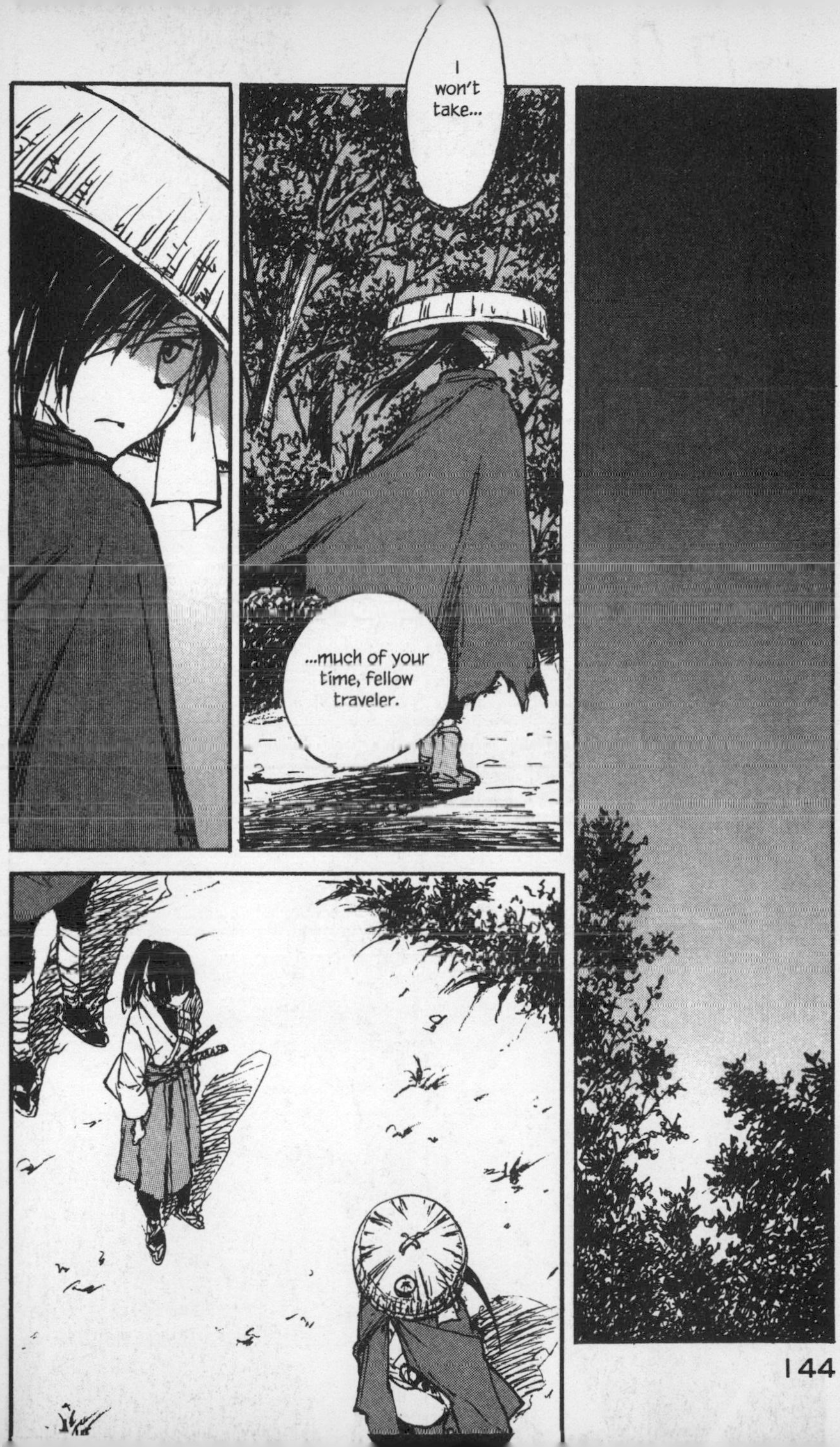
I won't take...
...much of your time, fellow traveler.

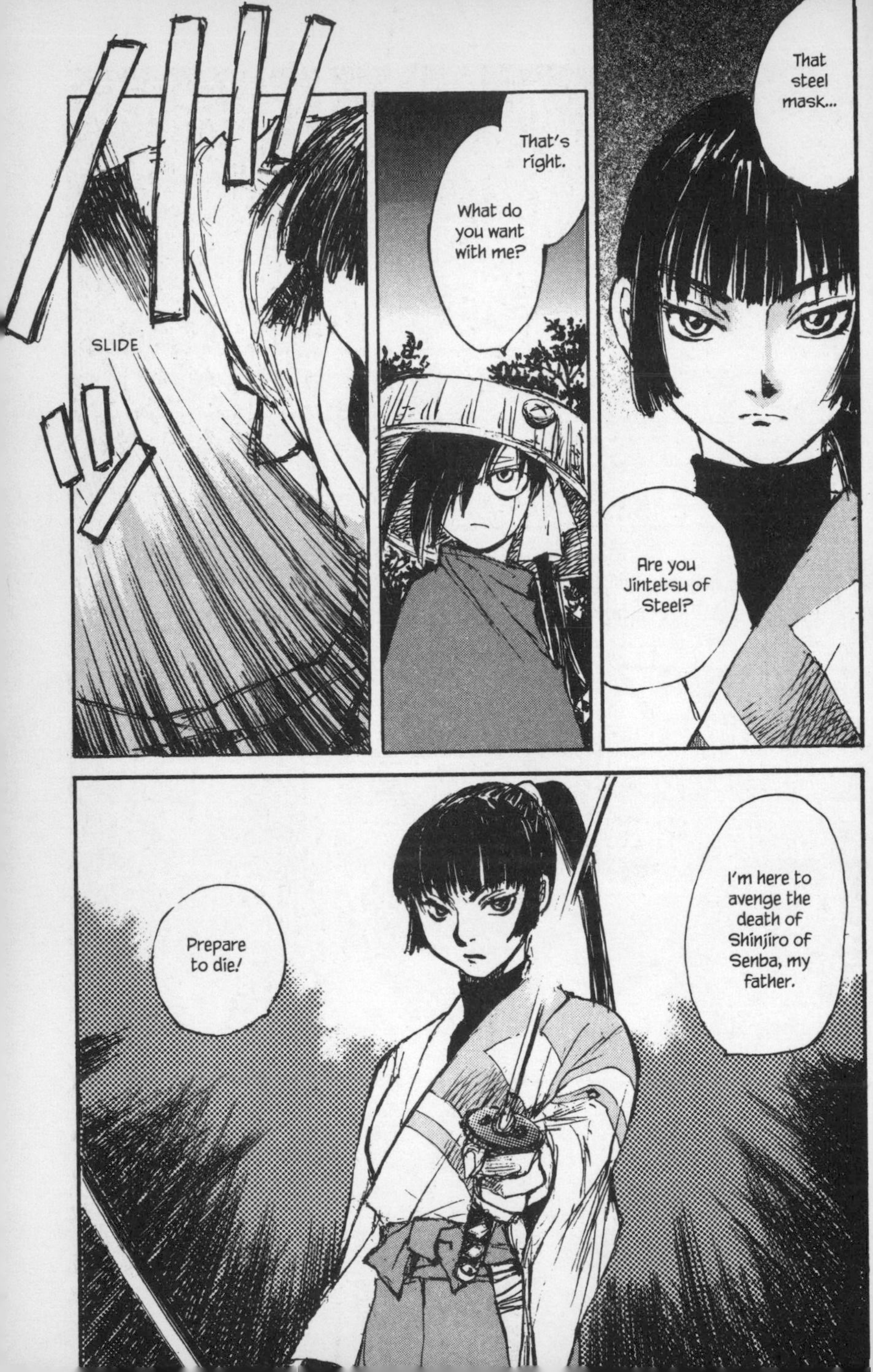
That steel mask...
Are you Jintetsu of Steel?
That's right.
What do you want with me?
SLIDE
I'm here to avenge the death of Shinjiro of Senba, my father.
Prepare to die!

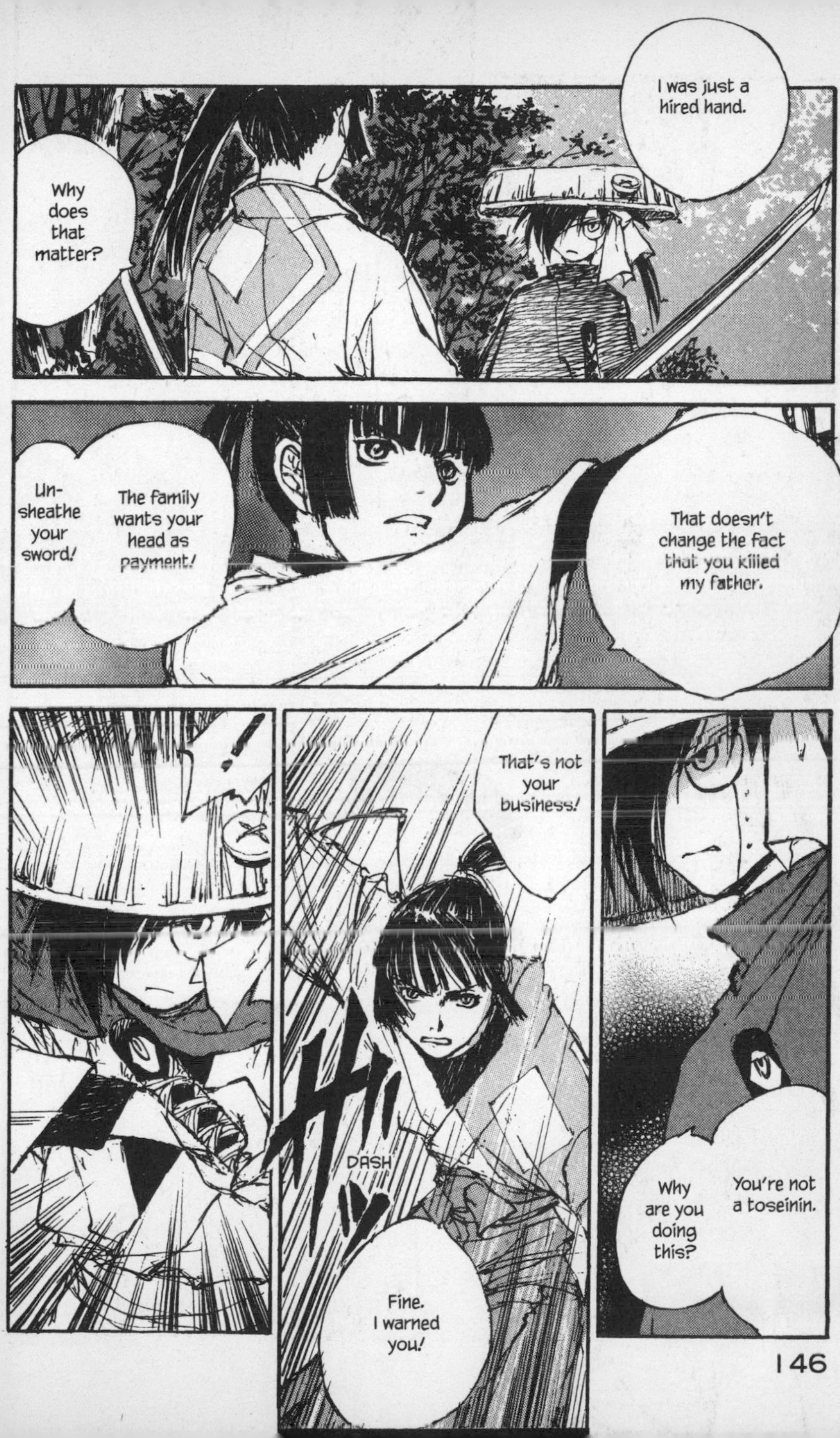
I was just a hired hand.
Why does that matter?
That doesn't change the fact that you killed my father.
The family wants your head as payment!
Un-sheathe your sword!
You're not a toseinin.
Why are you doing this?
That's not your business!
DASH
Fine. I warned you!

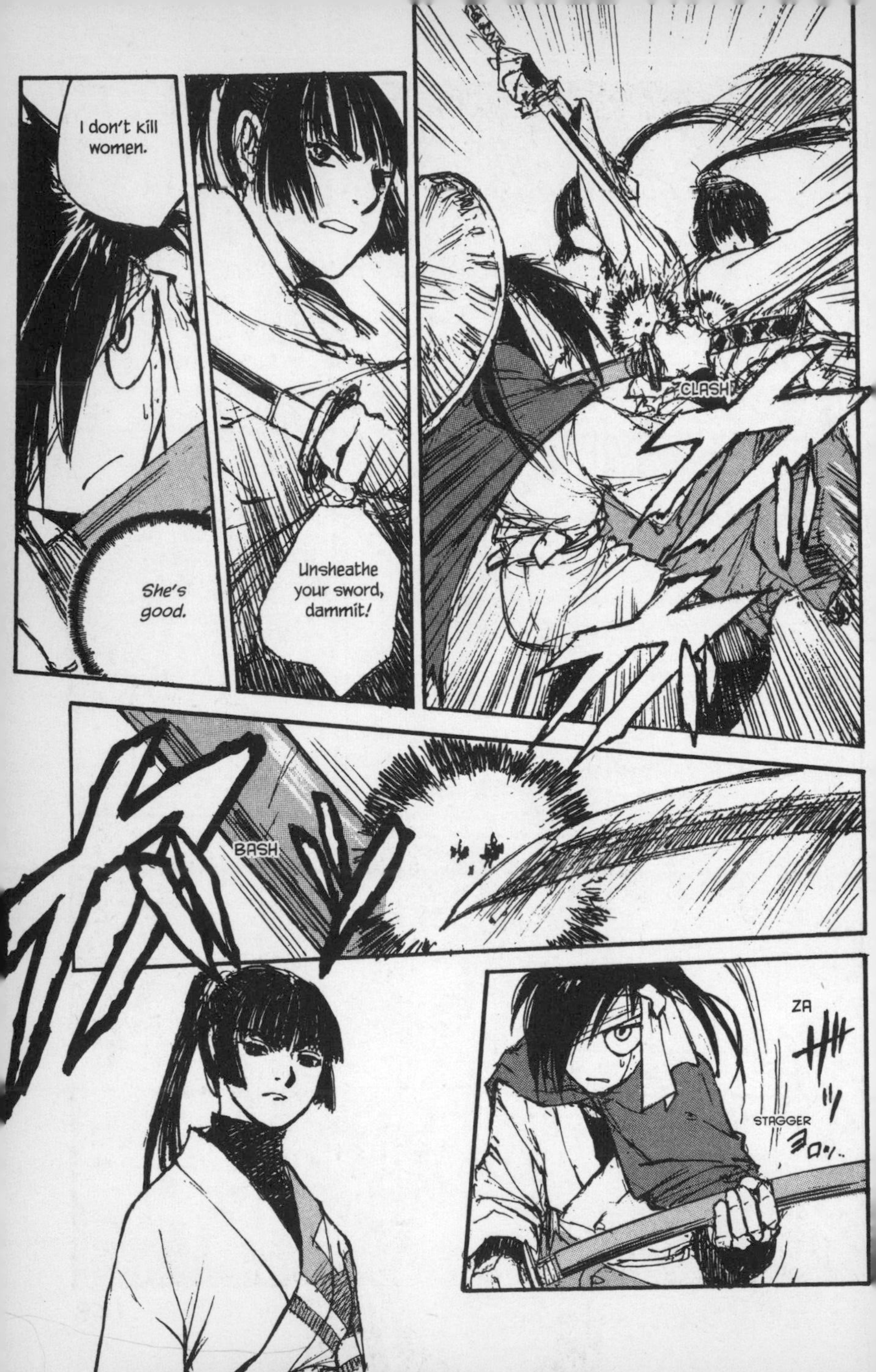
CLASH
Unsheathe your sword, dammit!
I don't kill women.
She's good.
BASH
ZA
STAGGER

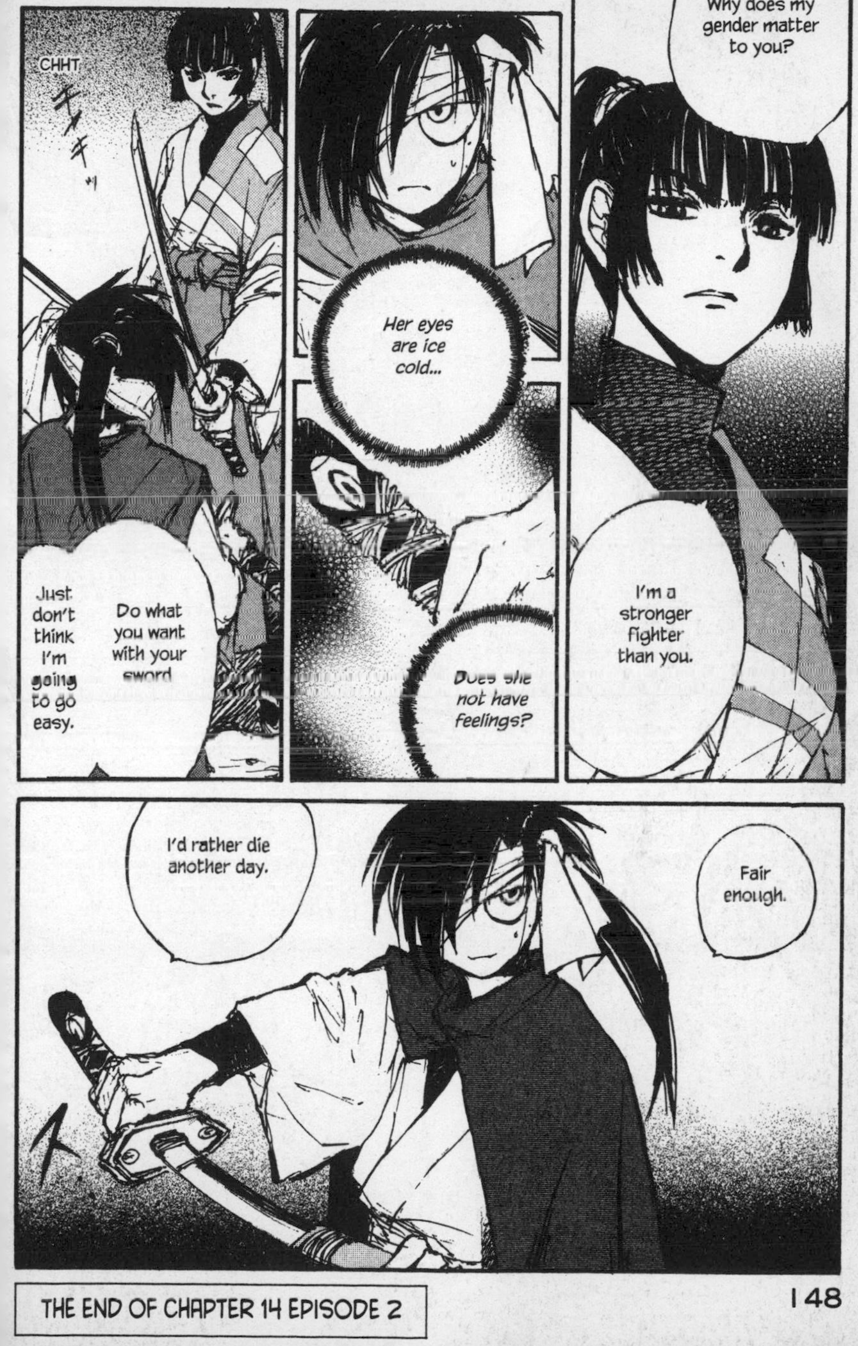
Why does my gender matter to you?
I'm a stronger fighter than you.
Her eyes are ice cold...
Does she not have feelings?
CHHT
Do what you want with your sword
Just don't think I'm going to go easy.
Fair enough.
I'd rather die another day.

THE END OF CHAPTER 14 EPISODE 2

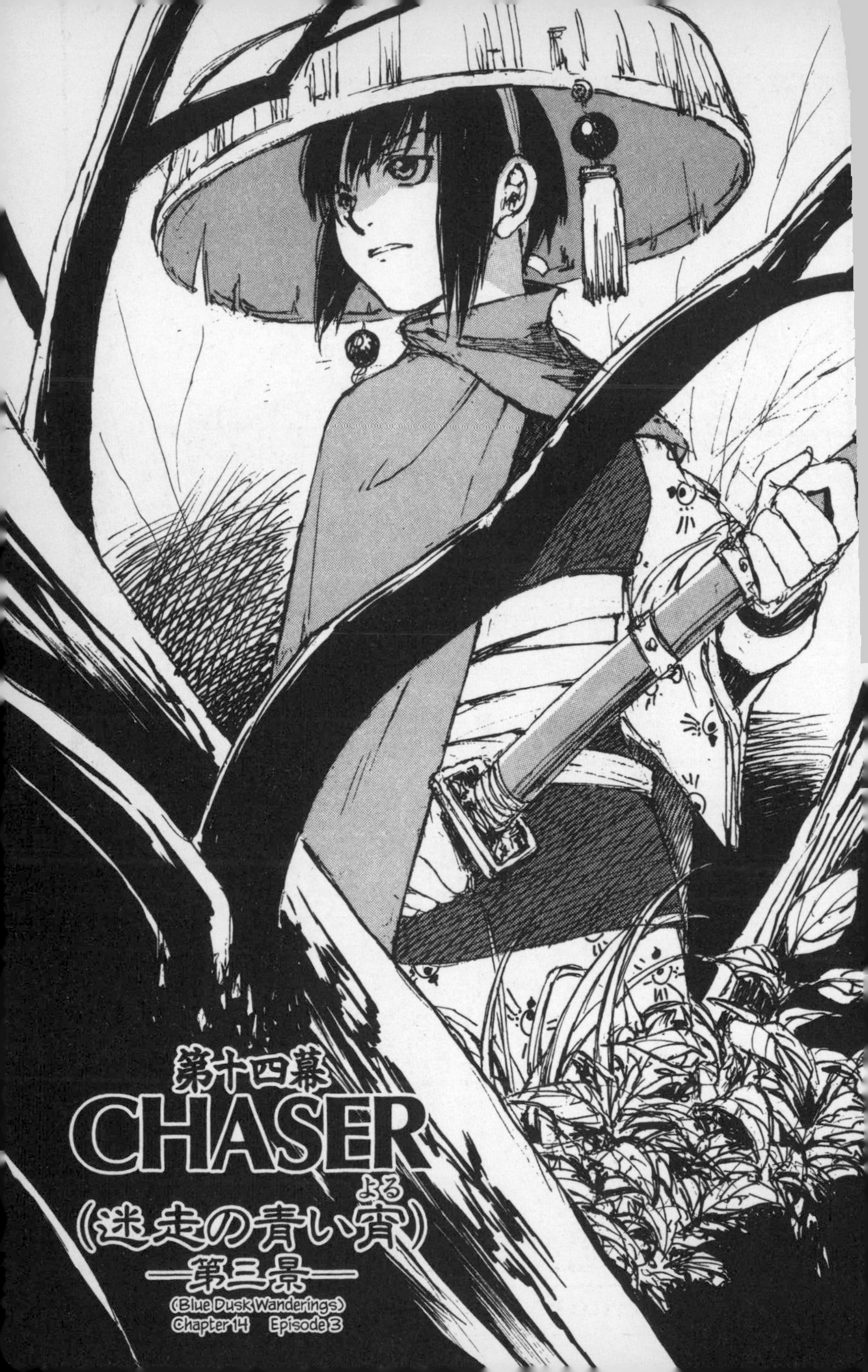
第十四幕
CHASER
よる
(迷走の青い宵)
—第三景—
(Blue Dusk Wanderings)
Chapter 14 Episode 3

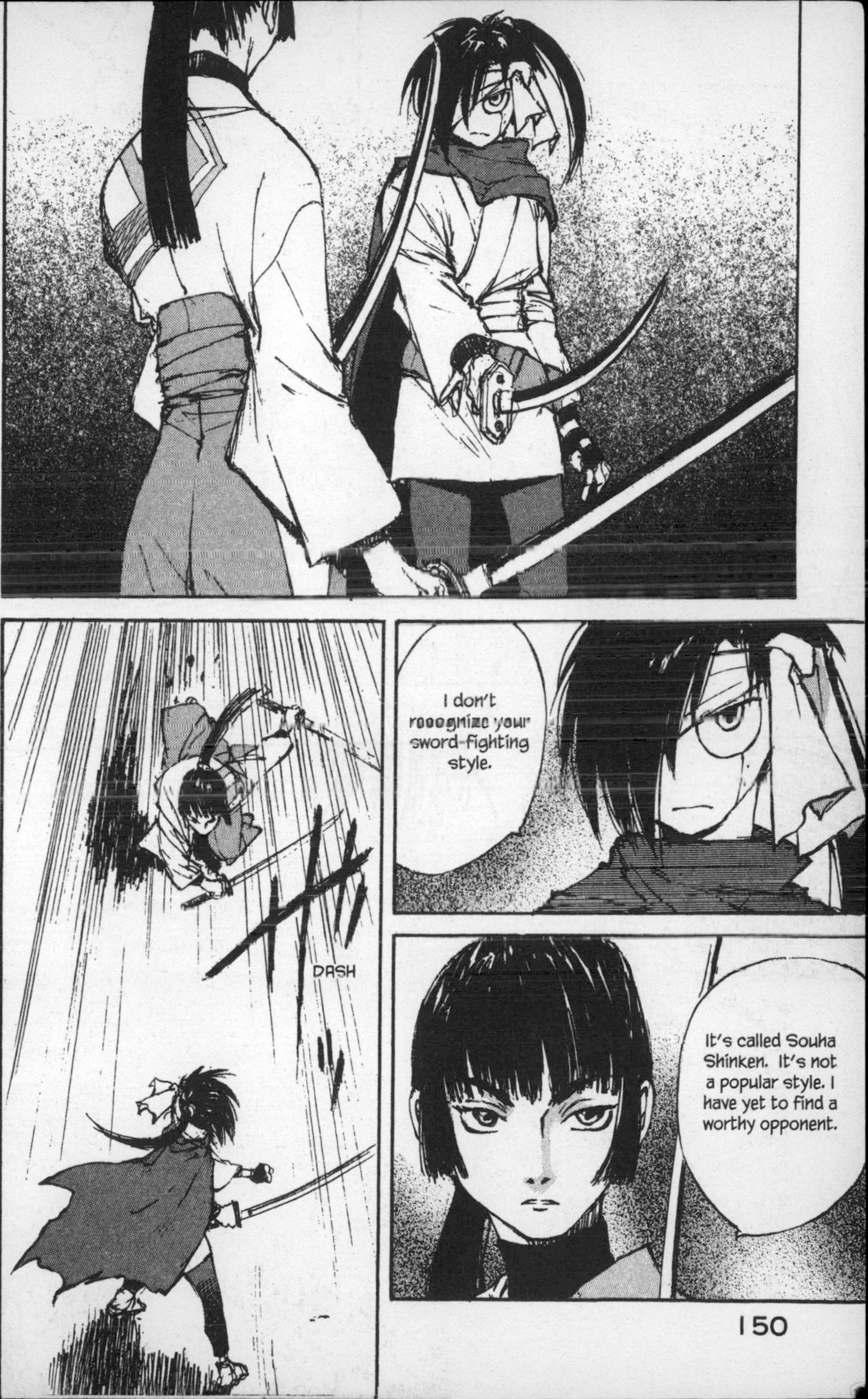
I don't recognize your sword-fighting style.
It's called Souha Shinken. It's not a popular style. I have yet to find a worthy opponent.
DASH

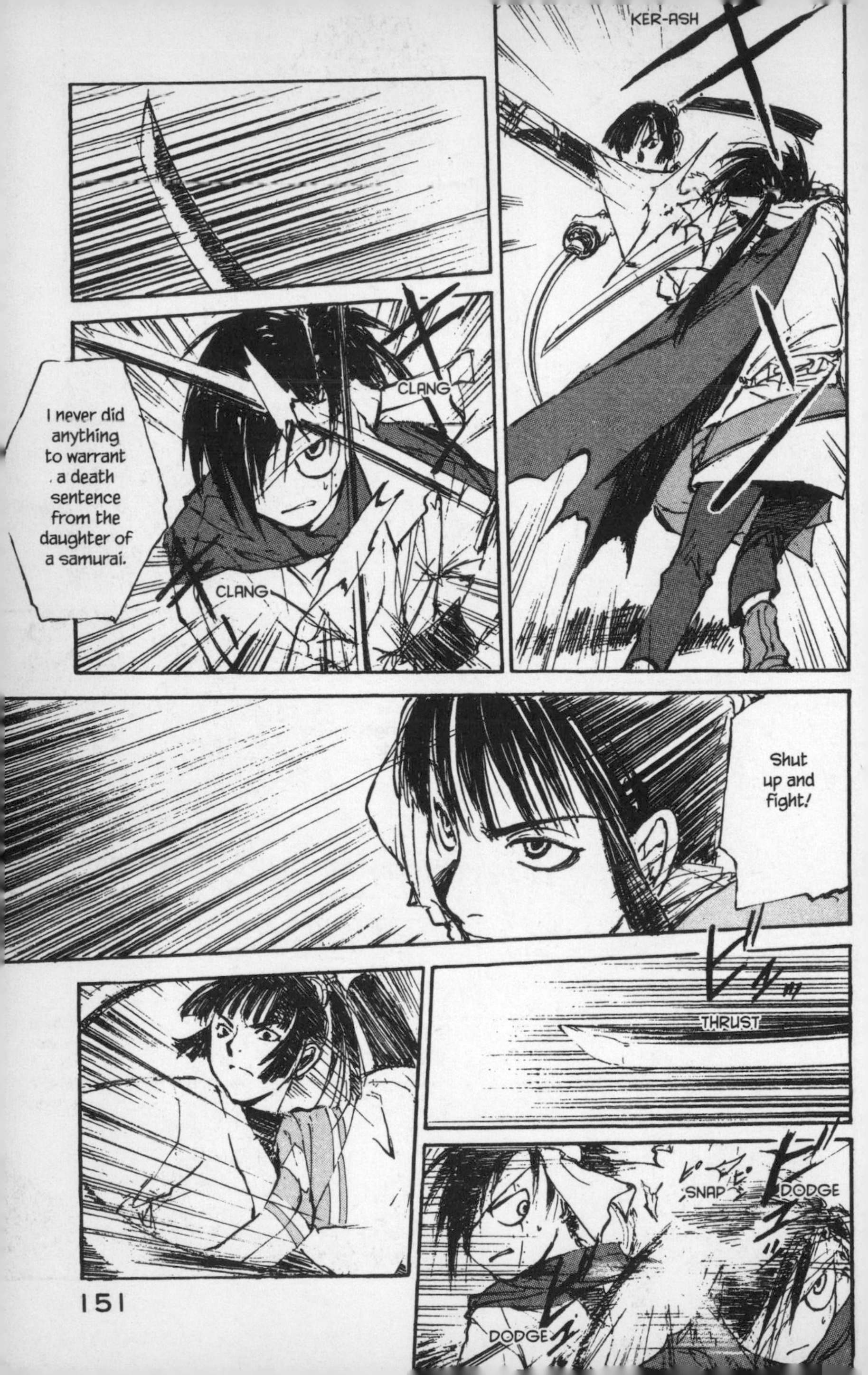
KER-ASH
CLANG
I never did anything to warrant a death sentence from the daughter of a samurai.
CLANG
Shut up and fight!
THRUST
DODGE
SNAP
DODGE

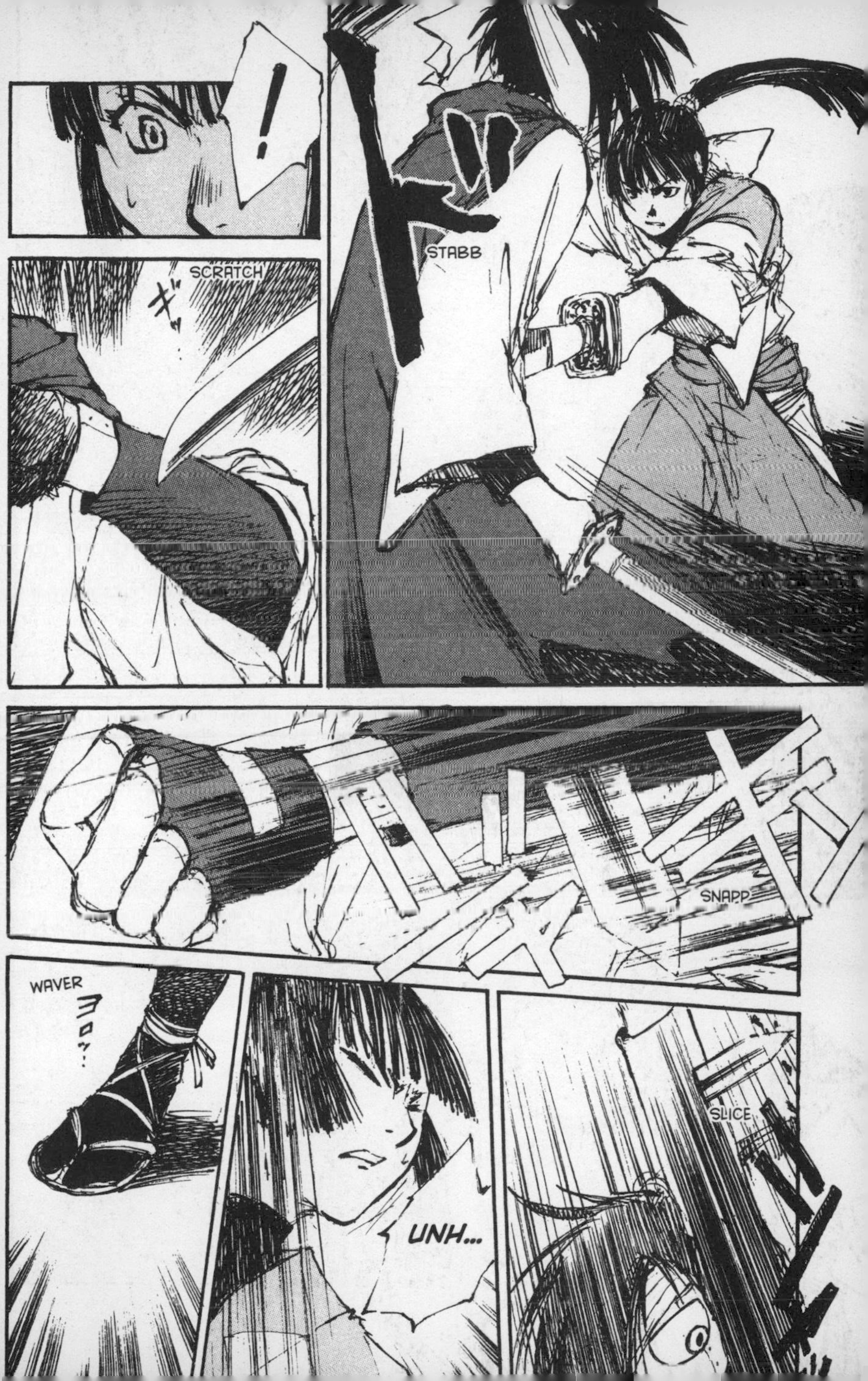
STABB
!
SCRATCH
ギッ
SNAPP
SLICE
UNH...
WAVER
ヨロッ…

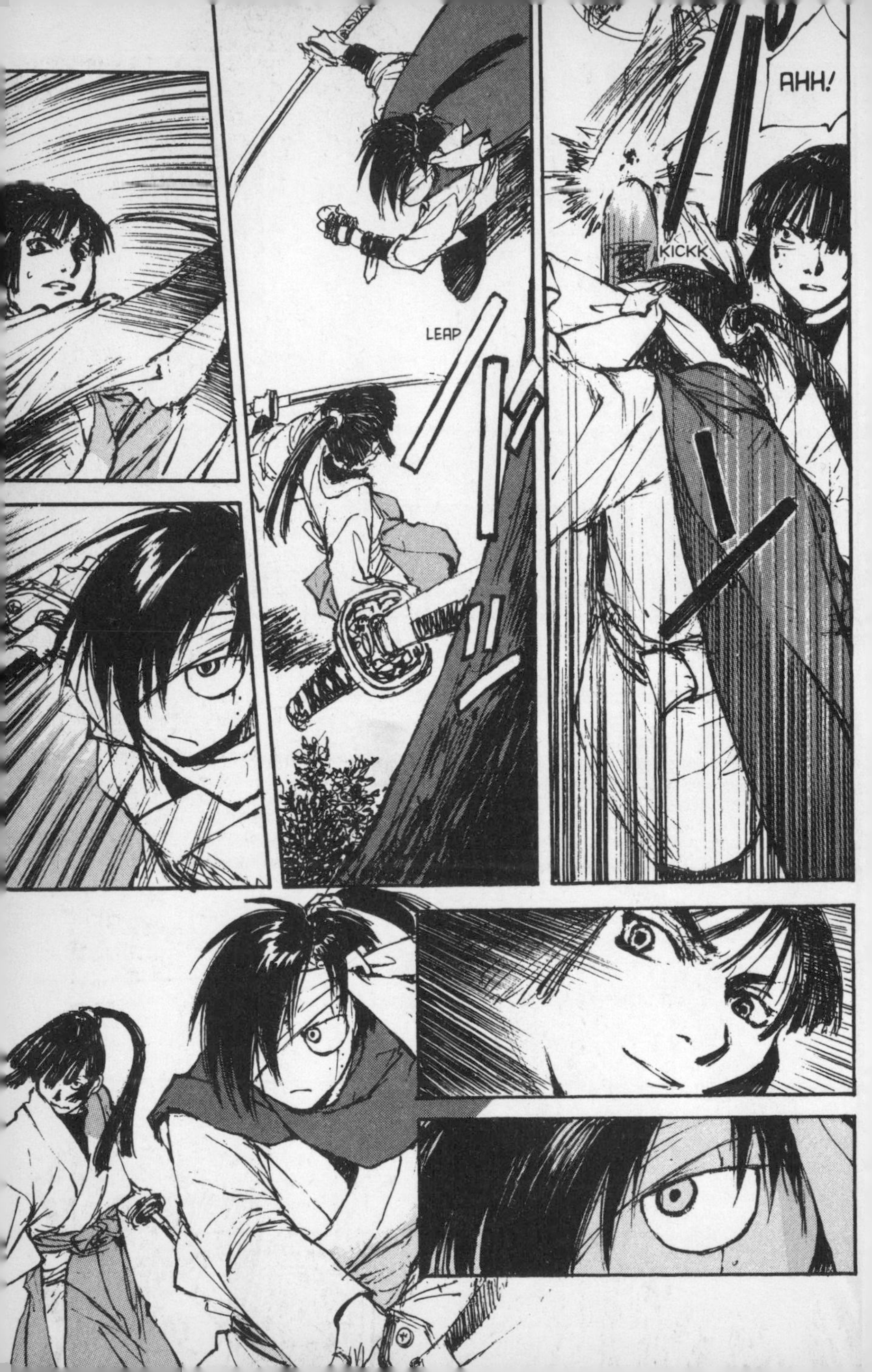
AHH!
KICKK
LEAP

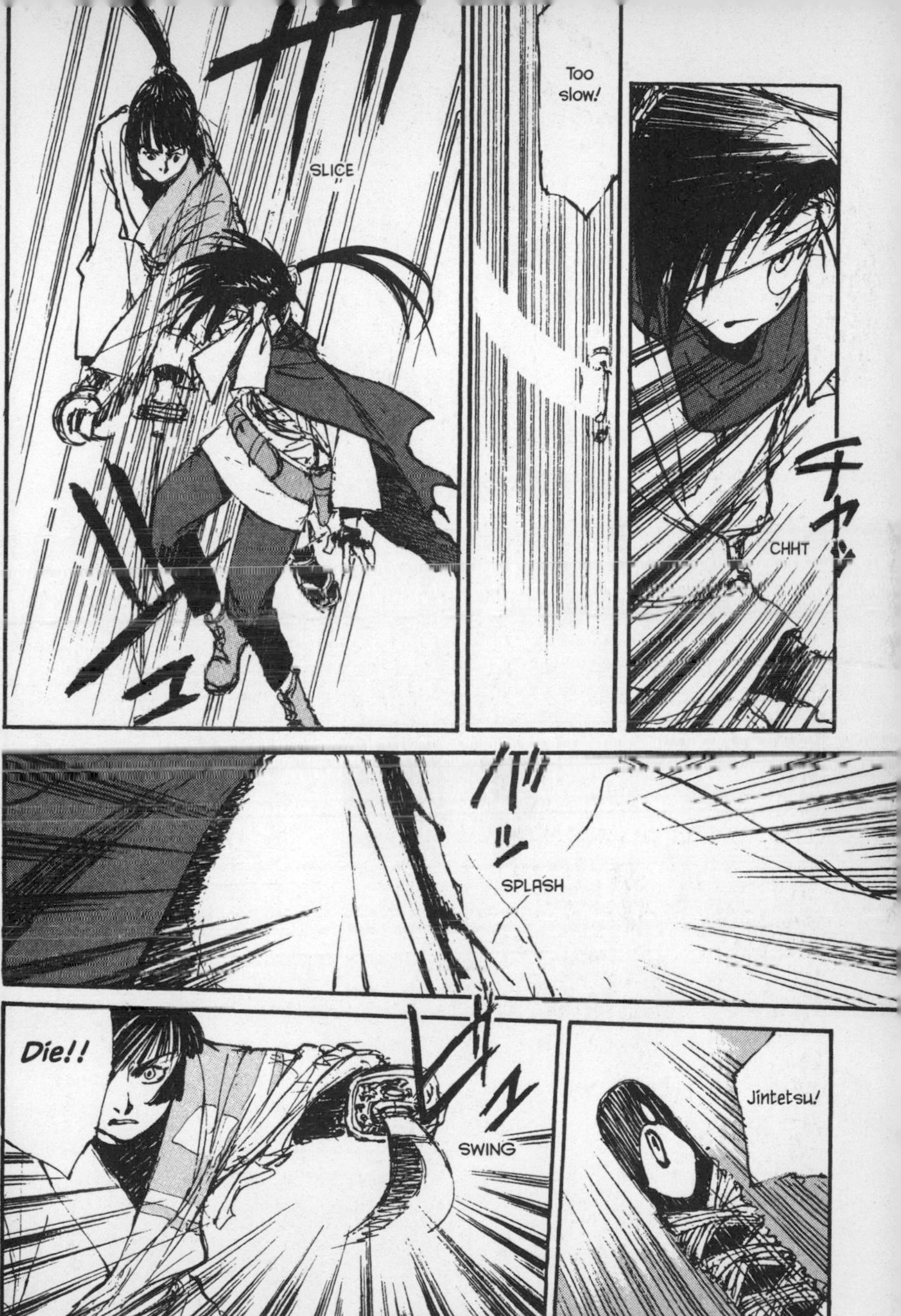
CHHT
Too slow!
SLICE
SPLASH
Jintetsu!
Die!!
SWING

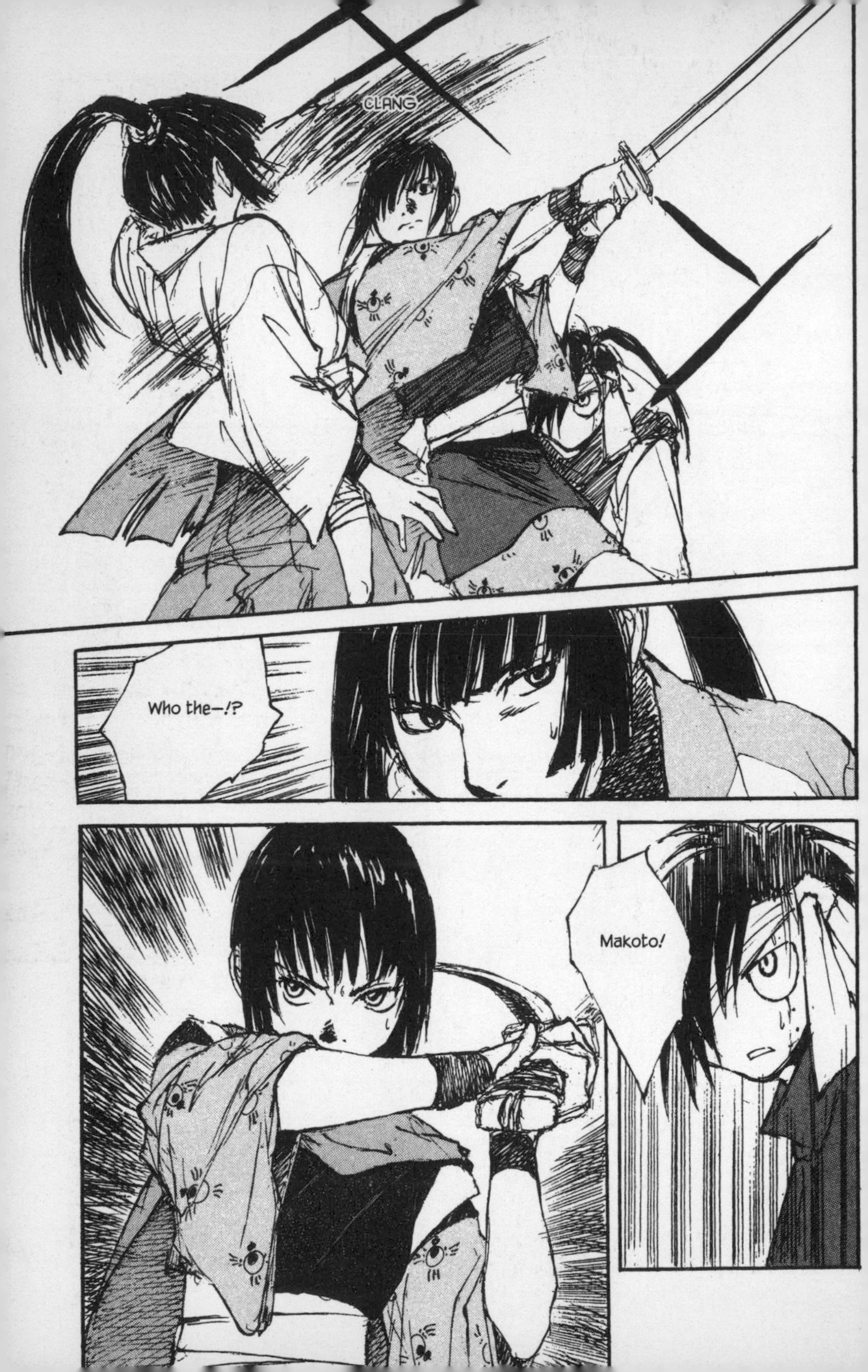
CLANG
Who the—!?
Makoto!

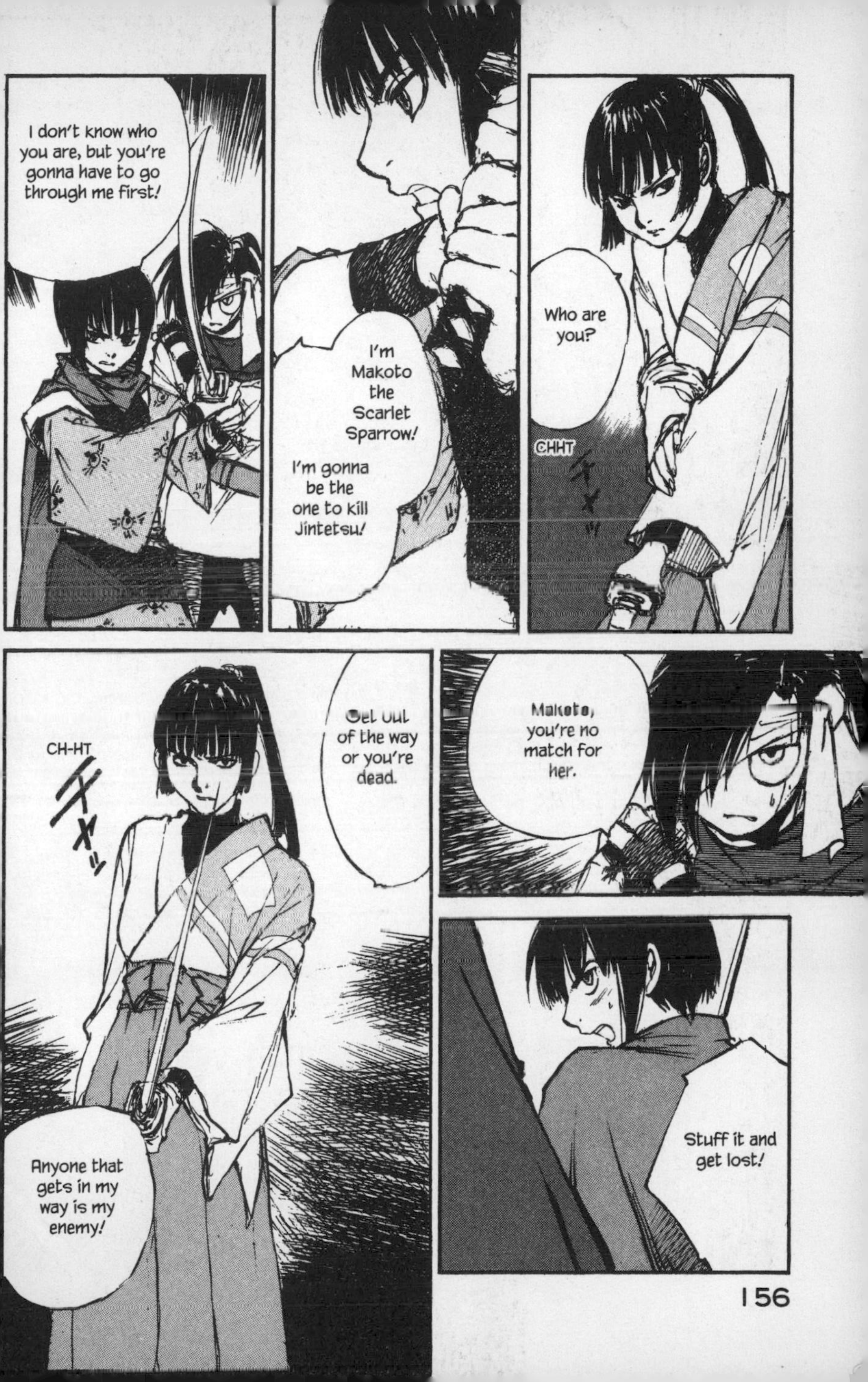
Who are you?
CHHT
I'm Makoto the Scarlet Sparrow!
I'm gonna be the one to kill Jintetsu!
I don't know who you are, but you're gonna have to go through me first!
Makoto, you're no match for her.
Stuff it and get lost!
Get out of the way or you're dead.
CH-HT
Anyone that gets in my way is my enemy!

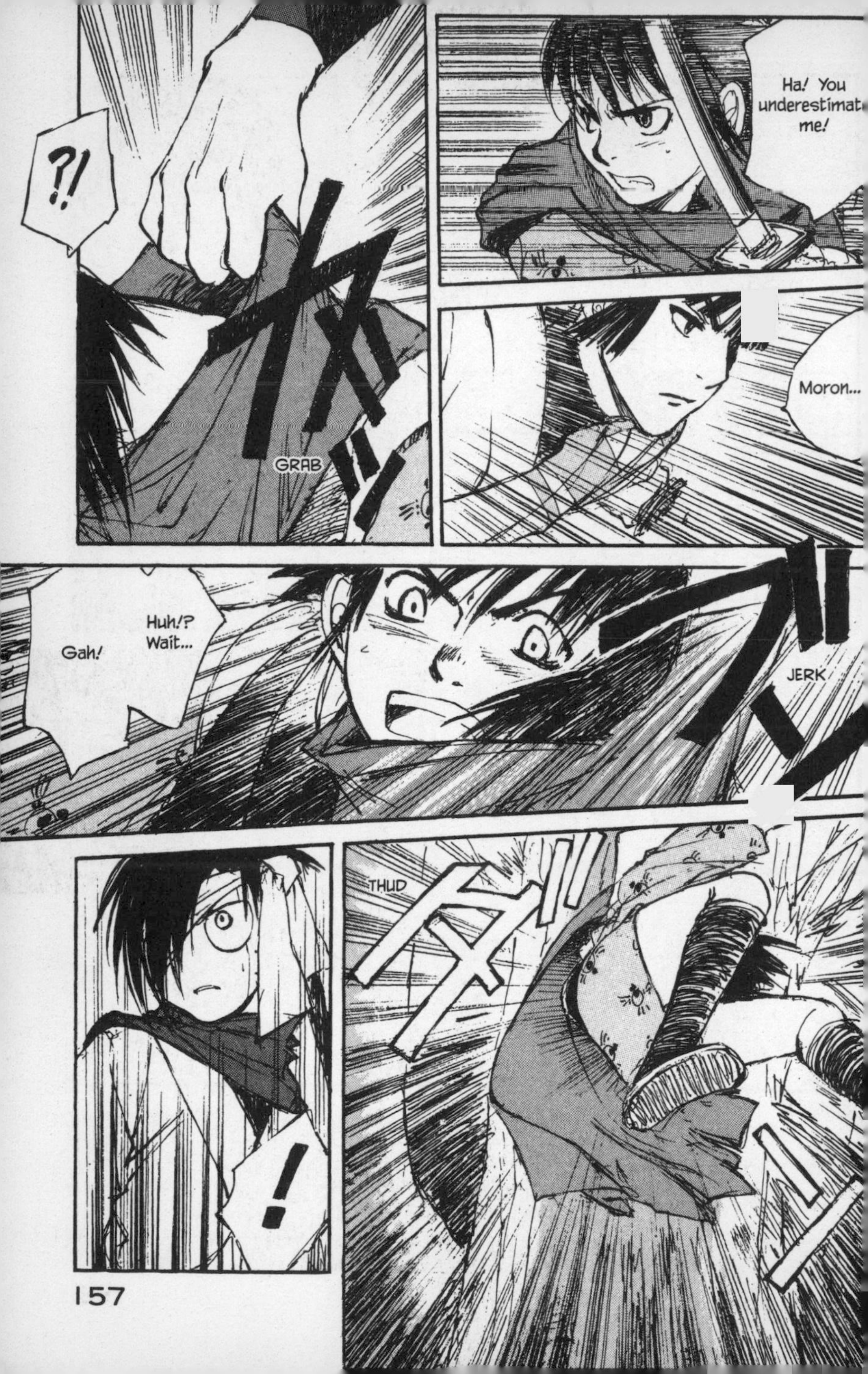
Ha! You underestimat me!
Moron...
?!
GRAB
JERK
Huh!? Wait...
Gah!
THUD
!

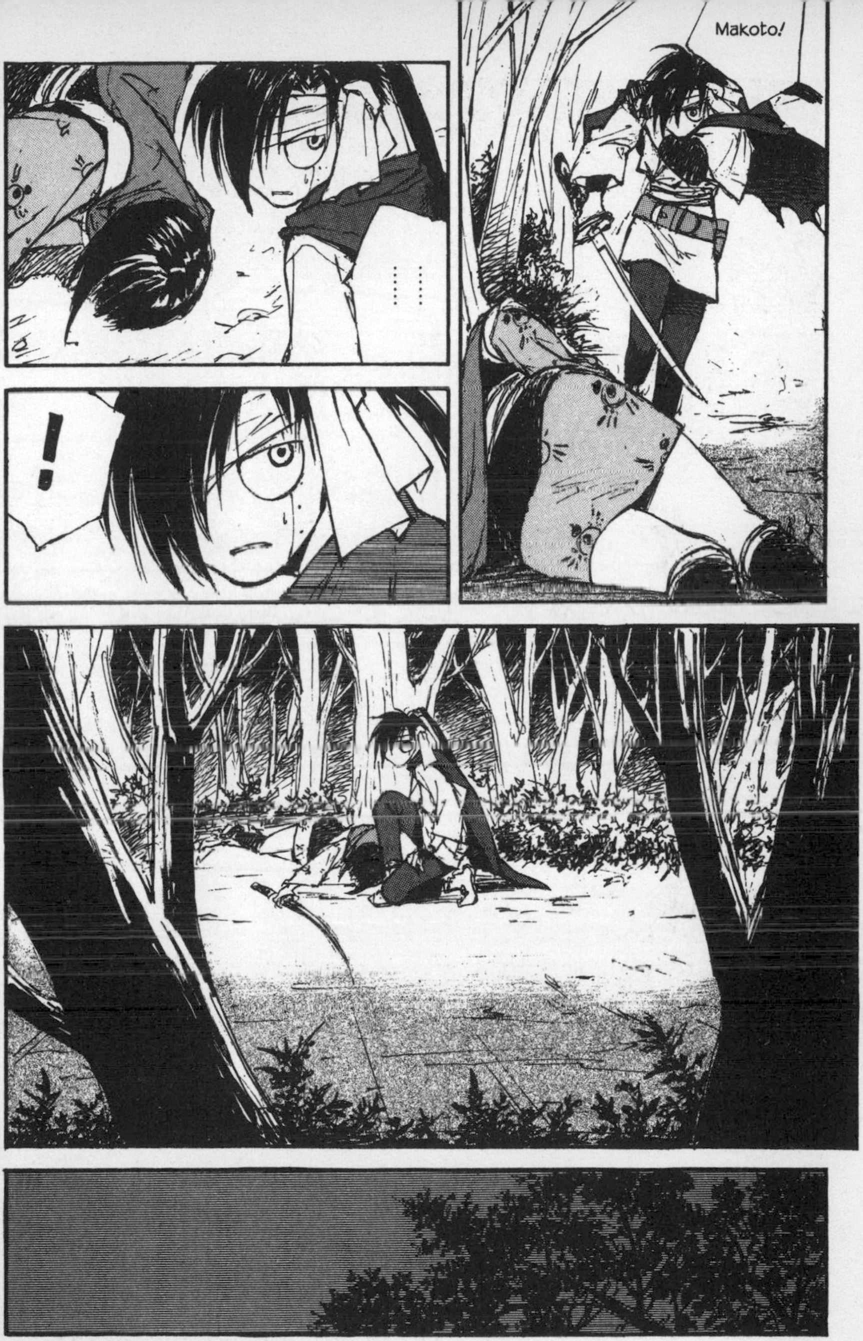
Makoto!
......
!

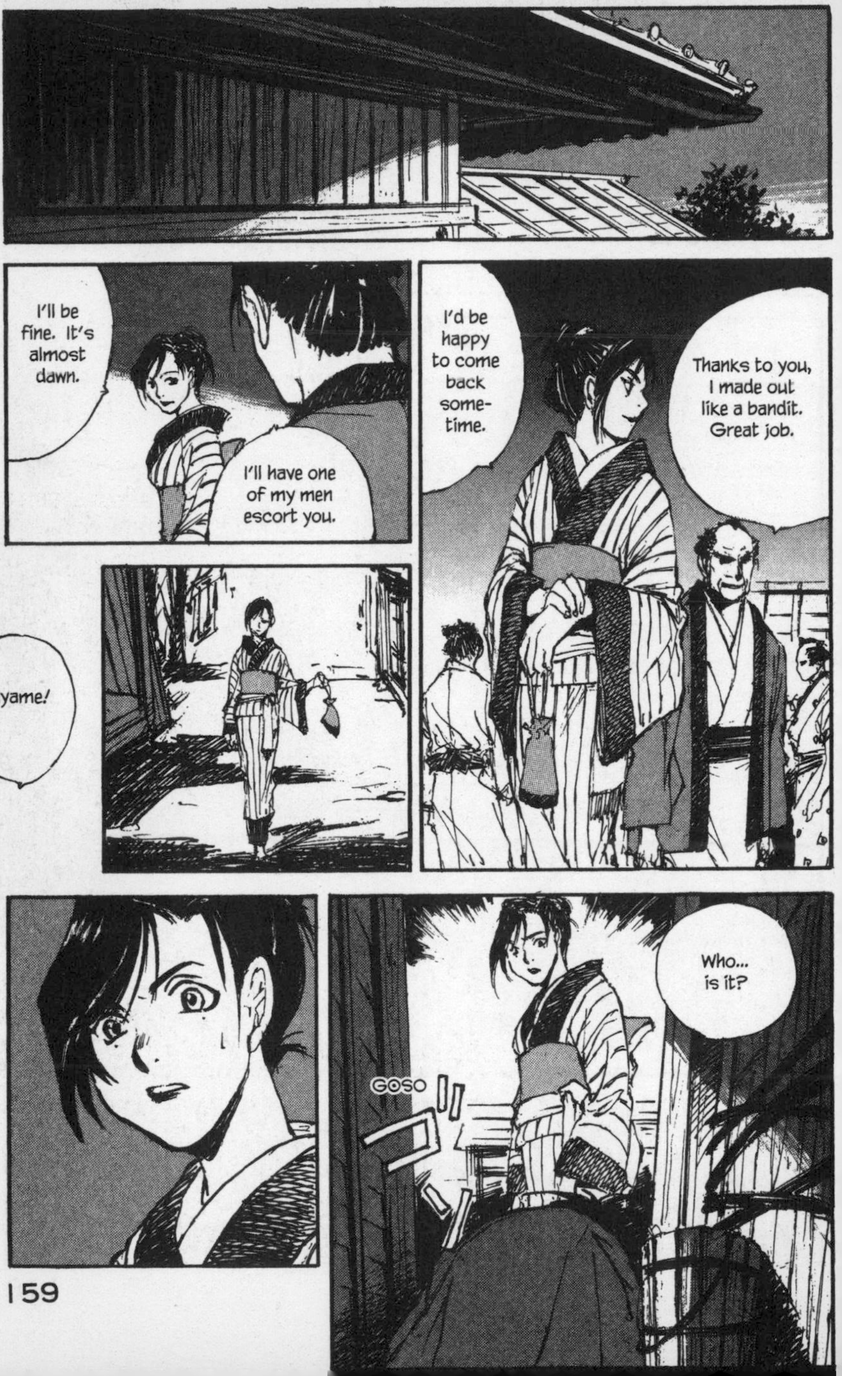
Thanks to you, I made out like a bandit. Great job.
I'd be happy to come back sometime.
I'll have one of my men escort you.
I'll be fine. It's almost dawn.
Ayame!
GOSO
Who... is it?

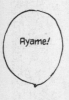

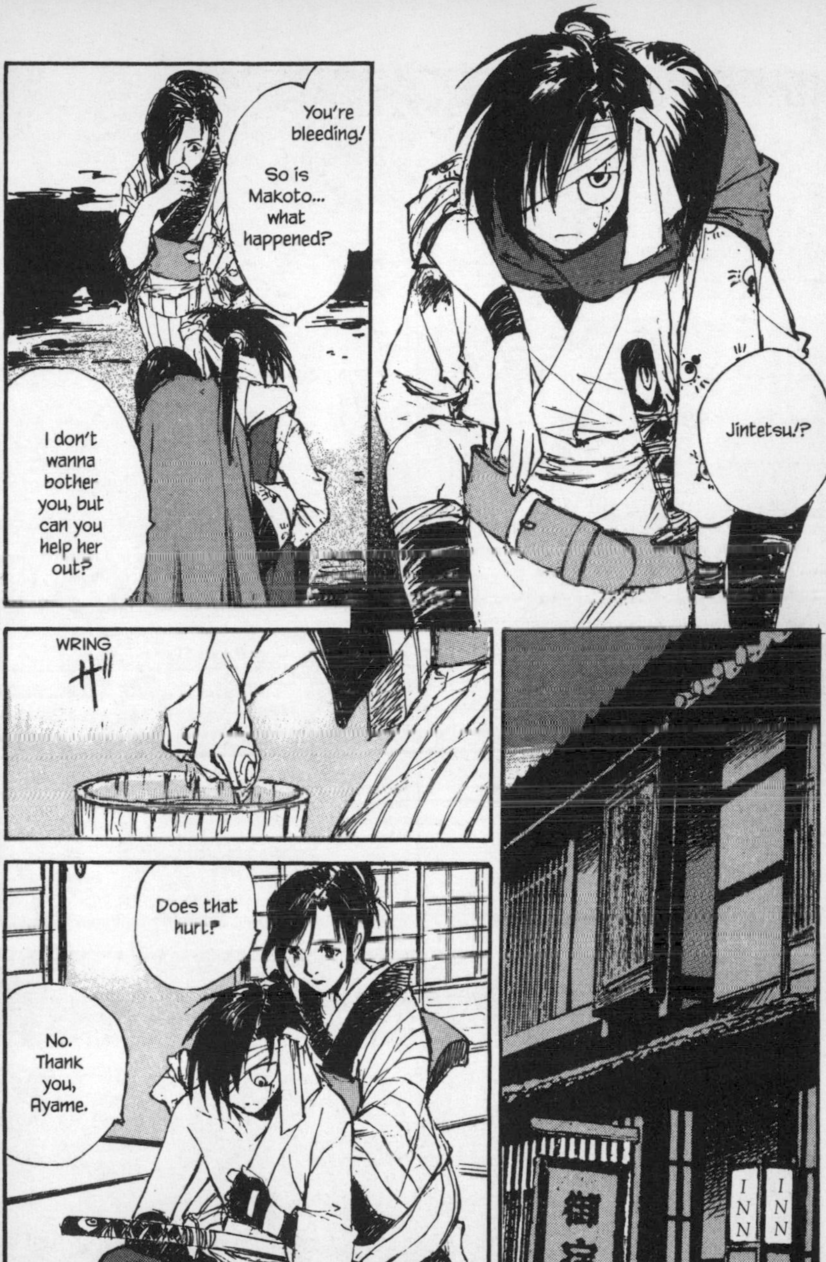
Jintetsu!?
You're bleeding!
So is Makoto... what happened?
I don't wanna bother you, but can you help her out?
INN
INN
御宿
WRING
Does that hurt!?
No. Thank you, Ayame.

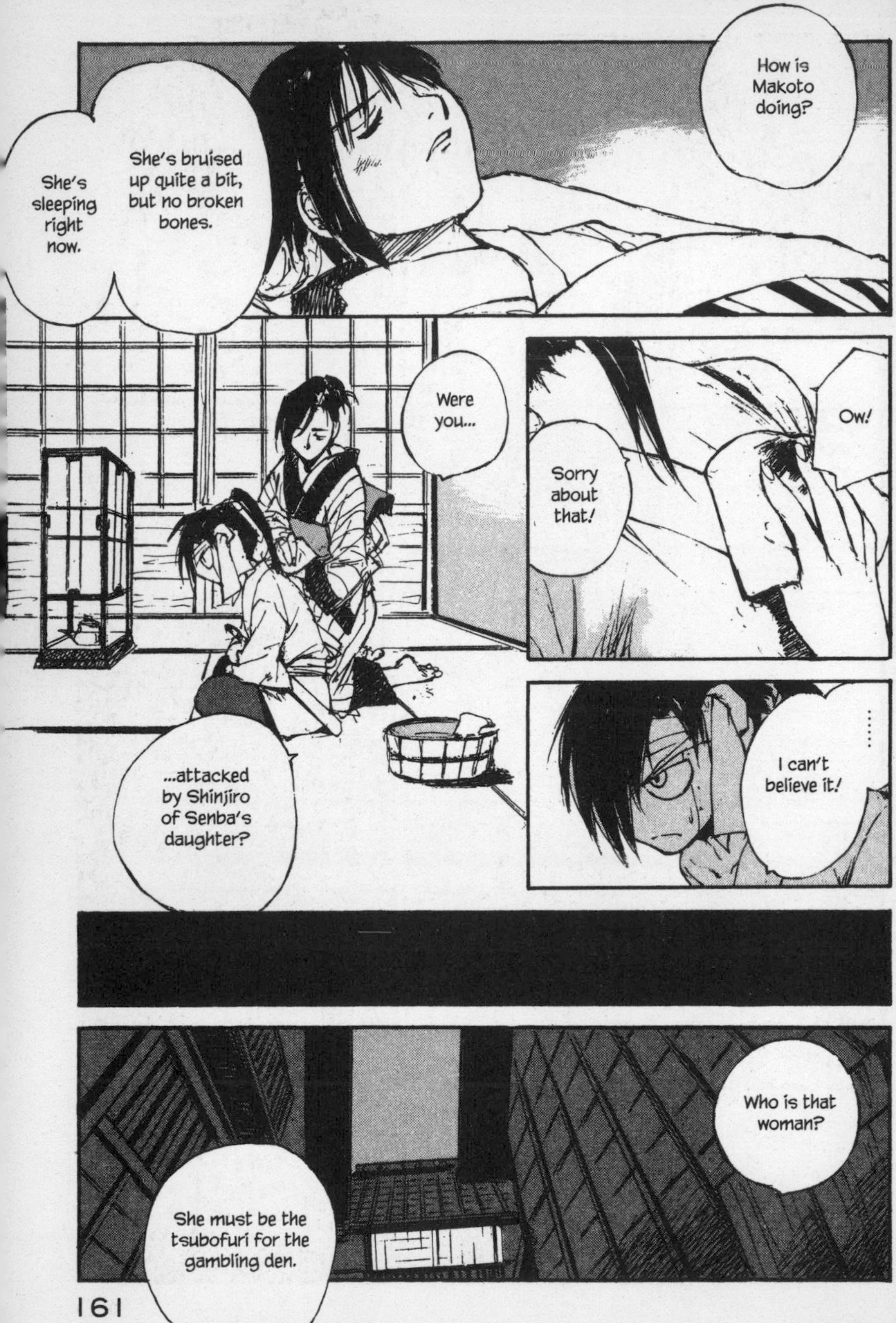
How is Makoto doing?
She's bruised up quite a bit, but no broken bones.
She's sleeping right now.
Ow!
Sorry about that!
……
I can't believe it!
Were you...
...attacked by Shinjiro of Senba's daughter?
Who is that woman?
She must be the tsubofuri for the gambling den.

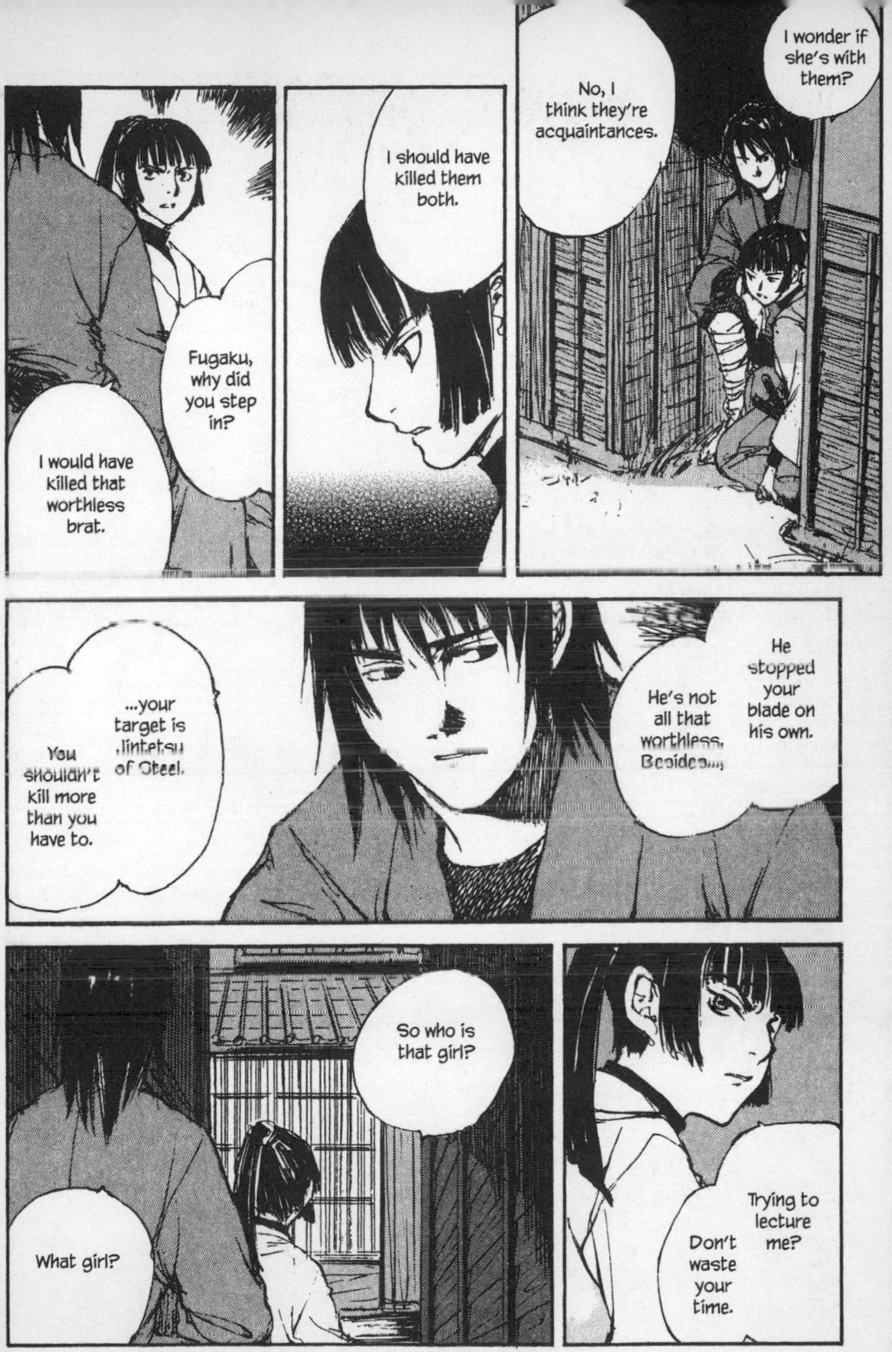
I wonder if she's with them?
No, I think they're acquaintances.
I should have killed them both.
Fugaku, why did you step in?
I would have killed that worthless brat.
He stopped your blade on his own.
He's not all that worthless. Besides...,
...your target is Jintetsu of Steel.
You shouldn't kill more than you have to.
Trying to lecture me?
Don't waste your time.
So who is that girl?
What girl?

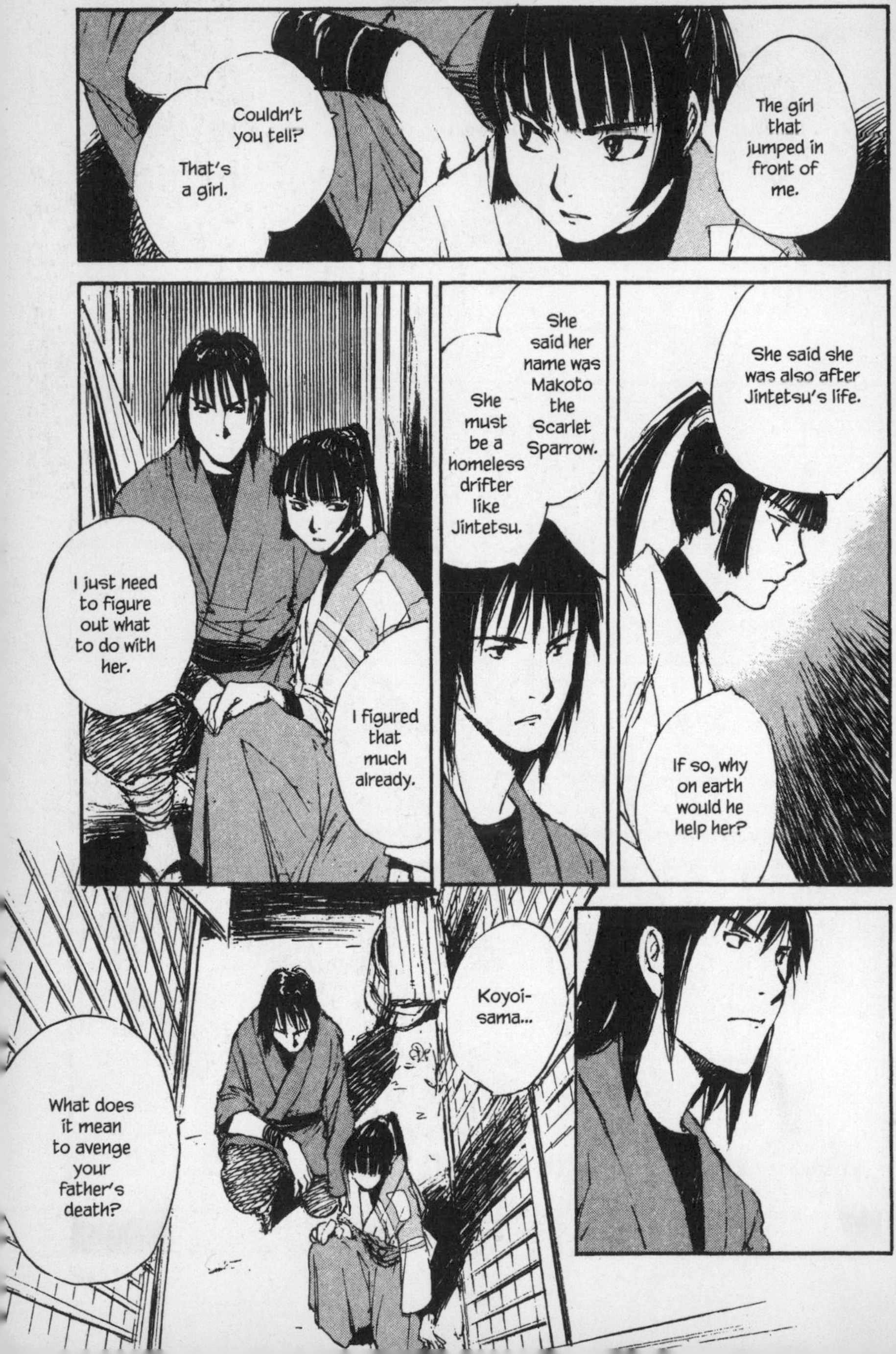
The girl that jumped in front of me.
Couldn't you tell? That's a girl.
She said she was also after Jintetsu's life.
If so, why on earth would he help her?
She said her name was Makoto the Scarlet Sparrow.
She must be a homeless drifter like Jintetsu.
I figured that much already.
I just need to figure out what to do with her.
Koyoi-sama...
What does it mean to avenge your father's death?

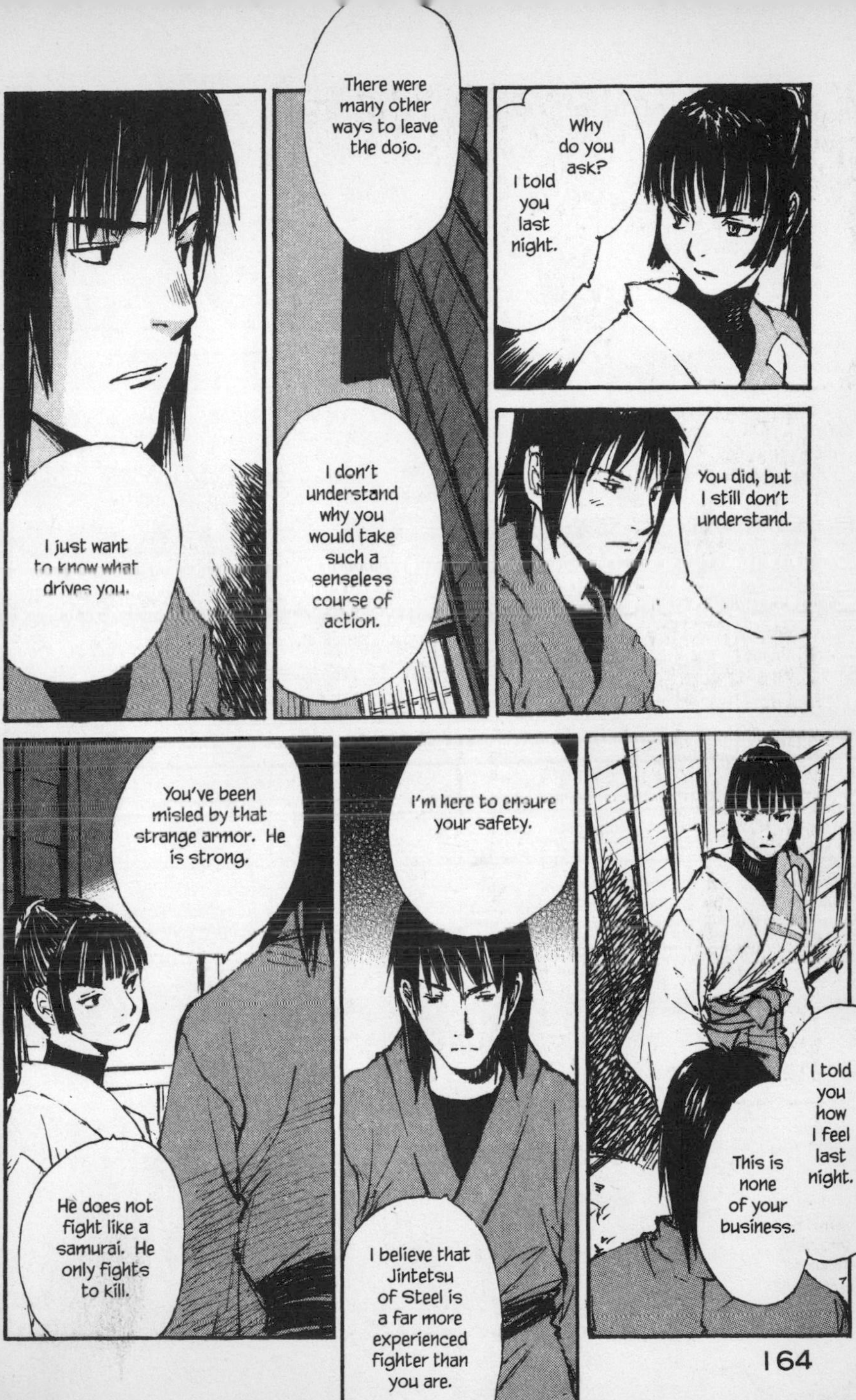
Why do you ask?
I told you last night.
You did, but I still don't understand.
There were many other ways to leave the dojo.
I don't understand why you would take such a senseless course of action.
I just want to know what drives you.
I told you how I feel last night.
This is none of your business.
I'm here to ensure your safety.
I believe that Jintetsu of Steel is a far more experienced fighter than you are.
You've been misled by that strange armor. He is strong.
He does not fight like a samurai. He only fights to kill.

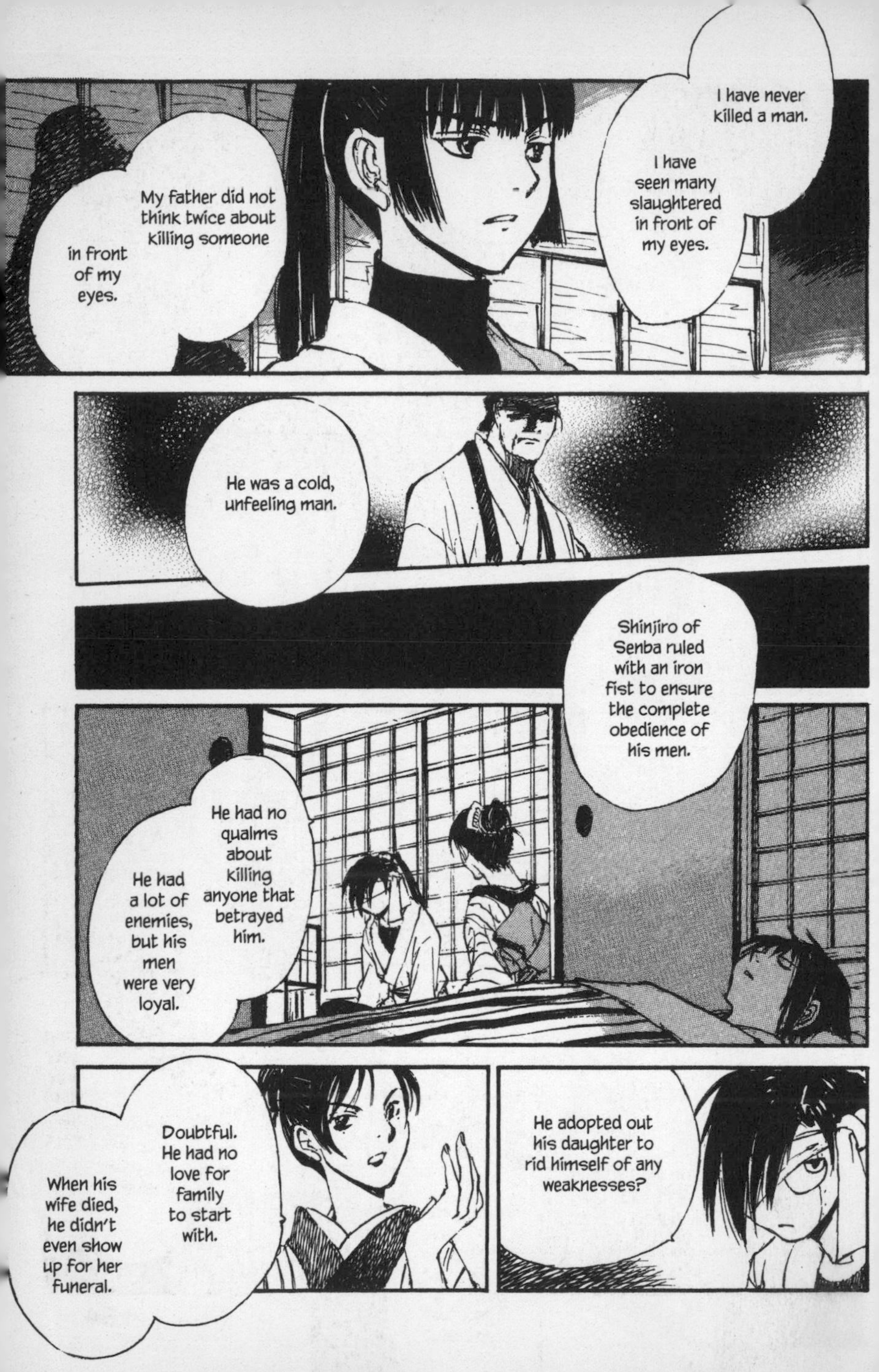
I have never killed a man.
I have seen many slaughtered in front of my eyes.
My father did not think twice about killing someone
in front of my eyes.
He was a cold, unfeeling man.
Shinjiro of Senba ruled with an iron fist to ensure the complete obedience of his men.
He had no qualms about killing anyone that betrayed him.
He had a lot of enemies, but his men were very loyal.
He adopted out his daughter to rid himself of any weaknesses?
Doubtful. He had no love for family to start with.
When his wife died, he didn't even show up for her funeral.

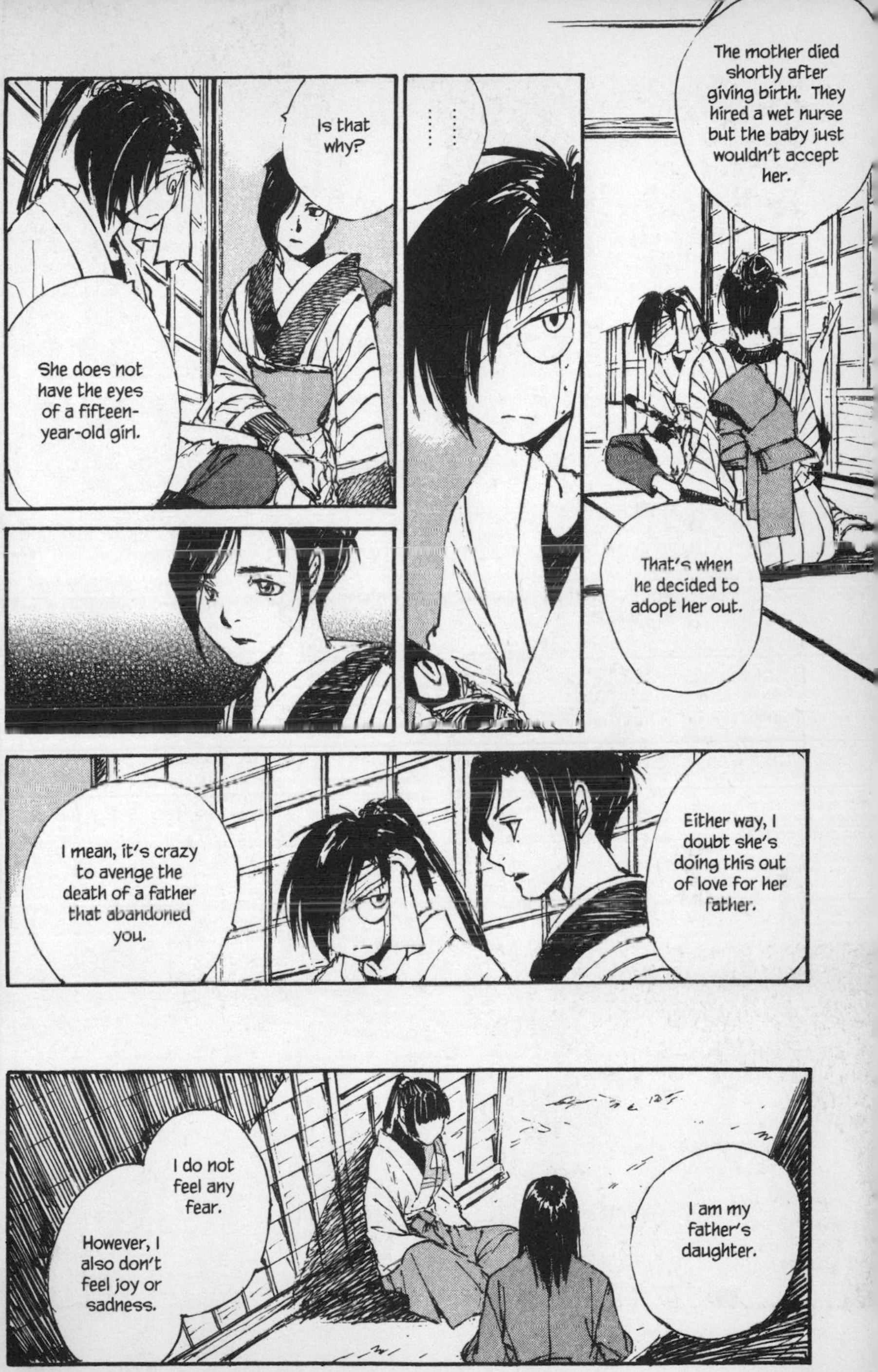
The mother died shortly after giving birth. They hired a wet nurse but the baby just wouldn't accept her.
That's when he decided to adopt her out.
......
Is that why?
She does not have the eyes of a fifteen-year-old girl.
Either way, I doubt she's doing this out of love for her father.
I mean, it's crazy to avenge the death of a father that abandoned you.
I am my father's daughter.
I do not feel any fear.
However, I also don't feel joy or sadness.

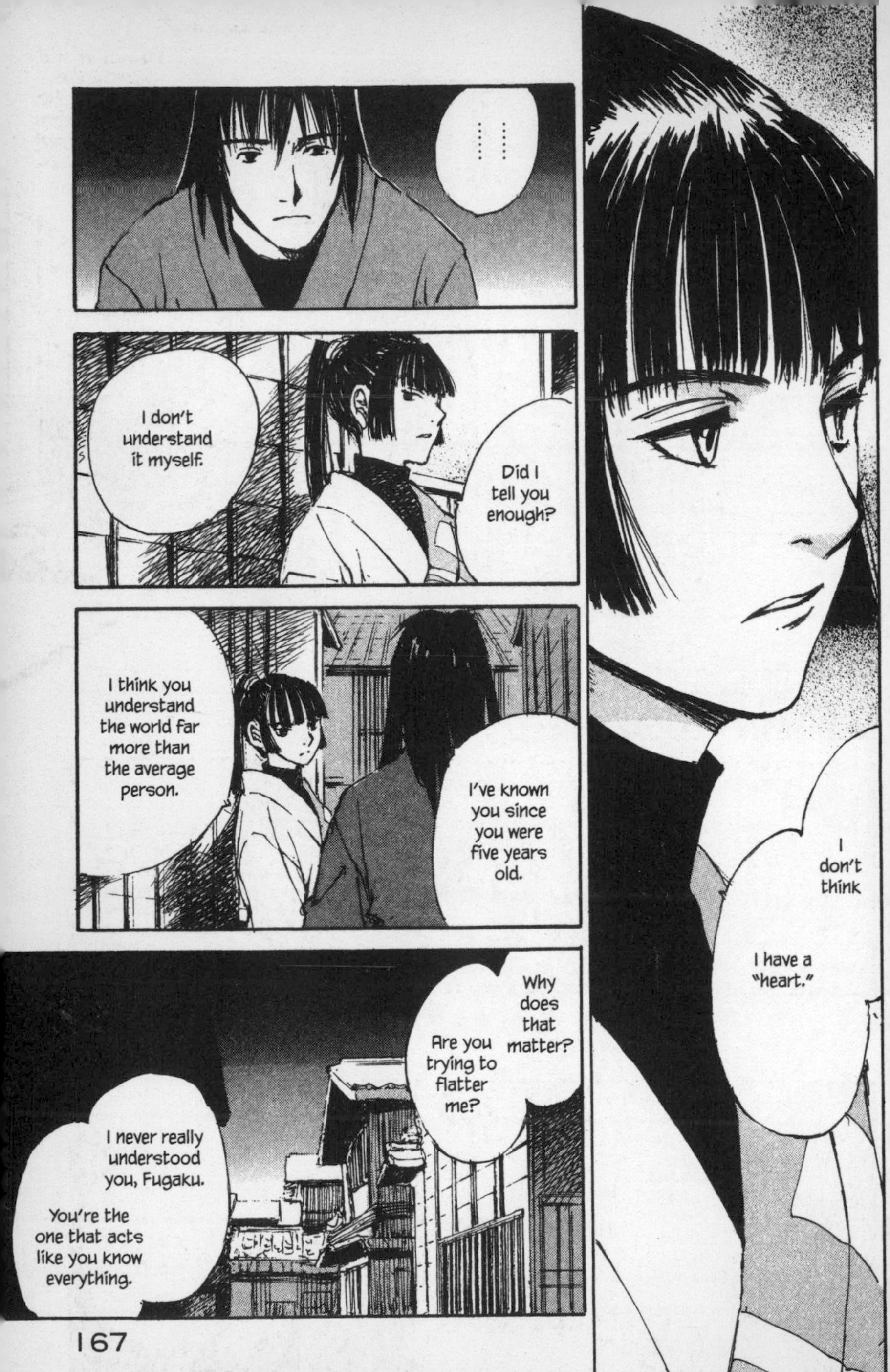
I don't think
I have a "heart."
......
Did I tell you enough?
I don't understand it myself.
I've known you since you were five years old.
I think you understand the world far more than the average person.
Why does that matter?
Are you trying to flatter me?
I never really understood you, Fugaku.
You're the one that acts like you know everything.

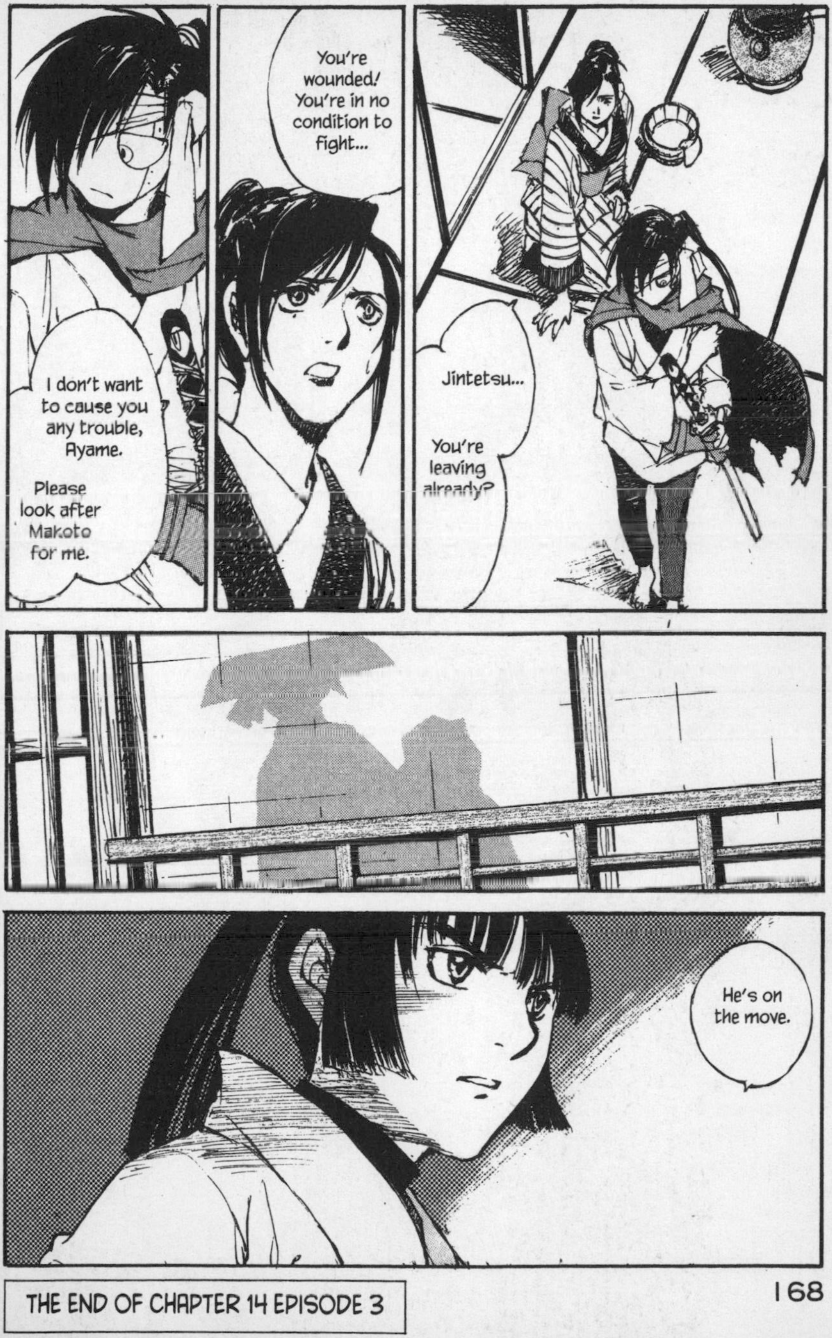
Jintetsu...
You're leaving already?
You're wounded! You're in no condition to fight...
I don't want to cause you any trouble, Ayame.
Please look after Makoto for me.
He's on the move.

THE END OF CHAPTER 14 EPISODE 3

第十四幕
CHASER
よる
(迷走の青い宵)
—第四景—
(Blue Dusk Wanderings)
Chapter 14 Episode 4

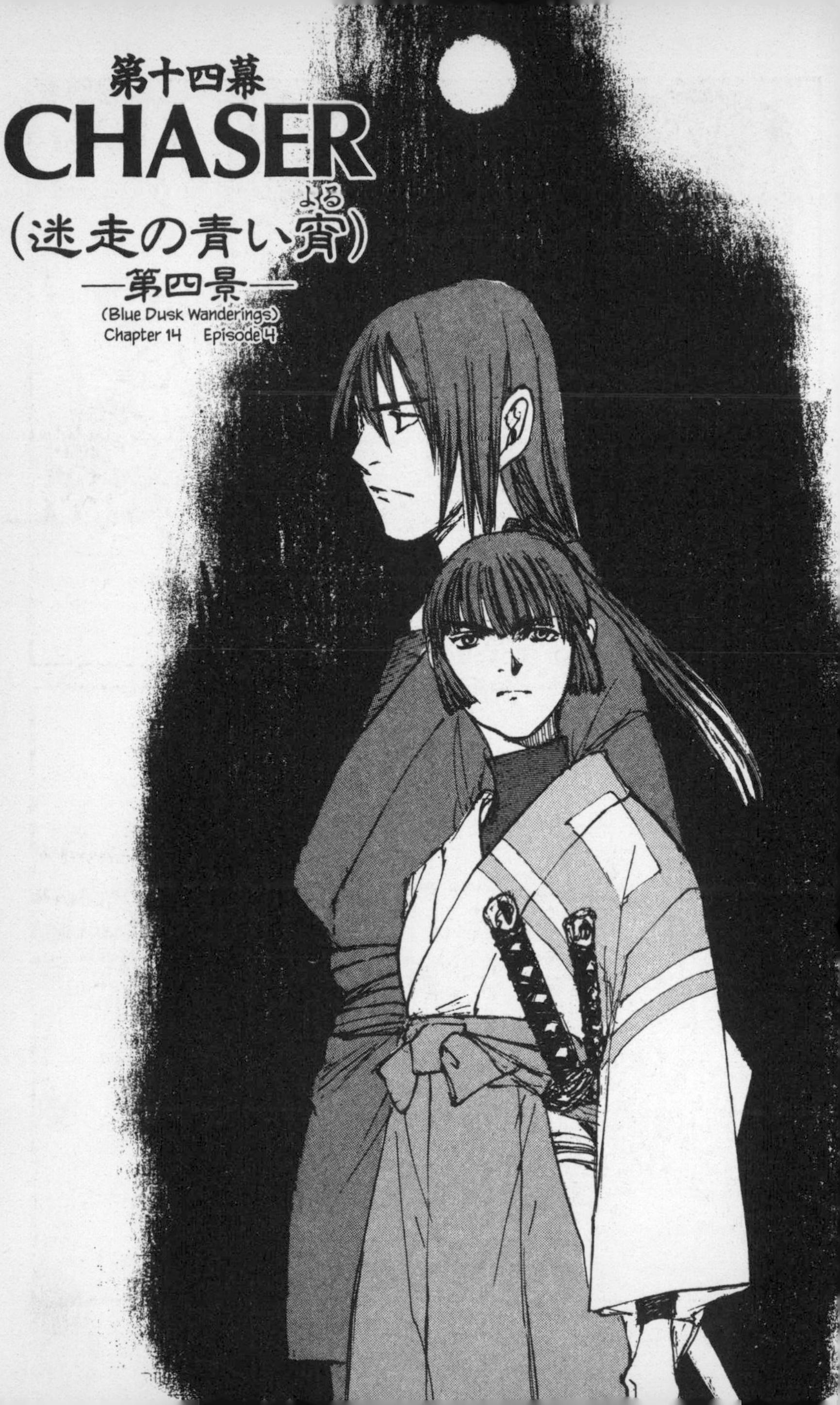

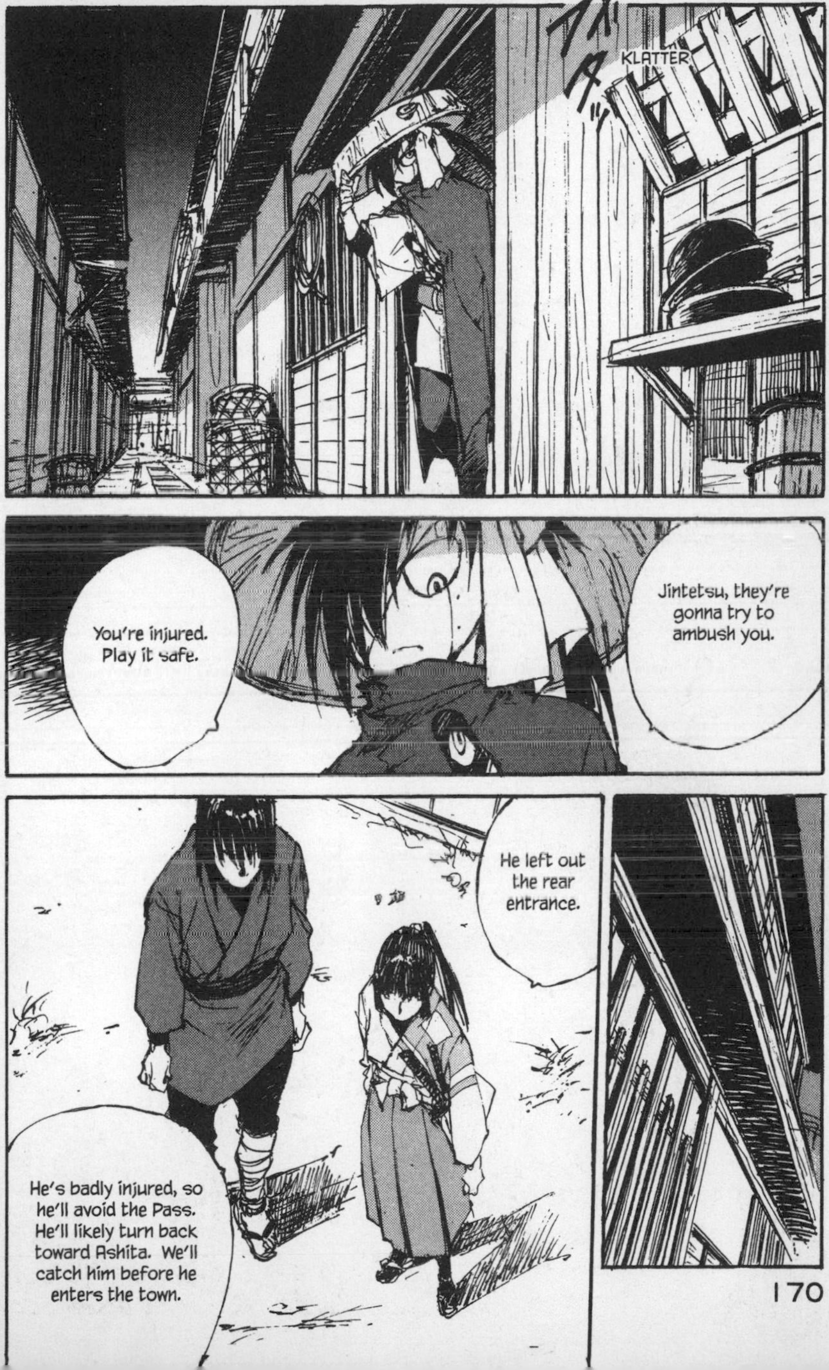
KLATTER
Jintetsu, they're gonna try to ambush you.
You're injured. Play it safe.
He left out the rear entrance.
He's badly injured, so he'll avoid the Pass. He'll likely turn back toward Ashita. We'll catch him before he enters the town.

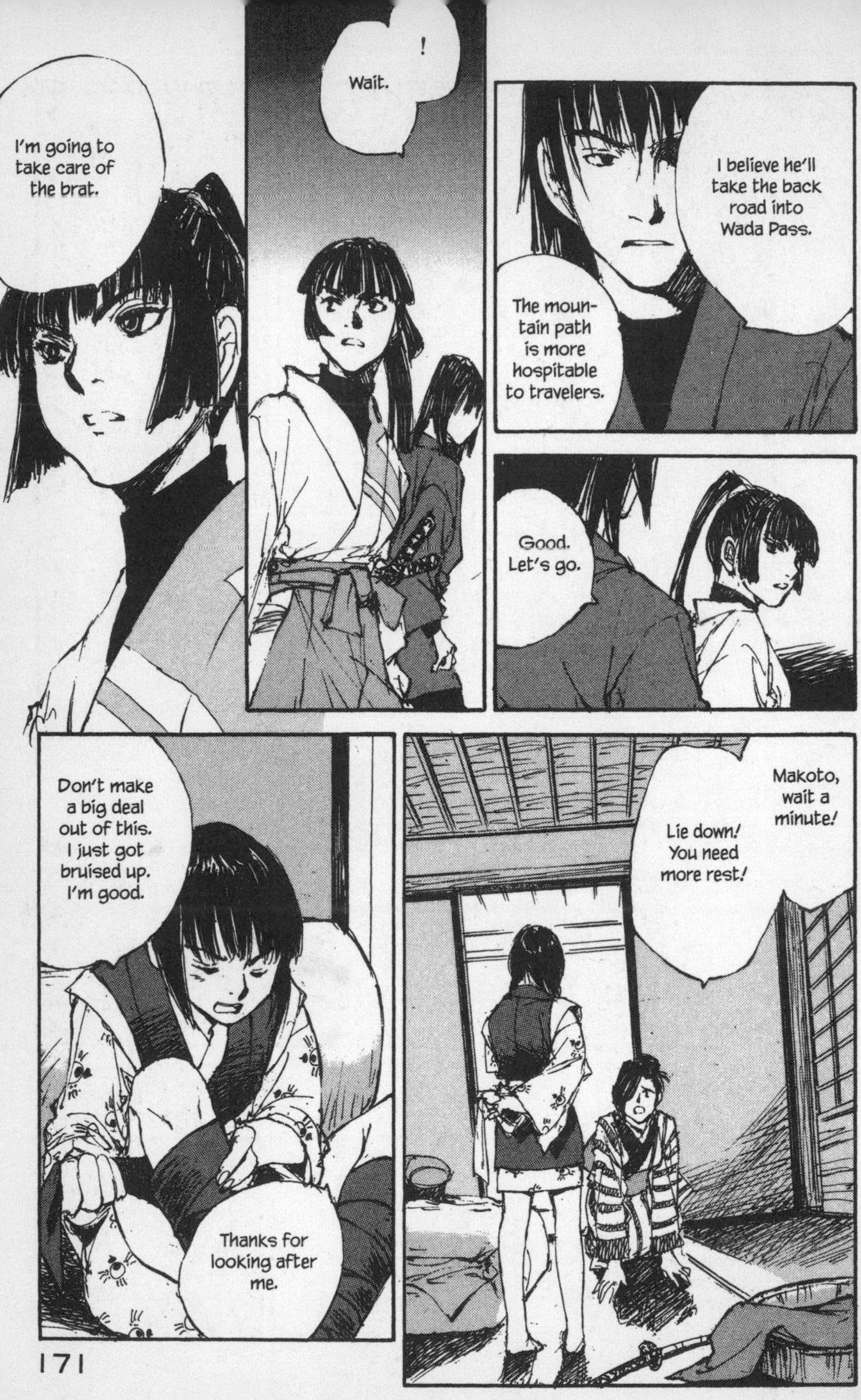
I believe he'll take the back road into Wada Pass.
The moun-tain path is more hospitable to travelers.
Good. Let's go.
!
Wait.
I'm going to take care of the brat.
Makoto, wait a minute!
Lie down! You need more rest!
Don't make a big deal out of this. I just got bruised up. I'm good.
Thanks for looking after me.

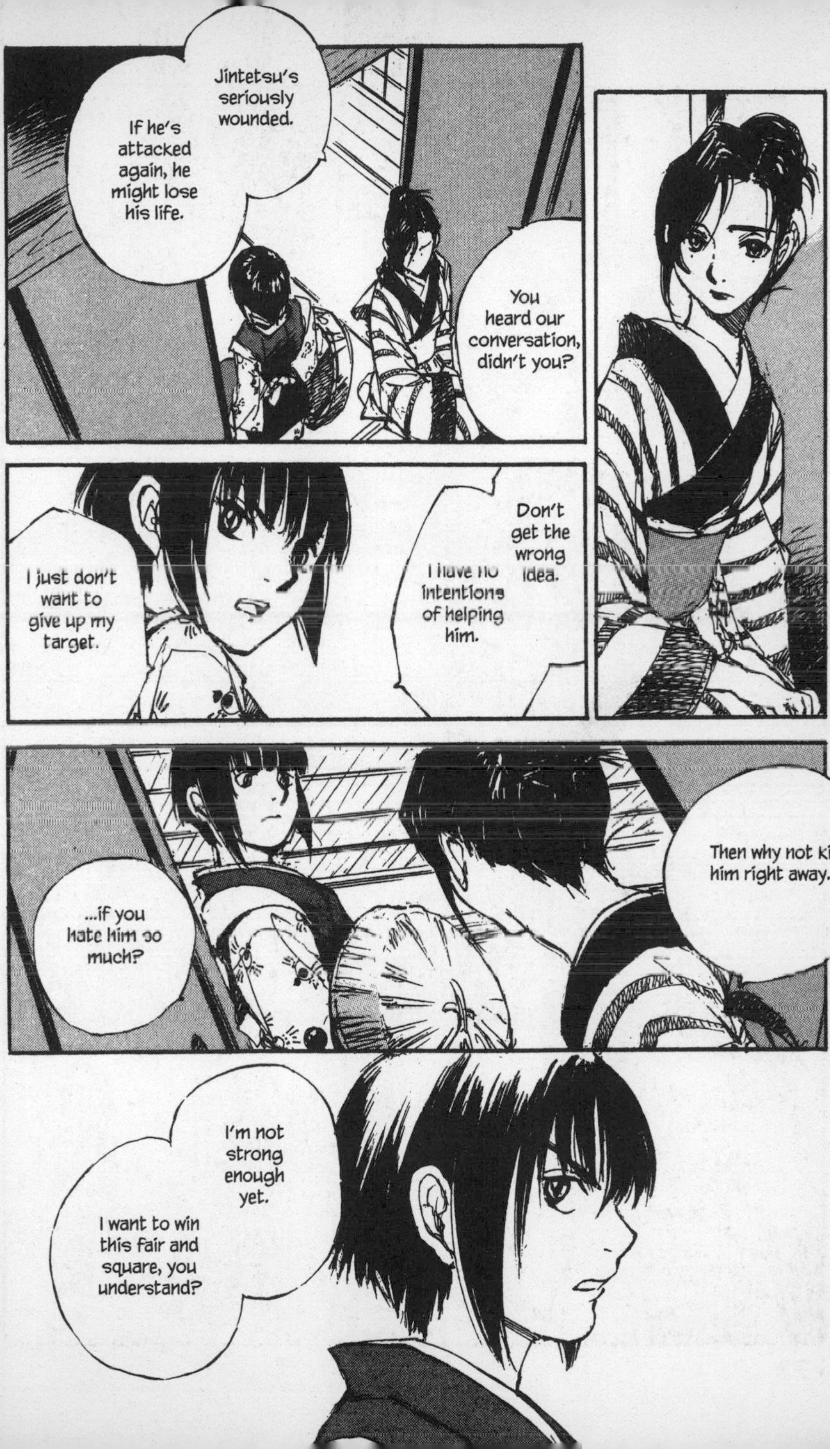
Jintetsu's seriously wounded.
If he's attacked again, he might lose his life.
You heard our conversation, didn't you?
Don't get the wrong idea.
I have no intentions of helping him.
I just don't want to give up my target.
Then why not kill him right away...
...if you hate him so much?
I'm not strong enough yet.
I want to win this fair and square, you understand?

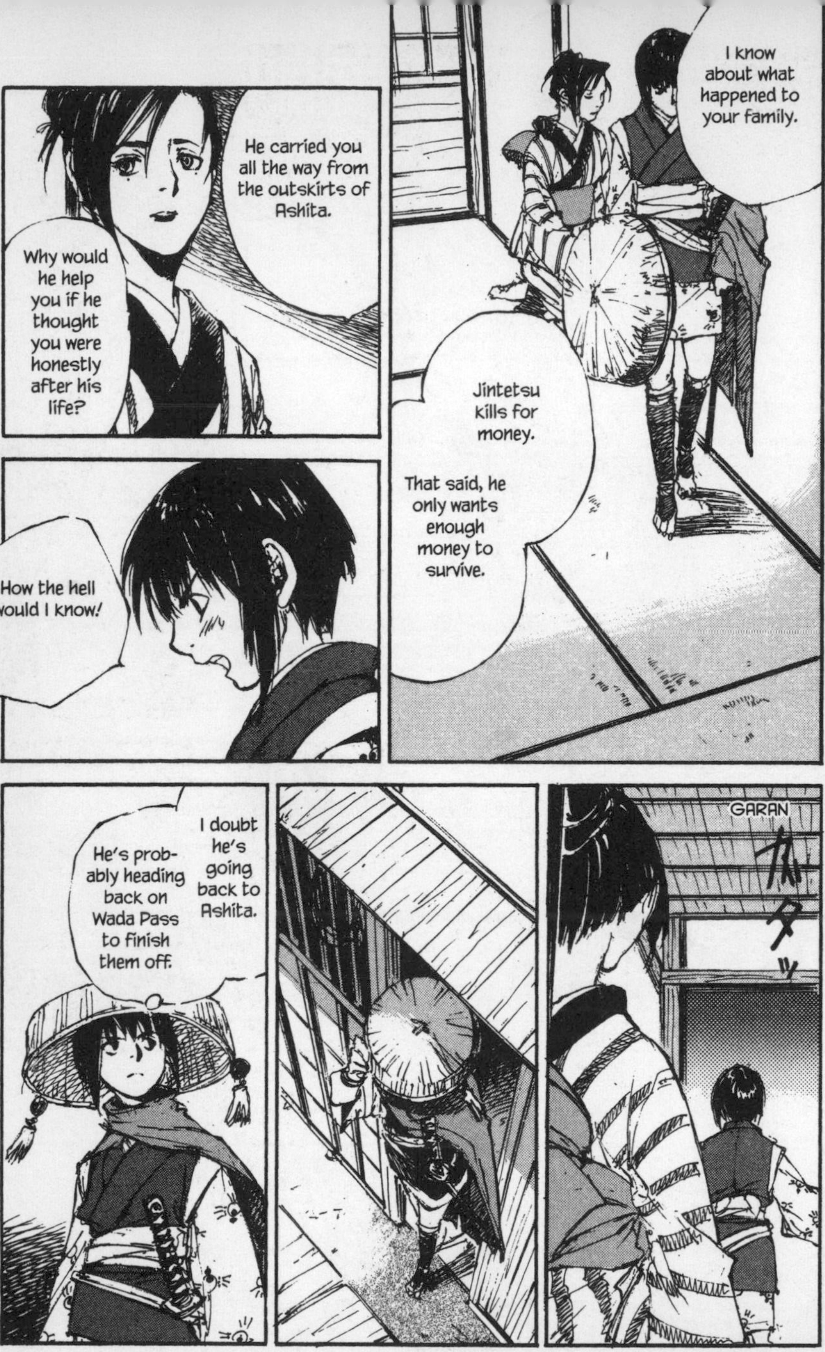

I know about what happened to your family.
Jintetsu kills for money.
That said, he only wants enough money to survive.
He carried you all the way from the outskirts of Ashita.
Why would he help you if he thought you were honestly after his life?
How the hell would I know!
GARAN
I doubt he's going back to Ashita.
He's probably heading back on Wada Pass to finish them off.

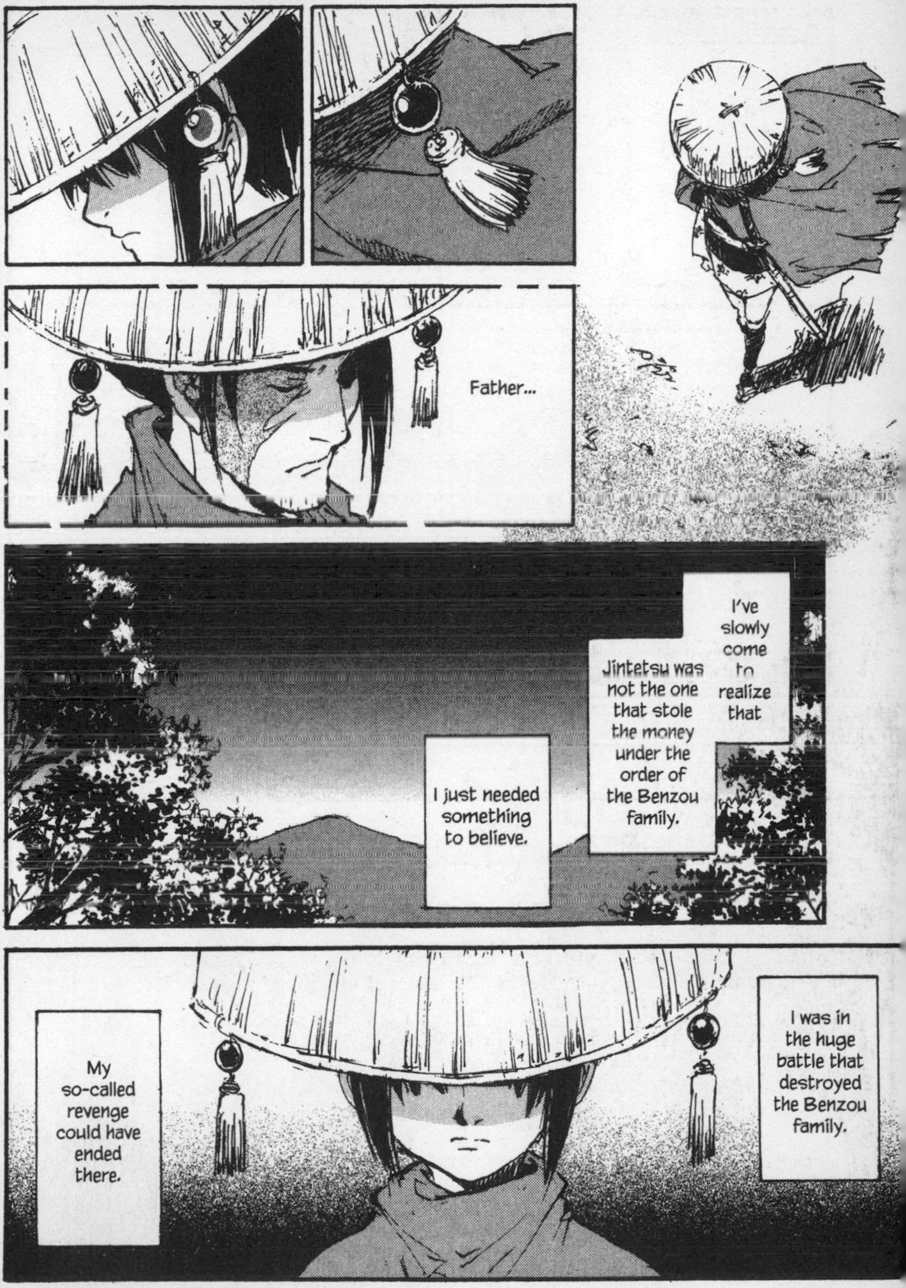
Father...
I've slowly come to realize that
Jintetsu was not the one that stole the money under the order of the Benzou family.
I just needed something to believe.
I was in the huge battle that destroyed the Benzou family.
My so-called revenge could have ended there.

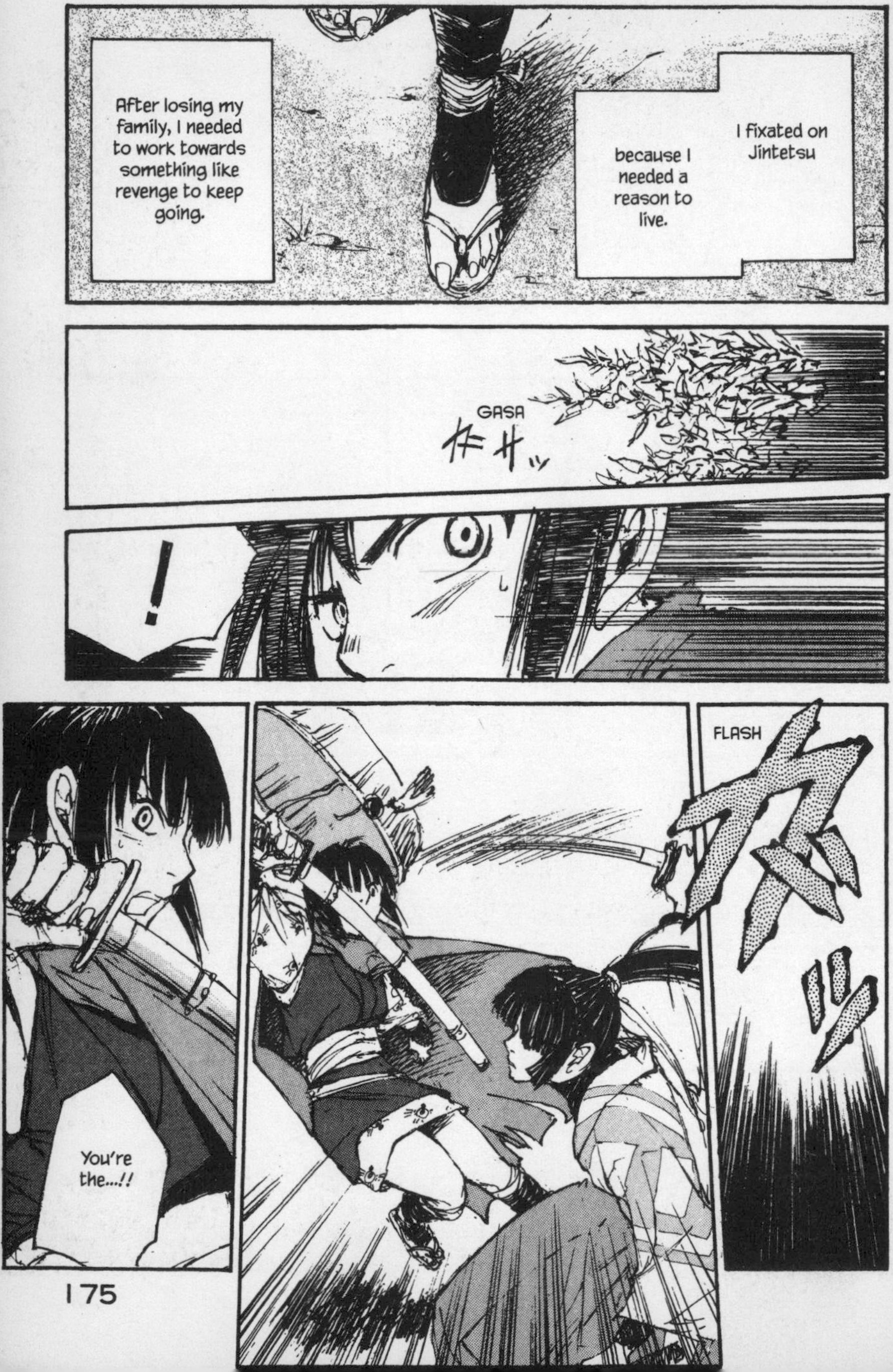
I fixated on Jintetsu
because I needed a reason to live.
After losing my family, I needed to work towards something like revenge to keep going.
GASA
!
FLASH
You're the...!!

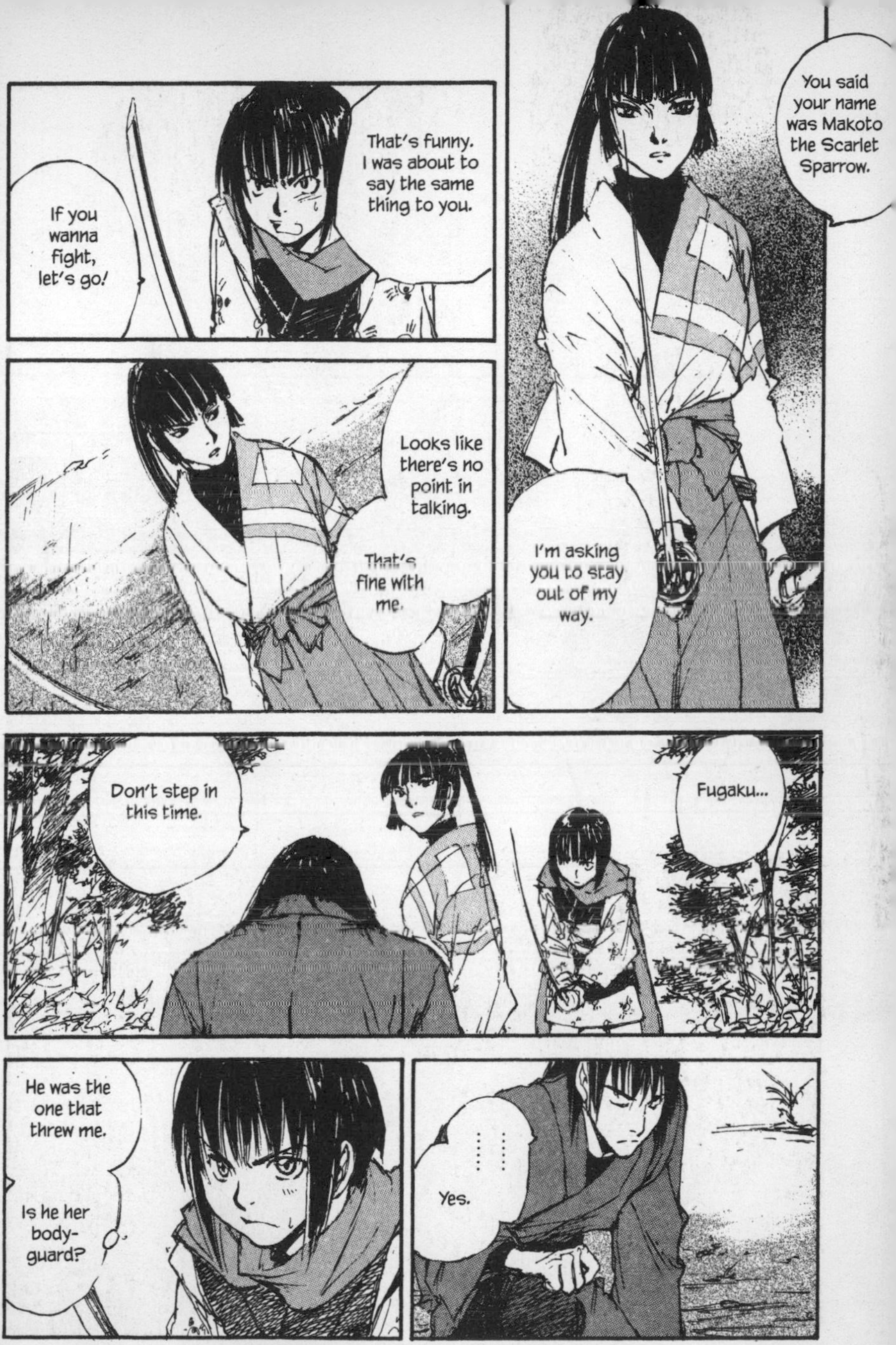
You said your name was Makoto the Scarlet Sparrow.
I'm asking you to stay out of my way.
That's funny. I was about to say the same thing to you.
If you wanna fight, let's go!
Looks like there's no point in talking.
That's fine with me.
Fugaku...
Don't step in this time.
......
Yes.
He was the one that threw me.
Is he her bodyguard?

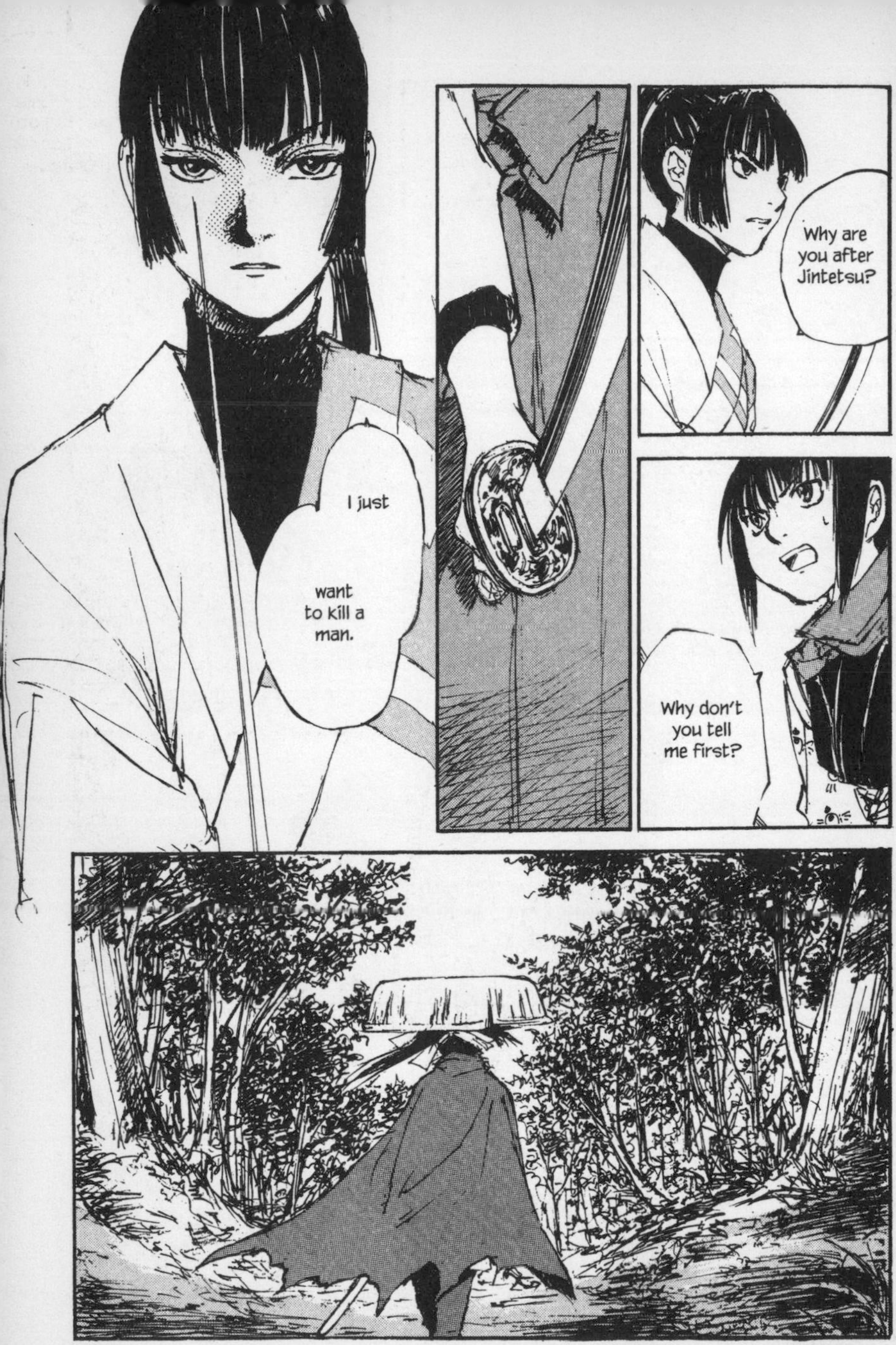
Why are you after Jintetsu?
Why don't you tell me first?
I just
want to kill a man.

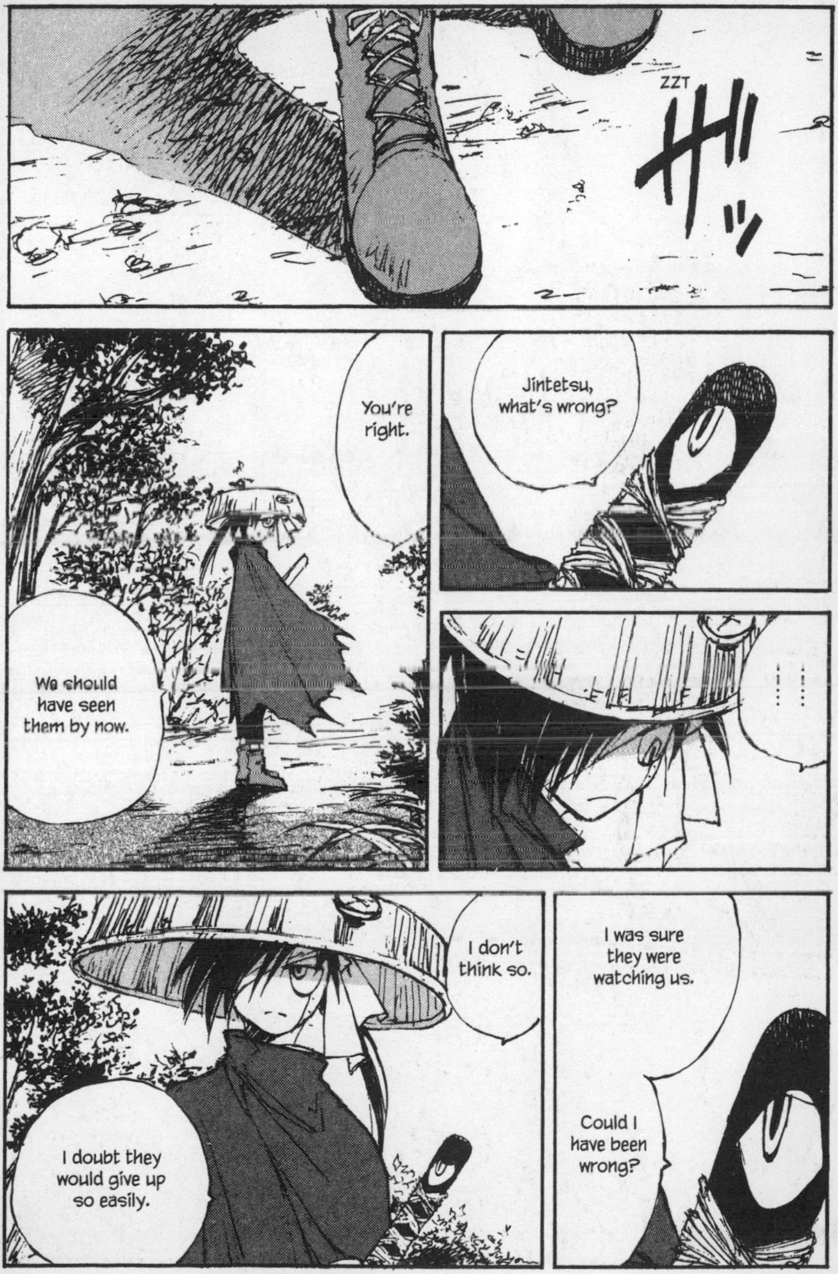
ZZT
ザッ
Jintetsu, what's wrong?
......
You're right.
We should have seen them by now.
I was sure they were watching us.
Could I have been wrong?
I don't think so.
I doubt they would give up so easily.

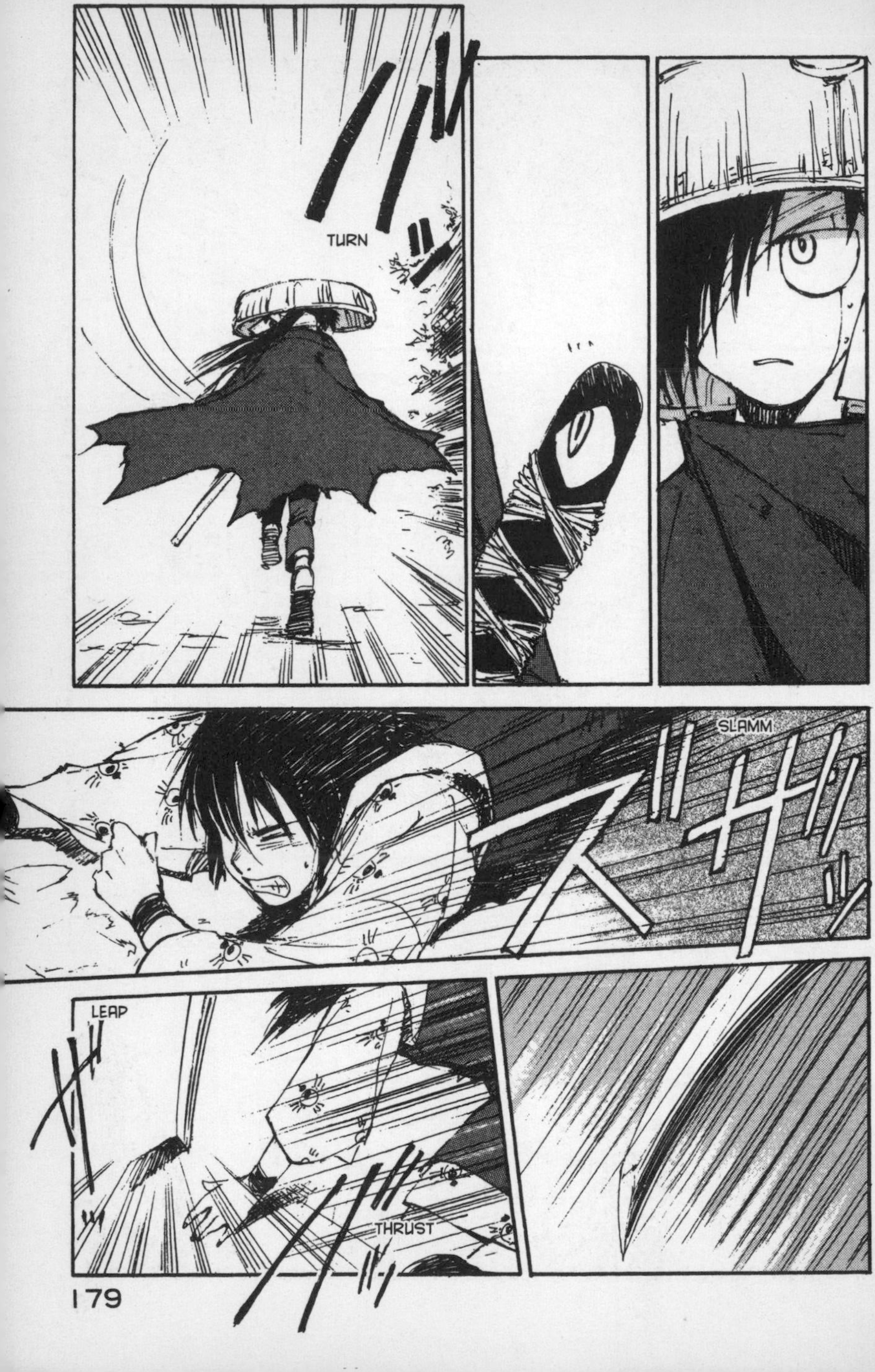
TURN
SLAMM
THRUST
LEAP

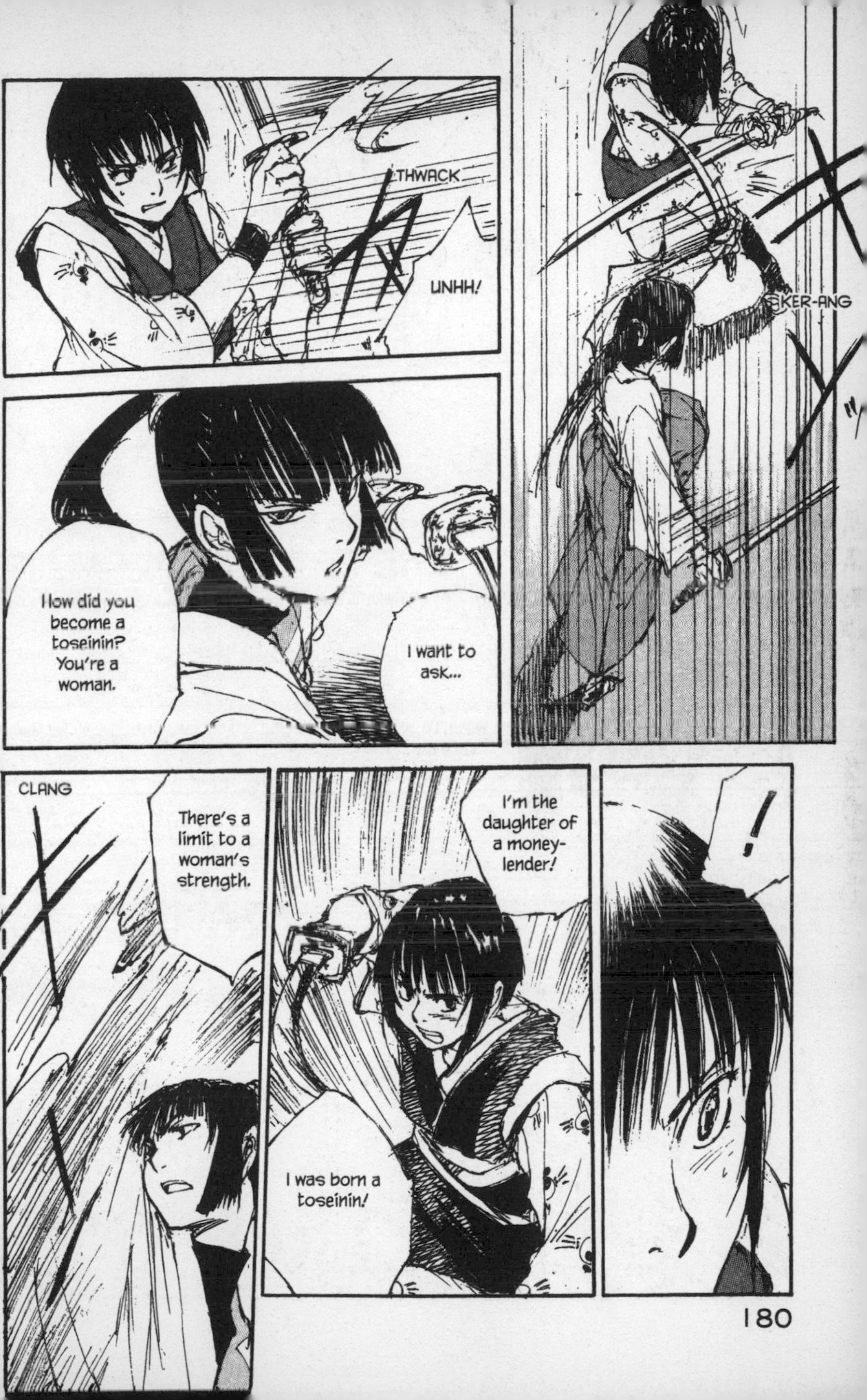
SKER-ANG
THWACK
UNHH!
I want to ask...
How did you become a toseinin? You're a woman.
!
I'm the daughter of a money-lender!
I was born a toseinin!
CLANG
There's a limit to a woman's strength.

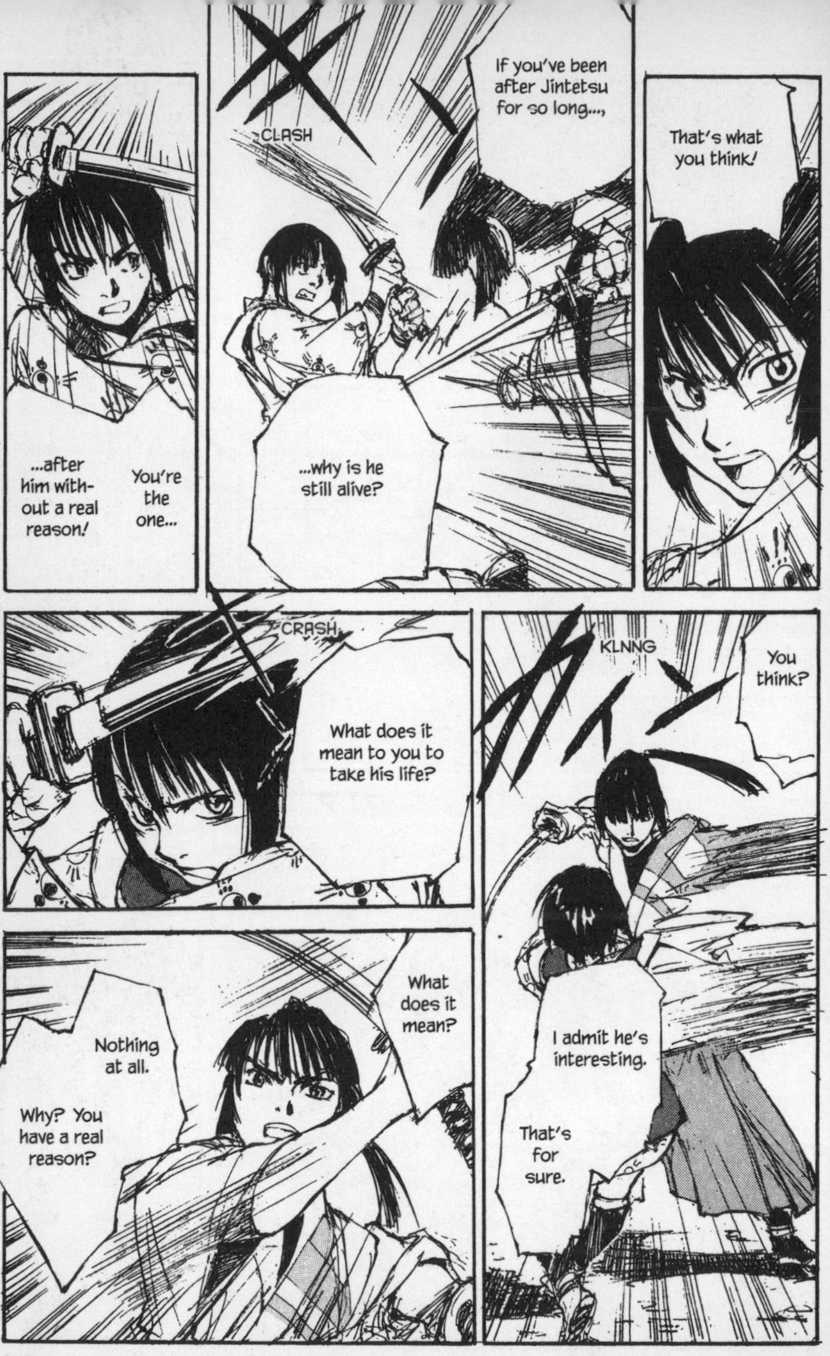
That's what you think!
If you've been after Jintetsu for so long...,
CLASH
...why is he still alive?
You're the one...
...after him with-out a real reason!
KLNNG
You think?
CRASH
What does it mean to you to take his life?
I admit he's interesting.
That's for sure.
What does it mean?
Nothing at all.
Why? You have a real reason?

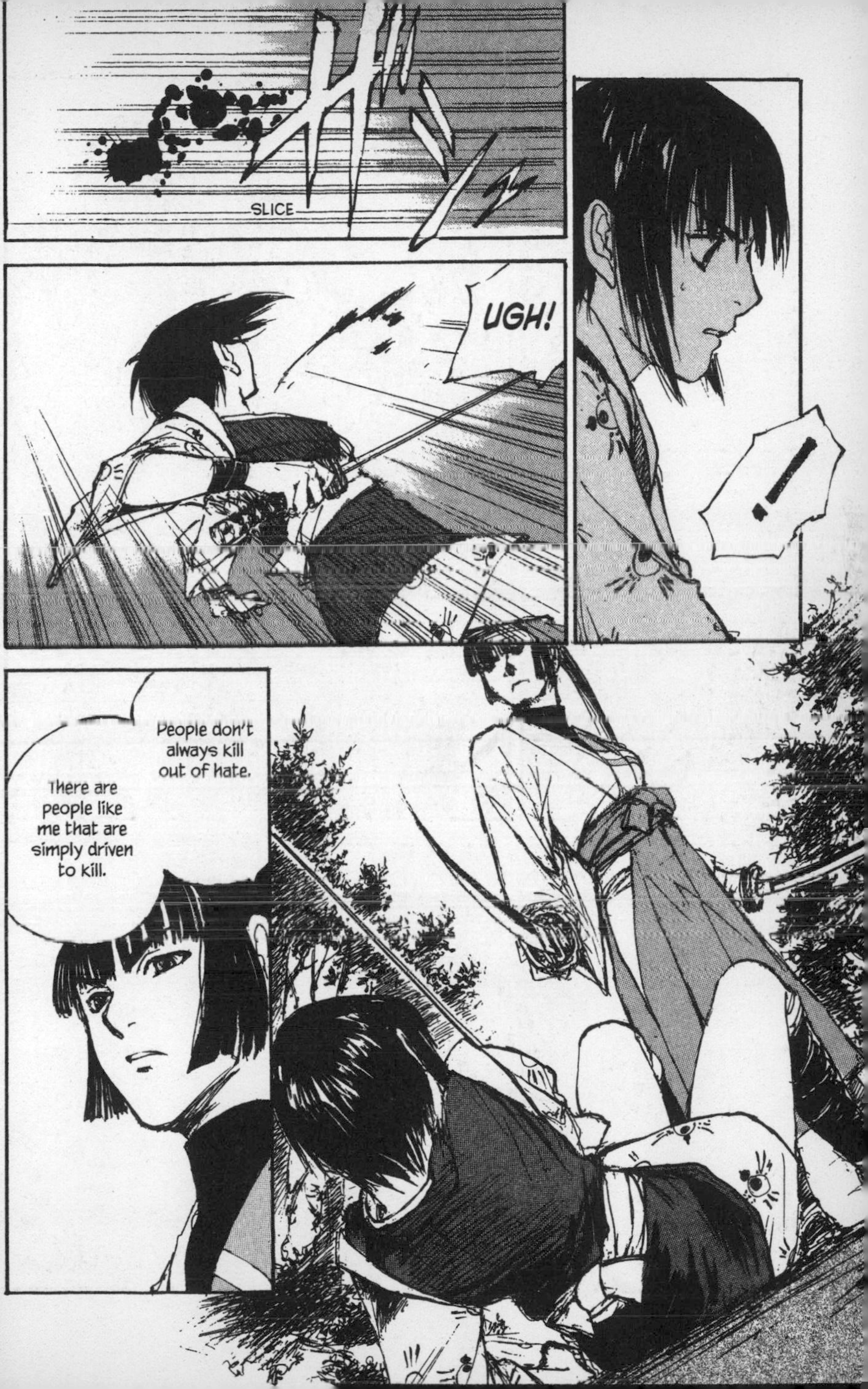
!
SLICE
UGH!
People don't always kill out of hate.
There are people like me that are simply driven to kill.

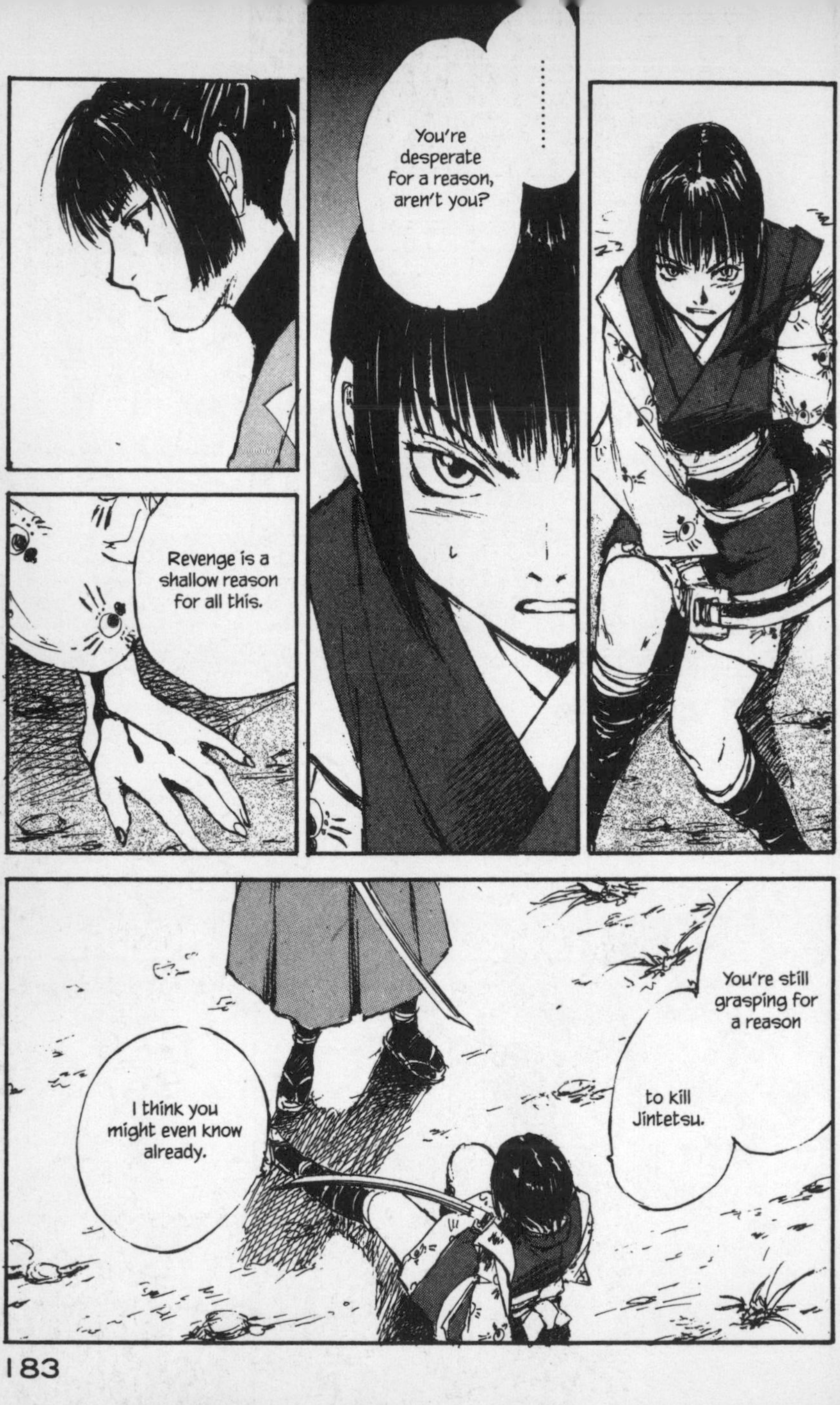
……
You're desperate for a reason, aren't you?
Revenge is a shallow reason for all this.
You're still grasping for a reason
to kill Jintetsu.
I think you might even know already.

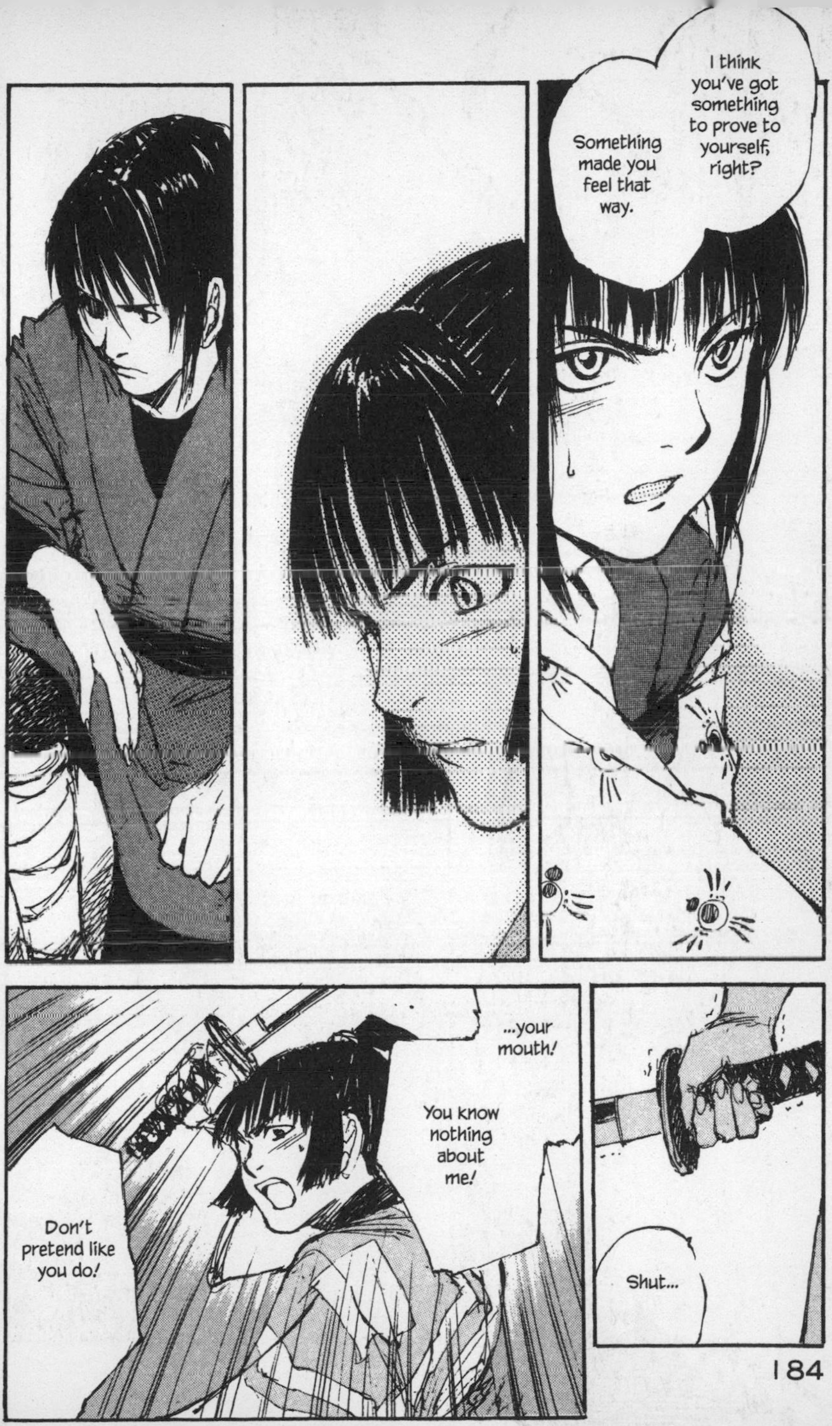
I think you've got something to prove to yourself, right?
Something made you feel that way.
Shut...
...your mouth!
You know nothing about me!
Don't pretend like you do!

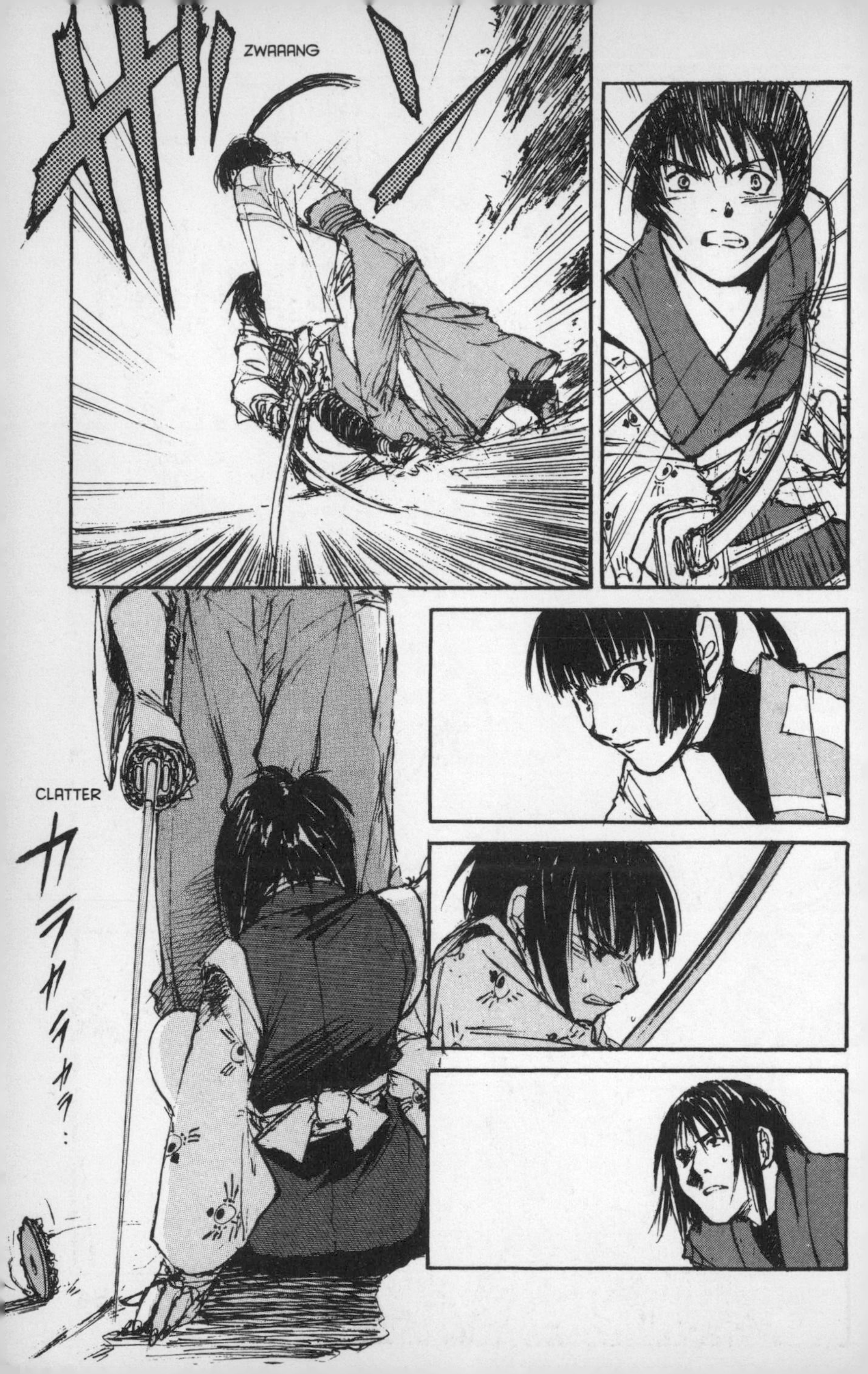
ZWAAANG
CLATTER

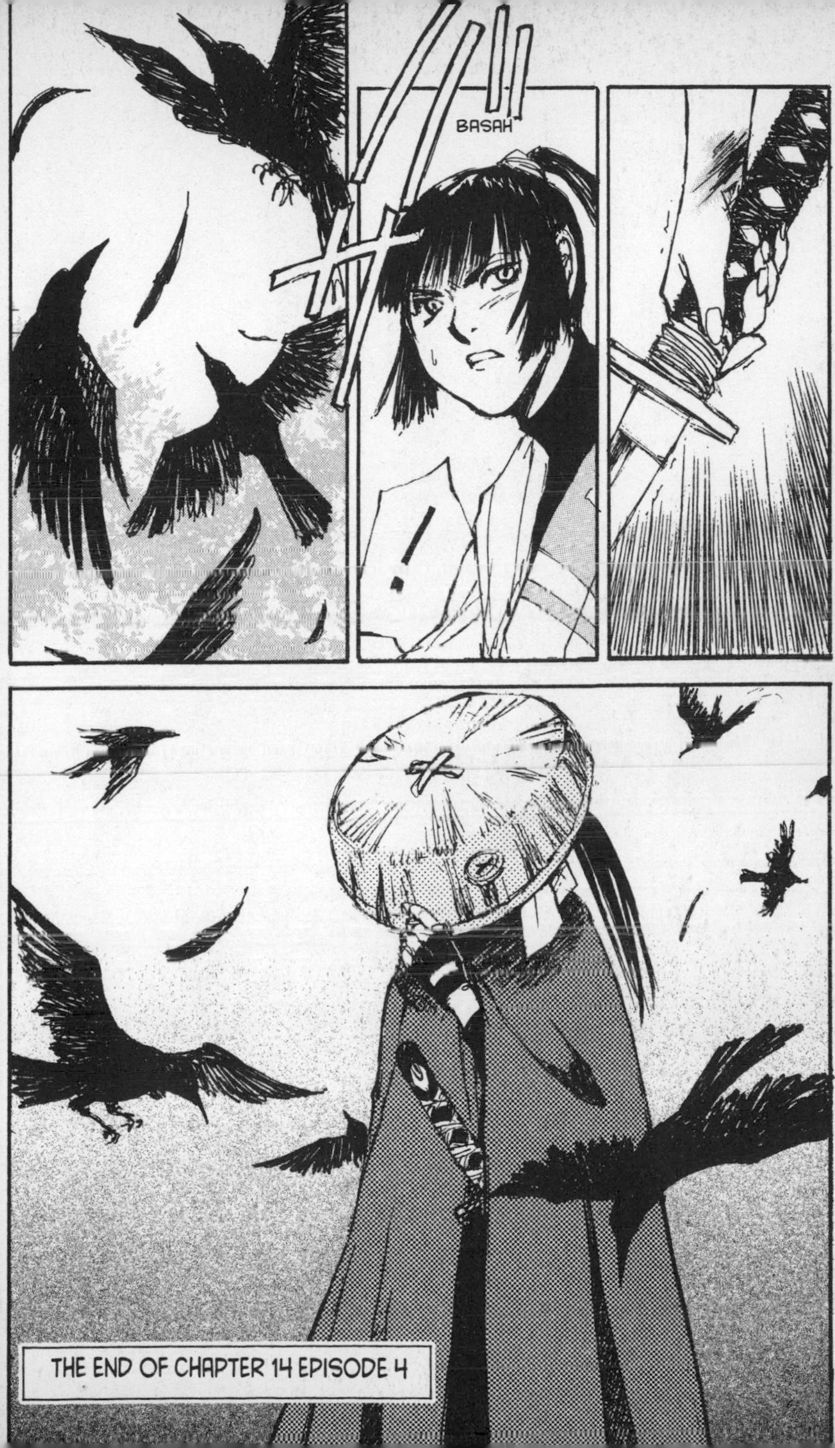
BASAH
!
THE END OF CHAPTER 14 EPISODE 4

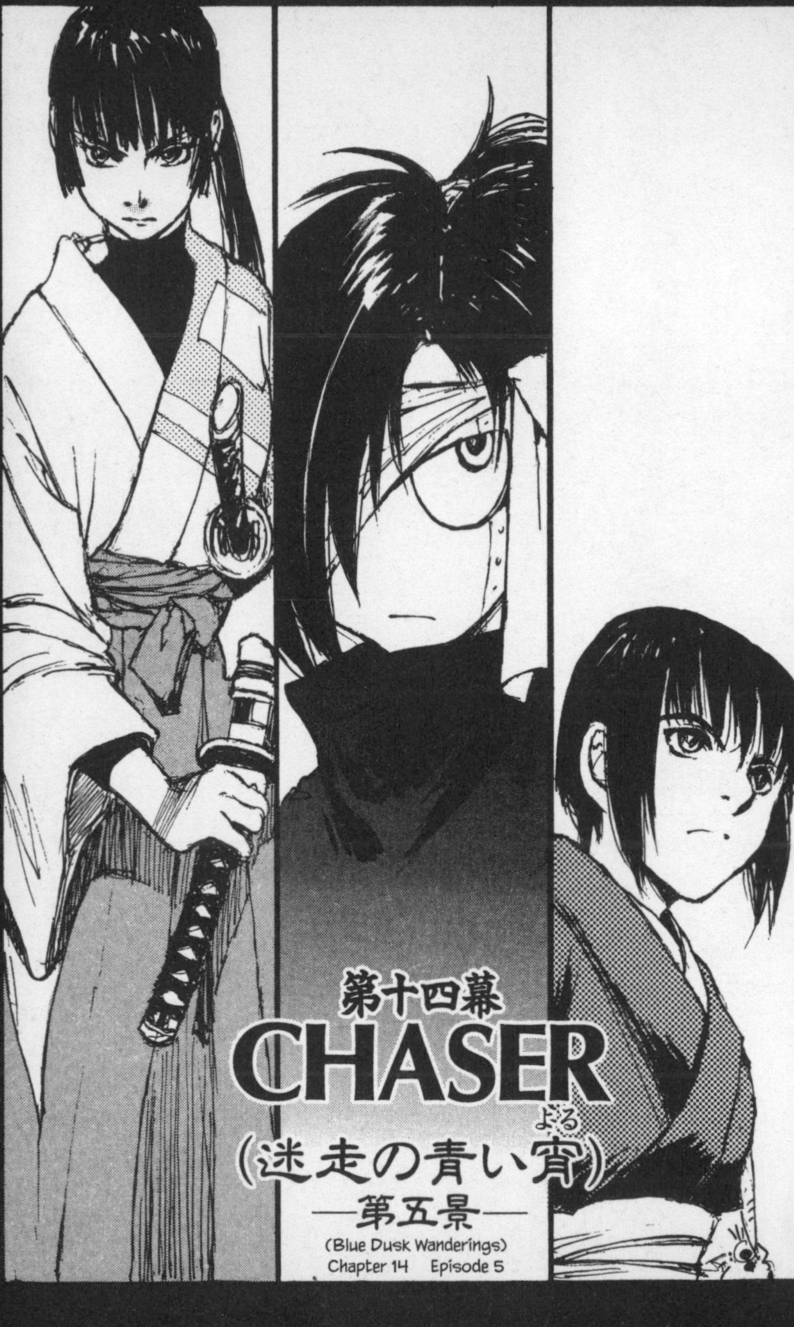
第十四幕
CHASER
(迷走の青い宵)
よる
—第五景—
(Blue Dusk Wanderings)
Chapter 14 Episode 5

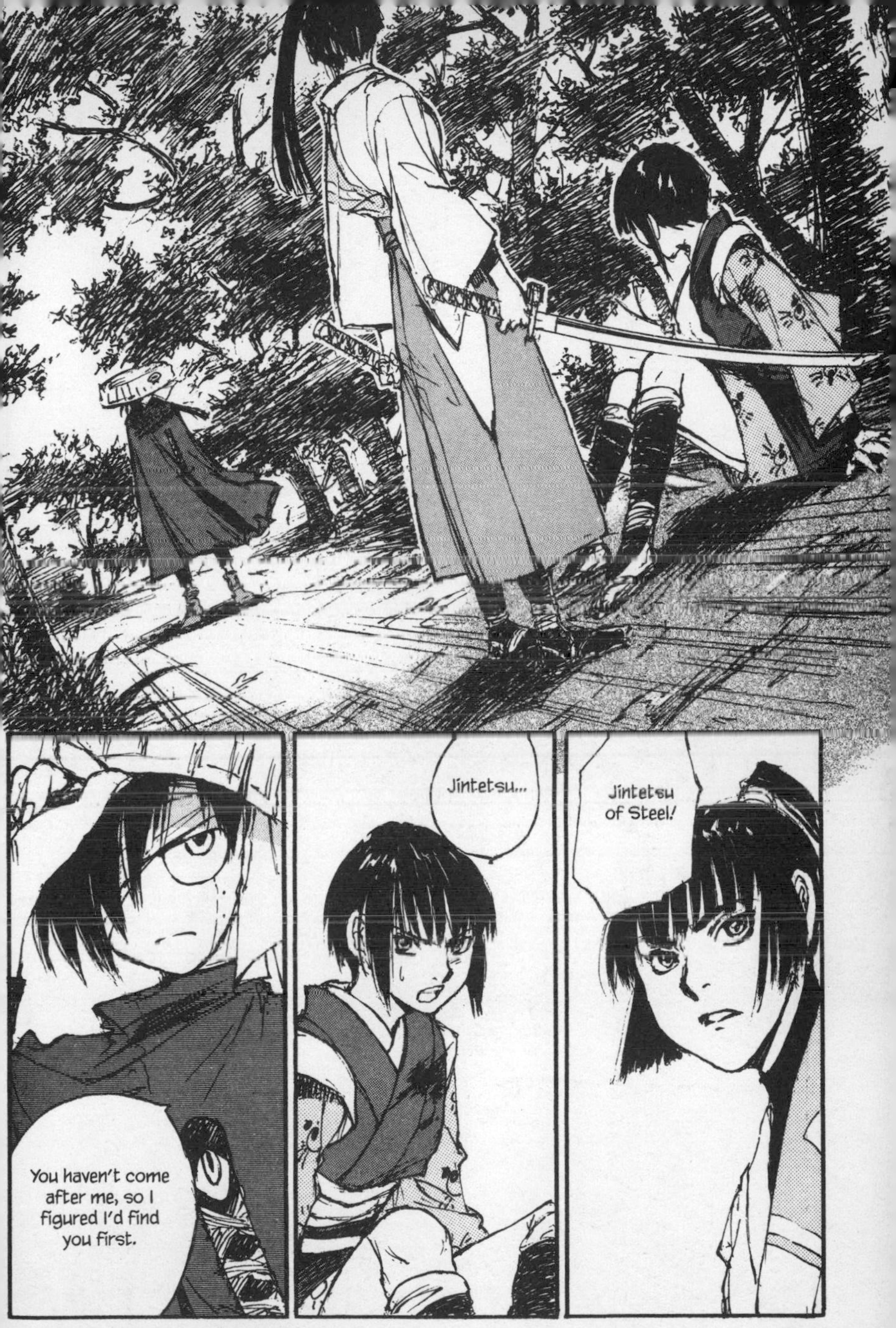
Jintetsu of Steel!
Jintetsu...
You haven't come after me, so I figured I'd find you first.

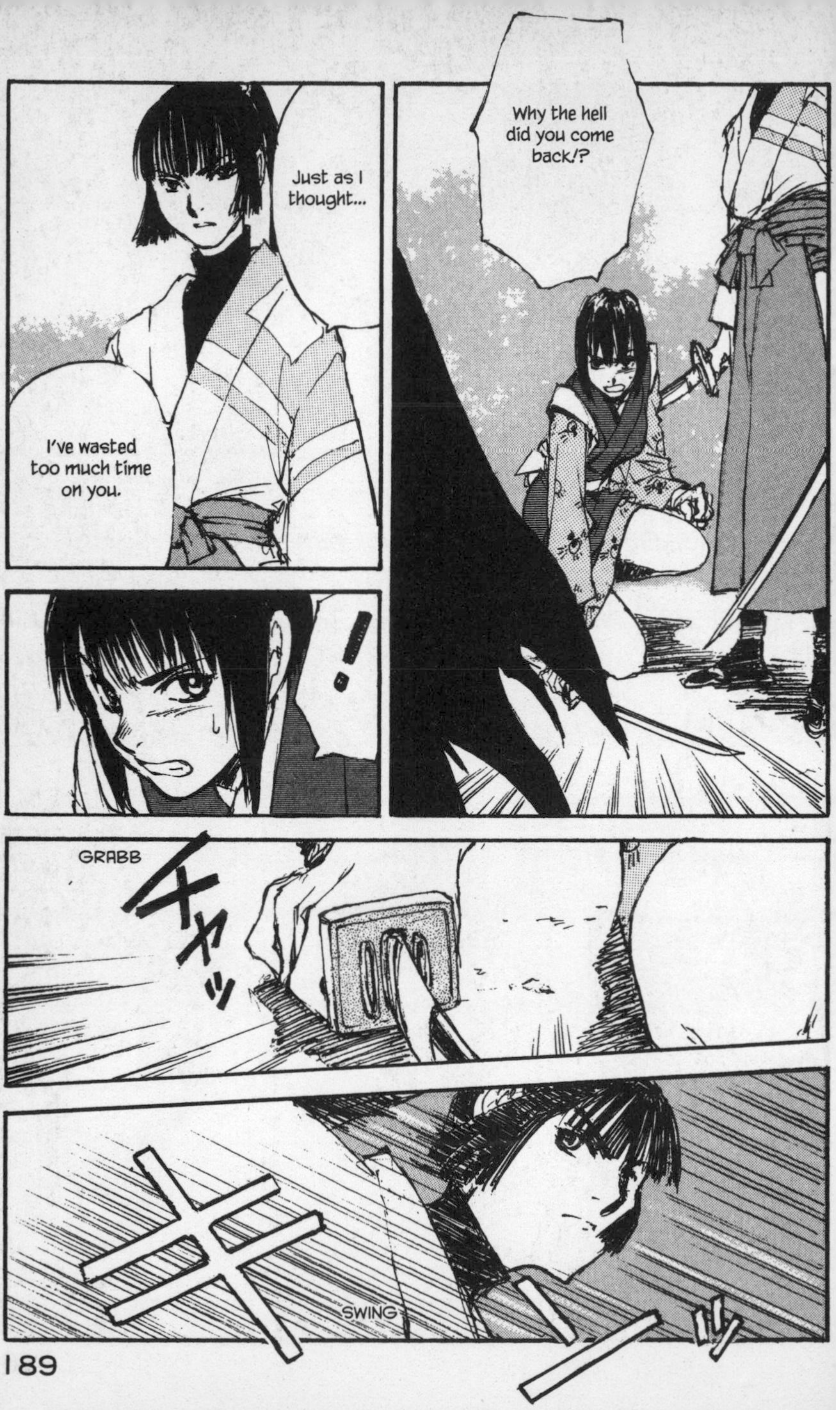
Why the hell did you come back!?
Just as I thought...
I've wasted too much time on you.
!
GRABB
SWING

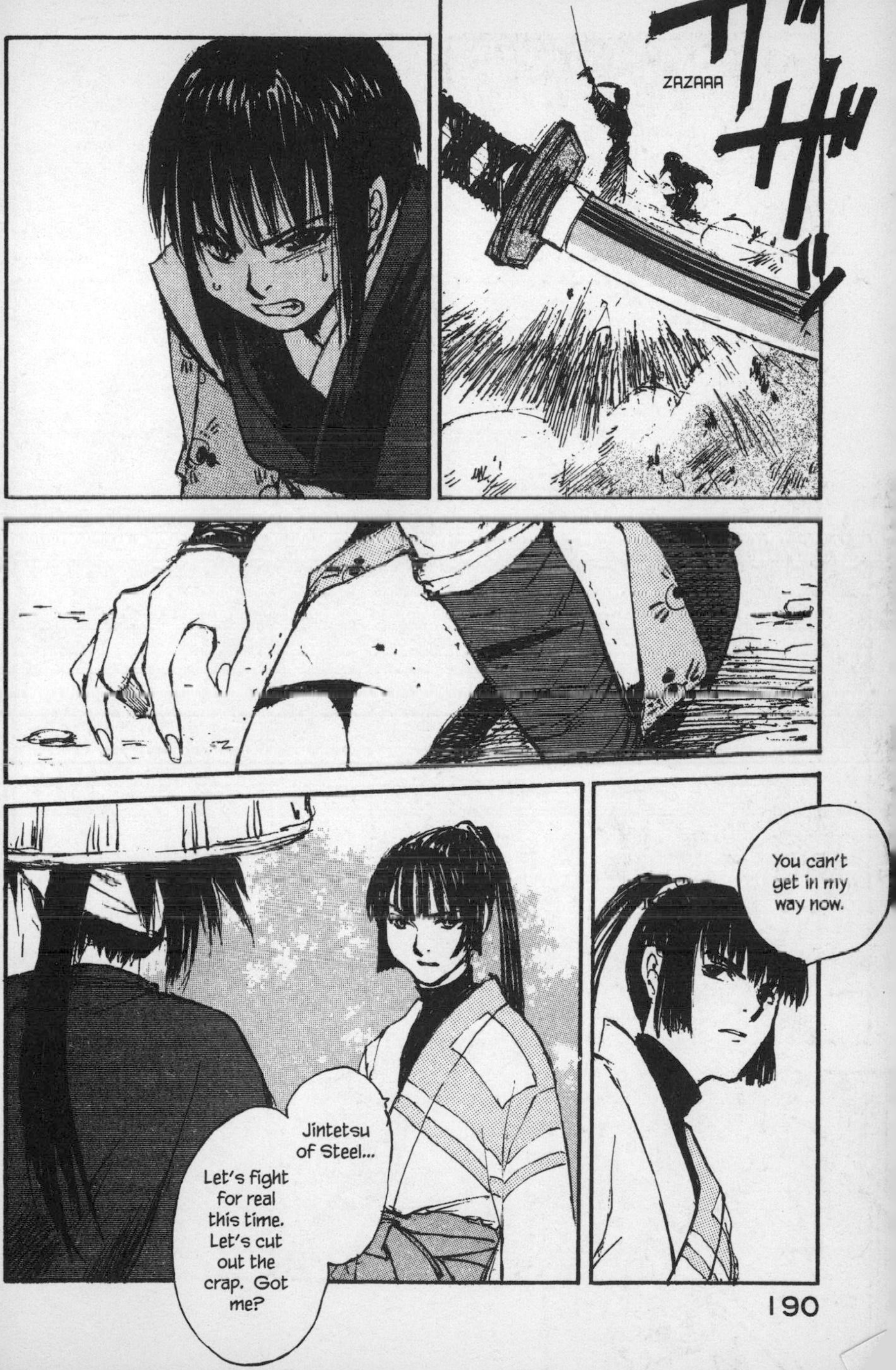
ZAZAAA
You can't get in my way now.
Jintetsu of Steel...
Let's fight for real this time. Let's cut out the crap. Got me?

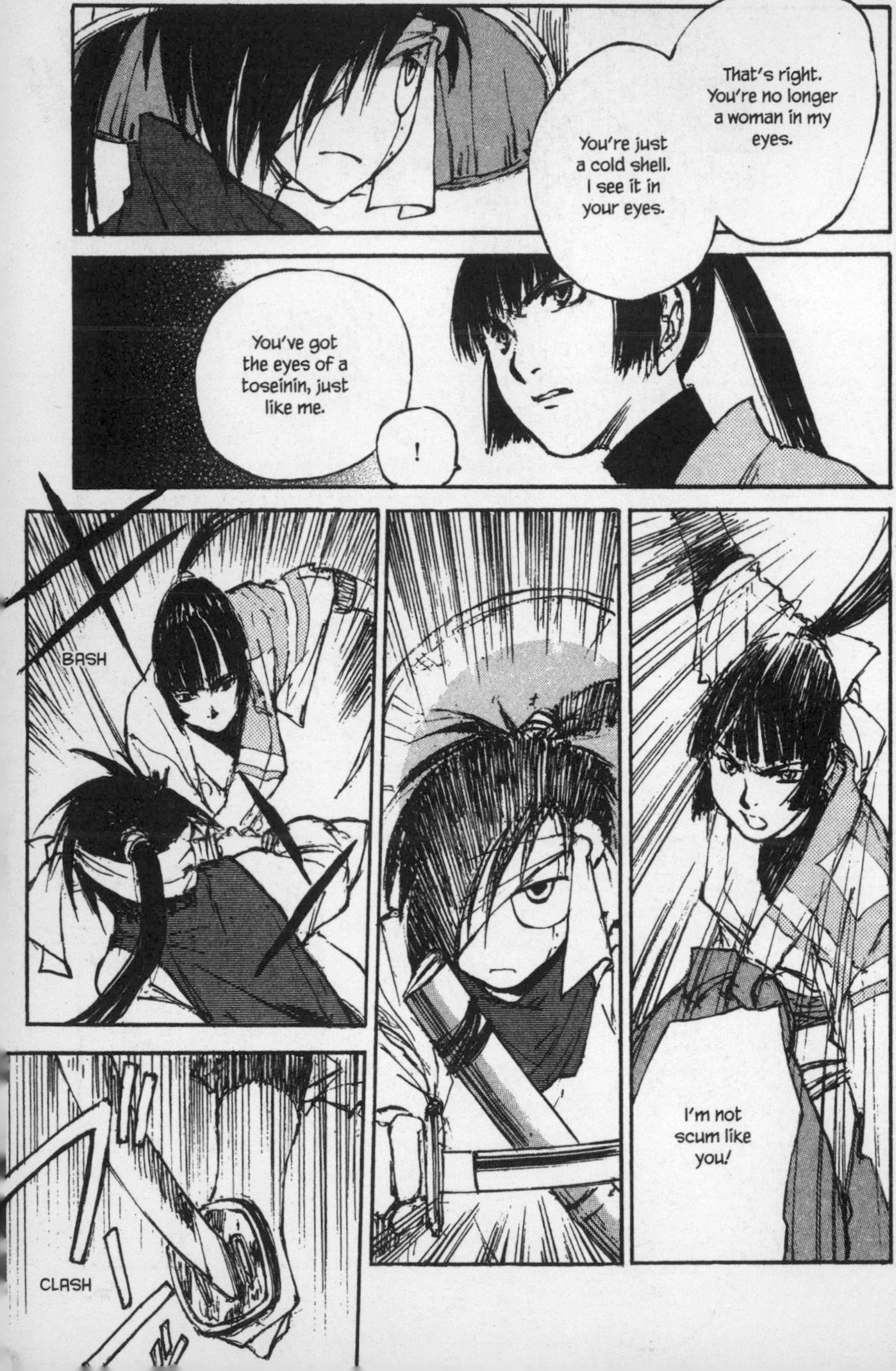
That's right. You're no longer a woman in my eyes.
You're just a cold shell. I see it in your eyes.
You've got the eyes of a toseinin, just like me.
!
I'm not scum like you!
BASH
CLASH

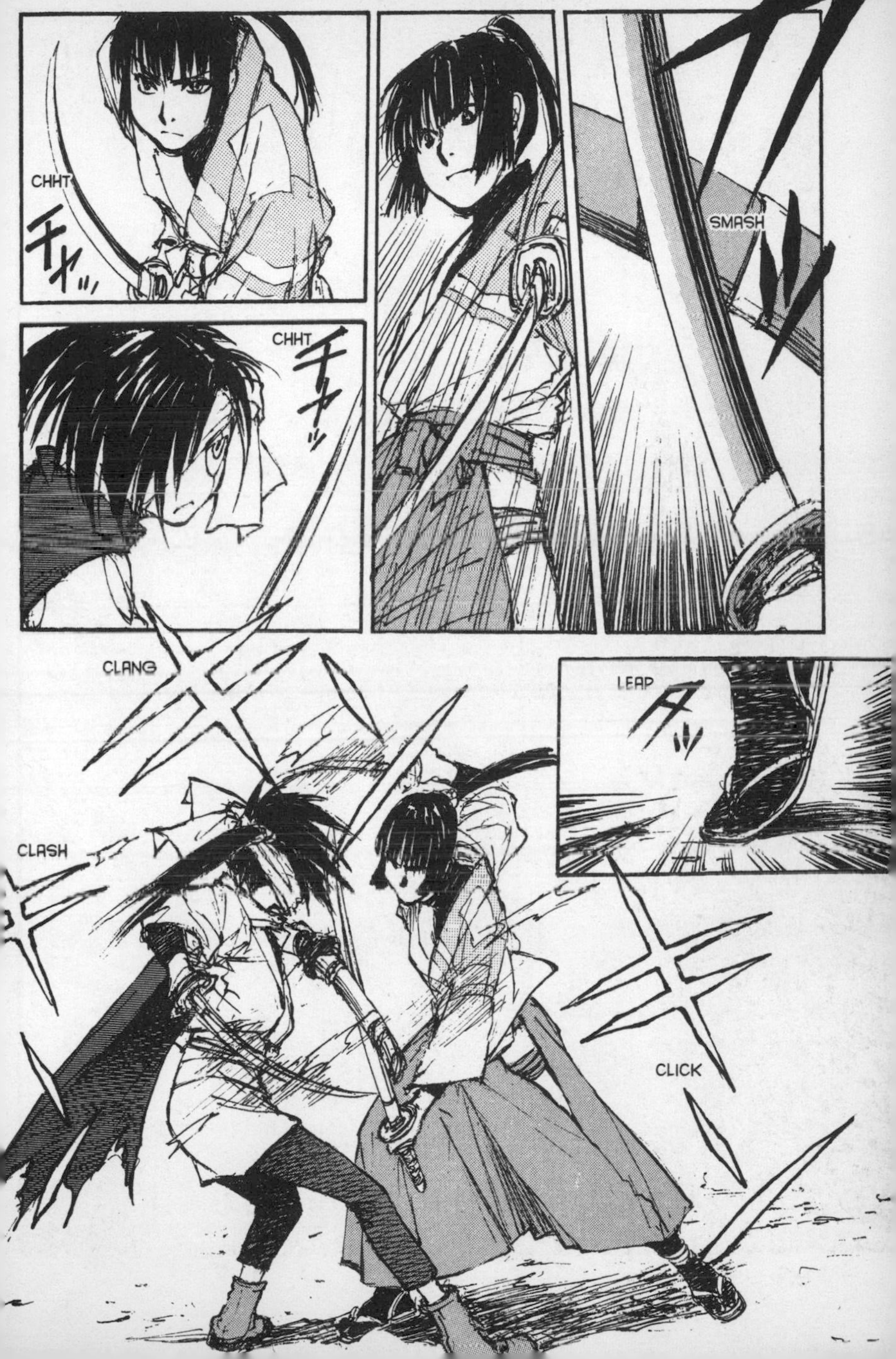
SMASH
CHHT
CHHT
LEAP
CLANG
CLASH
CLICK

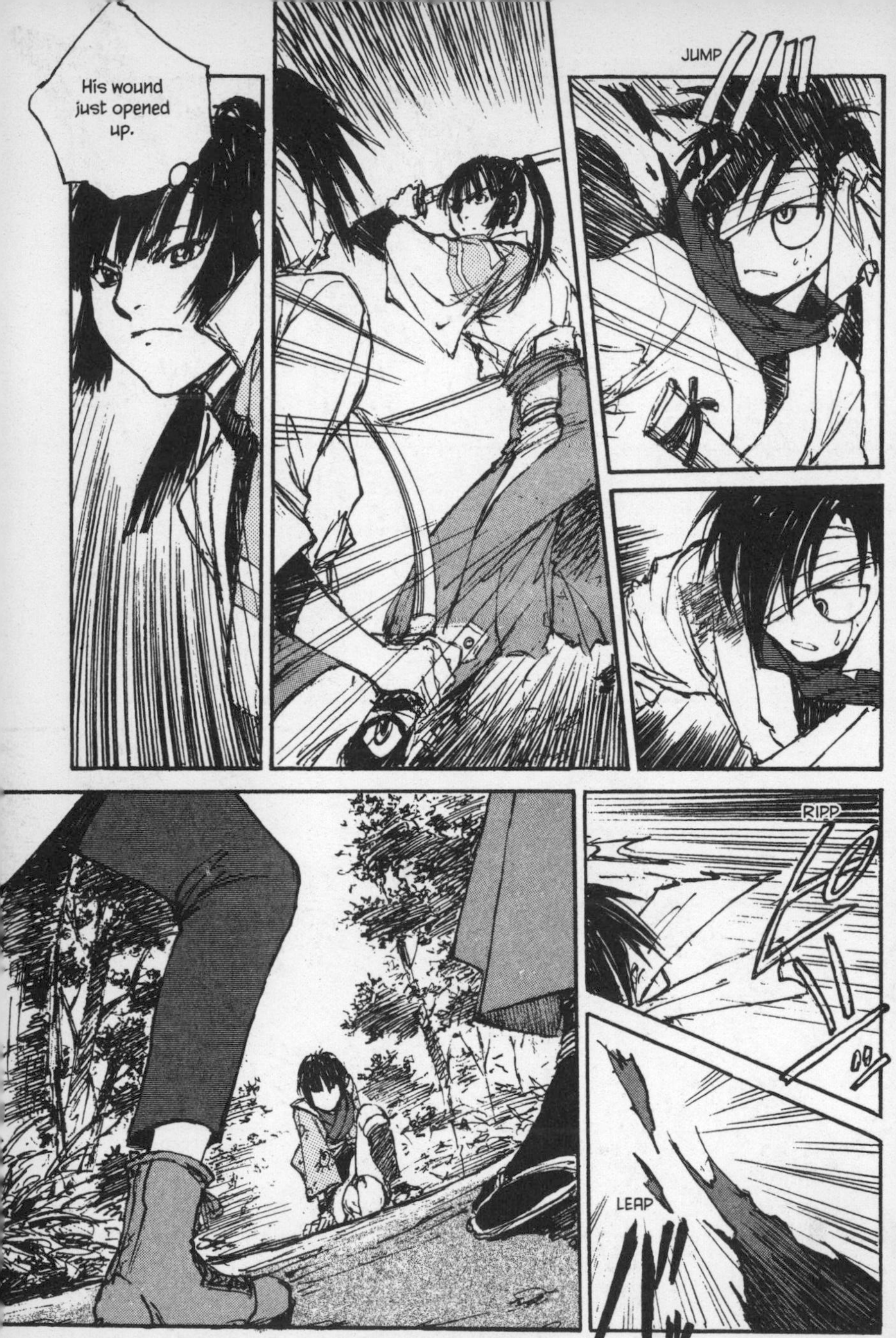
JUMP
His wound just opened up.
RIPP
LEAP

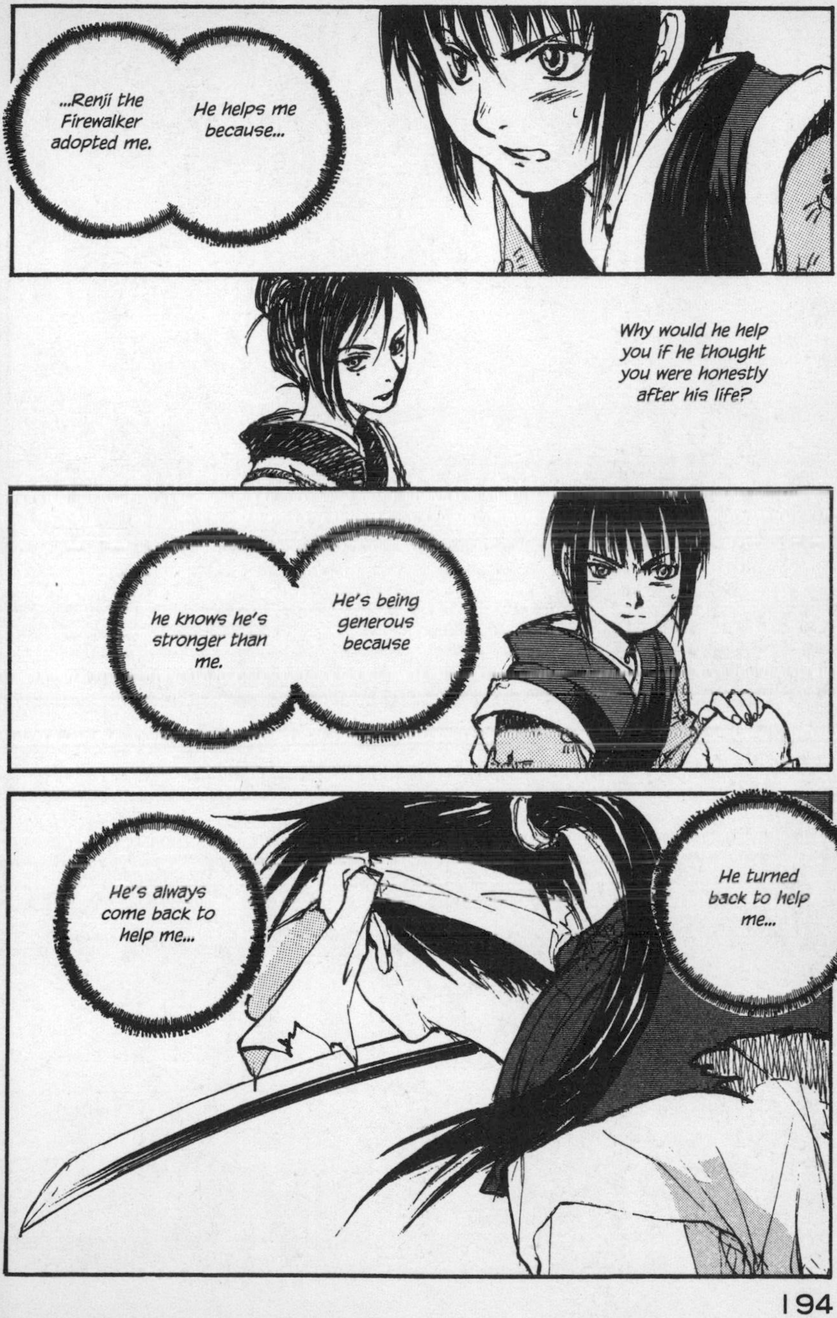
He helps me because...
...Renji the Firewalker adopted me.
Why would he help you if he thought you were honestly after his life?
He's being generous because
he knows he's stronger than me.
He turned back to help me...
He's always come back to help me...

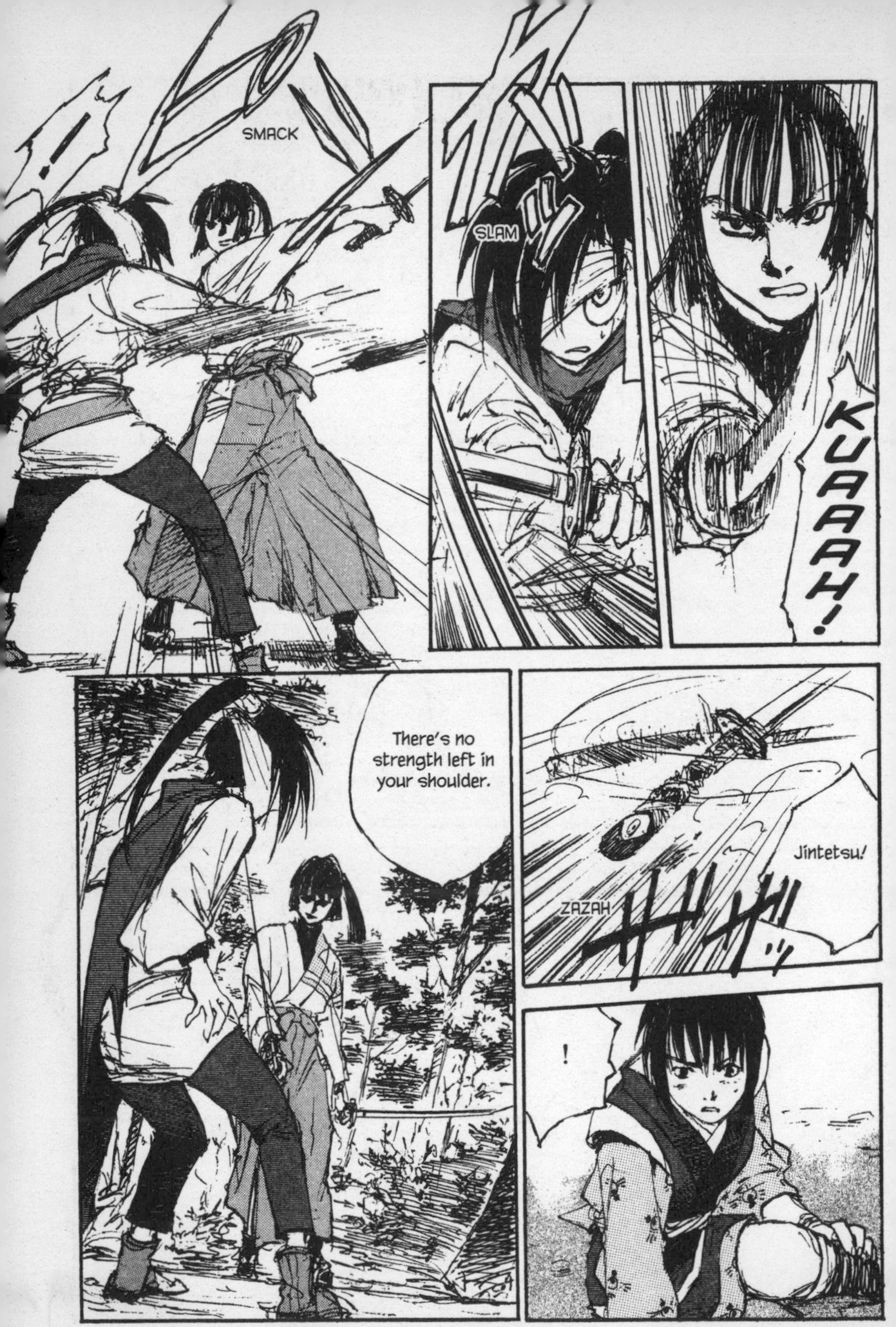
KUAAAAH!
SLAM
SMACK
Jintetsu!
ZAZAH
!
There's no strength left in your shoulder.

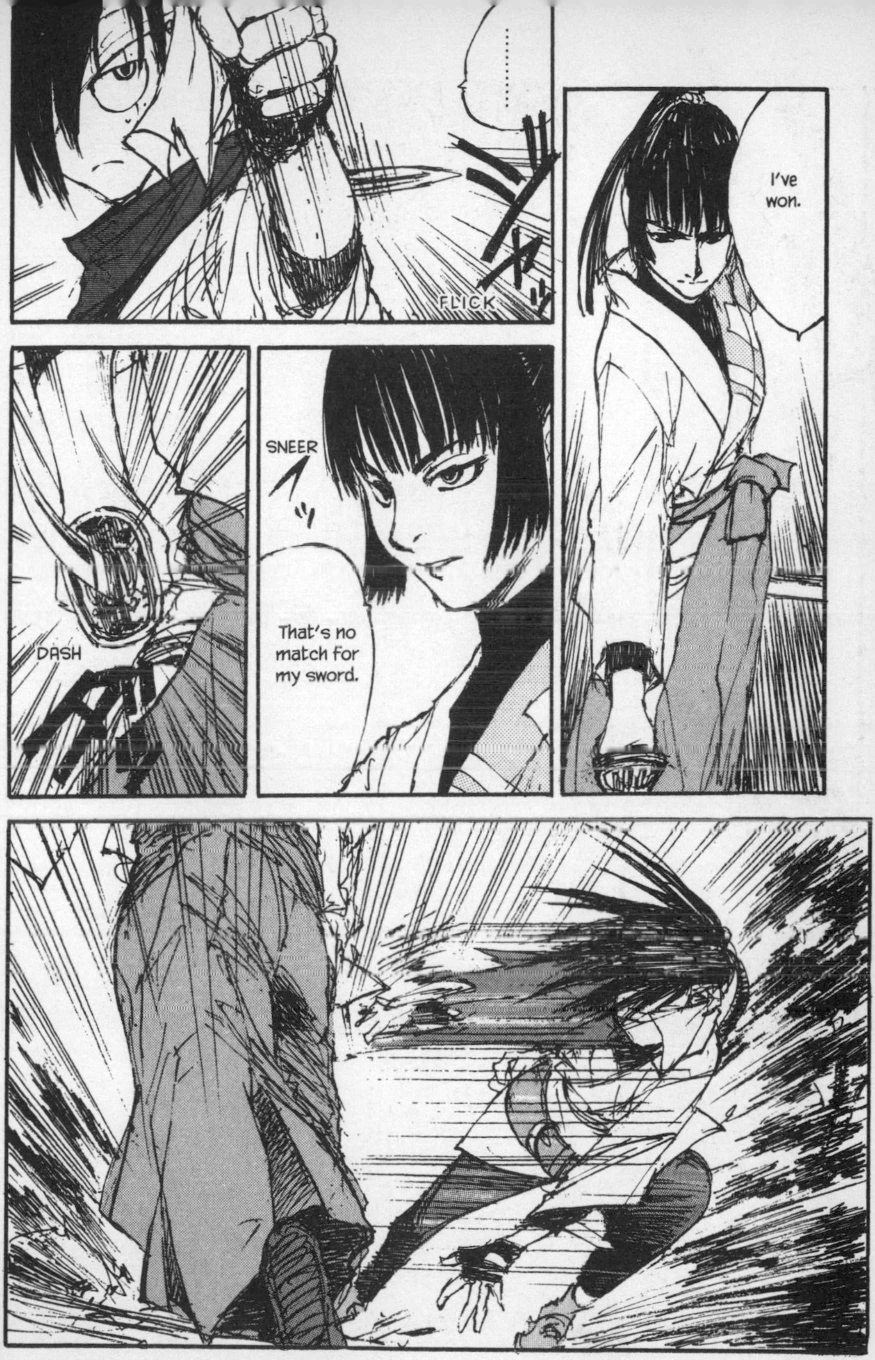
I've won.
FLICK
SNEER
That's no match for my sword.
DASH

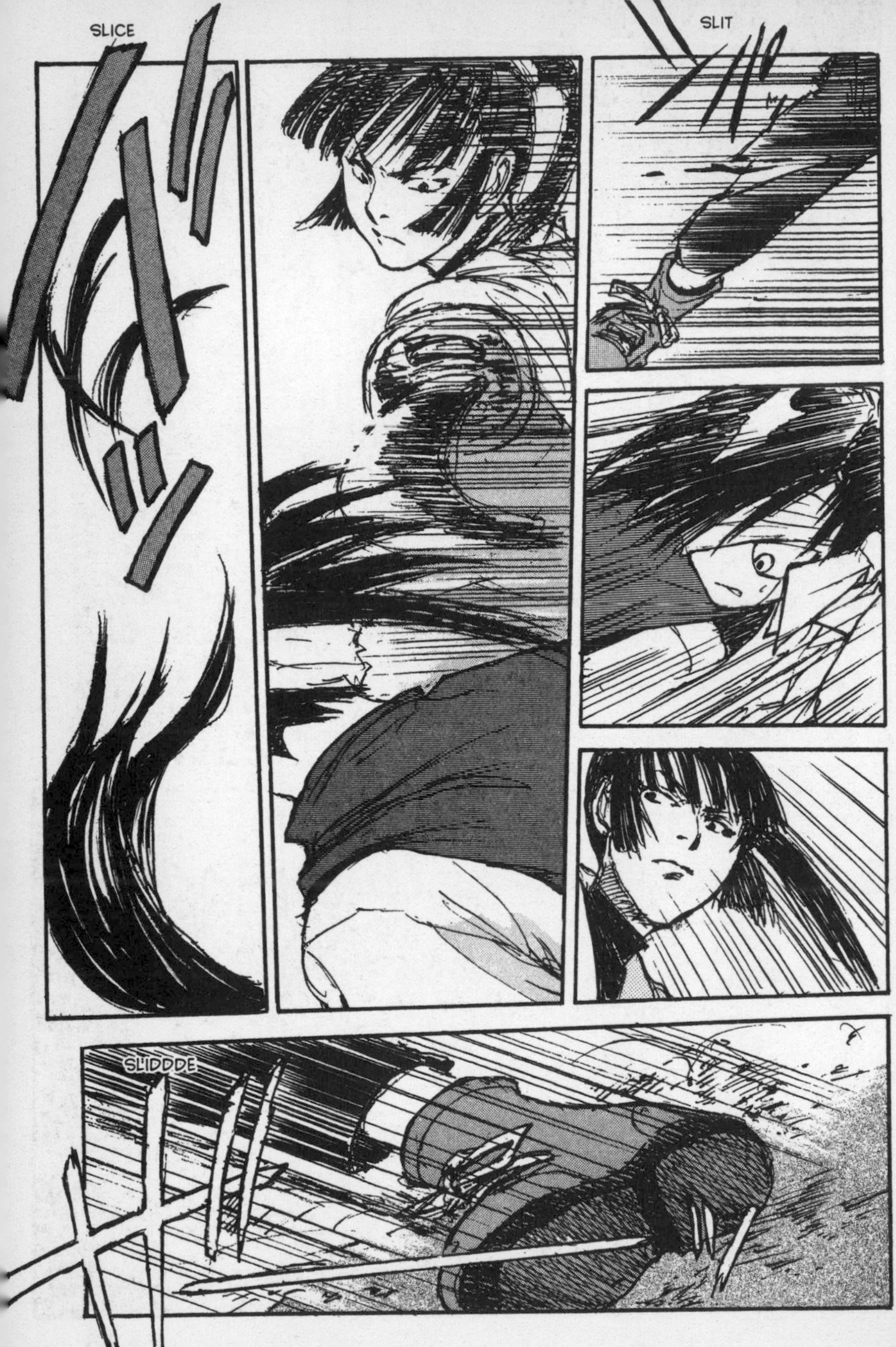
SLIT
SLICE
SLIDDDE

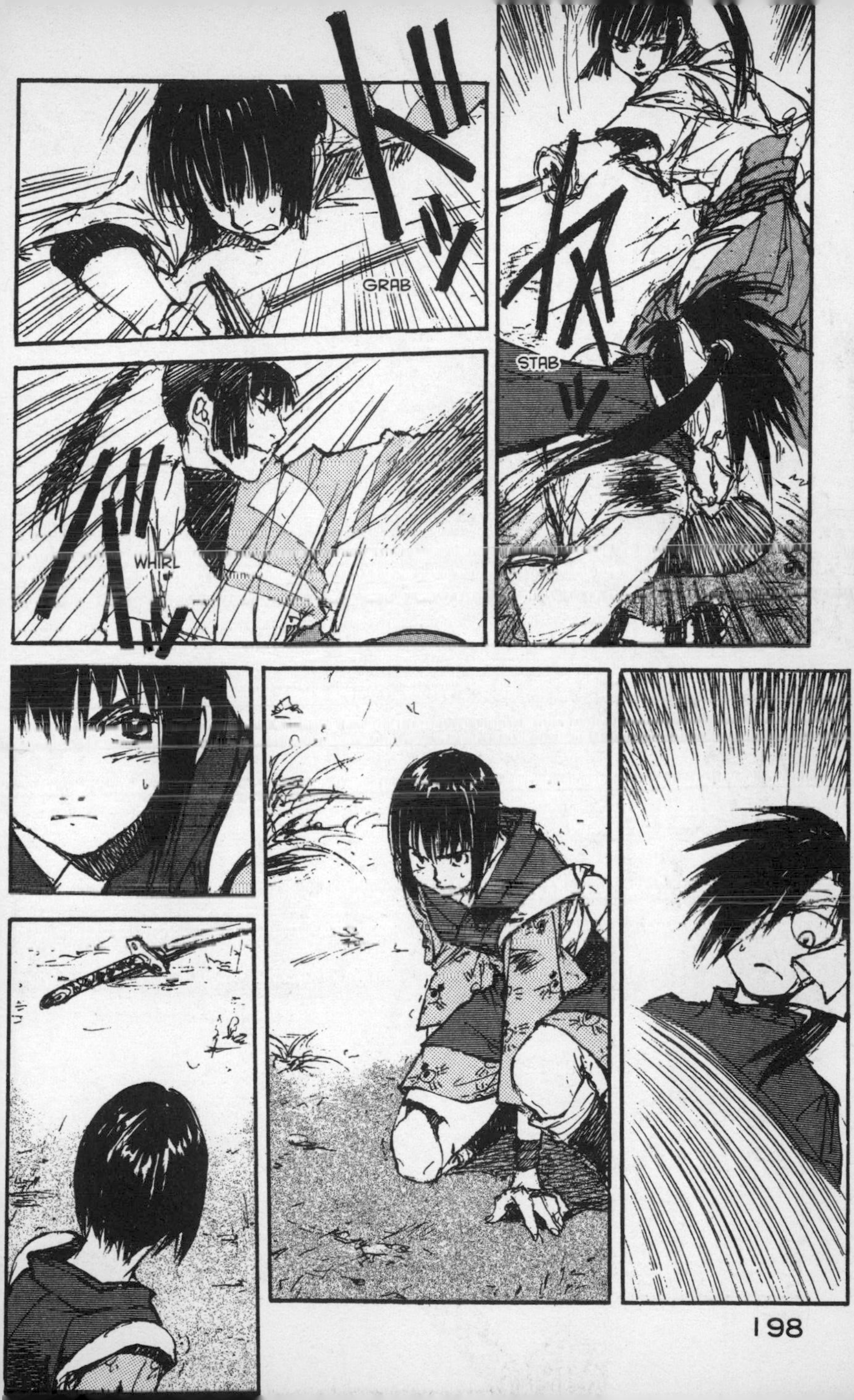
STAB
GRAB
WHIRL

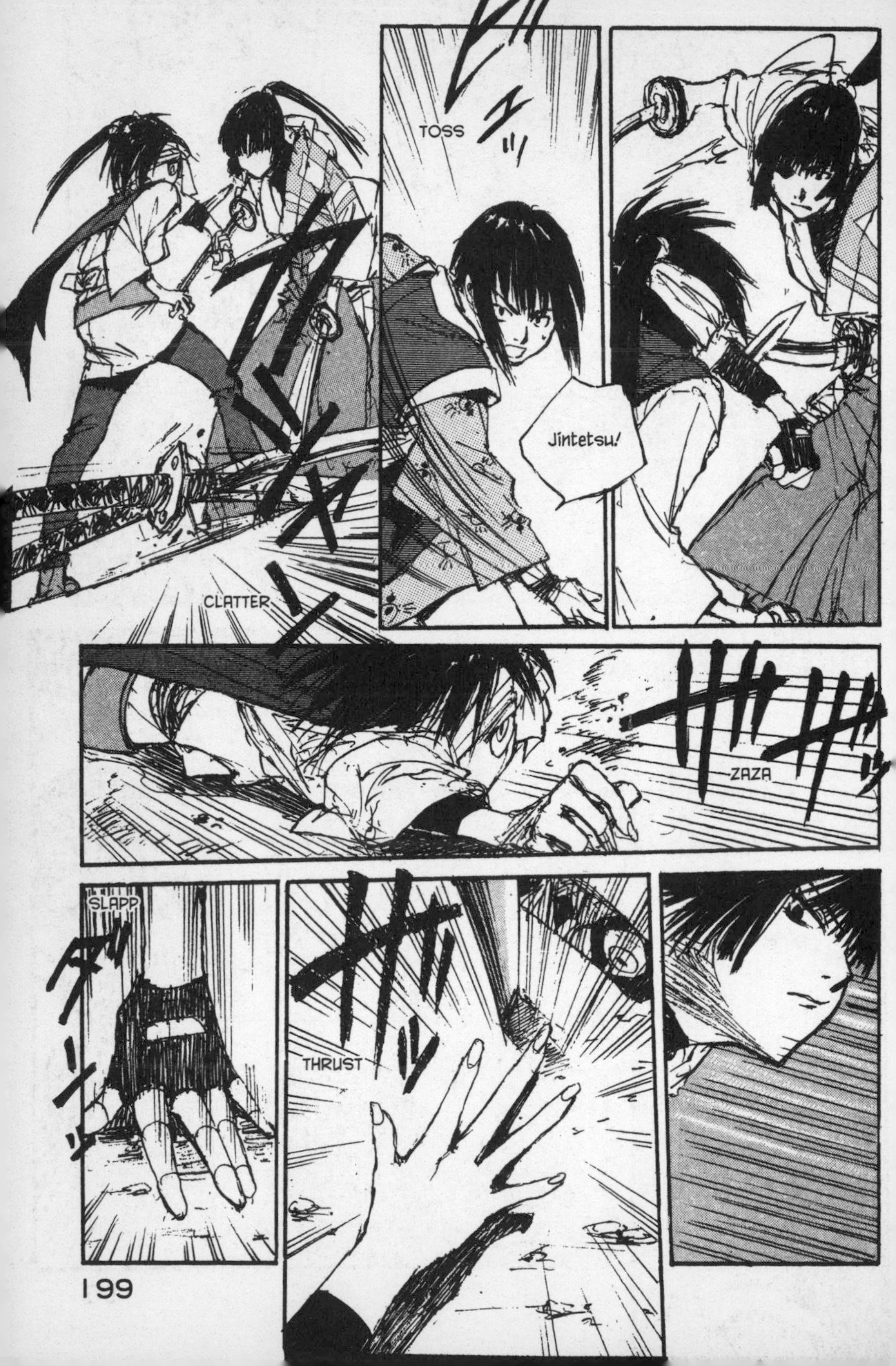
TOSS
Jintetsu!
CLATTER
ZAZA
THRUST
SLAPP

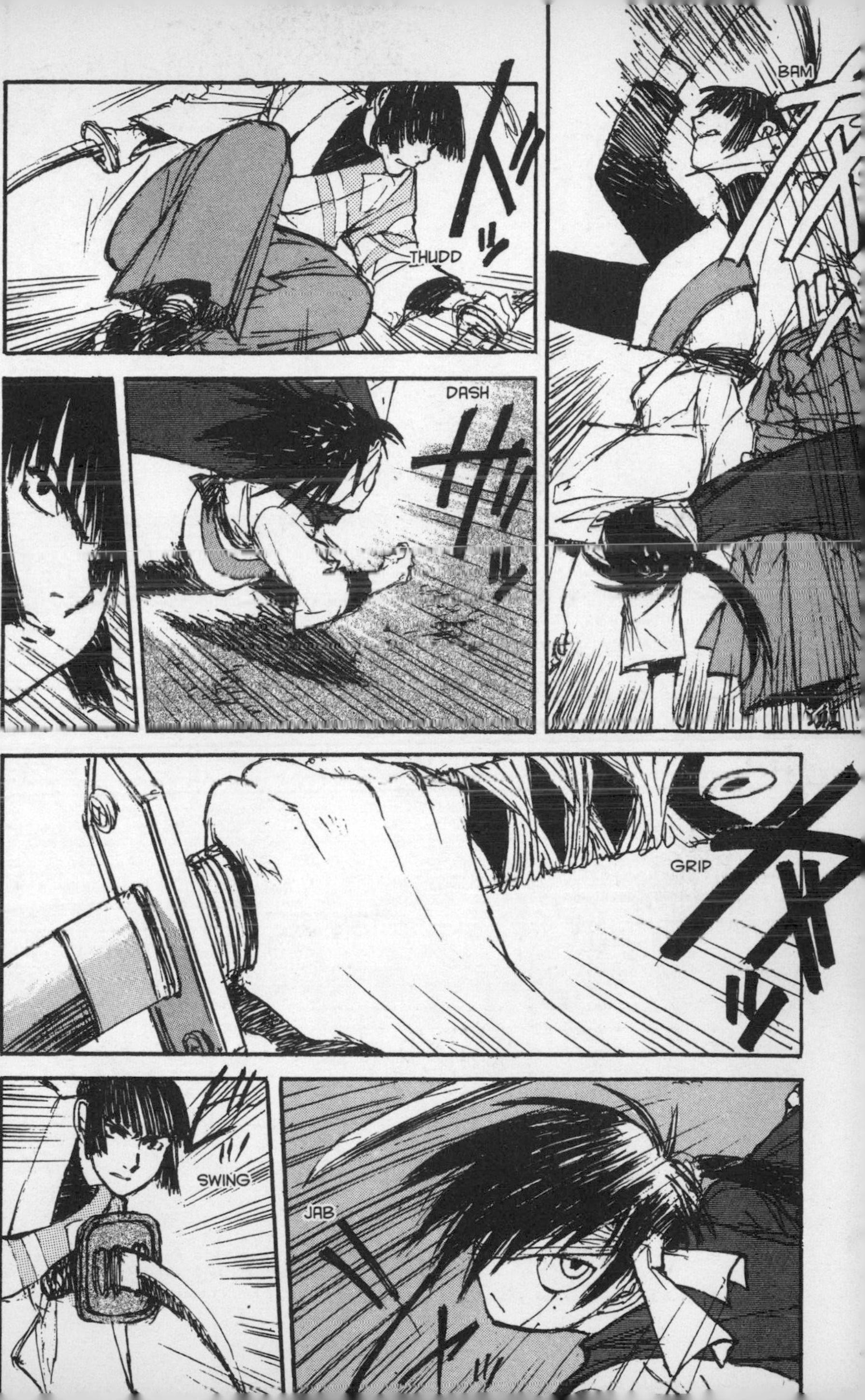
BAM
THUDD
DASH
GRIP
JAB
SWING

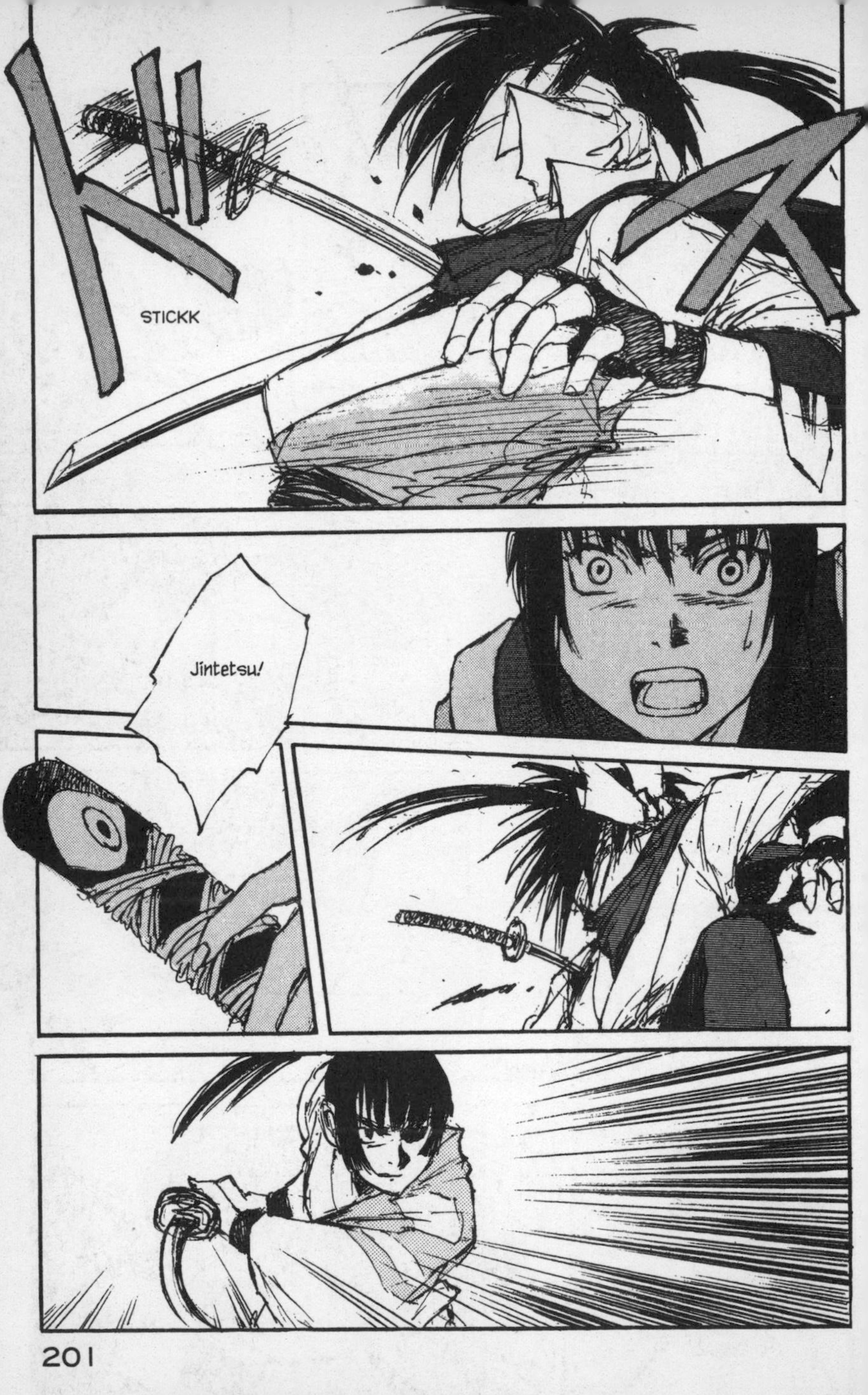
STICKK
Jintetsu!

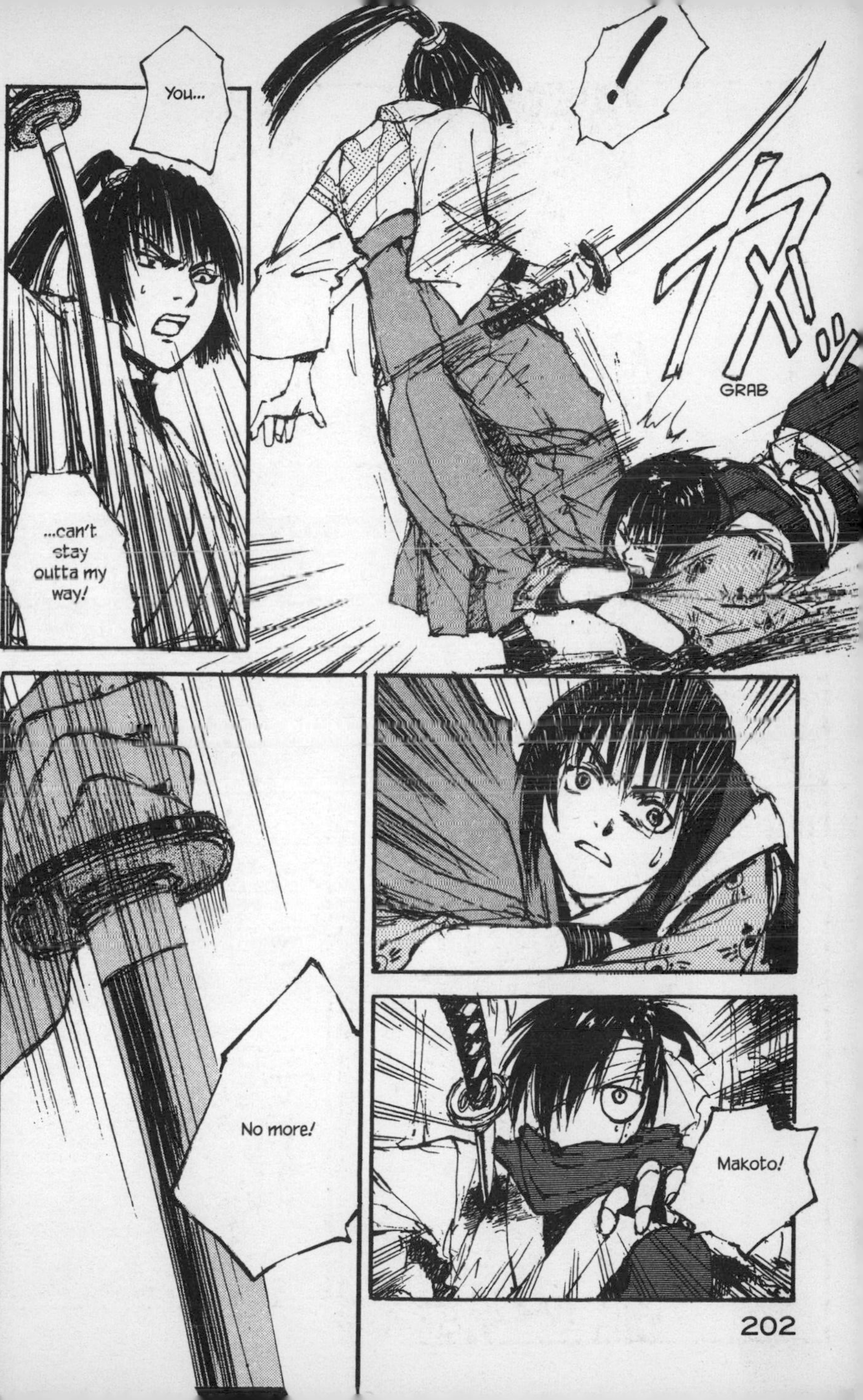
!
GRAB
You...
...can't stay outta my way!
Makoto!
No more!

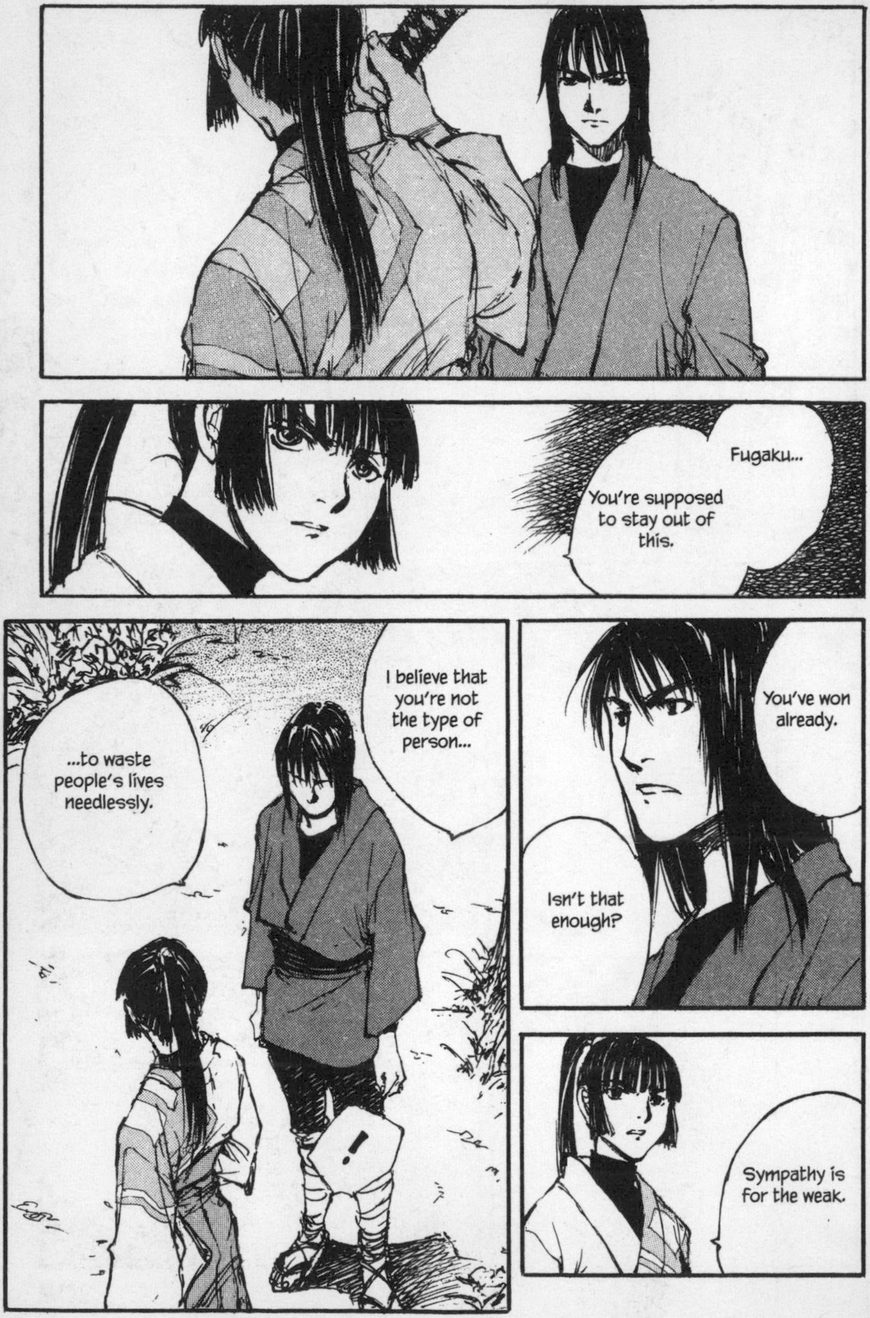

Fugaku...
You're supposed to stay out of this.
You've won already.
Isn't that enough?
Sympathy is for the weak.
I believe that you're not the type of person...
...to waste people's lives needlessly.
!

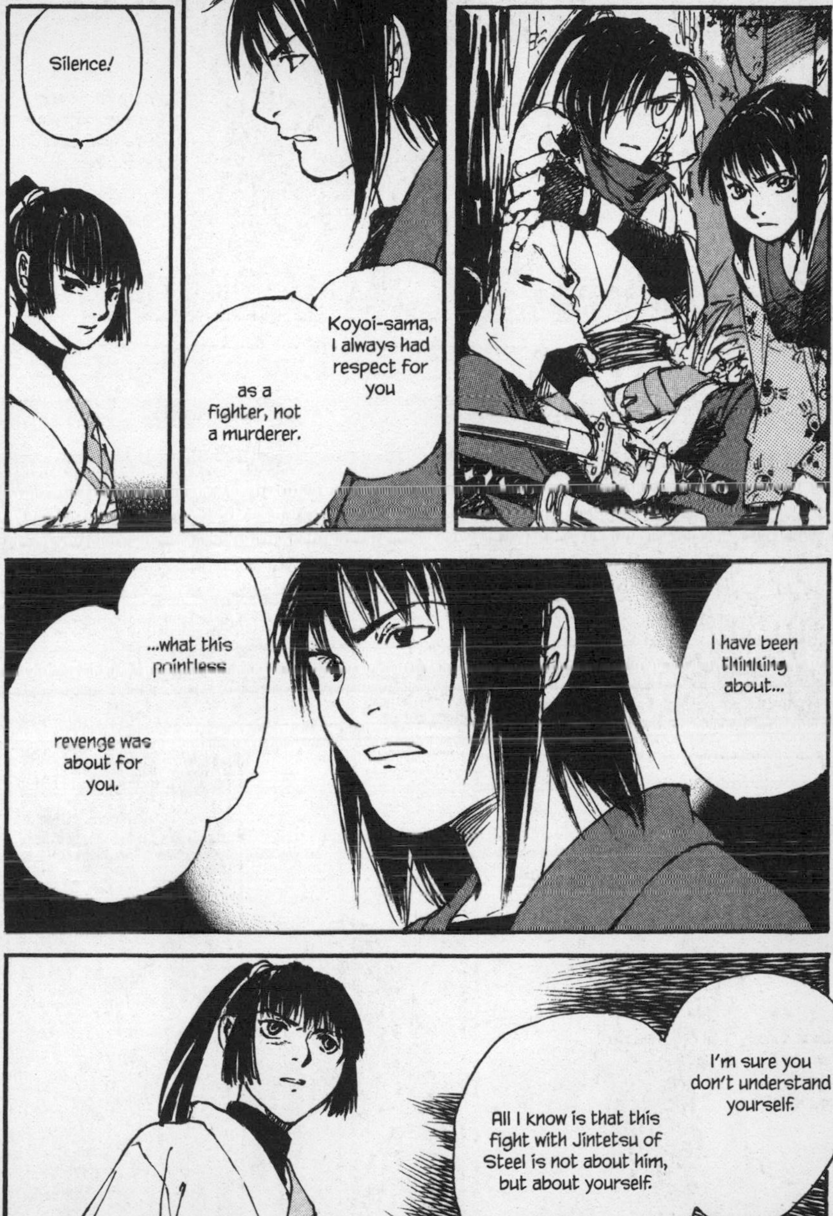

Koyoi-sama, I always had respect for you
as a fighter, not a murderer.
Silence!
I have been thinking about...
...what this pointless
revenge was about for you.
I'm sure you don't understand yourself.
All I know is that this fight with Jintetsu of Steel is not about him, but about yourself.

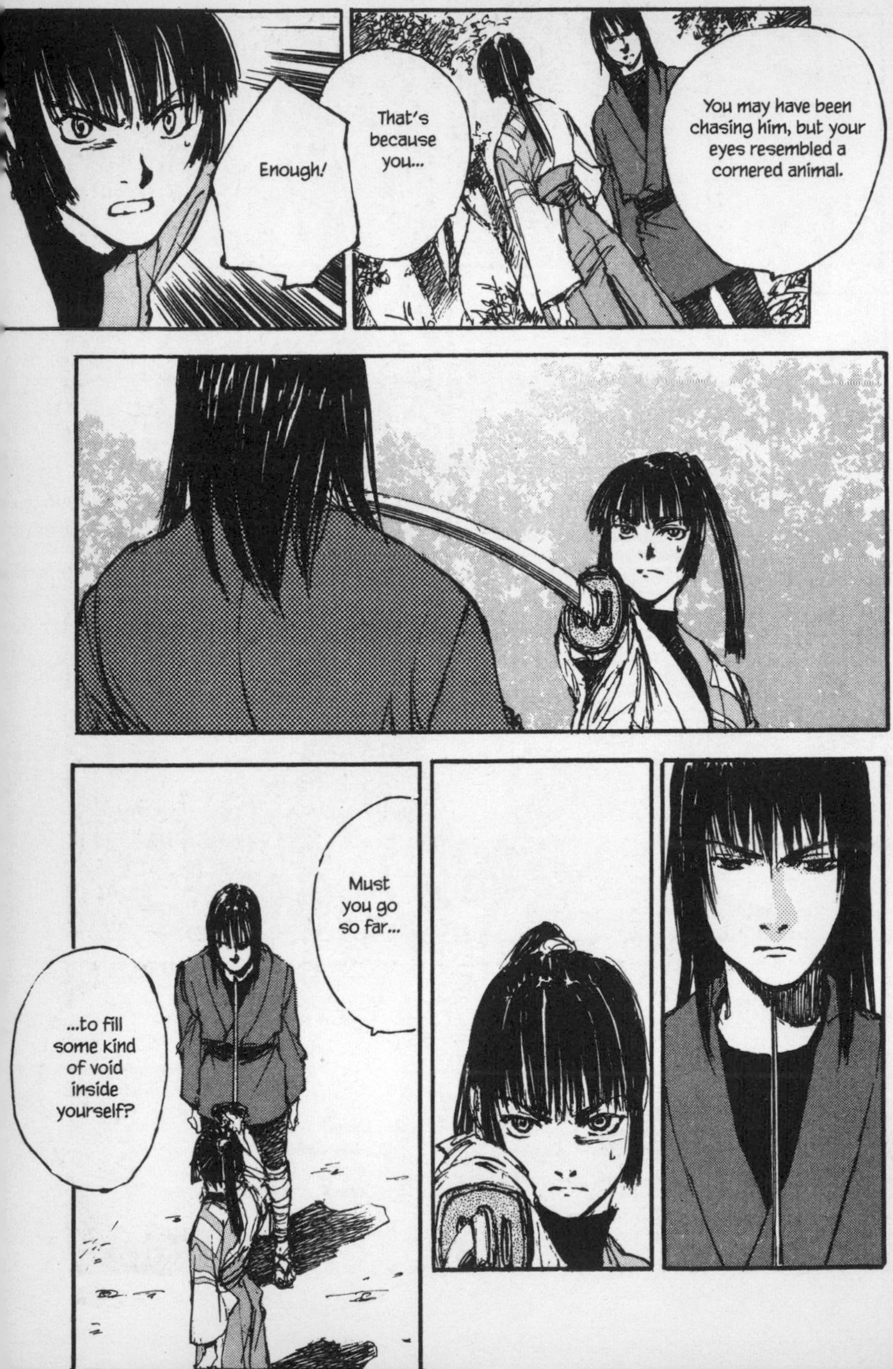
You may have been chasing him, but your eyes resembled a cornered animal.
That's because you...
Enough!
Must you go so far...
...to fill some kind of void inside yourself?

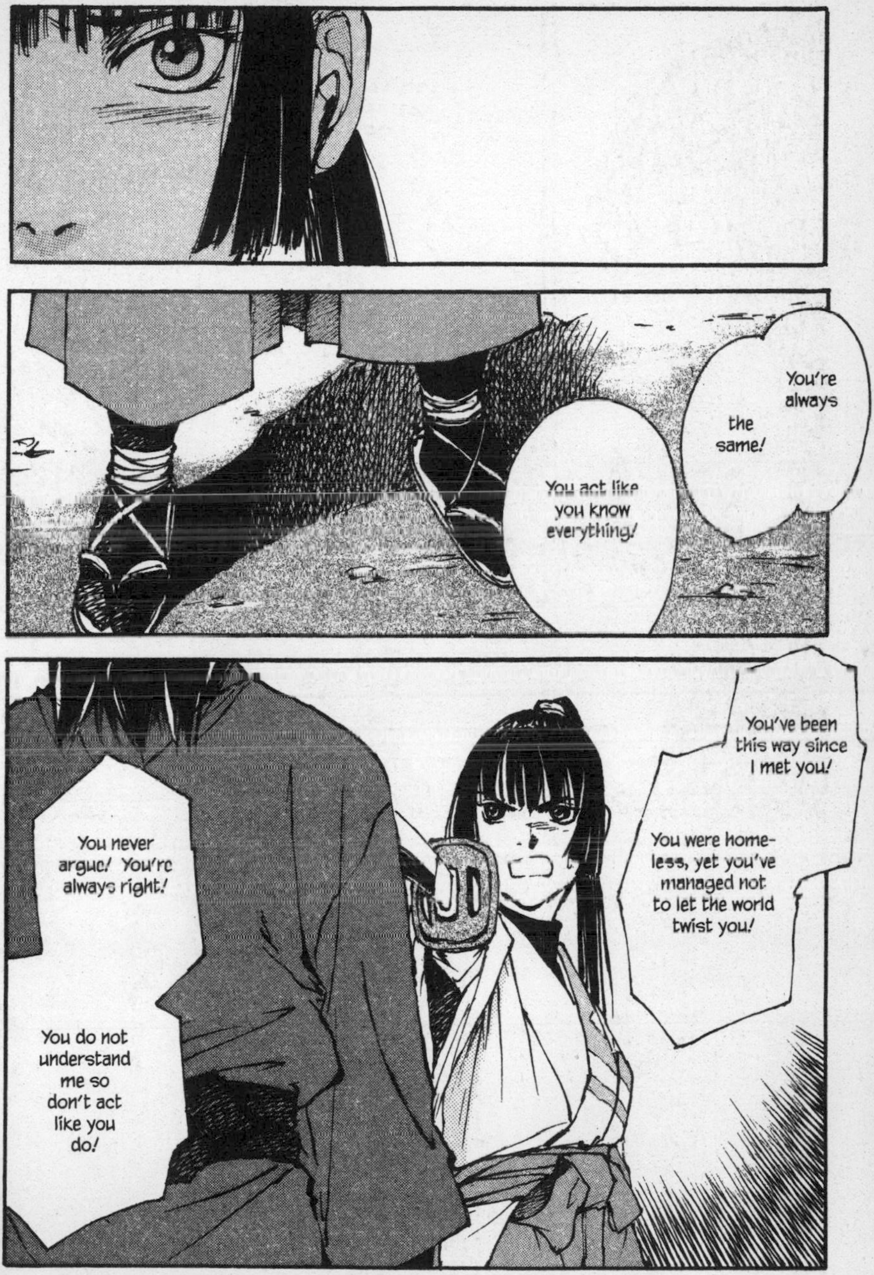
You're always the same!
You act like you know everything!
You've been this way since I met you!
You were home-less, yet you've managed not to let the world twist you!
You never argue! You're always right!
You do not understand me so don't act like you do!

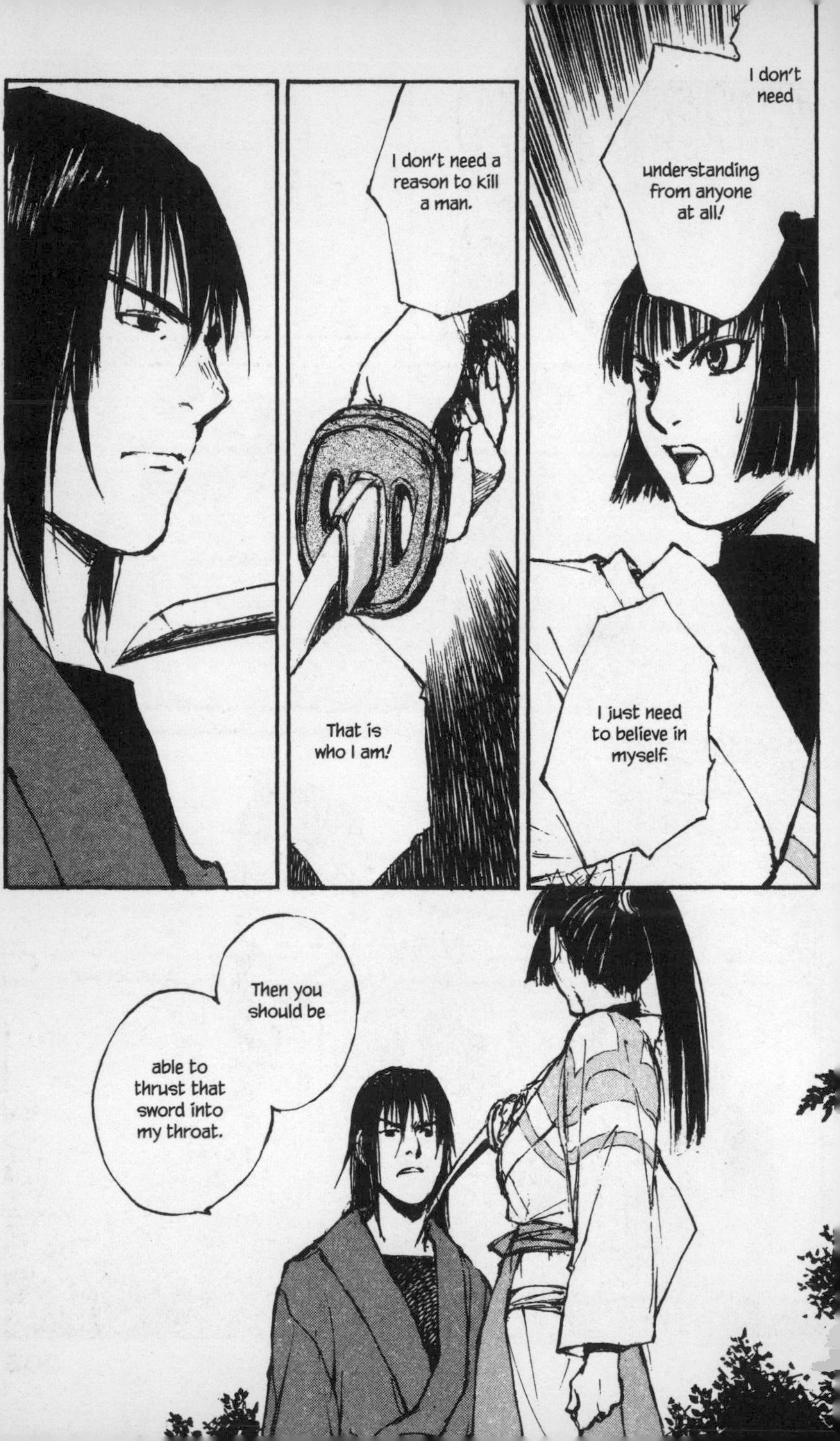
I don't need
understanding from anyone at all!
I just need to believe in myself.
I don't need a reason to kill a man.
That is who I am!
Then you should be
able to thrust that sword into my throat.

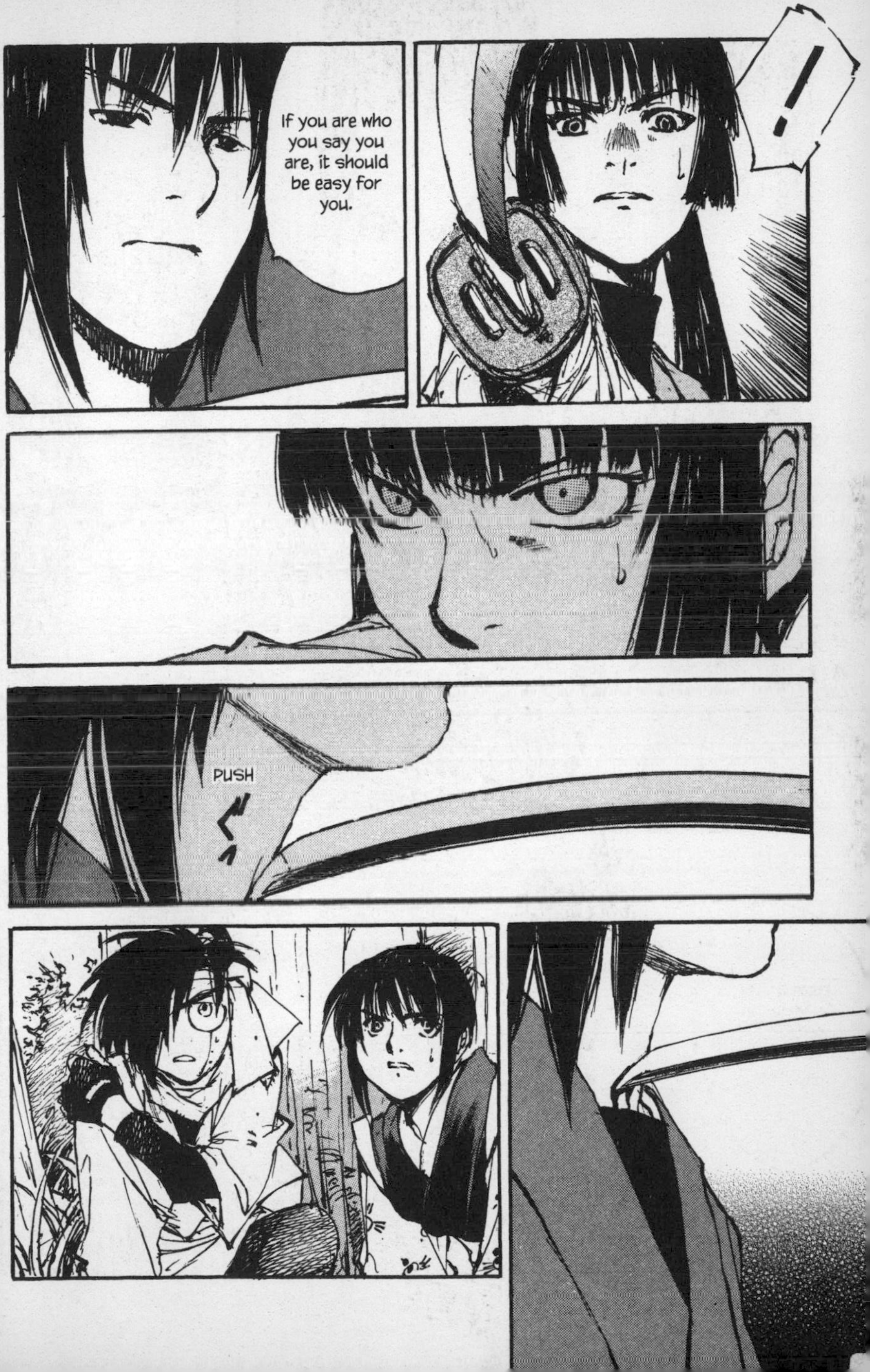
!
If you are who you say you are, it should be easy for you.
PUSH

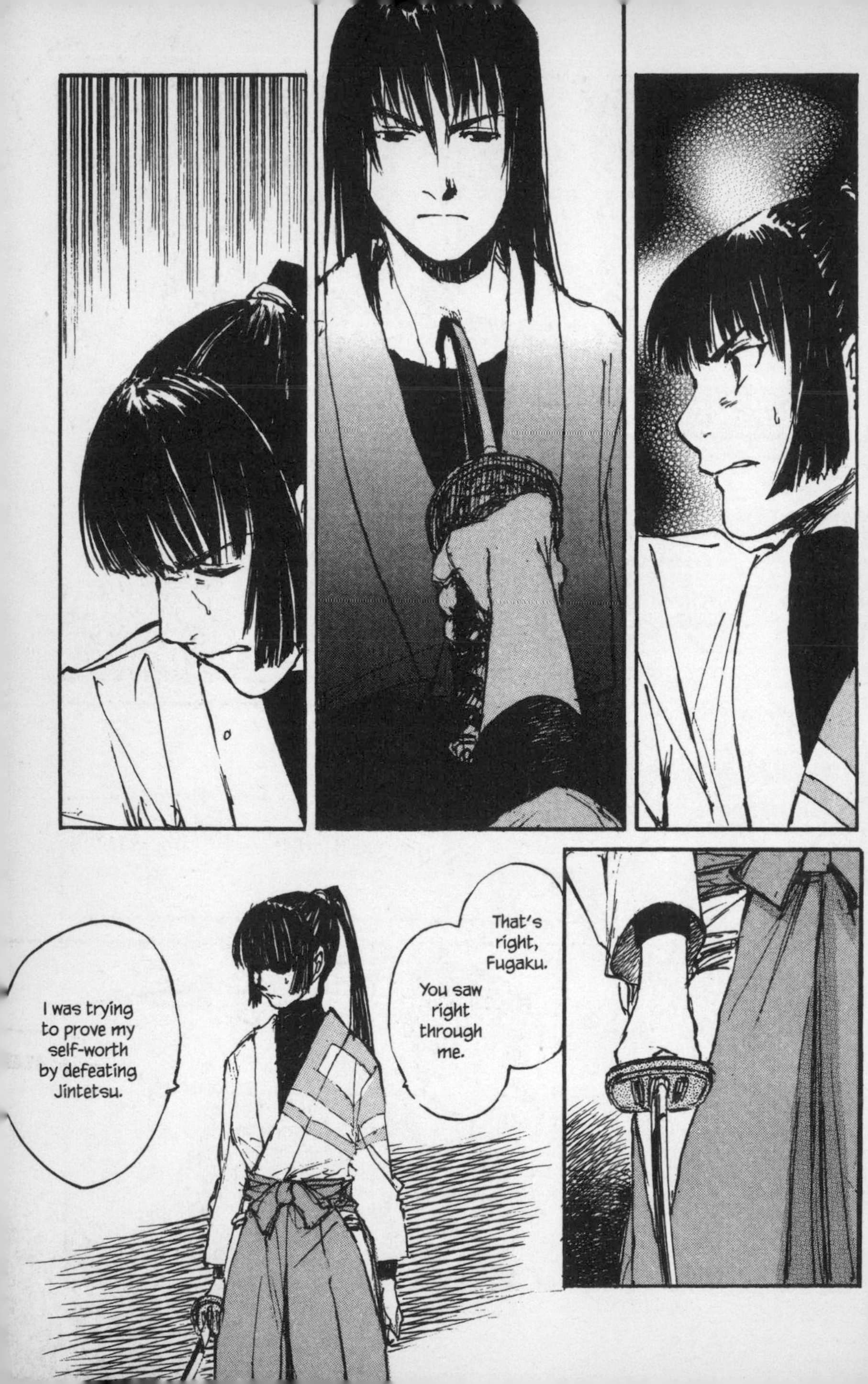
That's right, Fugaku.
You saw right through me.
I was trying to prove my self-worth by defeating Jintetsu.

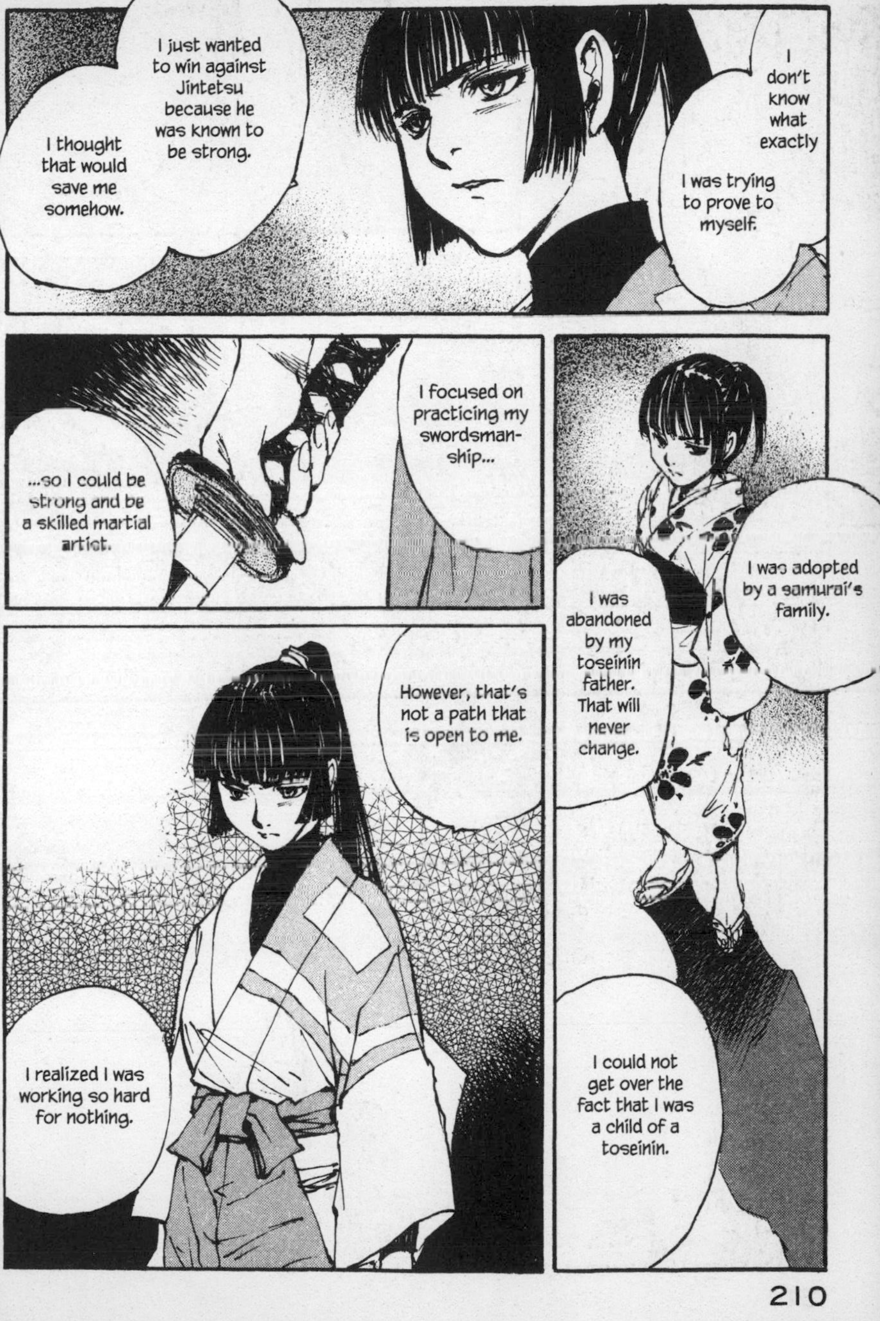
I don't know what exactly
I was trying to prove to myself.
I just wanted to win against Jintetsu because he was known to be strong.
I thought that would save me somehow.
I was adopted by a samurai's family.
I was abandoned by my toseinin father. That will never change.
I could not get over the fact that I was a child of a toseinin.
I focused on practicing my swordsman-ship...
...so I could be strong and be a skilled martial artist.
However, that's not a path that is open to me.
I realized I was working so hard for nothing.

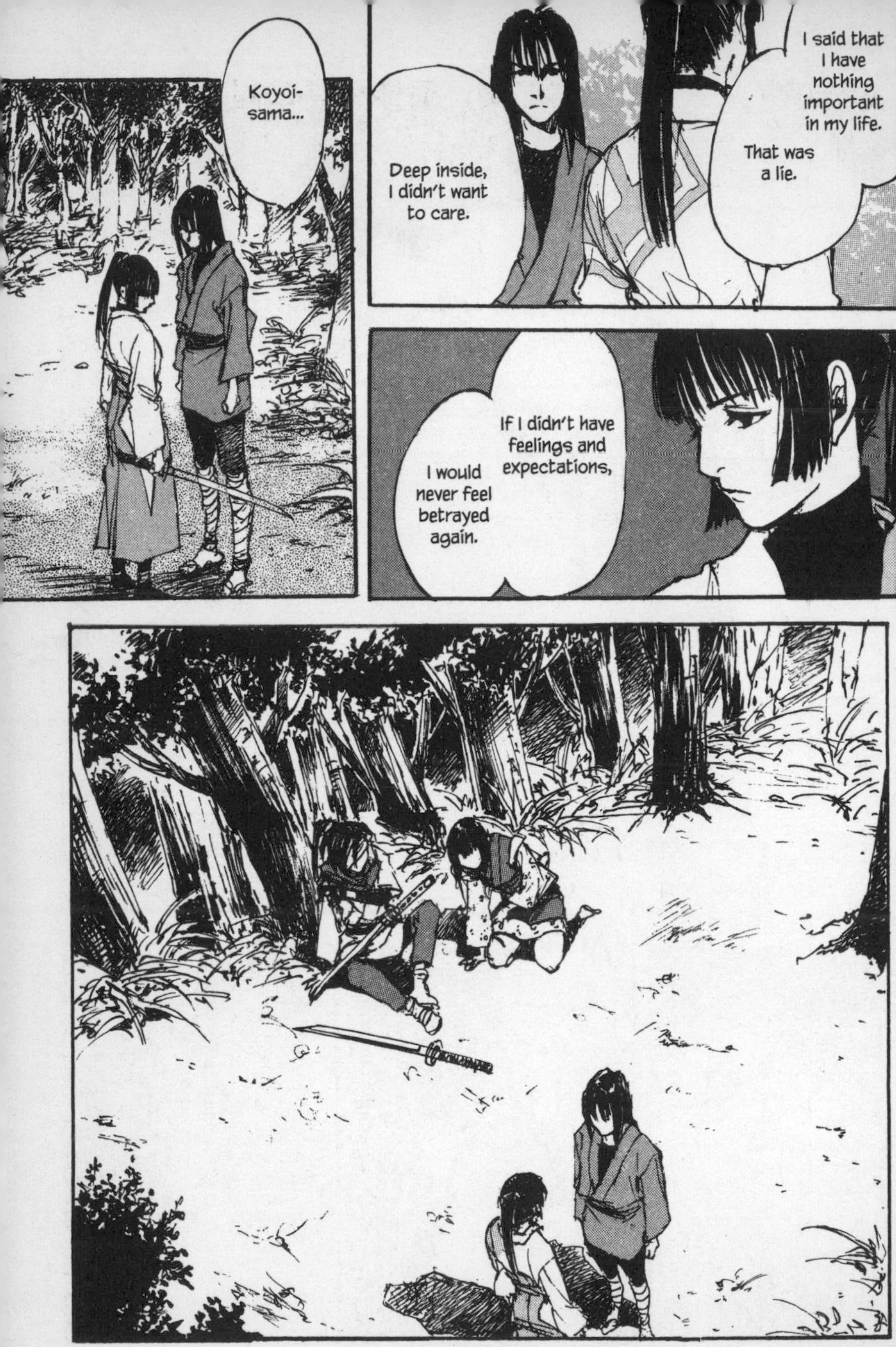

I said that I have nothing important in my life.
That was a lie.
Deep inside, I didn't want to care.
If I didn't have feelings and expectations,
I would never feel betrayed again.
Koyoi-sama...

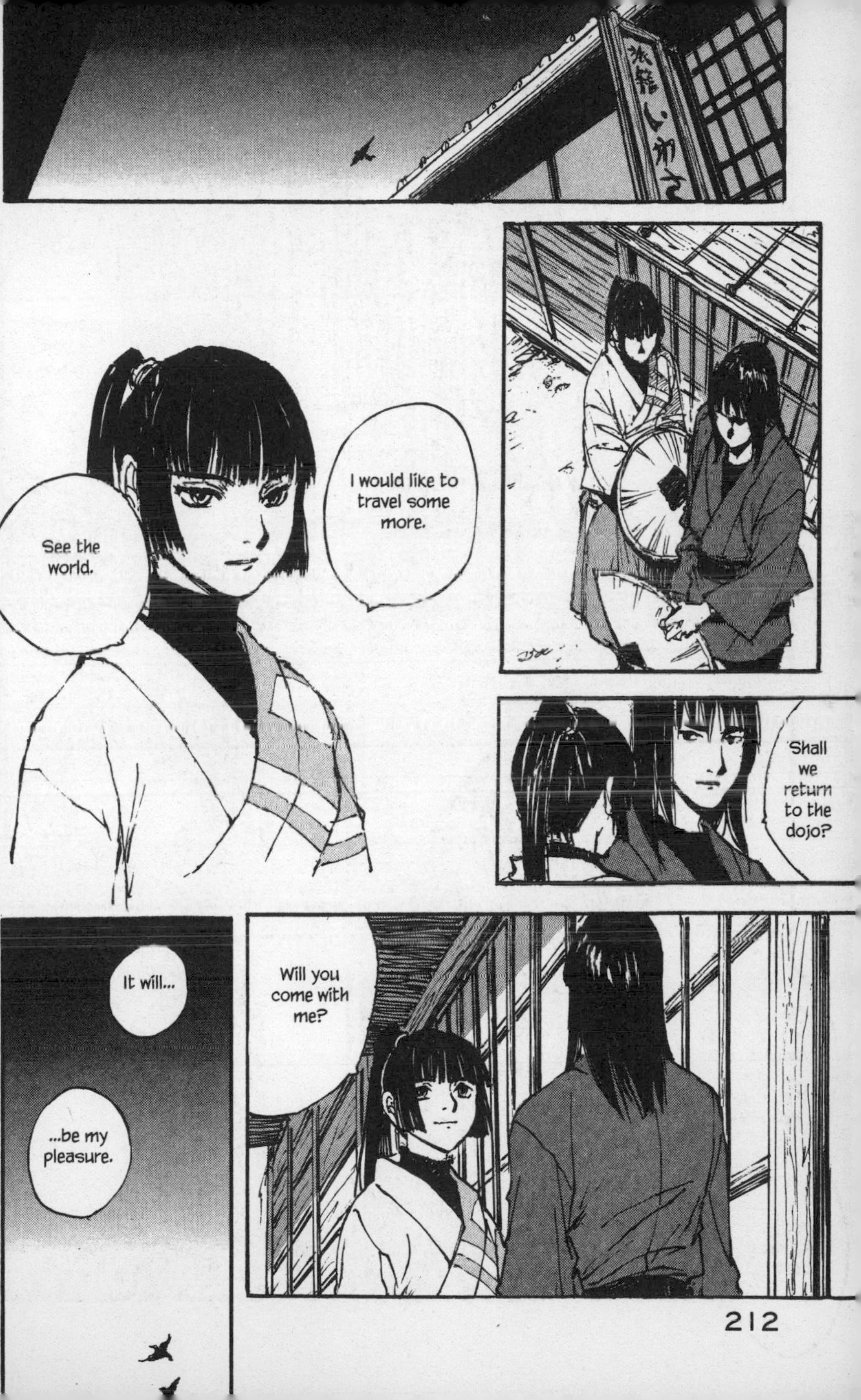
Shall we return to the dojo?
I would like to travel some more.
See the world.
Will you come with me?
It will...
...be my pleasure.

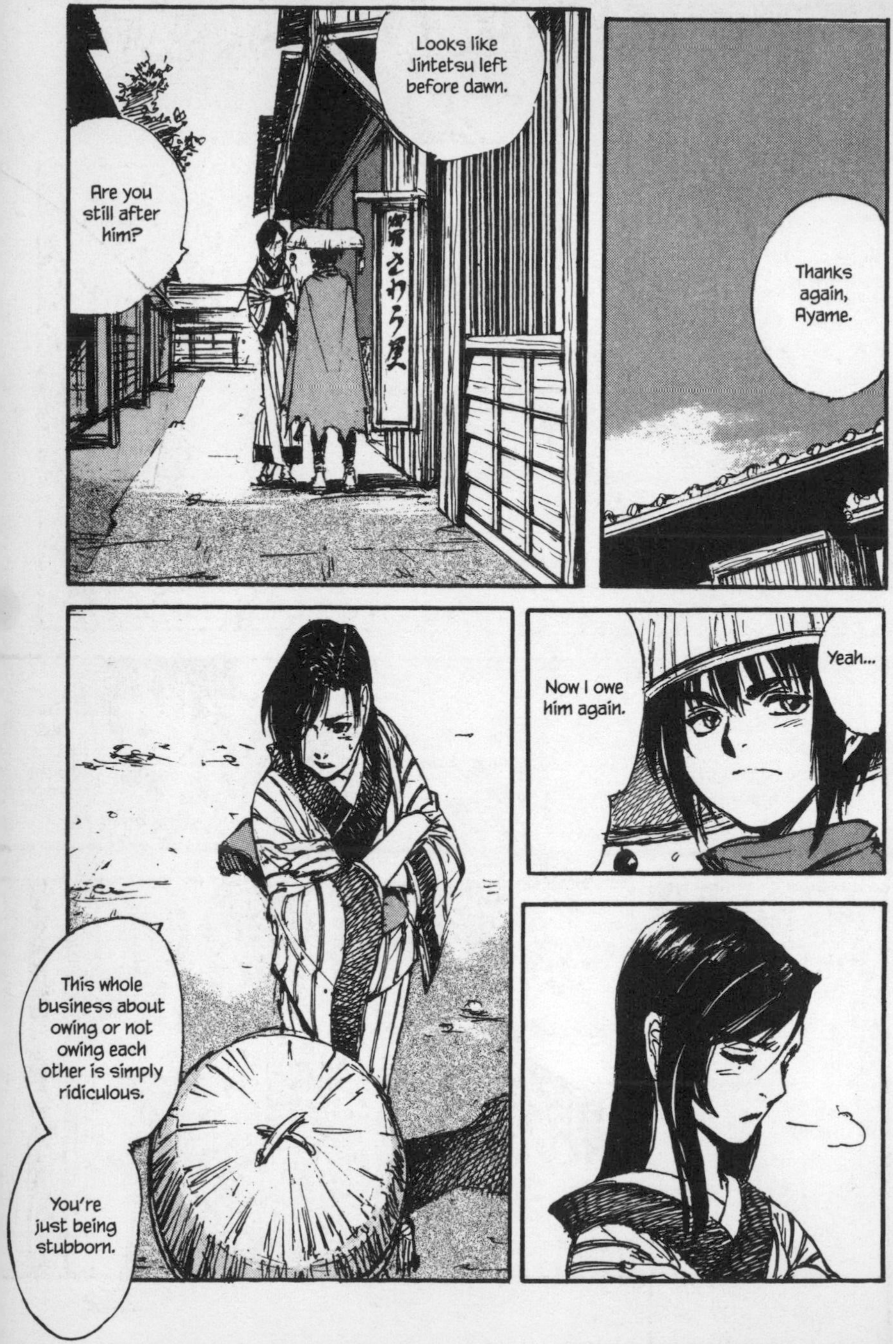
Thanks again, Ayame.
Looks like Jintetsu left before dawn.
Are you still after him?
Yeah...
Now I owe him again.
This whole business about owing or not owing each other is simply ridiculous.
You're just being stubborn.

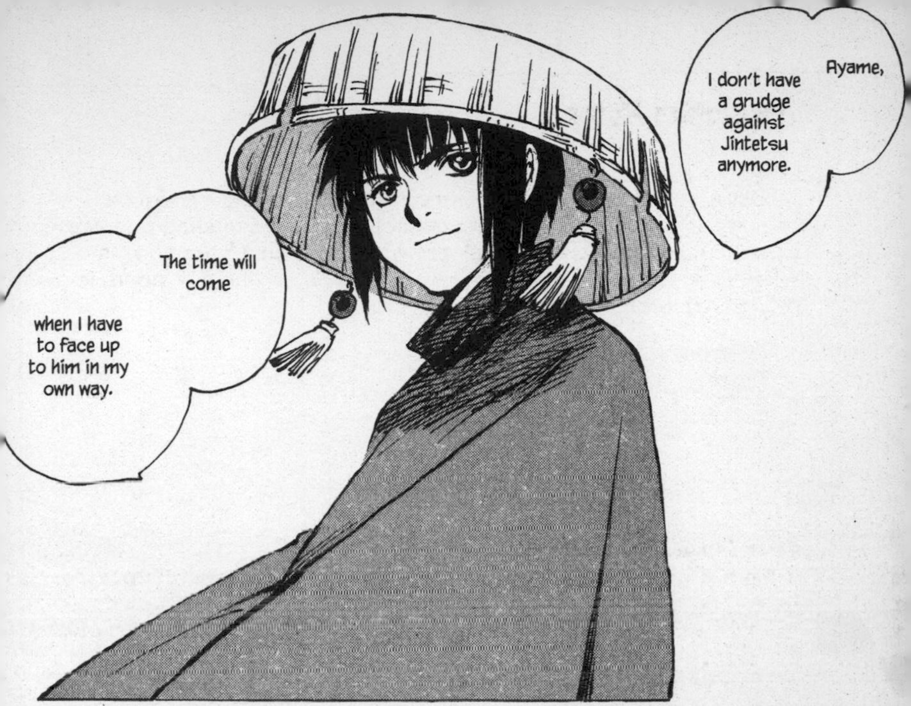
Ayame, I don't have a grudge against Jintetsu anymore.
The time will come when I have to face up to him in my own way.

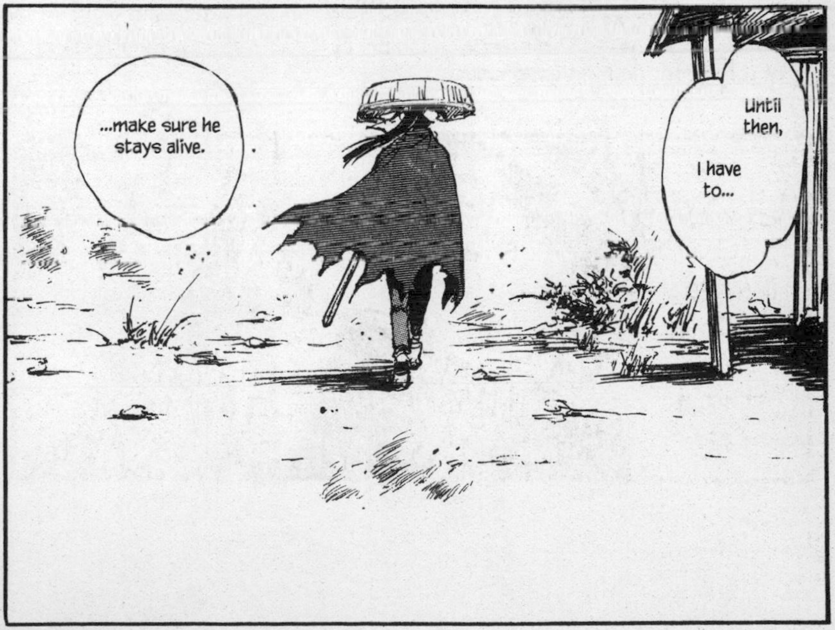
Until then, I have to...
...make sure he stays alive.

THE END OF KUROGANE VOL 5

Translation Notes

Japanese is a tricky language for most Westerners, and translation is often more art than science. For your edification and reading pleasure, here are notes on some of the places where we could have gone in a different direction in our translation of the work, or where a Japanese cultural reference is used.

Wild Dogs, page 20
In the background of this manga, you will often hear howls of dogs. Japan had a population of two indigenous wolf subspecies that populated the wilderness. One was called the Honshu Wolf, and it occupied the islands of Honshu, Kyushu and Shikoku. The other wolf was called the Ezo Wolf, aka Hokkaido Wolf, and it occupied the island of Hokkaido. Both wolf species were subspecies of the Grey Wolf. The Ezo Wolf became extinct through deliberate poisoning by farmers in 1889. The Honshu Wolf became extinct in 1903 due to a combination of rabies and human eradication.

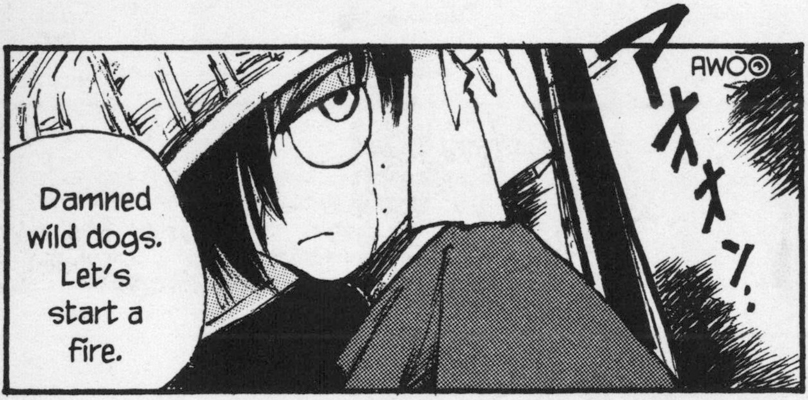
AWOO
Damned wild dogs. Let's start a fire.

Wild Mushrooms, page 21

Many poisonous mushrooms exist in Japan as well as the rest of the world. Poisonous mushrooms can closely resemble edible mushrooms, so only people with considerable experience, expertise and strong nerves should pick and eat wild mushrooms, as experienced mushroom hunters do occasionally get poisoned. To this day, people die of poisoning by misidentifying and eating wild mushrooms. Jintetsu's question to Renkaku about the mushrooms being edible is a fair question indeed.

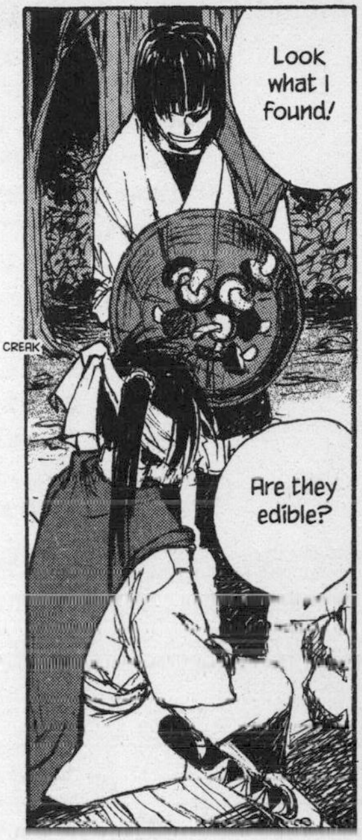
Look what I found!
CREAK
Are they edible?

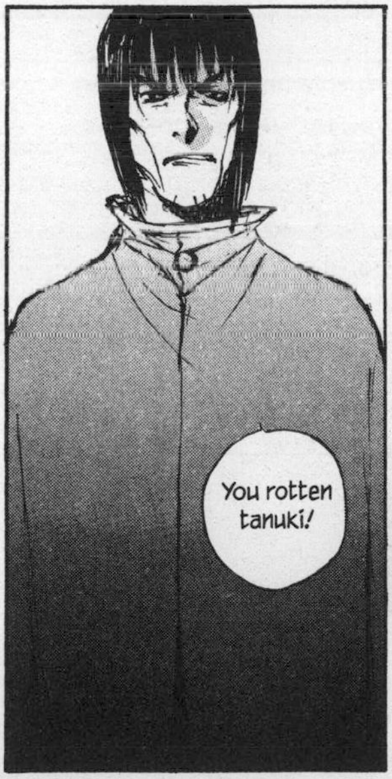
You rotten tanuki!

Tanuki, page 34

Tanuki, a Japanese subspecies of raccoon dogs (*Nyctereutes procyonoides*), have played a large role in Japanese mythology since ancient times. The tanuki in Japanese mythology is represented as a mischievous, jolly airhead that is slightly gullible. Liars and tricksters are often called a "tanuki" as a result of the tanuki's mythological affinity for tricks. Renkaku calls Yuji a "tanuki" when he discovers that he's been deceived.

Arranged Marriage, page 45
Arranged marriages were the norm in most of the world until fairly recently, and Japan is no exception. Marriages were seen as a way to forge alliances, and considered in a businesslike fashion rather than one based on love. Breaking an engagement was something that was not done without serious consequences, not just for the man and woman, but for their families and business. As a result, O-sen and Yuji had to take drastic steps in order to avoid the engagement that was arranged by O-sen's father.

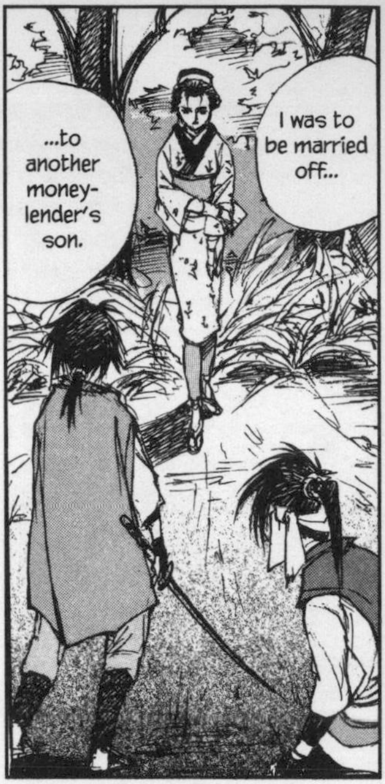
I was to be married off...
...to another money-lender's son.

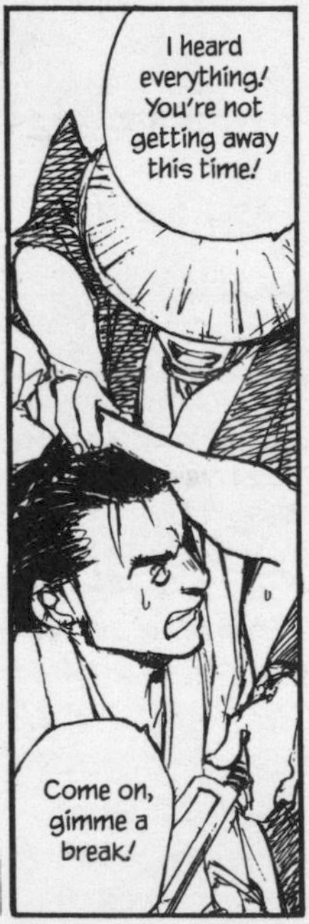
I heard everything! You're not getting away this time!
Come on, gimme a break!

Jutte, page 57
Jutte was a specialized weapon used by law enforcement during the Edo period. Jutte literally means ten hands, and the name reflects the weapon's versatile ability. The tool has no cutting edge. Instead, it has a single pronged hilt which is used to catch and snap off the blade of an opponent's weapon. It can also be used to catch a moving bladed weapon (sword, knife) and disarm the opponent by controlling his movement. The jutte is also seen clearly on page 107 of volume 4.

This is the final volume of KUROGANE! We hope you've enjoyed Jintetsu's adventures!

YA
Graphic
T

DETROIT PUBLIC LIBRARY
W9-BWR-863

Tomare!
[Stop!]

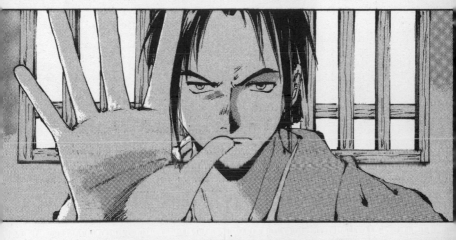

You are going the wrong way!

Manga is a completely different type of
reading experience.

To start at the beginning, go to the end!

That's right! Authentic manga is read
the traditional Japanese way—from right
to left. Exactly the opposite of how
American books are read. It's easy to
follow: Just go to the other end of the
book, and read each page—and each
panel—from right side to left side,
starting at the top right. Now you're
experiencing manga as it was
meant to be.

DEC '07
FR